Introduction to Logic

"Gensler's book is easy to read, his examples are very clear, his points made very simply. Gensler has the rare ability to find a simpler path to profound matters. He assists students by presenting easily-remembered strategies. His style encourages student confidence."

Thomas R. Foster, Ball State University

"Gensler's system is clear and straightforward. He presents his material in such a way that students feel encouraged as they grow in their ability to perform logical operations. If ever a logic book deserved the attribute user-'friendly' then this is the one."

Winfried Corduan, Taylor University

Introduction to Logic is a clear, interesting, and accessible introduction to one of the most challenging subjects in philosophy. Harry Gensler engages students through practical examples and important philosophical arguments, making the book ideal for students coming to logic for the first time. Using simpler methods for testing arguments (including the star test for syllogisms and an easier way to do proofs), students are led in a careful step-by-step way to master the complexities of logic. The book contains many exercises and study aids, including boxes for key ideas and a glossary. It is suitable for either basic or intermediate courses, since it covers a wide range of formal and informal areas:

- Syllogisms
- Propositional logic
- Quantificational logic
- Modal logic
- Deontic logic
- Belief logic

- The formalization of an ethical theory
- Metalogic
- Induction
- Meaning/definitions
- Fallacies/argumentation

The companion LogiCola instructional program, a scoring program, a teacher's manual, and various other teaching aids are available from the book's website: http://www.routledge.com/textbooks/gensler_logic

Harry J. Gensler, S.J., is Professor of Philosophy at John Carroll University in Cleveland. He is the author of *Gödel's Theorem Simplified* (1984), *Logic: Analyzing and Appraising Arguments* (1989), *Symbolic Logic: Classical and Advanced Systems* (1990), *Formal Ethics* (1996), and *Ethics: A Contemporary Introduction* (1998).

Introduction
to Logic

Harry J. Gensler

R Routledge
Taylor & Francis Group

LONDON AND NEW YORK

First published 2002
by Routledge
2 Park Square, Milton Park, Abingdon, Oxon, OX14 4RN

Simultaneously published in the USA and Canada
by Routledge
270 Madison Ave, New York, NY 10016

Reprinted 2003, 2004, 2005 (twice), 2006 (twice)

Routledge is an imprint of the Taylor & Francis Group, an informa business

© 2002 Harry J. Gensler

Typeset in Aldus Roman
by the author
Printed and bound in Great Britain by
TJ International Ltd, Padstow, Cornwall

British Library Cataloguing in Publication Data
A catalogue record for this book is available from the British Library.

Library of Congress Cataloging-in-Publication Data
A catalogue record for this book has been requested.

ISBN 10: 0-415-22674-0 (hbk)
ISBN 10: 0-415-22675-9 (pbk)

ISBN 13: 978-0-415-22674-5 (hbk)
ISBN 13: 978-0-415-22675-2 (pbk)

Contents

Chapter 9: Deontic and Imperative Logic 184

Chapter 10: Belief Logic 207

Chapter 11: A Formalized Ethical Theory 229

Chapter 12: Metalogic 253

Answers to Selected Problems 357

Glossary 388

Index of Names 398

Preface

This is a comprehensive *Introduction to Logic*. It covers:

- syllogisms;
- propositional and quantificational logic;
- modal, deontic, and belief logic;
- the formalization of an ethical theory;
- metalogic; and
- induction, meaning/definitions, and fallacies/argumentation.

Because of its broad scope, the book is well suited for either basic or intermediate courses in logic; the end of Chapter 1 talks about which chapters to use for which type of course.

Key features of the book include (a) clear, direct, concise writing; (b) interesting arguments, often about philosophy; and (c) simpler proof methods.

I wrote a companion computer program, LogiCola, to supplement classroom activity and enhance student learning. The "LogiCola Software" appendix has further information. You can get LogiCola (in Windows, DOS, and Macintosh formats), and the accompanying score processor and various teaching aids (including a teacher's manual), for free from either of these Web sites:

http://www.routledge.com/textbooks/gensler_logic
http://www.jcu.edu/philosophy/gensler/logicola.htm

I wish to thank in a special way several people who used various versions of this work (including its Prentice-Hall ancestors) and gave helpful suggestions and encouragement: Michael Bradie (Bowling Green State University), Robert Carnes (SUNY at Oswego), Winfried Corduan (Taylor University), Thomas Foster (Ball State University), Alex Orenstein (City University of New York), and Takashi Yagisawa (California State University). I also thank my students for their ideas on how to improve the book.

Harry J. Gensler
Philosophy Department
John Carroll University
Cleveland, OH 44118 USA

http://www.jcu.edu/philosophy/gensler

CHAPTER 1
Introduction

Logic is about reasoning – about going from premises to a conclusion. As we begin our study of logic, we need to get clearer on what logic is and why it's important. We also need to learn some concepts (like "valid" and "argument") that are central to the study of logic.

1.1   Logic

Logic[1] can be defined as *the analysis and appraisal of arguments*. When you do logic, you try to clarify reasoning and separate good from bad reasoning. As you work through this book, you'll examine philosophical reasoning on topics like free will and determinism, the existence of God, and the nature of morality. You'll also study reasoning on backpacking, water pollution, football, Supreme Court decisions, and the Bible. You'll come to see logic not as an irrelevant game with funny symbols, but rather as a useful tool to clarify and evaluate our reasoning – whether on everyday topics or on life's deeper questions.

Why study logic? I can think of three main reasons. First, logic can be fun. Doing logic is like playing a game or doing puzzles; logic will challenge your thinking processes in new ways. The rigor of logical systems will likely fascinate you. Most people find logic enjoyable.

Second, logic can deepen your understanding of philosophy. **Philosophy** can be defined as *reasoning about the ultimate questions of life*. Philosophers ask questions like "Why accept or reject free will?," "Can one prove or disprove God's existence?," and "How can one justify a moral belief?" If you don't know any logic, you'll have only a vague grasp of such issues; and you'll lack the tools needed to understand and evaluate philosophical reasoning. If you've studied philosophy, you'll likely recognize many of the pieces of philosophical reasoning in this book. If you haven't studied philosophy, you'll find this book a good introduction to the subject. In either case, you should get better at recognizing, understanding, and appraising philosophical reasoning.

---

[1] Important terms (like "**logic**") are introduced in bold type. Learn each such term and be able to give a definition. The Glossary at the end of the book has a collection of definitions.

Finally, logic can improve your analytical skills. While you've been reasoning about things all your life, this may be the first time that you focus on what reasoning is and try to become better at it. In most areas, it's a big advantage to be able to reason clearly; logic promotes intellectual skills that are important in law, business, medicine, and any other area that involves thinking and reasoning. This book is crammed with exercises; look at these as puzzles designed to help you think more clearly and logically.

1.2   Valid arguments

I begin my basic logic course with a multiple-choice test. The test has ten problems, each giving information (**premises**) and asking what **conclusion** necessarily follows. The problems are easy, but most students get almost half of them wrong.[1]

Here are two of the problems – with the right answers boxed:

If you overslept, you'll be late. You aren't late. Therefore: (a) You did oversleep. (b) You didn't oversleep. `[boxed]` (c) You're late. (d) None of these follows.	If you overslept, you'll be late. You didn't oversleep. Therefore: (a) You're late. (b) You aren't late. (c) You did oversleep. (d) None of these follows. `[boxed]`

While almost everyone gets the first problem right, many students wrongly pick "(b)" for the second problem. Here "You aren't late" doesn't necessary follow, since you might be late for some other reason; maybe your car didn't start. Most students, once they grasp this point, will see that (b) is wrong.[2]

Untrained logical intuitions are often unreliable. But logical intuitions can be developed; yours will likely improve as you work through this book. You'll also learn special techniques for testing arguments.

An **argument**, in the sense used in logic, is a set of statements consisting of premises and a conclusion; normally the premises give evidence for the conclusion. Arguments put into words a possible act of reasoning. Here's an example of a valid argument ("∴" is for *therefore*):

---

[1] The Web has my pretest at http://www.jcu.edu/philosophy/gensler/logic.htm in an interactive format. I suggest that you try it.
[2] These two arguments were taken from Matthew Lipman's fifth-grade logic textbook: *Harry Stottlemeier's Discovery* (Caldwell, NJ: Universal Diversified Services, 1974).

Valid argument 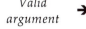 → If you overslept, you'll be late.
You aren't late.
∴ You didn't oversleep.

An argument is **valid** if it would be contradictory (impossible) to have the premises all true and conclusion false. In calling an argument *valid*, we aren't saying whether the premises are true. We're just saying that the conclusion *follows from* the premises – that if the premises were all true, then the conclusion also would have to be true. In saying this, we implicitly assume that there's no shift in the meaning or reference of the terms; hence we must use "overslept," "late," and "you" in the same way throughout the argument.

Our argument is valid because of its **logical form** – its arrangement of logical notions (like "if-then" and "not") and content phrases (like "You overslept" and "You're late"). We can display an argument's form by using words or symbols for logical notions, and letters for content phrases:

If you overslept, you'll be late.	If A then B **Valid**
You aren't late.	Not-B
∴ You didn't oversleep.	∴ Not-A

Our argument is valid because its *form* is correct. If we take another argument of the same form, but substituting other ideas for "A" and "B," then this second argument also will be valid. Here's an example:

If you're in France, you're in Europe.	If A then B **Valid**
You aren't in Europe.	Not-B
∴ You aren't in France.	∴ Not-A

Logic studies forms of reasoning. The content can deal with anything – backpacking, mathematics, cooking, physics, ethics, or whatever. When you learn logic, you're learning tools of reasoning that can be applied to any subject.

In our invalid example, the second premise denies the *first* part of the if-then (instead of the *second*); this small change makes all the difference:

If you overslept, you'll be late.	If A then B **Invalid**
You didn't oversleep.	Not-A
∴ You aren't late.	∴ Not-B

Intuitively, you might be late for some other reason – just as, in the following similar argument, you might be in Europe because you're in Italy:

If you're in France, you're in Europe.	If A then B **Invalid**
You aren't in France.	Not-A
∴ You aren't in Europe.	∴ Not-B

1.3 Sound arguments

Logicians distinguish *valid* arguments from *sound* arguments:

> An argument is **valid** if it would be contradictory to have the premises all true and conclusion false.
>
> An argument is **sound** if it's valid and has every premise true.

Calling an argument "valid" says nothing about whether its premises are true. But calling it "sound" says that it's valid (the conclusion follows from the premises) *and* has true premises. Here's an example of a *sound* argument:

$$\begin{array}{ll} \textit{Valid} & \text{If you're reading this, you aren't illiterate.} \\ \textit{and true} \;\;\rightarrow & \text{You're reading this.} \\ \textit{premises} & \therefore \text{You aren't illiterate.} \end{array}$$

When we try to prove a conclusion, we try to give a *sound* argument. We must make sure of two things: (a) that our premises are true, and (b) that our conclusion follows from our premises. If we have these two things, then our conclusion has to be true. The conclusion of a sound argument is always true.

An argument could be unsound in either of two ways; it might have a false premise or it might be invalid:

First premise false:	*Conclusion doesn't follow:*
All logicians are millionaires.	All millionaires eat well.
Gensler is a logician.	Gensler eats well.
∴ Gensler is a millionaire.	∴ Gensler is a millionaire.

When we criticize an opponent's argument, we try to show that it's *unsound*. We try to show: (a) that one of the premises is false, or (b) that the conclusion doesn't follow. If the argument has a false premise or is invalid, then our opponent hasn't proved the conclusion. But the conclusion still might be true – and our opponent might later discover a better argument for it. To show a view to be false, we must do more than just refute an argument for it; we must invent an argument of our own that shows the view to be false.

Besides asking whether premises are true, we could ask how certain they are, to ourselves or to others. We'd like our premises to be certain and obvious to everyone. We usually have to settle for less than this; our premises are often educated guesses or personal convictions. Our arguments are only as strong as their premises. This suggests a third strategy for criticizing an argument; we could try to show that one or more of the premises are very uncertain.

An argument often, especially in philosophy, leads to further arguments. Consider this argument against belief in God from St Thomas Aquinas (who mentioned it in order to show that it's unsound):[1]

> The belief that there's a God is unnecessary to explain our experience.
> All beliefs unnecessary to explain our experience ought to be rejected.
> ∴ The belief that there's a God ought to be rejected.

The argument is valid – the conclusion follows from the premises. Are the premises true? Aquinas might have clarified and then rejected the second premise as self-refuting; is this premise itself needed to explain our experience? Instead he rejected the first premise. He gave further arguments to show that belief in God *is* needed to explain our experience (of motion, causality, and so on). Are Aquinas's further arguments sound? We must leave debate on this to the philosophy of religion. Logic, however, can clarify the discussion. It can help us to express reasoning clearly, to determine whether a conclusion follows from the premises, and to focus on key premises to defend or criticize. Logic, while not itself resolving substantive issues, gives us intellectual tools to reason better about such issues.

I have two final points on terminology. We'll call statements *true* or *false* (not *valid* or *invalid*). And we'll call arguments *valid* or *invalid* (not *true* or *false*). While this is conventional usage, it pains a logician's ears to hear "invalid statement" or "false argument."

1.4 The plan of this book

This book, being an introduction, starts simply and doesn't presume any previous study of logic. It covers a broad range of topics in logic, from basic ones to rather advanced ones.

Chapter 2 covers syllogistic logic, an ancient branch of logic that focuses on "all," "no," and "some." Chapters 3 to 6 cover the classical systems of modern symbolic logic:

> Propositional logic: about "if-then," "and," "or," and "not."
> Quantificational logic: adding "all," "no," and "some."

Chapter 7 to 10 cover advanced (and increasingly more controversial) systems of philosophical interest:

---

[1] In this book, I often say that an argument is *from* a given philosopher. I mean that the person's writings contain or suggest the ideas in the argument; the phrasing is usually mine.

> Modal logic: about "necessary" and "possible."
> Deontic logic: about "ought" and "permissible."
> Belief logic: about consistent believing and willing.

Chapters 11 and 12 cover further advanced topics: an ethical formalization (featuring the golden rule) and metalogic (a study of logical systems with a view toward proving consistency and completeness). Chapter 13 covers inductive arguments (in which, at best, it's only highly probable that if the premises are true, then so is the conclusion). Chapter 14 covers meaning and definitions. Chapter 15 covers informal fallacies and further aspects of argumentation. In general, Chapters 2–5, 7, and 13–15 are suited for a basic logic course, while Chapters 6 and 8–12 are more advanced. Since this book is so comprehensive, there is much more material than could be covered in a one-term course.[1]

Logic requires careful reading. While I've tried to explain things as clearly and concisely as possible, some points are difficult – especially for a beginner; you may sometimes have to read an explanation a few times before the ideas sink in. Since logic is so cumulative (with one idea building on another), it's especially important to keep up with the work; and "keeping up" involves being able to work out the problems yourself. You'll find the accompanying LogiCola software (see the Appendix) a great help in this.

---

[1] Several chapters presume an understanding of earlier chapters. Chapter 4 builds on 3. Chapter 5 builds on 3 and 4. Chapter 6 builds on 3–5. Chapter 7 builds on 3 and 4. Chapter 8 builds on 3–7. Chapter 9 builds on 3–7. Chapter 10 builds on 3–7 and 9. Chapter 11 builds on 3–7 and 9–10. And Chapter 12 builds on 3 and 4.

CHAPTER 2
Syllogistic Logic

Syllogistic logic studies arguments whose validity depends on "all," "no," "some," and similar notions. This branch of logic, which goes back to Aristotle, was the first to be developed. It provides a fine preliminary to modern symbolic logic, which we begin in the next chapter.

2.1   Easier translations

We'll now create a little "syllogistic language," with precise rules for constructing arguments and testing validity. Our language will help us to test English arguments; here's how such an argument translates into our language:

All logicians are charming.		all L is C
Gensler is a logician.	➜	g is L
∴ Gensler is charming.		∴ g is C

Our language uses capital letters for general categories (like "logician") and small letters for specific individuals (like "Gensler"). It uses five words: "all," "no," "some," "is," and "not." Its grammatical sentences are called **wffs**, or **well-formed formulas**. Wffs are sequences having any of these eight forms (where other capital letters and other small letters may be used instead):[1]

all A is B	some A is B	x is A	x is y
no A is B	some A is not B	x is not A	x is not y

You must use one of these exact eight forms – but perhaps using other capitals for "A" and "B," and other small letters for "x" and "y":

Correct wffs:	all L is C	g is L	some P is not Q
Incorrect:	all l is c	G is L	not all P is Q

---

[1] Pronounce "wff" as "wŏŏf" – as in "wood" or "woofer." This book will consider letters with primes (like A′ and A′′) to be distinct additional letters.

Be careful about what sort of letter you use. In two cases, our rule for constructing wffs indirectly tells us whether to use a capital or a small letter:

Wffs beginning with a *word* (not a letter) use two capital letters: *Right:* all L is C *Wrong:* all l is c	Wffs beginning with a *letter* (not a word) begin with a small letter: *Right:* g is L *Wrong:* G is L

If a wff begins with a small letter, however, then the second letter can be either capital or small; so "a is B" and "a is b" are both wffs. In this case, we have to look at the meaning of the term:

Use capital letters for **general terms** (terms that *describe* or put in a *category*): B = a cute baby C = charming D = drives a Buick Use capitals for "a so and so," adjectives, and verbs.	Use small letters for **singular terms** (terms that pick out a *specific* person or thing): b = the world's cutest baby c = this child d = David Use small letters for "the so and so," "this so and so," and proper names.

So these translations are correct:

$$\text{Will Gensler is a cute baby} \quad = \quad \text{w is B}$$
$$\text{Will Gensler is the world's cutest baby} \quad = \quad \text{w is b}$$

We'll see later that whether we use a capital or a small letter can make a difference to the validity of an argument.

Be consistent when you translate English terms into logic; use the same letter for the same idea, and different letters for different ideas. It matters little what letter goes with what idea; "a cute baby" could be "B" or "C" or any other capital. To keep ideas straight, use letters that remind you of the English terms.

Syllogistic wffs all have the verb "is." English sentences with a different verb should be rephrased (to make "is" the main verb) and then translated:

	All dogs bark.	Al left the room.
=	All dogs is [are] *barkers.*	Al is a *person who left the room.*
=	all D is B	a is L

In the second example, "person who left the room" is a capital letter, since more than one person might have left the room.

2.1a   Exercise – No LogiCola exercise[1]

Which of the following are wffs?

all c is D	This isn't a wff, since both letters after "all" have to be capitals.

1. no e is f
2. g is H
3. J is K
4. all M is not Q
5. some L is m
6. p is not Q
7. R is not S
8. not all T is U
9. some X is not Y

2.1b   Exercise – LogiCola A (EM & ET)

Translate these English sentences into wffs.

John left the room.	j is L

1. This is a sentence.
2. This isn't the first sentence.
3. No logical positivist believes in God.
4. The book on your desk is green.
5. All dogs hate cats.
6. Kant is the greatest philosopher.
7. Ralph was born in Detroit.
8. Detroit is the birthplace of Ralph.
9. Alaska is a state.
10. Alaska is the biggest state.
11. Carol is my only sister.
12. Carol lives in Big Pine Key.
13. The idea of goodness is itself good.
14. All Michigan players are intelligent.
15. Michigan's team is awesome.
16. Donna is Ralph's wife.

2.2   The star test

A syllogism, roughly, is an argument using syllogistic wffs. Here's an English argument and its translation into a syllogism (the Cuyahoga is a river in Cleveland that used to be so polluted that it caught on fire):

No pure water is burnable.	no P is B
Some Cuyahoga River water is burnable.	some C is B
∴ Some Cuyahoga River water is not pure water.	∴ some C is not P

More precisely, a **syllogism** is a vertical sequence of one or more wffs in which each letter occurs twice and the letters "form a chain" (each wff has at least one letter in common with the wff just below it, if there is one, and the first wff has at least one letter in common with the last wff). This diagram shows how the letters "form a chain":

---

[1] Exercise sections have a boxed sample problem worked out and refer to any corresponding LogiCola computer exercises. Some further problems are worked out at the back of the book.

$$\begin{array}{l} \text{no P is B} \\ \text{some C is B} \\ \therefore \text{ some C is not P} \end{array}$$

The last wff in a syllogism is the *conclusion*; any other wffs are *premises*. Here are three further examples of syllogisms:

$$\begin{array}{lll} \text{a is C} & \text{some G is F} & \\ \text{b is not C} & \therefore \text{ some F is G} & \therefore \text{ all A is A} \\ \therefore \text{ a is not b} & & \end{array}$$

The last example is a premise-less syllogism. A premise-less syllogism is *valid* if and only if it's impossible for its conclusion to be false.

We need to learn a technical term before getting to our validity test:

> A letter is **distributed** in a wff if it occurs just after "all" or anywhere after "no" or "not."

The distributed letters below are underlined:

$$\begin{array}{llll} \text{all } \underline{A} \text{ is B} & \text{some A is B} & \text{x is A} & \text{x is y} \\ \text{no } \underline{A} \text{ is } \underline{B} & \text{some A is not } \underline{B} & \text{x is not } \underline{A} & \text{x is not } \underline{y} \end{array}$$

Note which letters are underlined (distributed). By our definition:

- The first letter after "all" is distributed, but not the second.
- Both letters after "no" are distributed.
- The letter after "not" is distributed.

Once you know which terms are distributed, you're ready to learn the star test for validity. The star test is a gimmick, but a quick and effective one; for now it's better just to learn the test and not worry about why it works.

The **star test** for syllogisms goes as follows:

> Star the *distributed* letters in the premises and *undistributed* letters in the conclusion. Then the syllogism is **VALID** if and only if every capital letter is starred *exactly* once and there is *exactly* one star on the right-hand side.

The general strategy goes: first star, then count.

Consider these two syllogisms (where I underlined the distributed letters):

all $\underline{A}$ is B			no $\underline{A}$ is $\underline{B}$
some C is A	← star distributed →		no $\underline{B}$ is C
∴ some C is B	← star undistributed →		∴ no $\underline{A}$ is $\underline{C}$

First star the *distributed* (underlined) letters in the premises and *undistributed* (not-underlined) letters in the conclusion:

all $\underline{A}^*$ is B **Valid**		no $\underline{A}^*$ is $\underline{B}^*$ **Invalid**
some C is A		no $\underline{B}^*$ is C^*
∴ some C^* is B^*		∴ no $\underline{A}$ is $\underline{C}$

Then count. A valid argument must satisfy two conditions:

- Each capital letter is starred in one and only one occurrence. (Small letters can be starred any number of times.)
- Exactly one right-hand letter (letter after "is" or "is not") is starred.

The first syllogism passes the test and is valid. The second fails the test (since "B" is starred twice and there are two right-hand stars) and is invalid.

Here are two short but confusing examples:

a is not $\underline{b}^*$ **Valid**	∴ all $\underline{A}$ is A^* **Valid**
∴ b^* is not $\underline{a}$	

Since the first syllogism has no capital letters, each capital in it is starred exactly once; recall that small letters can be starred any number of times. Since the second syllogism has no premises, we just star the conclusion; here "A" is starred exactly once and there is exactly one right-hand star.

Logic takes "some" to mean "one or more" – and so takes this to be valid:[1]

Gensler is a logician.	g is L **Valid**
Gensler is mean.	g is M
∴ Some logicians are mean.	∴ some L^* is M^*

Similarly, logic takes this next argument to be invalid:

Some logicians are mean.	some L is M **Invalid**
∴ Some logicians are not mean.	∴ some L^* is not $\underline{M}$

If *one or more* logicians are mean, it needn't be that *one or more* aren't mean; maybe *all* logicians are mean.

---

[1] In English, "some" can have various meanings, including "one or more," "two or more," "at least a few," "one or more but not all," "two or more but not all," and "a few but not all." Only the first meaning makes our argument valid.

As you begin doing the star test, you may want to first underline the distributed letters – and then star the underlined letters in the premises and the not-underlined ones in the conclusion. Later you can skip the underlining and just star the letters. After practice, the star test takes about five seconds to do.[1]

2.2a Exercise – No LogiCola exercise

Which of these are syllogisms?

| no P is B |
| some C is B |
| ∴ some C is not P |

This is a syllogism. (Each formula is a wff, each letter occurs twice, and the letters form a chain.)

1. all C is D
    ∴ some C is not E

2. g is not l
    ∴ l is not g

3. no Y is E
    all G is Y
    ∴ no Y is E

4. ∴ all S is S

5. k is not L
    all M is L
    some N is M
    Z is N
    ∴ k is not Z

2.2b Exercise – LogiCola BH

Underline the distributed letters in the following wffs.

| some R is not S |

| some R is not <u>S</u> |

1. w is not s
2. some C is B
3. no R is S
4. a is C
5. all P is B
6. r is not D
7. s is w
8. some C is not P

2.2c Exercise – LogiCola B (H and S)

Valid or invalid? Use the star test.

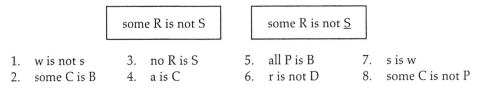

1. no P is B
    some C is not B
    ∴ some C is P

2. x is W
    x is not Y
    ∴ some W is not Y

3. no H is B
    no H is D
    ∴ some B is not D

---

[1] The star test is my invention; it came to me one day while I was watching a movie on television. For an explanation of why it works, see my "A simplified decision procedure for categorical syllogisms," *Notre Dame Journal of Formal Logic* 14 (1973): pages 457–66 – or my explanation at http://www.jcu.edu/philosophy/gensler/star.htm on the Web.

4.   some J is not P
     all J is F
     ∴ some F is not P

5.   g is not s
     ∴ s is not g

6.   all L is M
     g is L
     ∴ g is M

7.   all L is M
     g is not L
     ∴ g is not M

8.   some N is T
     some C is not T
     ∴ some N is not C

9.   all C is K
     s is K
     ∴ s is C

10. all D is A
     ∴ all A is D

11. s is C
     s is H
     ∴ some C is H

12. some C is H
     ∴ some C is not H

13. a is b
     b is c
     c is d
     ∴ a is d

14. no A is B
     some B is C
     some D is not C
     all D is E
     ∴ some E is A

2.3   English arguments

I suggest that you work out English arguments in a dual manner. First use intuition. Read the argument and ask whether it seems valid; sometimes this will be clear, but sometimes it won't. Then symbolize the argument and do the validity test. If your intuition and the validity test agree, then you have a stronger basis for your answer. If they disagree, then something went wrong; so you have to reconsider your intuition, your translation, or your use of the validity test. Using this two-prong attack trains your logical intuitions and gives you a double-check on the results.

When you translate into logic, use the same letter for the same idea, and different letters for different ideas. The "same idea" may be phrased in different ways; often it's redundant or stilted to phrase an idea in the exact same way throughout an argument. If you can't remember which letter translates which phrase, underline the phrase in the argument and write the letter above it; or write out separately which letter goes with which phrase.

Translate singular terms into small letters, and general terms into capital letters (see Section 2.1). Compare these two arguments:

Will is *the world's cutest baby*.	w is b **Valid**
The child over there is *the world's cutest baby*.	o is b
∴ Will is the child over there.	∴ w* is o*

Will is *a cute baby*.	w is B **Invalid**
The child over there is *a cute baby*.	o is B
∴ Will is the child over there.	∴ w* is o*

Intuitively, the first is valid and the second invalid. The symbolizations are identical, except that the first uses a small "b" (for "the world's cutest baby" – which refers to a specific baby) while the second uses a capital "B" (for "a cute baby" – which could describe various babies). We'd get both arguments wrong if we used the wrong case for this letter. We'd likely catch both mistakes if we did the problems intuitively as well as mechanically.

2.3a   Exercise – LogiCola BE

First appraise intuitively. Then translate into logic and use the star test to determine validity.

No pure water is burnable. Some Cuyahoga River water is burnable. ∴ Some Cuyahoga River water is not pure water.	no P* is B* **Valid** some C is B ∴ some C* is not P

1. All segregation laws degrade human personality.
    All laws that degrade human personality are unjust.
    ∴ All segregation laws are unjust.   [From Dr Martin Luther King.]

2. All Communists favor the poor.
    All Democrats favor the poor.
    ∴ All Democrats are Communists.   [This reasoning could persuade if expressed emotionally in a political speech. It's less apt to persuade if put into a clear premise-conclusion form.]

3. All too-much-time penalties are called before play starts.
    No penalty called before play starts can be refused.
    ∴ No too-much-time penalty can be refused.

4. No one under 18 is permitted to vote.
    No faculty member is under 18.
    The philosophy chairperson is a faculty member.
    ∴ The philosophy chairperson is permitted to vote.   [Applying a law (like ones about voting) requires logical reasoning. Lawyers and judges need to be logical.]

5. All acts that maximize good consequences are right.
    Some punishing of the innocent maximizes good consequences.
    ∴ Some punishing of the innocent is right.   [This argument and the next give a mini-debate on utilitarianism, which holds that all acts that maximize the total of good consequences for everyone are right. Moral philosophy would try to evaluate the premises; logic just focuses on whether the conclusion follows.]

6. No punishing of the innocent is right.
    Some punishing of the innocent maximizes good consequences.
    ∴ Some acts that maximize good consequences aren't right.

7. All huevos revueltos are buenos para el desayuno.
    All café con leche is bueno para el desayuno.
    ∴ All café con leche is huevos revueltos.   [To test whether this argument is valid, you don't have to understand its meaning; you only have to grasp the form. In doing formal (deductive) logic, you don't have to know what you're talking about; you only have to know the logical form of what you're talking about.]

8. The belief that there's a God is unnecessary to explain our experience.
    All beliefs unnecessary to explain our experience ought to be rejected.
    ∴ The belief that there's a God ought to be rejected.   [St Thomas Aquinas mentioned this argument in order to dispute the first premise.]

9. The belief in God gives practical life benefits (courage, peace, zeal, love, ...).
    All beliefs that give practical life benefits are pragmatically justifiable.
    ∴ The belief in God is pragmatically justifiable.   [From William James, an American pragmatist philosopher.]

10. All sodium salt gives a yellow flame when put into the flame of a Bunsen burner.
    This material gives a yellow flame when put into the flame of a Bunsen burner.
    ∴ This material is sodium salt.

11. All abortions kill innocent human life.
    No killing of innocent human life is right.
    ∴ No abortions are right.

12. All acts that maximize good consequences are right.
    All socially useful abortions maximize good consequences.
    ∴ All socially useful abortions are right.

13. That drink is transparent.
    That drink is tasteless.
    All vodka is tasteless.
    ∴ Some vodka is transparent.

14. Judy isn't the world's best cook.
    The world's best cook lives in Detroit.
    ∴ Judy doesn't live in Detroit.

15. All men are mortal.
    My mother is a man.
    ∴ My mother is mortal.

16. All gender-neutral terms can be applied naturally to individual women.
    The term "man" can't be applied naturally to individual women. (We can't naturally say "My mother is a man" – see the previous argument.)
    ∴ The term "man" isn't a gender-neutral term.   [This is from the philosopher Janice Molton's discussion of sexist language.]

17. Some moral questions are controversial.
    No controversial question has a correct answer.
    ∴ Some moral questions don't have a correct answer.

18. The idea of a perfect circle is a human concept.
    The idea of a perfect circle doesn't derive from sense experience.
    All ideas gained in our earthly existence derive from sense experience.
    ∴ Some human concepts aren't ideas gained in our earthly existence.   [This argument is from Plato. It led him to think that the soul gained ideas in a previous existence apart from the body, and so can exist apart from matter.]

19. All beings with a right to life are capable of desiring continued existence.
    All beings capable of desiring continued existence have a concept of themselves as a continuing subject of experiences.
    No human fetus has a concept of itself as a continuing subject of experiences.
    ∴ No human fetus has a right to life. [From Michael Tooley.]

20. The bankrobber wears size-twelve hiking boots.
    You wear size-twelve hiking boots.
    ∴ You're the bankrobber. [This is circumstantial evidence.]

21. All moral beliefs are products of culture.
    No products of culture express objective truths.
    ∴ No moral beliefs express objective truths.

22. Some books are products of culture.
    Some books express objective truths.
    ∴ Some products of culture express objective truths. [How could we change this argument to make it valid?]

23. Dr Martin Luther King believed in objective moral truths (about the wrongness of racism).
    Dr Martin Luther King disagreed with the moral beliefs of his culture.
    No people who disagree with the moral beliefs of their culture are absolutizing the moral beliefs of their own culture.
    ∴ Some who believed in objective moral truths aren't absolutizing the moral beliefs of their own culture.

24. All claims that would still be true even if no one believed them are objective truths.
    "Racism is wrong" would still be true even if no one believed it.
    "Racism is wrong" is a moral claim.
    ∴ Some moral claims are objective truths.

25. Some shivering people with uncovered heads have warm heads.
    All shivering people with uncovered heads are losing much body heat through their heads.
    All who are losing much body heat through their heads ought to put on a hat to stay warm.
    ∴ Some people who have warm heads ought to put on a hat to stay warm. [This was from a ski magazine.]

2.3b   Mystery story exercise – No LogiCola exercise

Herman had a party at his house. Alice, Bob, Carol, David, George, and others were there; one or more of these stole money from Herman's bedroom. You have the data in this big box, which may or may not give conclusive evidence about a given suspect:

1. Alice doesn't love money.
2. Bob loves money.
3. Bob isn't the richest person at the party.
4. Carol knew where the money was.
5. David works for Herman.
6. David isn't the nastiest person at the party.

7. All who stole money love money.
8. The richest person at the party didn't steal money.
9. All who stole money knew where the money was.
10. All who work for Herman hate Herman.
11. All who hate Herman stole money.
12. The nastiest person at the party stole money.

Did Alice steal money? If you can, prove your answer using a valid syllogism with premises from the big box.

Alice *didn't* steal money:

a is not L* – #1
all S* is L – #7
∴ a* is not S

1. Did Bob steal money? If you can, prove your answer using a valid syllogism with premises from the big box.
2. Did Carol steal money? If you can, prove your answer using a valid syllogism with premises from the big box.
3. Did David steal money? If you can, prove your answer using a valid syllogism with premises from the big box.
4. Based on our data, did more than one person steal money? Can you prove this using syllogistic logic?
5. Suppose that, from our data, we could deduce that a person stole money and also deduce that this same person didn't steal money. What would that show?

2.4 Harder translations

Suppose we want to test this argument:

Every human is mortal.   all H is M
Only humans are philosophers.   all P is H
∴ All philosophers are mortal.   ∴ all P is M

To symbolize such arguments, we need to translate idioms like "every" and "only" into our standard "all," "no," and "some." Here "every" is easy – since it just means "all." But "only" is more difficult. "Only humans are philosophers" really means "All philosophers are humans."

This box lists some common ways to express "all" in English:

Different ways to say "all A is B":	
Every (each, any) A is B.	Only B's are A's.
Whoever is A is B.	None but B's are A's.
A's are B's.[1]	No one is A unless he or she is B.
Those who are A are B.	Nothing is A unless it's B.
If a person is A, then he or she is B.	A thing isn't A unless it's B.
If you're A, then you're B.	It's false that some A is not B.

The forms on the left are fairly easy. The ones at the top right (with "only" and "none but") are tricky because they require switching the order of the letters:

$$
\begin{array}{ll}
 & \text{Only men are sumo wrestlers.} \\
= & \text{All sumo wrestlers are men.} \\
\neq & \text{All men are sumo wrestlers.}
\end{array}
\qquad
\begin{array}{ll}
 & \text{only M is S} \\
= & \text{all S is M}
\end{array}
$$

So "only" translates as "all," but with the terms reversed; "none but" works the same way. The forms at the bottom right (starting with "no … unless") are tricky too, because here "no" really means "all":

$$
\begin{array}{ll}
 & \text{No one is a sumo wrestler unless} \\
 & \quad \text{they are men.} \\
= & \text{All sumo wrestlers are men.}
\end{array}
\qquad
\begin{array}{ll}
 & \text{no one is S unless} \\
 & \quad \text{they are M} \\
= & \text{all S is M}
\end{array}
$$

So "no" with "unless" translates as "all." Don't reverse the letters here; only reverse letters with "only" and "none but."

This box lists some common ways to say "no A is B":

Different ways to say "no A is B":	
A's aren't B's.	No one that's A is B.
Every (each, any) A is non-B.	There isn't a single A that's B.
Whoever is A isn't B.	Not any A is B.
If a person is A, then he or she isn't B.	It's false that there's an A that's B.
If you're A, then you aren't B.	It's false that some A is B.

Never use "all A is not B." This form isn't a wff, and in English is ambiguous between "no A is B" and "some A is not B."

These last two boxes give some common ways to say "some":

---

[1] Logicians take "A's are B's" to mean "all A is B" – even though in ordinary English it also could mean "most A is B" or "some A is B."

some A is B =	*some A is not B* =
A's are sometimes B's.	One or more A's aren't B's.
One or more A's are B's.	There are A's that aren't B's.
There are A's that are B's.	Not all A's are B's.
It's false that no A is B.	It's false that all A is B.

Formulas "no A is B" and "some A is B" are contradictories: saying that one is false is equivalent to saying that the other is true:

It's false that no days are sunny	=	Some days are sunny.
It's false that some days are sunny	=	No days are sunny.

Similarly, "all A is B" and "some A is not B" are contradictories:

It's false that all cats are white	=	Some cats are not white.
It's false that some cats are not white	=	All cats are white.

Study these translation rules carefully. Idiomatic sentences can be difficult to untangle, even though they're part of our everyday speech. Our rules cover most, but not all, cases. If you find an example that our rules don't cover, you'll have to puzzle out the meaning yourself; you might try substituting concrete terms, like "sumo wrestler" and "men," as we did above.

2.4a Exercise – LogiCola A (HM & HT)

Translate these English sentences into wffs.

Nothing is worthwhile unless it's difficult.	all W is D

1. Only free actions can justly be punished.
2. Not all actions are determined.
3. Socially useful actions are right.
4. None but Democrats favor the poor.
5. At least some of the shirts are on sale.
6. Not all of the shirts are on sale.
7. No one is happy unless they are rich.[1]
8. Only rich people are happy.
9. Every rich person is happy.
10. Not any selfish people are happy.
11. Whoever is happy is not selfish.
12. Altruistic people are happy.

---

[1] How would you argue against this example (and the next two)? Would you go to the rich part of town and find a rich person who was miserable? Or would you go to the poor part of town and find a poor person who was happy?

13.   All of the shirts (individually) cost $20.
14.   All of the shirts (together) cost $20.
15.   Blessed are the merciful.
16.   I mean whatever I say.
17.   I say whatever I mean.
18.   Whoever hikes the Appalachian Trail (AT) loves nature.
19.   No person hikes the AT unless he or she likes to walk.
20.   Not everyone who hikes the AT is in great shape.

2.5   Deriving conclusions

Suppose you're given these premises and want to derive a conclusion that
follows validly using the syllogistic rules:

> Some cave dwellers use fire.
> All who use fire have intelligence.

You might use intuition. Then you'd read the premises reflectively, say "therefore" to yourself, hold your breath, and hope that the conclusion comes. If you
get a conclusion, write it down; then translate the argument into syllogistic
logic and test for validity using the star test. Do as many exercises as you can in
this intuitive way; this will help develop your intuition.

If your intuition fails, you can use four steps based on the star test:

(1) Translate the premises and star:	(2) Figure out the letters in the conclusion:	(3) Figure out the form of the conclusion:	(4) Add the conclusion and do the star test:
some C is F all F* is I	"C" and "I"	some - is -	some C is F all F* is I some C* is I*

(1) Translate the premises into logic and star the distributed letters. Check to
see if rules are broken. If we have two right-hand stars, or a capital letter that
occurs twice without being starred exactly once, then no conclusion validly
follows – and so we can write "no conclusion." In our example, no rules are
broken; so we continue with the problem.

(2) Figure out which letters will occur in the conclusion; these will be the two
letters that occur just once in the premises. In our example, "C" and "I" will
occur in the conclusion.

(3) Figure out the form of the conclusion. In this case, since we have two
capitals, the conclusion will start with "all" or "no" or "some." This rule tells
what form to use if both conclusion-letters are capitals:

Use one of these conclusion forms if both conclusion-letters are capitals.	all A is B	Use "all" if every premise has "all."
	no A is B	Use "no" if the premises have a mix of "all" and "no" (or else a single "no").
	some A is B some A is not B	Use "some" if any premise has "some" or small letters. Then use "is not" if any premise has "no" or "not"; otherwise, use "is."

In our example, the conclusion will use "some" (since the "some C is F" premise has "some"); it will use "is," since no premise has "no" or "not."

In some cases, one or both of the conclusion-letters will be small. Then the conclusion will have a small letter, "is" or "is not," and then the other letter. Follow this rule about whether to use "is" or "is not":

| *Use one of these conclusion forms if some conclusion-letter is small.* | x is A
x is y
x is not A
x is not y | Use "is not" if any premise has "no" or "not"; otherwise, use "is." |

(4) Add the conclusion and test for validity; if it comes out invalid, try switching the order of the letters to see if this makes it valid. In our example, we add "some C is I" – and it comes out valid. Our conclusion in English is "Some cave dwellers have intelligence":

> Some cave dwellers use fire.
> All who use fire have intelligence.
> _____
> Some cave dwellers have intelligence.

"Some who have intelligence are cave dwellers" is equivalent and also correct. The order of the terms doesn't matter with these four forms:

> no A is B   some A is B   x is y   x is not y

Here's another problem:

> No one held for murder is given bail.
> Smith isn't held for murder.
> _____

Do you intuitively want to conclude "Smith is given bail"? If so, consider that Smith might be held for something else (like kidnapping) for which bail is denied; or maybe Smith isn't held for anything. If we work it out using the rules, we translate the premises into logic and star the distributed letters:

(1) Translate the premises and star:	(2) Figure out the letters in the conclusion:	(3) Figure out the form of the conclusion:	(4) Add the conclusion and do the star test:
no M* is B* s is not M*	← "M" is starred twice! ← Rules are broken!		no M* is B* s is not M* no conclusion

Here "M" is starred twice (and there are two right-hand stars), and so rules are broken. So no conclusion follows.

If no rules had been broken, then the conclusion would have a small "s" and a capital "B." The form would be "- is not -." So the conclusion would be "s is not B." But, since "M" is already starred twice, this would be invalid.

2.5a Exercise – LogiCola BD

Derive a conclusion in English (not in wffs) that follows validly from and uses all the premises. Leave blank or write "no conclusion" if no such conclusion validly follows.

No pure water is burnable. Some Cuyahoga River water is not burnable.	no P* is B* some C is not B* no conclusion

Do you want to conclude "Some Cuyahoga River water is pure water"? Consider that all non-burnable parts of the river might be polluted by something that doesn't burn.

1. All human acts are determined (caused by prior events beyond our control).
   No determined acts are free.
   _____

2. Some human acts are free.
   No determined acts are free.
   _____

3. All acts where you do what you want are free.
   Some acts where you do what you want are determined.
   _____

4. All men are rational animals.
   No woman is a man.
   _____

5. All philosophers love wisdom.
   John loves wisdom.
   _____

6. Luke was a gospel writer.
   Luke was not an apostle.

7. All cheap waterproof raincoats block the escape of sweat.
   No raincoat that blocks the escape of sweat keeps you dry when hiking uphill.

8. All that is or could be experienced is thinkable.
   All that is thinkable is expressible in judgments.
   All that is expressible in judgments is expressible with subjects and predicates.
   All that is expressible with subjects and predicates is about objects and properties.

9. All moral judgments influence our actions and feelings.
   Nothing from reason influences our actions and feelings.

10. No feelings that diminish when we understand their origins are rational.
    All culturally taught racist feelings diminish when we understand their origin.

11. I weigh 180 pounds.
    My mind does not weigh 180 pounds.

12. No acts caused by hypnotic suggestion are free.
    Some acts where you do what you want are caused by hypnotic suggestion.

13. All unproved beliefs ought to be rejected.
    "There is a God" is an unproved belief.

14. All unproved beliefs ought to be rejected.
    "All unproved beliefs ought to be rejected" is an unproved belief.

15. Jones likes raw steaks.
    Jones likes champagne.

16. Some human beings seek revenge in a self-destructive way.
    No one seeking revenge in a self-destructive way is motivated only by self-interest.
    All purely selfish people are motivated only by self-interest.

17. All virtues are praised.
    No emotions are praised.

18. God is a perfect being.
    All perfect beings are self-sufficient.
    No self-sufficient being is influenced by anything outside of itself.

19. God is a perfect being.
    All perfect beings know everything.
    All beings that know everything are influenced by everything.

20. All basic moral norms hold for all possible rational beings as such.
    No principles based on human nature hold for all possible rational beings as such.

21. All programs that discriminate simply because of race are wrong.
    All racial affirmative action programs discriminate simply because of race.

22. Some racial affirmative action programs are attempts to make amends for past
    injustices toward a given group.
    No attempts to make amends for past injustices toward a given group discrimi-
    nate simply because of race. (Instead, they discriminate because of past injus-
    tices toward a group.)

23. Some actions approved by reformers are right.
    Some actions approved by society aren't approved by reformers.

24. Some wrong actions are errors made in good faith.
    No error made in good faith is blameworthy.

25. All moral judgments are such that disputes about them are impossible to resolve
    by reason.
    No objective truths are such that disputes about them are impossible to resolve
    by reason.

Here problems 1–3 give the three classic views on free will: hard determinism, inde-
terminism, and soft determinism; 8 and 20 are from Immanuel Kant; 9 is from David
Hume; 10 is from Richard Brandt; 17 and 18 are from Aristotle; and 19 is from Charles
Hartshorne.

2.6   Venn diagrams

Now we'll learn a second validity test. **Venn diagrams** are a way of testing syllogisms that involves diagramming the premises using three overlapping circles. Venn diagrams are more intuitive than the star test, even though the star test is easier to use. We'll apply Venn diagrams only to **traditional syllogisms** (two-premise syllogisms with no small letters).

Here's how to do the Venn-diagram test on a traditional syllogism:

> Draw three overlapping circles, labeling each with one of the syllogism's letters. Then diagram the premises following the directions below; as you draw the premises, try *not* to draw the conclusion. The syllogism is **VALID** if and only if drawing the premises *automatically* draws the conclusion.

First we draw three overlapping circles:

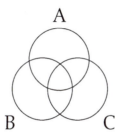

Visualize circle A containing all A things, circle B containing all B things, and circle C containing all C things. Within the circles are seven distinct areas:

- The central area is where all three circles overlap; this contains whatever has all three features (A and B and C).
- Further out are areas where two circles overlap; these contain whatever has only two features (for example, A and B but not C).
- Furthest out are areas inside only one circle; these contain whatever has only one feature (for example, A but not B or C).

Each of the seven areas can be either empty or non-empty. We shade the areas that we know to be empty. We put an "×" in the areas that we know to contain at least one entity. An area without either shading or an "×" is unknown; it may be either empty or non-empty, but we don't know which it is.

After we've drawn our three overlapping circles, we first draw "all" and "no" premises, by shading empty areas (showing that there are no existing things in these areas):

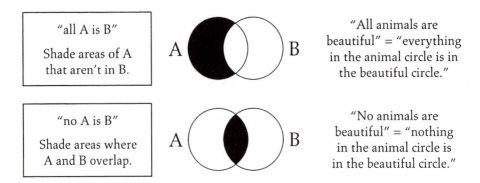

| "all A is B" | | "All animals are |
| Shade areas of A that aren't in B. | | beautiful" = "everything in the animal circle is in the beautiful circle." |

| "no A is B" | | "No animals are |
| Shade areas where A and B overlap. | | beautiful" = "nothing in the animal circle is in the beautiful circle." |

Lastly, we diagram "some" premises, by putting an "×" (symbolizing an existing thing) in some area that isn't already shaded:

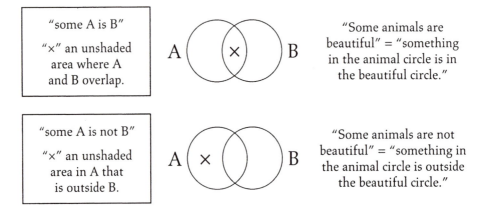

| "some A is B" | | "Some animals are |
| "×" an unshaded area where A and B overlap. | | beautiful" = "something in the animal circle is in the beautiful circle." |

| "some A is not B" | | "Some animals are not |
| "×" an unshaded area in A that is outside B. | | beautiful" = "something in the animal circle is outside the beautiful circle." |

In some cases, consistent with the above directions, we could put the "×" in either of two distinct areas. When this happens, the argument will be invalid; to show this, put the "×" in an area that *doesn't* draw the conclusion. The syllogism is valid if drawing the premises *automatically* draws the conclusion; it's invalid if we *can* draw the premises without drawing the conclusion.

Let's try the test on this valid "hard determinism" argument:

All human acts are determined.   all H is D   **Valid**
No free acts are determined.   no F is D
∴ No human acts are free.   ∴ no H is F

First we draw three overlapping circles:

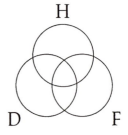

Then we draw the premise "all H is D" – by shading areas of H that are outside D:

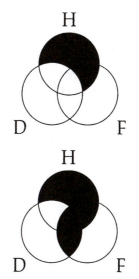

Then we draw the premise "no F is D" – by shading where F and D overlap:

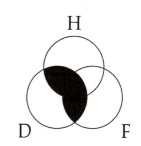

But then we've automatically drawn the conclusion "no H is F" – since we've shaded where H and F overlap. So the argument is valid.

Here's an invalid argument:

No human acts are determined.
No free acts are determined.
∴ No human acts are free.

Invalid

no H is D
no F is D
∴ no H is F

Here we draw "no H is D" (by shading where H and D overlap) and "no F is D" (by shading where F and D overlap). But then we haven't automatically drawn "no H is F" (since we haven't shaded all the areas where H and F overlap). So the argument is invalid.

Here's a valid argument using "some":

No determined acts are free.
Some human acts are free.
∴ Some human acts are not determined.

Valid

no D is F
some H is F
∴ some H is not D

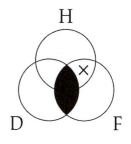

Recall that we first draw premises with "all" and "no" (by shading areas) before drawing premises with "some" (by putting an "×" in non-shaded areas).

So here we first draw "no D is F" (by shading where D and F overlap) and then "some H is F" (by putting an "×" in the only non-shaded area where H and F overlap). But then we've automatically drawn "some H is not D" – since we've put an "×" in some area of H that is outside D. So the argument is valid.

Here's an invalid argument using "some":

No determined acts are free.
Some human acts are not determined.
∴ Some human acts are free.

no D is F **Invalid**
some H is not D
∴ some H is F

We first draw "no D is F" – by shading where D and F overlap):

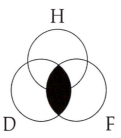

Then we have to draw "some H is not D" – by putting an "×" in some area of H that is outside D. There are two ways we could do this:

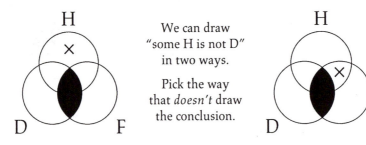

We can draw "some H is not D" in two ways.

Pick the way that *doesn't* draw the conclusion.

When there are two places to put an "×," always pick the way that *doesn't* draw the conclusion. So here we pick the first way:

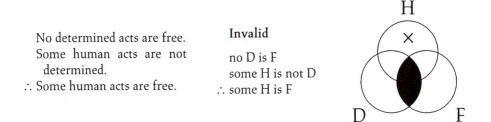

No determined acts are free.
Some human acts are not determined.
∴ Some human acts are free.

Invalid

no D is F
some H is not D
∴ some H is F

Since it's possible to draw the premises without drawing the conclusion, the argument is invalid.

2.6a   Exercise – LogiCola BC

Test for validity using Venn diagrams.

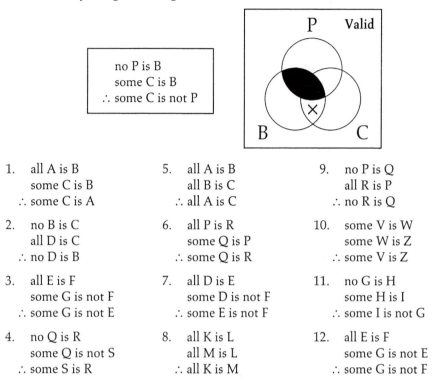

no P is B
some C is B
∴ some C is not P

P   Valid

B   C

1. all A is B
    some C is B
    ∴ some C is A

2. no B is C
    all D is C
    ∴ no D is B

3. all E is F
    some G is not F
    ∴ some G is not E

4. no Q is R
    some Q is not S
    ∴ some S is R

5. all A is B
    all B is C
    ∴ all A is C

6. all P is R
    some Q is P
    ∴ some Q is R

7. all D is E
    some D is not F
    ∴ some E is not F

8. all K is L
    all M is L
    ∴ all K is M

9. no P is Q
    all R is P
    ∴ no R is Q

10. some V is W
     some W is Z
     ∴ some V is Z

11. no G is H
     some H is I
     ∴ some I is not G

12. all E is F
     some G is not E
     ∴ some G is not F

2.7   Idiomatic arguments

Our arguments so far have been phrased in a clear premise-conclusion format. Unfortunately, real-life arguments are seldom so neat and clean. Instead we may find convoluted wording or extraneous material. Important parts of the argument may be omitted or only hinted at. And it may be hard to pick out the premises and conclusion. It often takes hard work to reconstruct a clearly stated argument from a passage.

Logicians like to put the conclusion last:

Socrates is human. All   s is H
humans are mortal. *So*   all H is M
Socrates is mortal.   ∴ s is M

But people sometimes put the conclusion first, or in the middle:

Socrates must be mortal.	Socrates is human. *So he*	s is H
After all, he's human and	*must be mortal* – since all	all H is M
all humans are mortal.	humans are mortal.	∴ s is M

In these examples, "must" and "so" indicate the conclusion (which always goes *last* when we translate the argument into logic). Here are some typical words that help us pick out the premises and conclusion:

These often indicate premises:		*These often indicate conclusions:*
Because, for, since, after all …	∴	Hence, thus, so, therefore …
I assume that, as we know …		It must be, it can't be …
For these reasons …		This proves (or shows) that …

When you don't have this help, ask yourself what is argued *from* (these are the premises) and what is argued *to* (this is the conclusion).

In reconstructing an argument, first pick out the conclusion. Then translate the premises and conclusion into logic; this may involve untangling idioms like "Only A's are B's" (which translates into "all B is A"). If some letters occur only once, you may have to add unstated but implicit premises; using the "principle of charity," interpret unclear reasoning in the way that gives the best argument. Finally, test for validity.

Here's an example of a twisted argument:

"You aren't allowed in here! After all, only members are allowed."

First we pick out the premises and conclusion:

Only members are allowed in here.	all A is M
∴ You aren't allowed in here.	∴ u is not A

Since "M" and "u" occur only once, we need to add an implicit premise linking these to produce a syllogism. We add a plausible premise and test for validity:

You aren't a member. (implicit)	u is not M*	**Valid**
Only members are allowed in here.	all A* is M	
∴ You aren't allowed in here.	∴ u* is not A	

2.7a   Exercise – LogiCola B (F & I)

First appraise intuitively; then translate into logic (making sure to pick out the conclusion correctly) and determine validity using the star test. Supply implicit premises where needed. Be sure to use correct wffs and syllogisms.

Whatever is good in itself ought to be desired. But whatever ought to be desired is capable of being desired. So only pleasure is good in itself, since only pleasure is capable of being desired.	all G* is O **Valid** all O* is C all C* is P ∴ all G is P* The conclusion is *"Only pleasure is good in itself"*: *"all G is P."*

1. Racial segregation in schools generates severe feelings of inferiority among black students. Whatever generates such feelings treats students unfairly on the basis of race. Anything that treats students unfairly on the basis of race violates the 14th Amendment. Whatever violates the 14th Amendment is unconstitutional. As a result, racial segregation in schools is unconstitutional.   [This is the reasoning behind the 1954 Brown vs. Topeka Board of Education Supreme Court decision.]

2. You couldn't have studied! The evidence for this is that you got an F- on the test.

3. God can't condemn agnostics for non-belief. For God is all-good, anyone who is all-good respects intellectual honesty, and no one who does this condemns agnostics for non-belief.

4. Only what is under a person's control is subject to praise or blame. Thus the consequences of an action aren't subject to praise or blame, since not all the consequences of an action are under a person's control.

5. No synthetic garment absorbs moisture. So no synthetic garment should be worn next to the skin while skiing.

6. Not all human concepts can be derived from sense experience. My reason for saying this is that the idea of "self-contradictory" is a human concept but isn't derived from sense experience.

7. Analyses of humans in purely physical-chemical terms are neutral about whether we have inner consciousness. So, contrary to Hobbes, we must conclude that no analysis of humans in purely physical-chemical terms fully explains our mental activities. Clearly, explanations that are neutral about whether we have inner consciousness don't fully explain our mental activities.

8. Only what is based on sense experience is knowledge about the world. It follows that no mathematical knowledge is knowledge about the world.

9. Not all the transistors in your radio can be silicon. After all, every transistor that works well at high temperatures is silicon and yet not all the transistors in your radio work well at high temperatures.

10. Moral principles aren't part of philosophy. This follows from these considerations: Only objective truths are part of philosophy. Nothing is an objective truth unless it's experimentally testable. Finally, of course, moral principles aren't experimentally testable.   [From the logical positivist A. J. Ayer.]

11. At least some women are fathers. This follows from these facts: (1) Jones is a father, (2) Jones had a sex change to female, and (3) whoever had a sex change to female is (now) a woman.

12. Only language users employ generalizations. Not a single animal uses language. At least some animals reason. So not all reasoners employ generalizations. [From John Stuart Mill.]

13. Only pure studies in form have true artistic worth. This proves that a thing doesn't have true artistic worth unless it's abstract, for it's false that there's something that's abstract but that isn't a pure study in form.

14. Anything that relieves pressure on my blisters while I hike would allow me to finish my PCT (Pacific Crest Trail) hike from Mexico to Canada. Any insole with holes cut out for blisters would relieve pressure on my blisters while I hike. I conclude that any insole with holes cut out for blisters would allow me to finish my PCT hike from Mexico to Canada.   [So I reasoned – and it worked.]

15. We know (from observing the earth's shadow on the moon during a lunar eclipse) that the earth casts a curved shadow. But spheres cast curved shadows. These two facts prove that the earth is a sphere.

16. Whatever is known is true, and whatever is true corresponds to the facts. We may conclude that no belief about the future is known.

17. No adequate ethical theory is based on sense experience, because any adequate ethical theory provides necessary and universal principles, and nothing based on sense experience provides such principles.   [From Immanuel Kant.]

18. At least some active people are hypothermia victims. Active people don't shiver. It follows that not all hypothermia victims shiver.   [From a ski magazine.]

19. Iron objects conduct electricity. We know this from what we learned last week – namely, that iron objects are metallic and that nothing conducts electricity unless it's metallic.

20. Only things true by linguistic convention are necessary truths. This shows that "God exists" can't be a necessary truth. After all, existence claims aren't true by linguistic convention.

21. No bundle of perceptions eats food. Hume eats food, and Hume is a human person. From this it follows (contrary to David Hume's theory) that no human person is a bundle of perceptions.

22. Whatever events we could experience as empirically real (as opposed to dreams or hallucinations) are events that could fit coherently into our experience. So an uncaused event isn't something we could experience as empirically real. I assume that it's false that some uncaused event could fit coherently into our experience. [From Immanuel Kant.]

23. I think I'm seeing a chair. But there are some people who think they're seeing a chair who are deceived by their senses. And surely people deceived by their senses don't really know that they're seeing an actual chair. So I don't really know that I'm seeing an actual chair.

24. No material objects can exist unperceived. I say this for three reasons: (1) Material objects can be perceived. (2) Only sensations can be perceived. And finally, (3) no sensation can exist unperceived.   [Bertrand Russell criticized this argument for an idealist metaphysics.]

25. Only those who can feel pleasure or pain deserve moral consideration. Not all plants can feel pleasure or pain. So not all plants deserve moral consideration.

26. True principles don't have false consequences. There are plausible principles with false consequences. Hence not all true principles are plausible.

27. Only what divides into parts can die. Everything that's material divides into parts. No human soul is material. This shows that no human soul can die.

2.8   The Aristotelian view

Historically, "Aristotelian" and "modern" logicians disagree about the validity of some syllogism forms. They disagree because of conflicting views about allowing empty terms (general terms that don't refer to any existing beings).

Compare these two arguments:

All underwater fish are animals.	All unicorns are animals.
∴ Some animals are underwater fish.	∴ Some animals are unicorns.

Intuitively, the first seems valid while the second seems invalid. Yet both have the same form – one that tests out as "invalid" using our star test:

all U* is A   **Invalid**
∴ some A* is U*

What is going on here?

When we read the first argument, we tend to presuppose that there is at least one underwater fish. Given this, as an assumed additional premise, it follows validly that some animals are underwater fish. When we read the second argument, we don't assume that there is at last one unicorn.[1] Without this additional assumption, it doesn't follow that some animals are unicorns.

Logically, what we have is this:

     ←

This is *valid* if we assume as a further premise that there are U's. It's *invalid* if we don't assume this.

The **Aristotelian view**, which assumes that each general term in a syllogism refers to at least one existing being, calls the argument "valid." The **modern view**, which allows empty terms like "unicorn" that don't refer to existing beings, calls the argument "invalid."

I prefer the modern view, since we often reason without presupposing that our general terms refer to existing entities. Someone may write a paper disputing the existence of angels; it would be awkward if we couldn't reason using the term "angel" without presupposing that there are angels. Or a teacher may say, "All students with straight-100s may skip the final exam"; this rule doesn't presuppose that anyone in fact will get straight-100s. On the other hand, in many cases we *can* presuppose that our general terms all refer; then the Aristotelian test seems more realistic.

---

[1] Unicorns are mythical creatures that are like horses but have a single horn on the forehead. Since there are no such beings, "unicorn" is an empty term and doesn't refer to existing beings.

Suppose we have an argument with true premises that's invalid on the modern view but valid on the Aristotelian view. Should we draw the conclusion or not? We should draw the conclusion if we know that each general term in the premises refers to at least one existing being; otherwise, we shouldn't.

Some logic books use the Aristotelian view, but most use the modern view. It makes a difference in very few cases; all the syllogisms in this chapter prior to this section test out the same on either view.

Use this version of the star test for the Aristotelian view:

> Star the distributed letters in the premises and undistributed letters in the conclusion. Then on the Aristotelian view (that is, presuming as an implicit premise that all the general terms refer), the syllogism is **VALID** if and only if every capital letter is starred *at least once* and there is exactly one star on the right-hand side.

The Aristotelian view requires capital letters to be starred *at least once* (once or twice), while the modern view requires them to be starred *exactly once*.

If you want to use Venn diagrams for the Aristotelian view, add this rule:

> Any circle with only one non-shaded area must have an "×" put in this area.

This is equivalent to assuming that the circle in question isn't entirely empty.

CHAPTER 3
Basic Propositional Logic

Propositional logic studies arguments whose validity depends on "if-then," "and," "or," "not," and similar notions. This chapter covers the basics, and the next covers proofs. Our later systems will build on what we learn here.

3.1   Easier translations

We'll now create a little "propositional language," with precise rules for constructing arguments and testing validity. Our language will help us to test English arguments.

Our language uses capital letters for true-or-false statements and parentheses for grouping. And it uses five special symbols: "~" (squiggle), "·" (dot), "∨" (vee), "⊃" (horseshoe), and "≡" (threebar):

~P	=	Not-P
(P · Q)	=	Both P and Q
(P ∨ Q)	=	Either P or Q
(P ⊃ Q)	=	If P then Q
(P ≡ Q)	=	P if and only if Q

A grammatically correct formula of our language is called a **wff**, or **well-formed formula**. Wffs are sequences that we can construct using these rules:[1]

1. Any capital letter is a wff.
2. The result of prefixing any wff with "~" is a wff.
3. The result of joining any two wffs by "·" or "∨" or "⊃" or "≡" and enclosing the result in parentheses is a wff.

These rules let us build wffs like the following:

---

[1] Pronounce "wff" as "wŏŏf" – as in "wood" or "woofer." This book will consider letters with primes (like A´ and A´´) to be distinct additional letters.

$$
\begin{array}{rcl}
P & = & \text{I went to Paris.} \\
{\sim}Q & = & \text{I didn't go to Quebec.} \\
(P \cdot {\sim}Q) & = & \text{I went to Paris and I didn't go to Quebec.} \\
(N \supset (P \cdot {\sim}Q)) & = & \text{If I'm Napoleon, then I went to Paris and} \\
& & \text{I didn't go to Quebec.}
\end{array}
$$

Parentheses are tricky. Note how these formulas differ:

Wrong:	(~Q)	~P · Q	P · Q ⊃ R
Right:	~Q	(~P · Q)	(P · (Q ⊃ R))
		~(P · Q)	((P · Q) ⊃ R)

"~Q" doesn't need parentheses. A wff requires a pair of parentheses (to avoid ambiguity) for each "·," "∨," "⊃," or "≡." These two differ:

$$
\begin{array}{rcl}
({\sim}P \cdot Q) & = & \text{Both not-P and Q} \\
{\sim}(P \cdot Q) & = & \text{Not both P and Q}
\end{array}
$$

The first is very definite and says that P is false and Q is true. The second just says that not both are true (at least one is false). Don't read both the same way, as "not P and Q." Read "both" for the left-hand parenthesis, or use pauses:

$$
\begin{array}{rcl}
({\sim}P \cdot Q) & = & \text{Not-P (pause) and (pause) Q} \\
{\sim}(P \cdot Q) & = & \text{Not (pause) P and Q}
\end{array}
$$

Logic is easier if you read the formulas correctly. These two also differ:

$$
\begin{array}{rcl}
(P \cdot (Q \supset R)) & = & \text{P, and if Q then R} \\
((P \cdot Q) \supset R) & = & \text{If P-and-Q, then R}
\end{array}
$$

The first says P is definitely true, but the second leaves us in doubt about this. Here's a useful rule for translating from English into logic:

> Put "(" wherever you see "both," "either," or "if."

Here are examples:

$$
\begin{array}{rcl}
\text{Either not A or B} & = & ({\sim}A \vee B) \\
\text{Not either A or B} & = & {\sim}(A \vee B) \\
\text{If both A and B, then C} & = & ((A \cdot B) \supset C) \\
\text{Not both not A and B} & = & {\sim}({\sim}A \cdot B)
\end{array}
$$

Here's another useful rule, with examples:

> Group together parts on either side of a comma.

$$\text{If A, then B and C} = (A \supset (B \cdot C))$$
$$\text{If A then B, and C} = ((A \supset B) \cdot C)$$

If you're confused on where to divide a sentence that lacks a comma, ask yourself where a comma would naturally go – and then translate accordingly:

$$\begin{array}{ccccc} \text{If it snows then I'll} & & \text{If it snows, then I'll} & & \\ \text{go outside and I'll ski} & = & \text{go outside and I'll ski} & = & (S \supset (G \cdot K)) \end{array}$$

Be sure to have your capital letters stand for whole statements:

$$\begin{array}{lll} \textit{Wrong:} & \text{Gensler is happy} & = & (G \cdot H) \\ \textit{Right:} & \text{Gensler is happy} & = & G \end{array}$$

Here's a more subtle example:

$$\begin{array}{lll} \textit{Wrong:} & \text{Bob and Lauren got married to each other} & = & (B \cdot L) \\ \textit{Right:} & \text{Bob and Lauren got married to each other} & = & M \end{array}$$

The first is wrong because the English sentence doesn't mean "Bob got married and Lauren got married" (which omits "to each other"). So "and" in our example doesn't connect whole sentences – as it does here:

$$\text{Bob and Lauren were sick} = (B \cdot L)$$

This means "Bob was sick and Lauren was sick."

Long sentences, like this one, can be confusing to translate:

> If attempts to prove "God exists" fail in the same way as our best proofs for "There are other conscious beings besides myself," then belief in God is reasonable if and only if belief in other conscious beings is reasonable.

Focus on logical terms, like "if-then" and "not," and translate part by part. Our long sentence has this form:

$$\text{If ..., then ... if and only if ....} = (F \supset (G \equiv O))$$

Don't let complex wording intimidate you. Instead, divide and conquer.

It doesn't matter what letters you use, as long as you're consistent. Use the same letter for the same idea, and different letters for different ideas. If you use "P" for "I went to Paris," then use "~P" for "I didn't go to Paris."

Our translation rules have exceptions and need to be applied with common sense. So don't translate "I saw them both" as "S(" – which isn't even a wff.

3.1a   Exercise – LogiCola C (EM & ET)[1]

Translate these English sentences into wffs.

Both not A and B.	(~A · B)

1.   Not both A and B.
2.   Both A and either B or C.
3.   Either both A and B or C.
4.   If A, then B or C.
5.   If A then B, or C.
6.   If not A, then not either B or C.
7.   If not A, then either not B or C.
8.   Either A or B, and C.
9.   Either A, or B and C.
10. If A then not both not B and not C.
11. If you get an error message, then the disk is bad or it's a Macintosh disk.
12. If I bring my digital camera, then if my batteries don't die then I'll take pictures of my backpack trip and put the pictures on my Web site.
13. If you both don't exercise and eat too much, then you'll gain weight.
14. The statue isn't by either Cellini or Michelangelo.
15. If I don't have either $2 in exact change or a bus pass, I won't ride the bus.
16. If Michigan and Ohio State play each other, then Michigan will win.
17. Either you went through both Dayton and Cinci, or you went through Louisville.
18. If she had hamburgers then she ate junk food, and she ate French fries.
19. I'm going to Rome or Florence and you're going to London.
20. Everyone is male or female.

3.2   Simple truth tables

Let "P" stand for "I went to Paris" and "Q" for "I went to Quebec." Each could be *true* or *false* (the two **truth values**) – represented by "1" and "0." There are four possible truth-value combinations:

P Q	
0 0	Both are false
0 1	Just Q is true
1 0	Just P is true
1 1	Both are true

In the first case, I went to neither Paris nor Quebec. In the second, I went to Quebec but not Paris. And so on.

---

[1] Exercise sections have a boxed sample problem worked out and refer to any corresponding LogiCola computer exercises. Some further problems are worked out at the back of the book.

A **truth table** gives a logical diagram for a wff. It lists all possible truth-value combinations for the letters and says whether the wff is true or false in each case. The truth table for "·" ("and") is very simple:

P Q	(P · Q)
0 0	0
0 1	0
1 0	0
1 1	1

"I went to Paris and I went to Quebec."

"(P · Q)" is a **conjunction**; P and Q are its **conjuncts**.

"(P · Q)" claims that *both* parts are true. So "I went to Paris *and* I went to Quebec" is false in the first three cases (where one or both parts are false) – and true only in the last case. These truth equivalences give the same information:

$$(0 \cdot 0) = 0 \qquad \text{(false} \cdot \text{false)} = \text{false}$$
$$(0 \cdot 1) = 0 \qquad \text{(false} \cdot \text{true)} = \text{false}$$
$$(1 \cdot 0) = 0 \qquad \text{(true} \cdot \text{false)} = \text{false}$$
$$(1 \cdot 1) = 1 \qquad \text{(true} \cdot \text{true)} = \text{true}$$

Here "$(0 \cdot 0) = 0$" says that an AND statement is false if both parts are false. The next two say that an AND is false if one part is false and the other part is true. And "$(1 \cdot 1) = 1$" says that an AND is true if both parts are true.[1]

Here are the truth table and equivalences for "∨" ("or"):

P Q	(P ∨ Q)
0 0	0
0 1	1
1 0	1
1 1	1

$$(0 \vee 0) = 0$$
$$(0 \vee 1) = 1$$
$$(1 \vee 0) = 1$$
$$(1 \vee 1) = 1$$

"I went to Paris or I went to Quebec."

"(P ∨ Q)" is a **disjunction**; P and Q are its **disjuncts**.

"(P ∨ Q)" claims that *at least one* part is true. So "I went to Paris *or* I went to Quebec" is true if I went to one or both places; it's false if I went to neither place. Our "∨" thus symbolizes the *inclusive* sense of "or." English also can use "or" in an *exclusive* sense, which claims that at least one part is true *but not both*. Here is how both senses of "or" translate into our symbolism:

- **Inclusive "or"**: A or B or both   =   (A ∨ B)
- **Exclusive "or"**: A or B but not both   =   ((A ∨ B) · ~(A · B))

The exclusive sense requires a longer symbolization.[2]

Here are the truth table and equivalences for "⊃" ("if-then"):

---

[1] Our "·" is simpler than the English "and," which can mean things like "and then" (as it does in "Suzy got married and had a baby" – which differs from "Suzy had a baby and got married").

[2] People sometimes use "*Either* A or B" to indicate the exclusive "or." We won't do this; instead, we'll use "either" to indicate grouping and we'll translate it as a left-hand parenthesis.

P Q	(P ⊃ Q)
0 0	1
0 1	1
1 0	0
1 1	1

(0 ⊃ 0) = 1
(0 ⊃ 1) = 1
(1 ⊃ 0) = 0
(1 ⊃ 1) = 1

"If I went to Paris, then
I went to Quebec."

"(P ⊃ Q)" is a **conditional**;
P is the **antecedent**
and Q the **consequent**.

"(P ⊃ Q)" claims that what we *don't* have is the first part true and the second false. Suppose you say this:

"*If* I went to Paris, *then* I went to Quebec."

By our table, you speak truly if you went to neither place, or to both places, or to Quebec but not Paris. You speak falsely if you went to Paris but not Quebec. Does that seem right to you? Most people think so, but some have doubts.

Our truth table can produce strange results. Take this example:

If I had eggs for breakfast, then
the world will end at noon.   (E ⊃ W)

Suppose that I didn't have eggs, and so E is false. By our table, the conditional is then *true* – since if E is false then "(E ⊃ W)" is true. This is strange. We'd normally tend to take the conditional to be *false* – since we'd take it to claim that my having eggs would *cause* the world to end. So translating "if-then" as "⊃" doesn't seem satisfactory. There's something fishy going on here.

Our "⊃" symbolizes a simplified "if-then" that ignores elements like causal connections and temporal sequence. "(P ⊃ Q)" has a very simple meaning; it just *denies* that we have P-true-and-Q-false:

(P ⊃ Q)		~(P · ~Q)
If P is true, then Q is true.	=	We don't have P true and Q false.

Translating "if-then" this way is a useful simplification, since it captures the part of "if-then" that normally determines validity. The simplification usually works; in the few cases where it doesn't, we can use a more complex translation (as we'll sometimes do in the chapters on modal logic).

The truth conditions for "⊃" are hard to remember. These slogans may help:

Falsity implies anything.	(0 ⊃) = 1
Anything implies truth.	(⊃ 1) = 1
Truth doesn't imply falsity.	(1 ⊃ 0) = 0

The "Falsity implies anything" slogan, for example, means that the whole if-then is true if the first part is false; so "If I'm a billionaire, then ..." is true, regardless of what replaces "...," since I'm *not* a billionaire.

Here are the table and equivalences for "≡" ("if-and-only-if"):

P Q	(P ≡ Q)
0 0	1
0 1	0
1 0	0
1 1	1

$(0 \equiv 0) = 1$
$(0 \equiv 1) = 0$
$(1 \equiv 0) = 0$
$(1 \equiv 1) = 1$

"I went to Paris if and only if I went to Quebec."

"(P ≡ Q)" is a **biconditional**.

"(P ≡ Q)" claims that both parts have the *same* truth value: both are true or both are false. So "≡" is much like "equals."

Here are the table and equivalences for "~" ("not"):

P	~P
0	1
1	0

$\sim 0 = 1$
$\sim 1 = 0$

"I didn't go to Paris."

"~P" is a **negation**.

"~P" has the *opposite* value of "P." If "P" is true then "~P" is false, and if "P" is false then "~P" is true.

Most of the rest of this book presupposes that you know these truth equivalences; try to master them right away.

3.2a Exercise – LogiCola D (TE & FE)

Calculate each truth value.

(0 · 1)	(0 · 1) = 0

1.	(0 ∨ 1)	6.	(1 · 0)	11.	(0 ≡ 0)	16.	(1 ∨ 0)
2.	(0 · 0)	7.	(1 ⊃ 1)	12.	(1 ∨ 1)	17.	(1 ≡ 0)
3.	(0 ⊃ 0)	8.	(1 ≡ 1)	13.	(1 · 1)		
4.	~0	9.	(0 ∨ 0)	14.	(1 ⊃ 0)		
5.	(0 ≡ 1)	10.	(0 ⊃ 1)	15.	~1		

3.3 Truth evaluations

We can calculate the truth value of a wff if we know the truth value of its letters. Consider this problem:

Suppose that P=1, Q=0, and R=0.
What is the truth value of "((P ⊃ Q) ≡ ~R)"?

To figure this out, we write "1" for "P," "0" for "Q," and "0" for "R"; then we simplify from the inside out, using our equivalences, until we get "1" or "0":

$$((P \supset Q) \equiv \sim R) \quad \leftarrow \quad \text{original formula}$$
$$((1 \supset 0) \equiv \sim 0) \quad \leftarrow \quad \text{substitute "1" and "0" for the letters}$$
$$(0 \equiv 1) \quad \leftarrow \quad \text{put "0" for "}(1 \supset 0)\text{," and "1" for "}\sim 0\text{"}$$
$$0 \quad \leftarrow \quad \text{put "0" for "}(0 \equiv 1)\text{"}$$

Here the formula is false.

Some people work out truth values vertically, as above. Others work them out horizontally:

$$((1 \supset 0) \equiv \sim 0) = (0 \equiv 1) = 0$$

Still others work out the values in their heads.

Simplify parts inside parentheses first. With a wff of the form "$\sim(\ldots)$," first work out the part inside parentheses to get 1 or 0; then apply "$\sim$" to the result. Study these two examples:

Right: $\sim(1 \vee 0) = \sim 1 = 0$
Wrong: $\sim(1 \vee 0) = (\sim 0 \vee \sim 1) = (1 \vee 0) = 1$

Don't distribute "$\sim$" as the wrong example does it. Instead, first evaluate whatever is inside the parentheses.

3.3a   Exercise – LogiCola D (TM & TH)

Assume that A=1 and B=1 (A and B are both true) while X=0 and Y=0 (X and Y are both false). Calculate the truth value of each wff below.

$$((A \vee X) \supset \sim B)$$

$$((1 \vee 0) \supset \sim 1)$$
$$(1 \supset 0)$$
$$0$$

1. $\sim(A \cdot X)$
2. $(\sim A \cdot \sim X)$
3. $\sim(\sim A \cdot \sim X)$
4. $(A \supset X)$
5. $(\sim X \equiv Y)$

6. $(\sim B \supset A)$
7. $\sim(A \supset X)$
8. $(B \cdot (X \vee A))$
9. $(\sim(X \cdot A) \vee \sim B)$
10. $(\sim A \vee \sim(X \supset Y))$

11. $((A \cdot \sim X) \supset \sim B)$
12. $\sim(A \supset (X \vee \sim B))$
13. $(\sim X \vee \sim(\sim A \equiv B))$
14. $(\sim Y \supset (A \cdot X))$
15. $\sim((A \supset B) \supset (B \supset Y))$

3.4   Unknown evaluations

We can sometimes figure out a formula's truth value even if we don't know the truth value of some letters. Take this example:

Suppose that P=1 and Q=? (unknown).
What is the truth value of "(P ∨ Q)"?

We first substitute "1" for "P" and "?" for "Q":

$$(1 \lor ?)$$

We might just see that this is true, since an OR is true if at least one part is true. Or we might try it both ways. Since "?" could be "1" or "0," we write "1" above the "?" and "0" below it. Then we evaluate the formula for each case:

$$1 = 1$$
$$(1 \lor ?)$$
$$0 = 1$$

The formula is true, since it's true either way.
    Here's another example:

Suppose that P=1 and Q=?
What is the truth value of "(P · Q)"?

We first substitute "1" for "P" and "?" for "Q":

$$(1 \cdot ?)$$

We might see that this is unknown, since the truth value of the whole depends on the unknown letter. Or we might try it both ways; then we write "1" above the "?" and "0" below it – and we evaluate the formula for each case:

$$1 = 1$$
$$(1 \cdot ?)$$
$$0 = 0$$

The formula is unknown, since it could be either true or false.

3.4a   Exercise – LogiCola D (UE, UM, & UH)

Assume that T=1 (T is true), F=0 (F is false), and U=? (U is unknown). Calculate the truth value of each wff below.

(~T · U)	(~1 · ?) = (0 · ?) = 0

1. (U · F)	4. (~F · U)	7. (U ⊃ ~T)	10. (U ⊃ ~F)
2. (U ⊃ ~T)	5. (F ⊃ U)	8. (~F ∨ U)	11. (U · ~T)
3. (U ∨ ~F)	6. (~T ∨ U)	9. (T · U)	12. (U ∨ F)

3.5 Complex truth tables

A truth table for a wff is a diagram listing all possible truth-value combinations for the wff's letters and saying whether the wff would be true or false in each case. We've done simple tables already; now we'll do complex ones.

A formula with n distinct letters has 2^n possible truth-value combinations:

A	A B	A B C
0	0 0	0 0 0
1	0 1	0 0 1
	1 0	0 1 0
	1 1	0 1 1
		1 0 0
		1 0 1
		1 1 0
		1 1 1

One letter gives 2 (2^1) combinations.
Two letters give 4 (2^2) combinations.
Three letters give 8 (2^3) combinations.

n letters give 2^n combinations.

To get every combination, alternate 0's and 1's below the last letter the required number of times. Then alternate 0's and 1's below each earlier letter at half the previous rate: by twos, fours, and so on. This numbers each row in ascending order in base 2.

A truth table for "~(A ∨ ~B)" begins like this:

A B	~(A ∨ ~B)
0 0	
0 1	
1 0	
1 1	

The right side has the wff. The left side has each letter used in the wff; we write each letter just once, regardless of how often it occurs. Below the letters, we write all possible truth-value combinations. Finally we figure out the wff's truth value for each line. The first line has A and B both false – which makes the whole wff false:

~(A ∨ ~B)	← original formula
~(0 ∨ ~0)	← substitute "0" for each letter
~(0 ∨ 1)	← put "1" for "~0"
~1	← put "1" for "(0 ∨ 1)"
0	← put "0" for "~1"

The wff comes out "1," "0," and "0" for the next three lines – which gives us this truth table:

A B	~(A ∨ ~B)
0 0	0
0 1	1
1 0	0
1 1	0

So "~(A ∨ ~B)" is true if and only if A is false and B is true. The simpler wff "(~A · B)" is equivalent, in that it's true in the same cases. Both wffs are true in some cases and false in others – making them **contingent statements**.

The truth table for "(P ∨ ~P)" is true in all cases – which makes the formula a **tautology**:

P	(P ∨ ~P)
0	1
1	1

"I went to Paris or I didn't go to Paris."

This formula, called the **law of the excluded middle**, says that every statement is true or false. This law holds in propositional logic, since we stipulated that capital letters stand for true-or-false statements. The law doesn't always hold in English, since English allows statements that are too vague to be true or false. Is "It's raining" true if there's a slight drizzle? Is "My shirt is white" true if it's a light cream color? Such claims can be too vague to be true or false. So the law is an idealization when applied to English.

The truth table for "(P · ~P)" is false in all cases – which makes the formula a **self-contradiction**:

P	(P · ~P)
0	0
1	0

"I went to Paris and I didn't go to Paris."

"P and not-P" is always false in propositional logic, which presupposes that "P" stands for the same statement throughout. English is looser and lets us shift the meaning of a phrase in the middle of a sentence. "I went to Paris and I didn't go to Paris" may express a truth if it means this:

> "I went to Paris (in that I landed once at the Paris airport) – but I didn't really go there (in that I saw almost nothing of the city)."

Because of the shift in meaning, this would better translate as "(P · ~Q)."

3.5a   Exercise – LogiCola D (FM & FH)

Do a truth table for each formula.

P Q R	((P ∨ Q) ⊃ R)
0 0 0	1
0 0 1	1
0 1 0	0
0 1 1	1
1 0 0	0
1 0 1	1
1 1 0	0
1 1 1	1

((P ∨ Q) ⊃ R)

1. (P ≡ ~Q)	4. ((P · ~Q) ⊃ R)	7. (~Q ⊃ ~P)
2. (~P · Q)	5. ((P ≡ Q) ⊃ Q)	8. (P ≡ (P · P))
3. (P ∨ (Q · ~R))	6. ((P ∨ ~Q) ⊃ R)	9. ~(P · (Q ∨ ~R))

3.6 The truth-table test

Take a propositional argument. Construct a truth table showing the truth value of the premises and conclusion for all possible cases. The argument is **VALID** if and only if no possible case has the premises all true and conclusion false.

Suppose we want to test this invalid argument:

If you're a dog, then you're an animal.	(D ⊃ A)
You're not a dog.	~D
∴ You're not an animal.	∴ ~A

First we do a truth table for the premises and conclusion. We start as follows:

D A	(D ⊃ A), ~D ∴ ~A
0 0	
0 1	
1 0	
1 1	

Then we evaluate the three wffs on each truth combination. The first combination has D=0 and A=0, which makes all three wffs true:

(D ⊃ A)	~D	~A
(0 ⊃ 0)	~0	~0
1	1	1

So the first line of our truth table looks like this:

D A	(D ⊃ A),	~D	∴	~A
0 0	1	1		1

We work out the other three lines:

D A	(D ⊃ A),	~D	∴	~A	
0 0	1	1		1	
0 1	1	1		0	← Invalid
1 0	0	0		1	
1 1	1	0		0	

The argument is invalid, since some possible case has the premises all true and conclusion false. The case in question is one where you aren't a dog but you are an animal (perhaps a cat).

Consider this valid argument:

If you're a dog, then you're an animal.	(D ⊃ A)
You're a dog.	D
∴ You're an animal.	∴ A

Again we do a truth table for the premises and conclusion:

D A	(D ⊃ L),	D	∴	A	Valid
0 0	1	0		0	
0 1	1	0		1	
1 0	0	1		0	
1 1	1	1		1	

Here the argument is valid, since no possible case has the premises all true and conclusion false.

There's a short-cut form of the truth-table test. Recall that all we're looking for is 110 (premises all true and conclusion false). The argument is invalid if 110 sometimes occurs; otherwise, it's valid. To save time, we can first evaluate an easy wff and cross out any lines that couldn't be 110. In our previous example, we might work out "D" first:

D A	(D ⊃ A),	D	∴	A
0 0	– – – – – – – –0– – – – –			
0 1	– – – – – – – –0– – – – –			
1 0		1		
1 1		1		

The first two lines can't be 110 (since the second digit is 0); so we cross them out and ignore the remaining values. The last two lines could be 110, so we need to work them out further. Next we might evaluate "A":

D A	(D ⊃ A), D ∴ A
0 0	— — — — — — — 0 — — — — —
0 1	— — — — — — — 0 — — — — —
1 0	1 0
1 1	— — — — — — — 1 — — — 1 —

The last line can't be 110 (since the last digit is 1); so we cross it out. Then we have to evaluate "(D ⊃ A)" for only one case – for which it comes out false. Since we never get 110, the argument is valid:

D A	(D ⊃ A), D ∴ A	Valid
0 0	— — — — — — — 0 — — — — —	
0 1	— — — — — — — 0 — — — — —	
1 0	— — — 0 — — — 1 — — — 0 —	
1 1	— — — — — — — 1 — — — 1 —	

The short-cut method can save much time if otherwise we'd have to evaluate a long formula for eight or more cases.

With a two-premise argument, we look for 110. With three premises, we look for 1110. Whatever the number of premises, we look for a case where the premises are all true and conclusion false. The argument is valid if and only if this case never occurs.

The truth-table test can get tedious for long arguments. Arguments with 6 letters need 64 lines – and ones with 10 letters need 1024 lines. So we'll use the truth-table test only on fairly simple arguments.[1]

3.6a Exercise – LogiCola D (AE, AM, & AH)

First appraise intuitively. Then translate into logic (using the letters given) and use the truth-table test to determine validity.

		L R	(L ∨ R), ~L ∴ R	Valid
It's in my left hand or my right hand.		0 0	0 1 0	
It's not in my left hand.		0 1	1 1 1	we never
∴ It's in my right hand.		1 0	1 0 0	get 110
		1 1	1 0 1	

1. If you're a collie, then you're a dog.
   You're a dog.
   ∴ You're a collie. [Use C and D.]

---

[1] An argument that tests out "invalid" is either invalid or else valid on grounds that go beyond the system in question. Let me give an example to illustrate the second possibility. "This is green, therefore something is green" translates into propositional logic as "T ∴ S" and tests out invalid. But the argument is in fact valid – as we later could show using quantificational logic.

2. If you're a collie, then you're a dog.
   You're not a dog.
   ∴ You're not a collie.   [Use C and D.]

3. If television is always right, then Anacin is better than Bayer.
   If television is always right, then Anacin isn't better than Bayer.
   ∴ Television isn't always right.   [Use T and B.]

4. If it rains and your tent leaks, then your down sleeping bag will get wet.
   Your tent won't leak.
   ∴ Your down sleeping bag won't get wet.   [Use R, L, and W.]

5. If I get Grand Canyon reservations and get a group together, then I'll explore
   canyons during spring break.
   I've got a group together.
   I can't get Grand Canyon reservations.
   ∴ I won't explore canyons during spring break.   [Use R, T, and E.]

6. There is an objective moral law.
   If there is an objective moral law, then there is a source of the moral law.
   If there is a source of the moral law, then there is a God. (Other possible sources,
   like society or the individual, are claimed not to work.)
   ∴ There is a God.   [Use M, S, and G; this argument is from C. S. Lewis.]

7. If ethics depends on God's will, then something is good because God desires it.
   Something isn't good because God desires it. (Instead, God desires something
   because it's already good.)
   ∴ Ethics doesn't depend on God's will.   [Use D and B; this argument is from
   Plato's *Euthyphro*.]

8. It's an empirical fact that the basic physical constants are precisely in the narrow
   range of what is required for life to be possible. (This "anthropic principle" has
   considerable evidence behind it.)
   The best explanation for this fact is that the basic physical constants were caused
   by an intelligent being intending to produce life. (The main alternatives are the
   "chance coincidence" and "parallel universe" explanations.)
   If these two things are true, then it's reasonable to believe that the basic structure
   of the world was set up by an intelligent being (God) intending to produce life.
   ∴ It's reasonable to believe that the basic structure of the world was set up by an
   intelligent being (God) intending to produce life.   [Use E, B, and R; this argument is from Peter Glynn.]

9. I'll go to Paris during spring break if and only if I'll win the lottery.
   I won't win the lottery.
   ∴ I won't go to Paris during spring break.   [Use P and W.]

10. If we have a simple concept proper to God, then we've directly experienced God
    and we can't rationally doubt God's existence.
    We haven't directly experienced God.
    ∴ We can rationally doubt God's existence.   [Use S, E, and R.]

11. If there is a God, then God created the universe.
    If God created the universe, then matter didn't always exist.
    Matter always existed.
    ∴ There is no God.   [Use G, C, and M.]

12. If this creek is flowing, then either the spring upstream has water or this creek
    has some other water source.
    This creek has no other water source.
    This creek isn't flowing.
    ∴ The spring upstream has no water.   [Use F, S, and O.]

3.7   The truth-assignment test

> Take a propositional argument. Set each premise to
> 1 and the conclusion to 0. The argument is **VALID**
> if and only if no consistent way of assigning 1 and
> 0 to the letters will make this work – so we can't
> make the premises all true and conclusion false.

Suppose we want to test this valid argument:

It's in my left hand or my right hand.	$(L \lor R)$
It's not in my left hand.	$\sim L$
∴ It's in my right hand.	∴ R

First we set each premise to 1 and the conclusion to 0 (just to see if this works):

$$(L \lor R) = 1$$
$$\sim L = 1$$
$$\therefore R = 0$$

Then we figure out the values of as many letters as we can. The conclusion has
R false. We show this by writing a 0-superscript after each R:

$$(L \lor R^0) = 1$$
$$\sim L = 1$$
$$\therefore R^0 = 0$$

The second premise has ~L true – and so L is false. So we write a 0-superscript
after each L (showing that L is false):

$$(L^0 \lor R^0) = 1$$
$$\sim L^0 = 1$$
$$\therefore R^0 = 0$$

Then the first premise is false, since an OR is false if both parts are false:

$$\frac{0}{(L^0 \vee R^0)} \neq 1 \quad \textbf{Valid}$$
$$\sim L^0 = 1$$
$$\therefore R^0 = 0$$

Since 0 isn't 1, we slash the "=." It's impossible to make the premises all true and conclusion false, since this would make the first premise both 1 and 0. So the argument is valid.

In doing the test, first assign 1 to the premises and 0 to the conclusion. Then figure out the truth values for the letters – and then the truth values for the longer formulas. If you have to cross something out, then the assignment isn't possible, and so the argument is valid.

Consider this invalid argument:

It's in my left hand or my right hand.	$(L \vee R)$
It's not in my left hand.	$\sim L$
$\therefore$ It's not in my right hand.	$\therefore \sim R$

Again, we first set each premise to 1 and the conclusion to 0:

$$(L \vee R) = 1$$
$$\sim L = 1$$
$$\therefore \sim R = 0$$

Then L is false (since ~L is true) – and R is true (since ~R is false). But then the first premise comes out true:

$$\frac{1}{(L^0 \vee R^1)} = 1 \quad \textbf{Invalid}$$
$$\sim L^0 = 1$$
$$\therefore \sim R^1 = 0$$

Since we *can* make the premises all true and conclusion false, the argument is invalid. A truth-table gives the same result when L=0 and R=1:

L R	$(L \supset R)$,	$\sim L$	$\therefore$	$\sim R$	
0 1	1	1		0	← **Invalid**

The truth-assignment test gives this result more quickly.[1]

Here's another invalid argument:

---

[1] Some find lines like "~L⁰ = 1" confusing. Here the *larger complex* " ~L" is true but *the letter* "L" is false. When I write an 0-superscript above the letter, I mean that the letter is false.

> It's in my left hand or my right hand.   (L ∨ R)
> ∴ It's in my right hand.   ∴ R

If we work this out, we get R false – but we get no value for L:

$$(L \vee R^0) = 1$$
$$\therefore R^0 = 0$$

Since the value for L matters, we could try both values (first *true* and then *false*); the argument is invalid if *either* value makes the premises all true and conclusion false. Here making L *true* gives this result:

$$\frac{1}{(L^1 \vee R^0)} = 1 \quad \textbf{Invalid}$$
$$\therefore R^0 = 0$$

In working out the truth values for the letters, try to make the premises all true and conclusion false. The argument is invalid if there's some way to do this.

3.7a   Exercise – LogiCola ES

Test for validity using the truth-assignment test.

(K ⊃ (I ∨ S))	(K¹ ⊃ (I⁰ ∨ S⁰)) ≠ 1 **Valid**
~I	~I⁰ = 1
K	K¹ = 1 (we can't
∴ S	∴ S⁰ = 0 have 1110)

1. ~(N ≡ H)
    N
    ∴ ~H

2. ((J • ~D) ⊃ Z)
    ~Z
    D
    ∴ ~J

3. ((T ∨ M) ⊃ Q)
    M
    ∴ Q

4. P
    ∴ (P • Q)

5. ((L • F) ⊃ S)
    S
    F
    ∴ L

6. ((A • U) ⊃ ~B)
    B
    A
    ∴ ~U

7. ((W • C) ⊃ Z)
    ~Z
    ∴ ~C

8. Q
    ∴ (P ⊃ Q)

9. (E ∨ (Y • X))
    ~E
    ∴ X

10. (~T ⊃ (P ⊃ J))
    P
    ~J
    ∴ T

11. ~P
    ∴ ~(Q ⊃ P)

12. ((~M • G) ⊃ R)
    ~R
    G
    ∴ M

13. ~(Q ≡ I)
    ~Q
    ∴ I

14. ((Q • R) ≡ S)
    Q
    ∴ S

15. A
    ~A
    ∴ B

3.7b Exercise – LogiCola EE

First appraise intuitively. Then translate into logic and use the truth-assignment test to determine validity.

<table>
<tr><td>

If our country will be weak,
then there will be war.
Our country will not be weak.
∴ There will not be war.

</td><td>

$(K^0 \supset R^1) = 1$ **Invalid**
$\sim K^0 = 1$ (we can
∴ $\sim R^1 = 0$ have 110)

</td></tr>
</table>

1. Some things are caused (brought into existence).
   Anything caused is caused by another.
   If some things are caused and anything caused is caused by another, then either there's a first cause or there's an infinite series of past causes.
   There's no infinite series of past causes.
   ∴ There's a first cause. [A "first cause" (often identified with God) is a cause that isn't itself caused by another. This argument is from St Thomas Aquinas.]

2. If you pass and it's intercepted, then the other side gets the ball.
   You pass.
   It isn't intercepted.
   ∴ The other side doesn't get the ball.

3. If God exists in the understanding and not in reality, then there can be conceived a being greater than God (namely, a similar being that also exists in reality).
   "There can be conceived a being greater than God" is false (since "God" is defined as "a being than which no greater can be conceived").
   God exists in the understanding.
   ∴ God exists in reality. [This is St Anselm's ontological argument – one of the most widely discussed arguments of all time.]

4. If existence is a perfection and God by definition has all perfections, then God by definition must exist.
   God by definition has all perfections.
   Existence is a perfection.
   ∴ God by definition must exist. [From René Descartes.]

5. If we have sensations of alleged material objects and yet no material objects exist, then God is a deceiver.
   God isn't a deceiver.
   We have sensations of alleged material objects.
   ∴ Material objects exist. [From René Descartes – who thus based our knowledge of the external material world on our knowledge of God.]

6. If "good" is definable in experimental terms, then ethical judgments are scientifically provable and ethics has a rational basis.
   Ethical judgments aren't scientifically provable.
   ∴ Ethics doesn't have a rational basis.

7.   If it's right for me to lie and not right for you, then there's a relevant difference between our cases.
     There's no relevant difference between our cases.
     It's not right for you to lie.
     ∴ It's not right for me to lie.

8.   If Newton's gravitational theory is correct and there's no undiscovered planet near Uranus, then the orbit of Uranus would be such-and-such.
     Newton's gravitational theory is correct.
     The orbit of Uranus isn't such-and-such.
     ∴ There's an undiscovered planet near Uranus.   [This reasoning led to the discovery of the planet Neptune.]

9.   If attempts to prove "God exists" fail in the same way as our best arguments for "There are other conscious beings besides myself," then belief in God is reasonable if and only if belief in other conscious beings is reasonable.
     Attempts to prove "God exists" fail in the same way as our best arguments for "There are other conscious beings besides myself."
     Belief in other conscious beings is reasonable.
     ∴ Belief in God is reasonable.   [From Alvin Plantinga.]

10. If you pack intelligently, then either this teddy bear will be useful on the hiking trip or you won't pack it.
     This teddy bear won't be useful on the hiking trip.
     You won't pack it.
     ∴ You pack intelligently.

11. If knowledge is sensation, then pigs have knowledge.
     Pigs don't have knowledge.
     ∴ Knowledge isn't sensation.   [From Plato.]

12. If capital punishment is justified and justice doesn't demand a vindication for past injustices, then capital punishment either reforms the offender or effectively deters crime.
     Capital punishment doesn't reform the offender.
     Capital punishment doesn't effectively deter crime.
     ∴ Capital punishment isn't justified.

13. If belief in God were a purely intellectual matter, then either all smart people would be believers or all smart people would be non-believers.
     Not all smart people are believers.
     Not all smart people are non-believers.
     ∴ Belief in God isn't a purely intellectual matter.   [From the Jesuit theologian John Powell.]

14. If you're lost, then you should call for help or head downstream.
     You're lost.
     ∴ You should call for help.

15. If maximizing human enjoyment is always good and the sadist's dog-torturing maximizes human enjoyment, then the sadist's act is good.
    The sadist's dog-torturing maximizes human enjoyment.
    The sadist's act isn't good.
    ∴ Maximizing human enjoyment isn't always good.

16. If there's knowledge, then either some things are known without proof or we can prove every premise by previous arguments infinitely.
    We can't prove every premise by previous arguments infinitely.
    There's knowledge.
    ∴ Some things are known without proof.   [From Aristotle.]

17. If you modified your computer or didn't send in the registration card, then the warranty is void.
    You didn't modify your computer.
    You sent in the registration card.
    ∴ The warranty isn't void.

18. If "X is good" means "Hurrah for X!" and it makes sense to say "If X is good," then it makes sense to say "If hurrah for X!"
    It makes sense to say "If X is good."
    It doesn't make sense to say "If hurrah for X!"
    ∴ "X is good" doesn't mean "Hurrah for X!"   [From Hector-Neri Castañeda.]

19. If we have an idea of substance, then "substance" refers either to a simple sensation or to a complex constructed out of simple sensations.
    "Substance" doesn't refer to a simple sensation.
    ∴ We don't have an idea of substance.   [From David Hume.]

20. If we have an idea of "substance" and our idea of "substance" doesn't derive from sensations, then "substance" is a thought category of pure reason.
    Our idea of "substance" doesn't derive from sensations.
    We have an idea of "substance."
    ∴ "Substance" is a thought category of pure reason.   [From Immanuel Kant.]

21. If "good" means "socially approved," then what is socially approved is necessarily good.
    What is socially approved isn't necessarily good.
    ∴ "Good" doesn't mean "socially approved."

22. [Generalizing the last argument, G. E. Moore argued that we can't define "good" in terms of any empirical term "F" – like "desired" or "socially approved."]
    If "good" means "F," then what is F is necessarily good.
    What is F isn't necessarily good. (We can consistently say "Some F things may not be good" without thereby violating the meaning of "good.")
    ∴ "Good" doesn't mean "F."

23. If moral realism (the belief in objective moral truths) were true, then it could explain the moral diversity in the world.
    Moral realism can't explain the moral diversity in the world.
    ∴ Moral realism isn't true.

3.8 Harder translations

Now we'll learn how to symbolize idiomatic English. We'll still sometimes use these earlier rules:

- Put "(" wherever you see "both," "either," or "if."
- Group together parts on either side of a comma.

Here are three additional rules, with examples:

> Translate "but" ("yet," "however," "although," and so on) as "and."

$$\text{Michigan played } but \text{ it lost} \quad = \quad (P \cdot L)$$

The translation loses the contrast (or surprise), but this doesn't affect validity.

> Translate "unless" as "or."

$$\text{You'll die } unless \text{ you breathe} \quad = \quad (D \lor B) \quad = \quad (B \lor D)$$
$$Unless \text{ you breathe you'll die} \quad = \quad (D \lor B) \quad = \quad (B \lor D)$$

"Unless" also is equivalent to "if not"; so we could use "$(\sim B \supset D)$" – "If you don't breathe, then you'll die."

> Translate "just if" and "iff" (a logician word) as "if and only if."

$$\text{I'll agree } just \ if \text{ you pay me \$1,000} \quad = \quad (A \equiv P)$$
$$\text{I'll agree } iff \text{ you pay me \$1,000} \quad = \quad (A \equiv P)$$

The order of the letters doesn't matter with "$\cdot$" or "$\lor$" or "$\equiv$."

Our next two rules are tricky. The first governs most conditional words:

> The part after "if" ("provided that," "assuming that," and so on) is the antecedent (the "if"-part, the part before the horseshoe).

$$\textit{If} \text{ you're a dog, then you're an animal} \quad = \quad (D \supset A)$$
$$\textit{Provided that} \text{ you're a dog, you're an animal} \quad = \quad (D \supset A)$$
$$\text{You're an animal, } \textit{if} \text{ you're a dog} \quad = \quad (D \supset A)$$
$$\text{You're an animal, } \textit{provided that} \text{ you're a dog} \quad = \quad (D \supset A)$$

"Only if" is different and follows its own rule:

> The part after "only if" is the consequent (the "then"-part, the part after the horseshoe).
>
> Equivalently: Write "⊃" for "only if."

You're alive *only if* you have oxygen   =   (A ⊃ O)
Only if you have oxygen are you alive   =   (A ⊃ O)

Using the second form of the rule, "Only if O, A" would become "⊃ O, A" – which we'd put as "(A ⊃ O). "

Sometimes the **contrapositive** form gives a more intuitive translation. The contrapositive of "(A ⊃ B)" is "(~B ⊃ ~A)"; both are equivalent (true in the same cases). Consider these translations:

You pass *only if* you take the exam   =

(P ⊃ E)   (If you pass then you take the exam.)
(~E ⊃ ~P)   (If you don't take the exam then you don't pass.)

The second translation sounds better in English, since we tend to read a temporal sequence into an if-then (even though "⊃" abstracts from this and claims only that we don't have the first part true and the second part false).

Here's the rule for translating "sufficient" and "necessary":

> "A is *sufficient* for B" means "If A then B."
> "A is *necessary* for B" means "If not A then not B."
> "A is *necessary and sufficient* for B" means "A if and only if B."

Oxygen is *sufficient for* life   =   (O ⊃ L)
Oxygen is *necessary for* life   =   (~O ⊃ ~L)
Oxygen is *necessary and sufficient for* life   =   (O ≡ L)

The order of the letters matters only with "⊃."

These translation rules are rough and don't always work. Sometimes you have to puzzle out the meaning on your own.

3.8a   Exercise – LogiCola C (HM & HT)

Translate these English sentences into wffs.

| A, assuming that B. | (B ⊃ A) |

1. If she goes, then you'll be alone but I'll be here.
2. Your car will start only if you have gas.

3. I will quit unless you give me a raise.
4. Taking the final is a sufficient condition for passing.
5. Taking the final is necessary for you to pass.
6. You're a man just if you're a rational animal.
7. Unless you have faith, you'll die.
8. She neither asserted it nor hinted at it.
9. Getting at least 96 is a necessary and sufficient condition for getting an A.
10. Only if you exercise are you fully alive.
11. I'll go, assuming that you go.
12. Assuming that your belief is false, you don't know.
13. Having a true belief is a necessary condition for having knowledge.
14. You get mashed potatoes or French fries, but not both.
15. You're wrong if you say that.

3.9 Idiomatic arguments

Our arguments so far have been phrased in a clear premise-conclusion format. Unfortunately, real-life arguments are seldom so neat and clean. Instead we may find convoluted wording or extraneous material. Important parts of the argument may be omitted or only hinted at. And it may be hard to pick out the premises and conclusion. It often takes hard work to reconstruct a clearly stated argument from a passage.

Logicians like to put the conclusion last:

Socrates is human. If he's	H
human, then he's mortal.	$(H \supset M)$
So Socrates is mortal.	$\therefore M$

But people sometimes put the conclusion first, or in the middle:

Socrates must be mortal.	Socrates is human. *So he*	H
After all, he's human. And	*must be mortal* – since if	$(H \supset M)$
if he's human, he's mortal.	he's human, he's mortal.	$\therefore M$

In these examples, "must" and "so" indicate the conclusion (which always goes *last* when we translate the argument into logic). Here are some typical words that help us pick out the premises and conclusion:

These often indicate premises:		These often indicate conclusions:
Because, for, since, after all ...	∴	Hence, thus, so, therefore ...
I assume that, as we know ...		It must be, it can't be ...
For these reasons ...		This proves (or shows) that ...

When you don't have this help, ask yourself what is argued *from* (these are the premises) and what is argued *to* (this is the conclusion).

In reconstructing an argument, first pick out the conclusion. Then translate the premises and conclusion into logic; this step may involve untangling idioms like "A unless B" (which translates into "A or B"). If you don't get a valid argument, try adding unstated but implicit premises; using the "principle of charity," interpret unclear reasoning in the way that gives the best argument. Finally, test for validity.

Here's an easy example:

The gun must have been shot recently! It's still hot.

First we pick out the premises and conclusion:

The gun is still hot.   H
∴ The gun was shot recently. ∴ S

Since this seems to presume an implicit premise, we add the most plausible one that we can think of that makes the argument valid. Then we translate into logic and test for validity:

If the gun is still hot, then it
 was shot recently. (implicit) $(H \supset S)$ **Valid**
The gun is still hot.   H
∴ The gun was shot recently. ∴ S

3.9a Exercise – LogiCola E (F & I)

First appraise intuitively; then translate into logic (making sure to pick out the conclusion correctly) and determine validity using the truth-assignment test. Supply implicit premises where needed.

<table>
<tr>
<td>

Knowledge is good in itself only if it's desired for its own sake. So knowledge is good in itself, since it's desired for its own sake.

</td>
<td>

$(G^0 \supset D^1) = 1$ **Invalid**
$D^1 = 1$
$\therefore G^0 = 0$

(The conclusion is "*So knowledge is good in itself*" – "*G.*")

</td>
</tr>
</table>

1. Knowledge can't be sensation. If it were, then we couldn't know something that we aren't presently sensing. [From Plato.]
2. Presuming that we followed the map, then unless the map is wrong there's a pair of lakes just over the pass. We followed the map. There's no pair of lakes just over the pass. Hence the map is wrong.
3. If they blitz but don't get to our quarterback, then our wide receiver will be open. So our wide receiver won't be open, as shown by the fact that they won't blitz.

4. My true love will marry me only if I buy her a Rolls Royce. It follows that she'll marry me, since I'll buy her a Rolls Royce.

5. The basic principles of ethics can't be self-evident truths, since if they were then they'd largely be agreed upon by intelligent people who have studied ethics.

6. That your views are logically consistent is a necessary condition for your views to be sensible. Your views are logically consistent. So your views are sensible.

7. If Ohio State wins but Nebraska doesn't, then the Ohio Buckeyes will be national champions. So it looks like the Ohio Buckeyes won't be national champs, since Nebraska clearly is going to win.

8. The filter capacitor can't be blown. This is indicated by the following facts. You'd hear a hum, presuming that the silicon diodes work but the filter capacitor is blown. But you don't hear a hum. And the silicon diodes work.

9. There will be a fire! My reason for saying this is that only if there's oxygen present will there be a fire. Of course there's oxygen present.

10. We have no moral knowledge. This is proved by the fact that if we did have moral knowledge then basic moral principles would be either provable or self-evident. But they aren't provable. And they aren't self-evident either.

11. It must be a touchdown! We know that it's a touchdown if the ball broke the plane of the end zone.

12. Assuming that it wasn't an inside job, then the lock was forced unless the thief stole the key. The thief didn't steal the key. We may infer that the robbery was an inside job, inasmuch as the lock wasn't forced.

13. It must be the case that we don't have any tea bags. After all, we'd have tea bags if your sister Carol drinks tea. Of course, Carol doesn't drink tea.

14. We can't still be on the right trail. We'd see the white Appalachian Trail blazes on the trees if we were still on the right trail.

15. If God is omnipotent, then he could make hatred inherently good – unless there's a contradiction in hatred being inherently good. But there's no contradiction in this. And God is omnipotent. I conclude that God could make hatred inherently good. [From William of Ockham, who saw morality as depending on God's will.]

16. Taking the exam is a sufficient condition for getting an A. You didn't take the exam. This means you don't get an A.

17. If Texas or Arkansas wins, then I win my $10 bet. I guess I win $10. Texas just beat Oklahoma 17-14!

18. Unless you give me a raise, I'll quit. Therefore I'm quitting!

19. There's no independent way to prove that our senses are reliable. So empirical knowledge is impossible – since, of course, empirical knowledge would be possible only if there were an independent way to prove that our senses are reliable.

20. It's virtuous to try to do what's good. On the other hand, it isn't virtuous to try to do what's socially approved. I conclude that, contrary to cultural relativism, "good" doesn't mean "socially approved." I assume, of course, that if "good" meant "socially approved" and it was virtuous to try to do what's good, then it would be virtuous to try to do what's socially approved.

21. Moral conclusions can be deduced from non-moral premises only if "good" is definable using non-moral predicates. But "good" isn't so definable. So moral conclusions can't be deduced from non-moral premises.

22. The world can't need a cause. If the world needed a cause, then so would God.

3.10   S-rules

We'll now learn some **inference rules,** which state that certain formulas can be derived from certain other formulas. These rules are important in their own right, since they reflect common forms of reasoning. The same rules will be building blocks for formal proofs, which we start in the next chapter; formal proofs reduce a complex argument to a series of small steps, each based on an inference rule.

The **S-rules,** which we'll study in this section, are used to *simplify* statements. Our first rule deals with "and"; here it is in English and in symbols:

This and that.	$\dfrac{(P \cdot Q)}{P,\, Q}$	AND statement, so
∴ This.		both parts are true.
∴ That.		

From an AND statement, we can infer each part: "It's cold and windy; therefore it's cold, therefore it's windy." Negative parts work the same way:

It isn't cold and it isn't windy. $\dfrac{(\sim C \cdot \sim W)}{\sim C,\, \sim W}$
∴ It isn't cold.
∴ It isn't windy.

But from a *negative* AND statement (where "~" is outside the parentheses), we can infer nothing about the truth or falsity of each part:

You're *not both* in Paris and in Quebec. $\dfrac{\sim(P \cdot Q)}{\text{nil}}$
∴ No conclusion.

You can't be in both cities at the same time. But you might be in Paris (and not Quebec), or in Quebec (and not Paris), or in some third place. From "~(P · Q)" we can't tell the truth value for P or for Q; we only know that *not both* are true (at least one is false).

Our second S-rule deals with "or":

Not either this or that.	$\dfrac{\sim(P \vee Q)}{\sim P,\, \sim Q}$	NOT-EITHER is true,
∴ Not this.		so both are false.
∴ Not that.		

From a NOT-EITHER statement, we can infer the opposite of each part: "It isn't either cold or windy, therefore it isn't cold, therefore it isn't windy." Negative parts work the same way: we infer the opposite of each part (the opposite of "~A" being "A"):

Not either not-A or not-B.

∴ A

∴ B

$$\frac{\sim(\sim A \vee \sim B)}{A, B}$$

But from a *positive* OR statement we can infer nothing about the truth or falsity of each part:

You're in either Paris or Quebec.

∴ No conclusion.

$$\frac{(P \vee Q)}{\text{nil}}$$

You might be in Paris (and not Quebec), or in Quebec (and not Paris). From "(P ∨ Q)" we can't tell the truth value for P or for Q; we only know that *at least one* is true.

Our third S-rule deals with "if-then":

False if-then.	$\dfrac{\sim(P \supset Q)}{P, \sim Q}$	FALSE IF-THEN,
∴ First part true.		so first part true,
∴ Second part false.		second part false.

Recall that our truth tables make an if-then false just in case the first part is true and the second false. Recall also that "(P ⊃ Q)" means "We *don't* have P-true-and-Q-false"; so "~(P ⊃ Q)" means "We *do* have P-true-and-Q-false."

This FALSE IF-THEN rule isn't very intuitive; I suggest memorizing it instead of appealing to logical intuitions or concrete examples. You'll use this rule so much in doing proofs that it'll soon become second nature.

If a FALSE IF-THEN has negative parts, we again infer the first part and the opposite of the second part:

$$\frac{\sim(\sim A \supset B)}{\sim A, \sim B} \qquad \frac{\sim(A \supset \sim B)}{A, B} \qquad \frac{\sim(\sim A \supset \sim B)}{\sim A, B}$$

This diagram might help you follow what is going on here:

$$\frac{\sim(\text{first part} \supset \text{second part})}{\begin{array}{cc} \text{write the} & \text{write the opposite} \\ \text{first part} & \text{of the second part} \end{array}}$$

But if the if-then is itself *positive* (there's no "~" outside the parentheses), then we can infer nothing about the truth or falsity of each part. So from "(A ⊃ B)" we can infer nothing about A or about B.

Let me sum up our three S-rules:

If we have		*we can infer*
AND	→	each part
NOT-EITHER	→	opposite of each part
FALSE IF-THEN	→	part-1 & opposite of part-2

So we can simplify these:

$$\frac{(P \cdot Q)}{P, Q} \qquad \frac{\sim(P \vee Q)}{\sim P, \sim Q} \qquad \frac{\sim(P \supset Q)}{P, \sim Q}$$

But we can't simplify these:

$$\frac{\sim(P \cdot Q)}{nil} \qquad \frac{(P \vee Q)}{nil} \qquad \frac{(P \supset Q)}{nil}$$

3.10a   Exercise – LogiCola F (SE & SH)

Draw any simple conclusions (a letter or its negation) that follow from these premises. If nothing follows, leave blank.

$$\boxed{\frac{(C \cdot \sim R)}{}} \qquad \boxed{\frac{(C \cdot \sim R)}{C, \sim R}}$$

1. $\sim(I \vee \sim V)$

2. $\sim(J \cdot \sim N)$

3. $(\sim O \vee \sim X)$

4. $\sim(H \supset \sim I)$

5. $(F \supset \sim G)$

6. $(\sim Q \cdot B)$

7. $\sim(\sim A \cdot \sim J)$

8. $(\sim T \supset \sim H)$

9. $\sim(\sim N \vee \sim E)$

10. $\sim(F \supset M)$

11. $(M \vee \sim W)$

12. $(\sim N \supset S)$

13. $(P \cdot U)$

14. $\sim(R \vee S)$

15. $(\sim D \cdot \sim Z)$

16. $(L \vee C)$

17. $\sim(\sim U \supset \sim L)$

18. $\sim(Q \cdot T)$

19. $\sim(\sim Y \supset G)$

20. $(\sim K \vee B)$

3.11   I-rules

The **I-rules** are used to *infer* a conclusion from two premises. There are six I-rules – two each for "•," "∨," and "⊃."

Our first two I-rules deal with "and":

Not both are true.	~(P • Q)	~(P • Q)	*Deny* AND.
This one is true.	P	Q	*Affirm* one part.
∴ The other isn't.	~Q	~P	∴ *Deny* other part.

With a NOT-BOTH, we must affirm one part. Here are examples:

You're *not both* in Paris   You're *not both* in Paris
and also in Quebec.   and also in Quebec.
You're in Paris.   You're in Quebec.
∴ You're not in Quebec.   ∴ You're not in Paris.

Negative parts work the same way; if we affirm one, we can deny the other:

$$\frac{\sim(\sim A \cdot \sim B) \quad \sim A}{B} \qquad \frac{\sim(A \cdot \sim B) \quad A}{B} \qquad \frac{\sim(A \cdot \sim B) \quad \sim B}{\sim A}$$

In each case, the second premise affirms (says the same as) one part. And the conclusion denies (says the opposite of) the other part.

If we deny one part, we can't draw a conclusion about the other part:

Not both are true.	~(P • Q)
The first is false.	~P
No conclusion.	nil

You may want to conclude Q; but maybe Q is false too (maybe both parts are false). Here's an example:

You're *not both* in Paris and also in Quebec.
You're not in Paris.
∴ No conclusion.

You needn't be in Quebec; maybe you're in Chicago. To get a conclusion from a NOT-BOTH, we must *affirm* one part.

Our second pair of I-rules deals with "or":

At least one is true.	$(P \lor Q)$	$(P \lor Q)$	*Affirm* OR.
This one isn't.	~P	~Q	*Deny* one part.
∴ The other is.	Q	P	∴ *Affirm* other part.

With an OR, we must deny one part. Here are examples:

At least one hand (left or right) has candy. The left hand doesn't. ∴ The right hand does.	At least one hand (left or right) has candy. The right hand doesn't. ∴ The left hand does.

Negative parts work the same; if we deny one part, we can affirm the other:

$(\sim A \lor \sim B)$	$(A \lor \sim B)$	$(A \lor \sim B)$
A	~A	B
~B	~B	A

In each case, the second premise denies (says the opposite of) one part. And the conclusion affirms (says the same as) the other part.

If we affirm one part, we can't draw a conclusion about the other part:

At least one is true.	$(L \lor R)$
The first is true.	L
No conclusion.	nil

You may want to conclude ~R; but maybe R is true too (maybe both parts are true). Here's an example:

> At least one hand (left or right) has candy.
> The left hand has candy.
> ∴ No conclusion.

We can't conclude "The right hand doesn't have candy," since maybe both hands have it. To get a conclusion from an OR, we must *deny* one part.

Our final I-rules are *modus ponens* (MP – affirming mode) and *modus tollens* (MT – denying mode). Both deal with "if-then":

IF-THEN.	$(P \supset Q)$
Affirm first.	P
∴ Affirm second.	Q

IF-THEN.	$(P \supset Q)$
Deny second.	~Q
∴ Deny first.	~P

With an if-then, we must affirm the first part or deny the second part:

If you're a dog, then you're an animal. You're a dog. ∴ You're an animal.	(D ⊃ A) D ——— A	If you're a dog, then you're an animal. You're not an animal. ∴ You're not a dog.	(D ⊃ A) ~A ——— ~D

Negative parts work the same. If we affirm the first, we can affirm the second:

$$\frac{(\sim A \supset \sim B) \quad \sim A}{\sim B} \qquad \frac{(A \supset \sim B) \quad A}{\sim B} \qquad \frac{(\sim A \supset B) \quad \sim A}{B}$$

And if we deny the second, we can deny the first:

$$\frac{(\sim A \supset \sim B) \quad B}{A} \qquad \frac{(A \supset \sim B) \quad B}{\sim A} \qquad \frac{(\sim A \supset B) \quad \sim B}{A}$$

If we deny the first part or affirm the second, we can't conclude anything about the other part:

If you're a dog, then you're an animal. You're not a dog. ∴ No conclusion.	(D ⊃ A) ~D ——— nil	If you're a dog, then you're an animal. You're an animal. ∴ No conclusion.	(D ⊃ A) A ——— nil

In the first case, you may want to conclude "You're not an animal"; but you might be a cat. In the second, you may want to conclude "You're a dog"; but again, you might be a cat. To get a conclusion from an if-then, we must *affirm the first part or deny the second part*: "(+ ⊃ -)."

Let me sum up our I-rules:

	If we have		*we can infer*
NOT-BOTH + one part	→	opposite of other part	
OR + opposite of one part	→	other part	
IF-THEN + part-1	→	part-2	
IF-THEN + opposite of part-2	→	opposite of part-1	

So we can infer with these:

$$\frac{\sim(P \cdot Q) \quad P}{\sim Q} \qquad \frac{(P \vee Q) \quad \sim P}{Q} \qquad \frac{(P \supset Q) \quad P}{Q} \qquad \frac{(P \supset Q) \quad \sim Q}{\sim P}$$

But we can't infer with these:

$$\frac{\sim(P \cdot Q)}{\sim P} \qquad \frac{(P \vee Q)}{P} \qquad \frac{(P \supset Q)}{\sim P} \qquad \frac{(P \supset Q)}{Q}$$

$$\text{nil} \qquad\qquad \text{nil} \qquad\qquad \text{nil} \qquad\qquad \text{nil}$$

Since formal proofs depend so much on the S- and I-rules, it's important to master these rules before starting the next chapter.

3.11a   Exercise – LogiCola F (IE & IH)

Draw any simple conclusions (a letter or its negation) that follow from these premises. If nothing follows, leave blank.

$$\boxed{\frac{(\sim Q \vee \sim M)}{Q}} \qquad \boxed{\frac{(\sim Q \vee \sim M)}{Q}\\ \sim M}$$

1. $\sim(W \cdot T)$ W	6. $\sim(B \cdot S)$ $\sim$S	11. $(\sim N \vee \sim A)$ A	16. $(\sim L \supset M)$ $\sim$M
2. $(\sim Y \supset K)$ Y	7. $(U \supset G)$ U	12. $\sim(V \cdot H)$ $\sim$V	17. $\sim(\sim F \cdot \sim O)$ $\sim$O
3. $(S \vee \sim L)$ $\sim$S	8. $\sim(\sim F \cdot \sim Q)$ $\sim$F	13. $(\sim A \supset \sim E)$ $\sim$E	18. $\sim(\sim S \cdot W)$ $\sim$W
4. $(X \supset E)$ E	9. $(C \supset \sim V)$ $\sim$C	14. $(K \vee \sim R)$ R	19. $(\sim I \vee K)$ K
5. $(\sim M \vee \sim B)$ $\sim$M	10. $(H \supset \sim B)$ H	15. $(Y \vee \sim C)$ $\sim$C	20. $\sim(A \cdot \sim Y)$ A

3.12   Combining S- and I-rules

Our next exercise mixes S- and I-rule inferences. This should cause you little trouble, so long as you remember to use S-rules to simplify *one* premise and I-rules to infer from *two* premises. Here's a quick review:

S-rules (Simplifying): S-1 to S-3   *I-rules (Inferring): I-1 to I-6*

$(P \cdot Q) \rightarrow P, Q$

$\sim(P \vee Q) \rightarrow \sim P, \sim Q$

$\sim(P \supset Q) \rightarrow P, \sim Q$

$\sim(P \cdot Q), P \rightarrow \sim Q$
$\sim(P \cdot Q), Q \rightarrow \sim P$

$(P \vee Q), \sim P \rightarrow Q$
$(P \vee Q), \sim Q \rightarrow P$

$(P \supset Q), P \rightarrow Q$
$(P \supset Q), \sim Q \rightarrow \sim P$

3.12a   Exercise – LogiCola F (CE & CH)

Draw any simple conclusions (a letter or its negation) that follow from these premises. If nothing follows, leave blank.

$(A \supset \sim B)$
$\sim A$
——————

(no conclusion)

1. $\sim(W \cdot \sim X)$
    $\sim W$
    ——————

5. $(D \vee \sim J)$
    D
    ——————

9. $(P \cdot \sim Q)$
    ——————

13. $(\sim L \cdot S)$
     ——————

2. $(\sim I \supset \sim N)$
    N
    ——————

6. $\sim(\sim C \supset D)$
    ——————

10. $\sim(\sim R \cdot A)$
     $\sim R$
     ——————

14. $(\sim L \vee \sim T)$
     L
     ——————

3. $\sim(\sim B \vee C)$
    ——————

7. $(X \supset F)$
    $\sim X$
    ——————

11. $(\sim S \vee T)$
     ——————

15. $(A \supset \sim B)$
     ——————

4. $\sim(L \cdot M)$
    ——————

8. $\sim(M \vee \sim I)$
    ——————

12. $\sim(R \cdot \sim G)$
     $\sim G$
     ——————

16. $\sim(U \cdot T)$
     T
     ——————

3.13   Extended inferences

From an AND statement, we can conclude that both parts are true; so from "$(P \cdot Q)$," we can get "P" and also "Q." The rule also works on larger formulas:

$((C \equiv D) \cdot (E \supset F))$ AND statement, so
——————————————   both parts are true.
$(C \equiv D), (E \supset F)$

Visualize the premise as a big AND with two parts – blurring out the details: "($$$$$ · #####)." We can infer each part, even if these parts are complex.

Here's another inference using an S-rule:

$$\frac{\sim((C \cdot D) \supset (E \supset F))}{(C \cdot D),\ \sim(E \supset F)} \qquad \text{FALSE IF-THEN, so first} \atop \text{part true, second part false.}$$

Again, blur the details; read the long formula as just "FALSE IF-THEN." From such a formula, we can conclude that the first part is true and the second false; so we write the first part and the opposite of the second.

Consider this formula (which I suggest you read to yourself as "IF-THEN"):

$$((C \cdot D) \supset (E \supset F))$$

Since this is an if-then, we can't break it down using an S-rule. But we can conclude something from it if we have the first part true:

$$\frac{((C \cdot D) \supset (E \supset F))}{(C \cdot D)} \qquad \frac{\text{IF-THEN.}}{\text{Affirm first.}} \atop \text{Affirm second.}$$

And we can infer if we have the second part false:

$$\frac{((C \cdot D) \supset (E \supset F))}{\sim(C \cdot D)} \qquad \frac{\text{IF-THEN.}}{\text{Deny second.}} \atop \text{Deny first.}$$

These are the only legitimate I-rule inferences. We get no conclusion if we deny the first part or affirm the second:

$$\frac{((C \cdot D) \supset (E \supset F))}{\text{nil}} \qquad \frac{((C \cdot D) \supset (E \supset F))}{\text{nil}}$$

Also, we get no conclusion if we just have "E" as an additional premise:

$$\frac{((C \cdot D) \supset (E \supset F))}{\text{nil}} \atop E$$

Here we don't know that "(E $\supset$ F)" is true – but just that it *would* be true *if* "(C $\cdot$ D)" were true.

3.13a Exercise – No LogiCola exercise

Draw any conclusions that follow from these premises by a single application of the S-or I-rules. If nothing follows in this way, then leave blank.

$$\frac{\sim(\sim A \lor (B \cdot C))}{}$$

$$\frac{\sim(\sim A \lor (B \cdot C))}{A, \sim(B \cdot C)}$$

1. $\dfrac{\sim((A \cdot B) \supset \sim C)}{}$

2. $\dfrac{(A \cdot B) \supset \sim C}{\sim(A \cdot B)}$

3. $\dfrac{\sim((G \lor H) \cdot (I \lor J))}{}$

4. $\dfrac{\sim((G \lor H) \cdot (I \lor J))}{(G \lor H)}$

5. $\dfrac{(A \cdot B) \lor (C \supset D)}{}$

6. $\dfrac{(A \cdot B) \lor (C \supset D)}{C}$

7. $\dfrac{\sim((A \supset B) \lor C)}{}$

8. $\dfrac{(A \supset B) \supset C}{(A \supset B)}$

9. $\dfrac{(G \equiv H) \supset \sim(I \cdot J)}{\sim(I \cdot J)}$

3.14 Logic gates and computers

Digital computers were developed using ideas from propositional logic. The key insight is that electrical devices can simulate logic formulas.

Computers represent "1" and "0" by different physical states; "1" might be a positive voltage and "0" a zero voltage. An **and-gate** would then be a physical device with two inputs and one output, where the output has a positive voltage if and only if *both* inputs have positive voltages:

$$\begin{array}{c} A \rightarrow \\ B \rightarrow \end{array} \boxed{\text{AND-GATE}} \rightarrow (A \cdot B)$$

An **or-gate** would be similar, except that the output has a positive voltage if and only if *at least one* input has a positive voltage. For any formula, we can construct an input-output device (a **logic gate**) that mimics that formula.

A computer basically converts input information into 1's and 0's, manipulates these 1's and 0's by logic gates and memory devices, and converts the resulting 1's and 0's back into a useful output. So propositional logic is central to the operation of computers. One of my logic teachers at the University of Michigan, Art Burks, was part of the team in the 1940s that produced the ENIAC – the first large-scale electronic computer. So logic had an important role in moving us into the computer age.

CHAPTER 4
Propositional Proofs

Formal proofs help us to develop reasoning skills and are a convenient way to test arguments of various systems. From now on, formal proofs will be our main method of testing arguments.

4.1   Two sample proofs

A formal proof breaks a complicated argument into a series of small steps. Since most steps are based on our S- and I-rules (see Sections 3.10–13), you may want to review these now and then as you learn to do formal proofs.

Let's start with a proof in English. Suppose that we want to show that the butler committed the murder. We know these facts:

    1.   The only people in the mansion were the butler and the maid.
    2.   If the only people in the mansion were the butler and the maid,
          then the butler or the maid did it.
    3.   If the maid did it, then she had a motive.
    4.   The maid didn't have a motive.

Using an indirect strategy, we first assume that the butler didn't do it. Then we show that this leads to a contradiction:

    5.   Assume: The butler didn't do it.
    6.   ∴ Either the butler or the maid did it.   {from 1 and 2}
    7.   ∴ The maid did it.   {from 5 and 6}
    8.   ∴ The maid had a motive.   {from 3 and 7}

Given our premises, we get a contradiction (between 4 and 8) if we assume that the butler *didn't* do it. So our premises entail that the butler *did* it. If we can be confident of the premises, then we can be confident that the butler did it.

This formal proof mirrors in symbols how we reasoned in English:

```
       1    T                 Valid
 *     2    (T ⊃ (B ∨ M))
 *     3    (M ⊃ H)
       4    ~H    ⇐
          [ ∴ B
       5  ┌ asm: ~B
 *     6  │ ∴ (B ∨ M)  {from 1 and 2}
       7  │ ∴ M  {from 5 and 6}
       8  └ ∴ H  {from 3 and 7}   ⇐
       9   ∴ B  {from 5; 4 contradicts 8}
```

First we block off the conclusion "B" (showing that we can't use it to derive further lines) and assume its opposite "~B." Then we derive further lines using the S- and I-rules until we get a contradiction. We get line 6 from 1 and 2 by the rule that goes "If-then, affirm first, so affirm second." We get 7 by the rule that goes "At least one is true, this one isn't, so the other is." And 8 follows by the rule that goes "If-then, affirm first, so affirm second." But 4 and 8 contradict. So 9 follows, using **RAA**, our new *reductio ad absurdum* (reduction to absurdity) rule, which says that an assumption that leads to a contradiction must be false. As we apply RAA, we block off lines 5 through 8 to show that we can't use them in deriving further lines. Thus we prove the argument valid.

There can be various ways to do a proof. Instead of deriving "H" in line 8, we could have used 3 and 4 to get "~M," which would contradict 7. Inferences and contradictions can use any earlier lines that aren't already blocked off.[1]

We starred lines 2, 3, and 6 when we used them. Starred lines largely can be ignored in deriving further steps. Here are the starring rules – with examples:

```
      Star any wff that you              Star the longer wff used
     simplify using an S-rule.             in an I-rule inference.

           *  (A · B)                         *  (A ⊃ B)
           ─────────                              A
              ∴ A                              ─────────
              ∴ B                                 ∴ B
```

Starred lines are redundant, since shorter lines have the same information. When doing proofs, focus on deriving things from *unstarred* complex wffs (where a "complex wff" is anything longer than a letter or its negation).[2]

Here's another formal proof. Again, we first assume that the conclusion is false; then we show that, given our premises, it couldn't be false, since this leads to a contradiction:

---

[1] Each derived step in this book has a brief justification saying what pervious steps were used. Some people like to refer to the inference rule (like "I-rules" or "I-5" or "MP") too. Other people like to skip justifications – since it's usually easy to tell where lines are from.

[2] Starring isn't a necessary part of proofs; but you may find it helpful – because it focuses your attention away from redundant lines that aren't going to help you derive further steps.

```
 *   1     ((A · B) ⊃ C)   Valid
     2     B     ⇐
           [ ∴ (C ∨ ~A)
 *   3     ┌ asm: ~(C ∨ ~A)
     4     │  ∴ ~C   {from 3}
     5     │  ∴ A   {from 3}
 *   6     │  ∴ ~(A · B)   {from 1 and 4}
     7     └  ∴ ~B   {from 5 and 6}   ⇐
     8     ∴ (C ∨ ~A)   {from 3; 2 contradicts 7}
```

We start by blocking off the conclusion (showing that we can't use it to derive further lines) and assuming its opposite. Then we derive further lines using the S- and I-rules until we get a contradiction. Line 3 simplifies into lines 4 and 5 (and then gets starred). Lines 1 and 4 give us 6 (and then 1 gets starred). Lines 5 and 6 give us 7 (and then 6 gets starred). But 2 and 7 contradict. Since assumption 3 leads to a contradiction, we apply RAA. We block off lines 3 through 7 to show that we can't use them in deriving further lines.[1] We derive our original conclusion in line 8. Thus we prove the argument valid.

If we try to prove an invalid argument, we won't succeed; instead, we'll be led to refute the argument. We'll see invalid arguments later.

4.2   Easier proofs

Now we'll learn the rules behind formal proofs. We'll use these inference rules, which hold regardless of what pairs of contradictory wffs replace "P" / "~P" and "Q" / "~Q" (here "→" means we can infer whole lines from left to right):

S-rules (Simplifying): S-1 to S-6

$$(P · Q) → P, Q$$
$$\sim(P ∨ Q) → \sim P, \sim Q$$
$$\sim(P ⊃ Q) → P, \sim Q$$

$$\sim\sim P → P$$

$$(P ≡ Q) → (P ⊃ Q), (Q ⊃ P)$$
$$\sim(P ≡ Q) → (P ∨ Q), \sim(P · Q)$$

I-rules (Inferring): I-1 to I-6

$$\sim(P · Q), P → \sim Q$$
$$\sim(P · Q), Q → \sim P$$

$$(P ∨ Q), \sim P → Q$$
$$(P ∨ Q), \sim Q → P$$

$$(P ⊃ Q), P → Q$$
$$(P ⊃ Q), \sim Q → \sim P$$

Read "(P · Q) → P, Q" as "from '(P · Q)' one may derive 'P' and also 'Q.'"

Three rules are new. Rule S-4 eliminates "~~" from the beginning of a wff. S-5 breaks a biconditional into two conditionals. S-6 breaks up the denial of a biconditional; since "(P ≡ Q)" says that P and Q have the same truth value,

---

[1] Since the problem is done, why bother to block off lines 3 to 7? The answer is that blocking off will become important later on, when we get to multiple-assumption arguments.

"~(P ≡ Q)" says that P and Q have different truth values – so one or the other is true, but not both. None of these three rules is used very much.[1]

Here are key definitions:

- A **premise** is a line consisting of a wff by itself (with no "asm:" or "∴").
- An **assumption** is a line consisting of "asm:" and then a wff.
- A **derived step** is a line consisting of "∴" and then a wff.
- A **formal proof** is a vertical sequence of zero or more premises followed by one or more assumptions or derived steps, where each derived step follows from previously not-blocked-off lines by RAA or one of the inference rules listed above, and each assumption is blocked off using RAA.[2]
- Two wffs are **contradictory** if they are exactly alike except that one starts with an additional "~."
- A **simple wff** is a letter or its negation; any other wff is **complex**.

Rule RAA says an assumption is false if it leads to contradictory wffs; these wffs may occur anywhere in the proof (as premises or assumptions or derived steps), so long as neither is blocked off. Here's a more precise formulation:

> **RAA**: Suppose that some pair of not-blocked-off lines have contradictory wffs. Then block off all the lines from the last not-blocked-off assumption on down and infer a step consisting in "∴" followed by a contradictory of that assumption.

Here's another example of a formal proof:

```
      1    A    ⇐        Valid
 *    2    (A ⊃ B)
           [ ∴ (A · B)
 *    3    ┌ asm: ~(A · B)
      4    │ ∴ B   {from 1 and 2}
      5    └ ∴ ~A  {from 3 and 4}   ⇐
      6    ∴ (A · B)   {from 3; 1 contradicts 5}
```

First we assume the contradictory of the conclusion. Then we derive things until we get a contradiction; here line 5 contradicts premise 1. Finally, we block off the wffs from the assumption on down and derive the opposite of the assumption; this gives us our original conclusion.

---

[1] S-1 to S-6 also work in the other direction (for example, "(A · B)" follows from "A" and "B"); but our proofs and software use the S-rules only to simplify. The LogiCola software does, however, let you use two additional rules for the biconditional: (1) Given "(A ≡ B)": if you have one side true you can get the other side true – and if you have one side false you can get the other side false. (2) Given "~(A ≡ B)": if you have one side true you can get the other side false – and if you have one side false you can get the other side true.

[2] By this definition, the stars, line numbers, blocked off original conclusion, and justifications aren't strictly part of the proof; instead, they are unofficial helps.

In this next example, it's easier to assume the simpler contradictory of the conclusion – to assume "C" instead of "~~C":

```
*   1     (A · ~B)   Valid
*   2     (C ⊃ B)
        [∴ ~C
    3   ┌ asm: C    ⇦
    4   │ ∴ A    {from 1}
    5   │ ∴ ~B   {from 1}
    6   └ ∴ ~C   {from 2 and 5}   ⇦
    7   ∴ ~C   {from 3; 3 contradicts 6}
```

Line 6 contradicts the assumption; line 4 wasn't needed and could be omitted.

Don't use the original conclusion to derive further steps or be part of a contradiction; blocking off the original conclusion reminds us not to use it in the proof. And be sure to assume a genuine contradictory of the conclusion:

Right:	Wrong:
[∴ (~A ⊃ B)	[∴ (~A ⊃ B)
asm: ~(~A ⊃ B)	asm: (A ⊃ B)

To form a contradictory, you may add a squiggle to the beginning. If the wff already begins with a squiggle (and not with a left-hand parenthesis), you may instead omit the squiggle.

For now, I suggest this strategy for constructing a proof for an argument:

1. START: Block off the conclusion and add "asm:" followed by the conclusion's simpler contradictory.

2. S&I: Go through the unstarred, complex,[1] not-blocked-off wffs and use these to derive new wffs using the S- and I-rules. Star any wff you simplify using an S-rule, or the longer wff used in an I-rule inference.

   Note: While you needn't derive wffs again that you already have, you can star wffs that would give you what you already have.

3. RAA: When some pair of not-blocked-off lines contradict, apply RAA and derive the original conclusion. Your proof is done!

This strategy can prove most valid propositional arguments. We'll see later that some arguments need multiple assumptions and a more complex strategy.

4.2a   Exercise – LogiCola F (TE & TH) and GEV

Prove each of these arguments to be valid (all are valid).

---

[1] Recall that a "complex wff" is anything longer than a letter or its negation.

```
*   1      (A ∨ B)   Valid
      [ ∴ (~A ⊃ B)
*   2    ┌ asm: ~(~A ⊃ B)
    3    │  ∴ ~A    {from 2}
    4    │  ∴ ~B    {from 2}
    5    └  ∴ B     {from 1 and 3}
    6      ∴ (~A ⊃ B)   {from 2; 4 contradicts 5}
```

(A ∨ B)
∴ (~A ⊃ B)

1. (A ⊃ B)
    ∴ (~B ⊃ ~A)

2. A
    ∴ (A ∨ B)

3. (A ⊃ B)
    (~A ⊃ B)
    ∴ B

4. ((A ∨ B) ⊃ C)
    ∴ (~C ⊃ ~B)

5. (A ∨ B)
    (A ⊃ C)
    (B ⊃ D)
    ∴ (C ∨ D)

6. (A ⊃ B)
    (B ⊃ C)
    ∴ (A ⊃ C)

7. (A ≡ B)
    ∴ (A ⊃ (A · B))

8. ~(A ∨ B)
    (C ∨ B)
    ~(D · C)
    ∴ ~D

9. (A ⊃ B)
    ~B
    ∴ (A ≡ B)

10. (A ⊃ (B ⊃ C))
    ∴ ((A · B) ⊃ C)

4.2b   Exercise – LogiCola F (TE & TH) and GEV

First appraise intuitively. Then translate into logic (using the letters given) and prove
to be valid (all are valid).

1. If Heather saw the butler putting the tablet into the drink and the tablet was
    poison, then the butler killed the deceased.
    Heather saw the butler putting the tablet into the drink.
    ∴ If the tablet was poison, then the butler killed the deceased.   [Use H, T, and B.]

2. If we had an absolute proof of God's existence, then our will would be irresistibly
    attracted to do right.
    If our will were irresistibly attracted to do right, then we'd have no free will.
    ∴ If we have free will, then we have no absolute proof of God's existence.   [Use P,
    I, and F. This argument is from Immanuel Kant and John Hick, who used it to
    explain why God doesn't make his existence more evident.]

3. If racism is clearly wrong, then either it's factually clear that all races have equal
    abilities or it's morally clear that similar interests of all beings ought to be given
    equal consideration.
    It's not factually clear that all races have equal abilities.
    If it's morally clear that similar interests of all beings ought to be given equal
    consideration, then it's clear that similar interests of animals and humans ought
    to be given equal consideration.
    ∴ If racism is clearly wrong, then it's clear that similar interests of animals and
    humans ought to be given equal consideration.   [Use W, F, M, and A. This
    argument is from Peter Singer, who fathered the animal liberation movement.]

4. The universe is orderly (like a watch that follows complex laws).
   Most orderly things we've examined have intelligent designers.
   We've examined a large and varied group of orderly things.
   If most orderly things we've examined have intelligent designers and we've
     examined a large and varied group of orderly things, then probably most
     orderly things have intelligent designers.
   If the universe is orderly and probably most orderly things have intelligent
     designers, then the universe probably has an intelligent designer.
   ∴ The universe probably has an intelligent designer.   [Use U, M, W, P, and D.
     This is a form of the argument from design for the existence of God.]

5. If God doesn't want to prevent evil, then he isn't all good.
   If God isn't able to prevent evil, then he isn't all powerful.
   Either God doesn't want to prevent evil, or he isn't able.
   ∴ Either God isn't all powerful, or he isn't all good.   [Use W, G, A, and P. This
     form of the problem-of-evil argument is from the ancient Greek Empiricus.]

6. If Genesis gives the literal facts, then birds were created before humans. (Genesis
     1:20–26)
   If Genesis gives the literal facts, then birds were not created before humans.
     (Genesis 2:5–20)
   ∴ Genesis doesn't give the literal facts.   [Use L and B. Origen, an early Christian
     thinker, gave similar textual arguments against taking Genesis literally.]

7. The world had a beginning in time.
   If the world had a beginning in time, there was a cause for the world's beginning.
   If there was a cause for the world's beginning, a personal being caused the world.
   ∴ A personal being caused the world.   [Use B, C, and P. This "kalam argument"
     for the existence of God is from William Craig and James Moreland; they
     defend premise 1 by various considerations, including the big-bang theory, the
     law of entropy, and the impossibility of an actual infinite.]

8. If the world had a beginning in time and it didn't just pop into existence without
     any cause, then the world was caused by God.
   If the world was caused by God, then there is a God.
   There is no God.
   ∴ Either the world had no beginning in time, or it just popped into existence with-
     out any cause.   [Use B, P, C, and G. This argument is from J. L. Mackie, who
     based his "There is no God" premise on the problem-of-evil argument.]

9. Closed systems tend toward greater entropy (a more randomly uniform distri-
     bution of energy). (This is the second law of thermodynamics.)
   If closed systems tend toward greater entropy and the world has existed through
     endless time, then the world would have achieved almost complete entropy (for
     example, everything would be about the same temperature).
   The world has not achieved almost complete entropy.
   If the world hasn't existed through endless time, then the world had a beginning
     in time.
   ∴ The world had a beginning in time.   [Use G, E, C, and B. This argument is from
     William Craig and James Moreland.]

10. If time stretches back infinitely, then today wouldn't have been reached.
    If today wouldn't have been reached, then today wouldn't exist.
    Today exists.
    If time doesn't stretch back infinitely, then there was a first moment of time.
    ∴ There was a first moment of time.   [Use I, R, T, and F.]

11. If there are already laws preventing discrimination against women, then if the
    Equal Rights Amendment (ERA) would rob women of many current privileges
    then passage of the ERA would be against women's interests and women ought
    to work for its defeat.
    The ERA would rob women of many current privileges (like draft exemption).
    ∴ If there are already laws preventing discrimination against women, then women
    ought to work for the defeat of the ERA.   [Use L, R, A, and W.]

12. If women ought never to be discriminated against, then we should work for
    current laws against discrimination and also prevent future generations from
    imposing discriminatory laws against women.
    The only way to prevent future generations from imposing discriminatory laws
    against women is to pass an Equal Rights Amendment (ERA).
    If we should prevent future generations from imposing discriminatory laws
    against women and the only way to do this is to pass an ERA, then we ought to
    pass an ERA.
    ∴ If women ought never to be discriminated against, then we ought to pass an ERA.
    [Use N, C, F, O, and E.]

13. If the claim that knowledge-is-impossible is true, then we understand the word
    "know" but there are no cases of knowledge.
    If we understand the word "know," then we understand "know" either from a
    verbal definition or from experienced examples of knowledge.
    If we understand "know" from a verbal definition, then there's an agreed-upon
    definition of "know."
    There's no agreed-upon definition of "know."
    If we understand "know" from experienced examples of knowledge, then there
    are cases of knowledge.
    ∴ The claim that knowledge-is-impossible is false.   [Use I, U, C, D, E, and A. This
    is a form of the paradigm-case argument.]

14. If *p* is the greatest prime, then *n* (we may stipulate) is one plus the product of all
    the primes less than *p*.
    If *n* is one plus the product of all the primes less than *p*, then either *n* is prime or
    else *n* isn't prime but has prime factors greater than *p*.
    If *n* is prime, then *p* isn't the greatest prime.
    If *n* has prime factors greater than *p*, then *p* isn't the greatest prime.
    ∴ *p* isn't the greatest prime.   [Use G, N, P, and F. This proof that there's no
    greatest prime number is from the ancient Greek mathematician Euclid.]

4.3   Easier refutations

If we try to prove an invalid argument, we won't succeed; instead, we'll be led to *refute* the argument. This version of an earlier example is invalid because it drops a premise; if we try a proof, we get no contradiction:

The only people in the mansion were the butler and the maid.

If the only people in the mansion were the butler and the maid, then the butler or the maid did it.

If the maid did it, then she had a motive.

∴ The butler did it.

	1	T	Invalid
*	2	(T ⊃ (B ∨ M))	
*	3	(M ⊃ H)	T, M, H, ~B
		[∴ B	
	4	asm: ~B	
*	5	∴ (B ∨ M) {from 1 and 2}	
	6	∴ M {from 4 and 5}	
	7	∴ H {from 3 and 6}	

We can show the argument to be invalid by giving a **refutation** – a set of truth conditions making the premises all true and conclusion false. To get the refutation, we take the simple wffs (letters or their negation) from not-blocked-off lines and put them in a box (their order doesn't matter); here the simple wffs come from lines 1, 4, 6, and 7. If the refutation has a letter by itself (like "T" or "M"), then we mark that letter *true* ("1") in the argument; if it has the negation of a letter (like "~B"), then we mark that letter *false* ("0"):

$$T^1 = 1 \qquad \text{Invalid}$$
$$(T^1 \supset (B^0 \vee M^1)) = 1$$
$$(M^1 \supset H^1) = 1$$
$$\therefore B^0 = 0$$

Our truth conditions make the premises all true and conclusion false – showing the argument to be invalid. We also could write the refutation in these ways:

T=1, M=1, H=1, B=0		T^1, M^1, H^1, B^0

Lawyers often use a similar form of reasoning to defend a client. They sketch a possible situation consistent both with the evidence and with their client's innocence; they conclude that the evidence doesn't establish their client's guilt. For the present example, a lawyer might argue as follows:

> We know that the only people in the mansion were the butler and the maid. But it's possible that the maid did the killing – not the butler – and that the maid had a motive. Since the known facts are consistent with this possibility, these facts don't establish that the butler did it.

Here's another invalid argument and its refutation:

$$
\begin{array}{lll}
1 & (A^0 \supset B^1) = 1 & \text{Invalid} \\
* \ \ 2 & (C^0 \vee B^1) = 1 & \\
& [\therefore (C^0 \vee A^0) = 0 & \boxed{B, \sim A, \sim C} \\
* \ \ 3 & \text{asm: } \sim(C \vee A) & \\
4 & \therefore \sim C \quad \{\text{from } 3\} & \\
5 & \therefore \sim A \quad \{\text{from } 3\} & \\
6 & \therefore B \quad \{\text{from } 2 \text{ and } 4\} &
\end{array}
$$

Again, we derive whatever we can. Since we don't get a contradiction, we take any simple wffs (letters or their negation) that aren't blocked off and put them in a box. This box gives truth conditions making the premises all true and conclusion false. This shows that the argument is invalid.

You may be tempted to use line 1 with 5 or 6 to derive a further conclusion – and a contradiction. But we can't derive anything validly here:

$$
\begin{array}{cc}
(A \supset B) & (A \supset B) \\
\dfrac{\sim A}{\text{nil}} & \dfrac{B}{\text{nil}}
\end{array}
$$

If we misapply the I-rules, we could incorrectly "prove" the invalid argument to be valid.

Let me summarize. Suppose we want to show that, given certain premises, the butler must be guilty. We assume that he's innocent and try to show that this leads to a contradiction. If we get a contradiction, then his innocence is impossible – and so he must be guilty. But if we get no contradiction, then we may be able to show how the premises could be true while yet he is innocent – thus showing that the argument against him is invalid.

I suggest this strategy for proving or refuting a propositional argument:

1. START: Block off the conclusion and add "asm:" followed by the conclusion's simpler contradictory.

2. S&I: Go through the unstarred, complex, not-blocked-off wffs and use these to derive new wffs using the S- and I-rules. Star any wff you simplify using an S-rule, or the longer wff used in an I-rule inference. If you get a contradiction, apply RAA (step 3). If you can derive nothing further and yet have no contradiction, then refute (step 4).

3. RAA: Since you have a contradiction, apply RAA. You've proved the argument valid.

4. REFUTE: You have no contradiction and yet can't derive anything else. Draw a box containing any simple wffs (letters or their negation) that aren't blocked off. In the original argument, mark each letter "1" or "0" or "?" depending on whether you have the letter or its negation or neither in the box. If these truth conditions make the premises all true and conclusion false, then this shows the argument to be invalid.

This strategy can prove or refute most propositional arguments. We'll see later that some arguments need a more complex strategy and multiple assumptions.

When we plug in the values of our refutation, we should get the premises all true and conclusion false. If that doesn't happen, then we did something wrong. The faulty line (a 0 or ? premise, or a 1 or ? conclusion) is the source of the problem; maybe we derived something incorrectly from this line, or didn't derive something we should have derived. So our strategy can sometimes tell us when something went wrong and where to look to fix the problem.

4.3a   Exercise – LogiCola GEI

Prove each of these arguments to be invalid (all are invalid).

$$(A \supset B)$$
$$\therefore (B \supset A)$$

$$
\begin{array}{ll}
1 & (A^0 \supset B^1) = 1 \quad \textbf{Invalid} \\
& [\therefore (B^1 \supset A^0) = 0 \\
* \quad 2 & \text{asm: } \sim(B \supset A) \quad \boxed{B, \sim A} \\
3 & \therefore B \quad \{\text{from 2}\} \\
4 & \therefore \sim A \quad \{\text{from 2}\}
\end{array}
$$

1. $(A \lor B)$
   $\therefore A$

2. $(A \supset B)$
   $(C \supset B)$
   $\therefore (A \supset C)$

3. $\sim(A \cdot \sim B)$
   $\therefore \sim(B \cdot \sim A)$

4. $(A \supset (B \cdot C))$
   $(\sim C \supset D)$
   $\therefore ((B \cdot \sim D) \supset A)$

5. $((A \supset B) \supset (C \supset D))$
   $(B \supset D)$
   $(A \supset C)$
   $\therefore (A \supset D)$

6. $(A \equiv B)$
   $(C \supset B)$
   $\sim(C \cdot D)$
   D
   $\therefore \sim A$

7. $((A \cdot B) \supset C)$
   $\therefore (B \supset C)$

8. $((A \cdot B) \supset C)$
   $((C \lor D) \supset \sim E)$
   $\therefore \sim(A \cdot E)$

9. $\sim(A \cdot B)$
   $(\sim A \lor C)$
   $\therefore \sim(C \cdot B)$

10. $\sim(\sim A \cdot \sim B)$
    $\sim C$
    $(D \lor \sim A)$
    $((C \cdot \sim E) \supset \sim B)$
    $\sim D$
    $\therefore \sim E$

4.3b   Exercise – LogiCola GEC

First appraise intuitively. Then translate into logic (using the letters given) and say whether valid (and give a proof) or invalid (and give a refutation).

1. If the butler shot Jones, then he knew how to use a gun.
   If the butler was a former marine, then he knew how to use a gun.
   The butler was a former marine.
   ∴ The butler shot Jones.   [Use S, K, and M.]

2. If virtue can be taught, then either there are professional virtue-teachers or there are amateur virtue-teachers.

   If there are professional virtue-teachers, then the Sophists can teach their students to be virtuous.

   If there are amateur virtue-teachers, then the noblest Athenians can teach their children to be virtuous.

   The Sophists can't teach their students to be virtuous and the noblest Athenians (such as the great leader Pericles) can't teach their children to be virtuous.

   ∴ Virtue can't be taught.   [Use V, P, A, S, and N. This is from Plato's *Meno*.]

3. It would be equally wrong for a sadist (through a drug injection that would blind you but not hurt your mother) to have blinded you permanently before or after your birth.

   If it would be equally wrong for a sadist (through such a drug injection) to have blinded you permanently before or after your birth, then it's false that one's moral right to equal consideration begins at birth.

   If infanticide is wrong and abortion isn't wrong, then one's moral right to equal consideration begins at birth.

   Infanticide is wrong.

   ∴ Abortion is wrong.   [Use E, R, I, and A.]

4. If you hold a moral belief and don't act on it, then you're inconsistent.

   If you're inconsistent, then you're doing wrong.

   ∴ If you hold a moral belief and act on it, then you aren't doing wrong.   [Use M, A, I, and W. Is the conclusion plausible? What more plausible conclusion follows from these premises?]

5. If Socrates escapes from jail, then he's willing to obey the state only when it pleases him.

   If he's willing to obey the state only when it pleases him, then he doesn't really believe what he says and he's inconsistent.

   ∴ If Socrates really believes what he says, then he won't escape from jail.   [Use E, W, R, and I. This argument is from Plato's *Crito*. Socrates had been jailed and sentenced to death for teaching philosophy. He discussed with his friends whether he ought to escape from jail instead of suffering the death penalty.]

6. Either Socrates's death will be perpetual sleep, or if the gods are good then his death will be an entry into a better life.

   If Socrates's death will be perpetual sleep, then he shouldn't fear death.

   If his death will be an entry into a better life, then he shouldn't fear death.

   ∴ He shouldn't fear death.   [Use P, G, B, and F. This argument is from Plato's *Crito* – except for which dropped premise?]

7. If predestination is true, then God causes us to sin.

   If God causes us to sin and yet damns sinners to eternal punishment, then God isn't good.

   ∴ If God is good, then either predestination isn't true or else God doesn't damn sinners to eternal punishment.   [Use P, C, D, and G. This attacks the views of the American colonial thinker Jonathan Edwards.]

8. If determinism is true, then we have no free will.
   If Heisenberg's interpretation of quantum physics is correct, some events aren't causally necessitated by prior events.
   If some events aren't causally necessitated by prior events, determinism is false.
   ∴ If Heisenberg's interpretation of quantum physics is correct, then we have free will. [Use D, F, H, and E.]

9. Government's function is to protect life, liberty, and the pursuit of happiness.
   The British colonial government doesn't protect these.
   The only way to change it is by revolution.
   If government's function is to protect life, liberty, and the pursuit of happiness and the British colonial government doesn't protect these, then the British colonial government ought to be changed.
   If the British colonial government ought to be changed and the only way to change it is by revolution, then we ought to have a revolution.
   ∴ We ought to have a revolution. [Use G, B, O, C, and R. This summarizes the reasoning behind the American Declaration of Independence. Premise 1 was claimed to be self-evident, premises 2 and 3 were backed by historical data, and premises 4 and 5 were implicit conceptual bridge premises.]

10. The apostles' teaching either comes from God or is of human origin.
    If it comes from God and we kill the apostles, then we will be fighting God.
    If it's of human origin, then it'll collapse of its own accord.
    If it'll collapse of its own accord and we kill the apostles, then our killings will be unnecessary.
    ∴ If we kill the apostles, then either our killings will be unnecessary or we will be fighting God. [Use G, H, K, F, C, and U. This argument, from Rabbi Gamaliel in Acts 5:34–9, is perhaps the most complex reasoning in the Bible.]

11. If materialism (the view that only matter exists) is true, then idealism is false.
    If idealism (the view that only minds exist) is true, then materialism is false.
    If mental events exist, then materialism is false.
    If materialists *think* their theory is true, then mental events exist.
    ∴ If materialists *think* their theory is true, then idealism is true. [Use M, I, E, and T.]

12. If determinism is true and cruelty is wrong, then the universe contains unavoidable wrong actions.
    If the universe contains unavoidable wrong actions, then we ought to regret the universe as a whole.
    If determinism is true and regretting cruelty is wrong, then the universe contains unavoidable wrong actions.
    ∴ If determinism is true, then either we ought to regret the universe as a whole (the pessimism option) or else cruelty isn't wrong and regretting cruelty isn't wrong (the "nothing matters" option). [Use D, C, U, O, and R. This sketches the reasoning in William James's "The Dilemma of Determinism." James thought that when we couldn't prove one side or the other to be correct (as on the issue of determinism) it was more rational to pick our beliefs in accord with practical considerations. He argued that these weighed against determinism.]

13. If a belief is proved, then it's worthy of acceptance.
     If a belief isn't disproved but is of practical value to our lives, then it's worthy of acceptance.
     If a belief is proved, then it isn't disproved.
     ∴ If a belief is proved or is of practical value to our lives, then it's worthy of acceptance.   [Use P, W, D, and V.]

14. If you're consistent and think that stealing is normally permissible, then you'll consent to the idea of others stealing from you in normal circumstances.
     You don't consent to the idea of others stealing from you in normal circumstances.
     ∴ If you're consistent, then you won't think that stealing is normally permissible. [Use C, N, and Y.]

15. If the meaning of a term is always the object it refers to, then the meaning of "Fido" is Fido.
     If the meaning of "Fido" is Fido, then if Fido is dead the meaning of "Fido" is dead.
     If the meaning of "Fido" is dead, then "Fido is dead" has no meaning.
     "Fido is dead" has meaning.
     ∴ The meaning of a term isn't always the object it refers to.   [Use A, B, F, M, and H. This is from Ludwig Wittgenstein, except for which dropped premise?]

16. God is all powerful.
     If God is all powerful, then he could have created the world in any logically possible way and the world has no necessity.
     If the world has no necessity, then we can't know the way the world is by abstract speculation apart from experience.
     ∴ We can't know the way the world is by abstract speculation apart from experience.   [Use A, C, N, and K. This is from the medieval William of Ockham.]

17. If God changes, then he changes for the worse or for the better.
     If he changes for the better, then he isn't perfect.
     If he's perfect, then he doesn't change for the worse.
     ∴ If God is perfect, then he doesn't change.   [Use C, W, B, and P.]

18. If belief in God has scientific backing, then it's rational.
     No conceivable scientific experiment could decide whether there is a God.
     If belief in God has scientific backing, then some conceivable scientific experiment could decide whether there is a God.
     ∴ Belief in God isn't rational.   [Use B, R, and D.]

19. Every event with finite probability eventually takes place.
     If the world powers don't get rid of their nuclear weapons, then there's a finite probability that humanity will eventually destroy the world.
     If every event with finite probability eventually takes place and there's a finite probability that humanity will eventually destroy the world, then humanity will eventually destroy the world.
     ∴ Either the world powers will get rid of their nuclear weapons, or humanity will eventually destroy the world.   [Use E, R, F, and H.]

20. If the world isn't ultimately absurd, then conscious life will go on forever and the world process will culminate in an eternal personal goal.
    If there is no God, then conscious life won't go on forever.
    ∴ If the world isn't ultimately absurd, then there is a God. [Use A, F, C, and G. This argument is from the Jesuit scientist, Pierre Teilhard de Chardin.]

21. If it rained here on this date 500 years ago and there's no way to know whether it rained here on this date 500 years ago, then there are objective truths that we cannot know.
    If it didn't rain here on this date 500 years ago and there's no way to know whether it rained here on this date 500 years ago, then there are objective truths that we cannot know.
    There's no way to know whether it rained here on this date 500 years ago.
    ∴ There are objective truths that we cannot know. [R, K, and O]

22. If you know that you don't exist, then you don't exist.
    If you know that you don't exist, then you know some things.
    If you know some things, then you exist.
    ∴ You exist. [Use K, E, and S.]

23. We have an idea of a perfect being.
    If we have an idea of a perfect being, then this idea is either from the world or from a perfect being.
    If this idea is from a perfect being, then there is a God.
    ∴ There is a God. [Use I, W, P, and G. This is from René Descartes, except for which dropped premise?]

24. The distance from A to B can be divided into an infinity of spatial points.
    One can cross only one spatial point at a time.
    If one can cross only one spatial point at a time, then one can't cross an infinity of spatial points in a finite time.
    If the distance from A to B can be divided into an infinity of spatial points and one can't cross an infinity of spatial points in a finite time, then one can't move from A to B in a finite time.
    If motion is real, then one can move from A to B in a finite time.
    ∴ Motion isn't real. [Use D, O, C, M, and R. This argument is from the ancient Greek Zeno of Elea, who denied the reality of motion.]

25. If the square root of 2 equals some fraction of positive whole numbers, then (we stipulate) the square root of 2 equals x/y and x/y is simplified as far as it can be.
    If the square root of 2 equals x/y, then $2 = x^2/y^2$.
    If $2 = x^2/y^2$, then $2y^2 = x^2$.
    If $2y^2 = x^2$, then x is even.
    If x is even and $2y^2 = x^2$, then y is even.
    If x is even and y is even, then x/y isn't simplified as far as it can be.
    ∴ The square root of 2 doesn't equal some fraction of positive whole numbers.
    [Use F, F′, S, T, T′, X, and Y.]

4.4 Multiple assumptions

We get stuck if we apply our present proof strategy to the following argument:

If the butler was at the party, then he fixed
the drinks and poisoned the deceased.   1   (A ⊃ (F · P))
If the butler wasn't at the party, then the   2   (~A ⊃ (S · R))
    detective would have seen him leave the   3   ~R
    mansion and would have reported this.   [∴ P
The detective didn't report this.   4   asm: ~P
∴ The butler poisoned the deceased.

After the assumption, we can't apply the S- or I-rules or RAA; and we don't have enough simple wffs for a refutation. So we're stuck. What can we do?

On our expanded proof strategy, when we get stuck we'll make another assumption. This assumption may lead to a contradiction; if so, we can apply RAA to derive the opposite and perhaps use this to complete the proof.

Let's focus on breaking up line 1. This line has two sides: "A" and "(F · P)." It would be useful to assume one side or its negation, in order to carry on the proof further; so we arbitrarily assume "~A" and see what happens. Since "~A" leads to a contradiction, we derive "A" – and having "A" lets us complete the proof in the normal way. Our multiple-assumption proof looks like this:

```
                           *   1     (A ⊃ (F · P))   Valid
                               2     (~A ⊃ (S · R))
                               3     ~R   ⇦
                                  [∴ P
To break up line 1, we         4   ┌ asm: ~P
assume one side or its    →    5   │ ┌ asm: ~A   {break up 1}
negation.                      6   │ │ ∴ (S · R)   {from 2 and 5}
                               7   │ │ ∴ S   {from 6}
                               8   │ └ ∴ R   {from 6}   ⇦
Since "~A" leads to a          9   │ ∴ A   {from 5; 3 contradicts 8}
contradiction, we derive  →  * 10   │ ∴ (F · P)   {from 1 and 9}
"A" and finish the proof.      11   │ ∴ F   {from 10}
                               12   └ ∴ P   {from 10}
                               13   ∴ P   {from 4; 4 contradicts 12}
```

The novel steps here are 5 through 9, which are used to derive "A." Study these steps careful before reading further.

Let's go through this again, but more slowly. Recall that we got stuck after our initial assumption. To carry on the proof further, it would be useful to break up line 1, by assuming one side or its negation. So we arbitrarily assume "~A." Then we use this second assumption "~A" with line 2 to derive further steps and get a contradiction (between 3 and 8):

Note the
double stars!

(We have two
not-blocked-off
assumptions.)

➜   **

```
        1    (A ⊃ (F · P))
 ➜ **   2    (~A ⊃ (S · R))
        3    ~R  ⇦
         [ ∴ P
        4    asm: ~P
        5       asm: ~A  {break up 1}
 ➜ **   6       ∴ (S · R)  {from 2 and 5}
        7       ∴ S  {from 6}
        8       ∴ R  {from 6}  ⇦
```

As usual, we star lines 2 and 6 when we use S- and I-rules on them. But now we use *two* stars – since now we have *two* not-blocked-off assumptions. This expanded starring rule covers multiple-assumptions proofs:

> When you star, use one star for
> each not-blocked-off assumption.

Multiple stars mean "You can ignore this line for now, but you may have to use it later."

Let's get back to our proof. Since "asm: ~A" leads to a contradiction (between 3 and 8), we use RAA to derive "A"; notice how we do it :

> When you get a contradiction:
>
> - block off the lines from the last assumption on down,
> - derive the opposite of this last assumption, and
> - erase star strings with more stars than the number of remaining assumptions.

```
        1    (A ⊃ (F · P))
        2    (~A ⊃ (S · R))
        3    ~R  ⇦
         [ ∴ P
        4    asm: ~P
        5    ┌ asm: ~A  {break up 1}
        6    │ ∴ (S · R)  {from 2 and 5}
        7    │ ∴ S  {from 6}
        8    └ ∴ R  {from 6}  ⇦
        9    ∴ A  {from 5; 3 contradicts 8}
```

Since our second assumption (line 5) led to a contradiction, we block off from this assumption on down (lines 5 to 8); now we can't use these lines, which depend on an outdated assumption, to derive further steps or get a contradiction. In line 9, we derive "A" (the opposite of assumption "~A"). Finally, we erase "**" from lines 2 and 6 – since now we have only one not-blocked-off assumption; we may have to use these formerly starred lines again.[1]

Now that we have "A" in line 9, we use this with line 1 to derive further steps and get a second contradiction; then we apply RAA to complete the proof:

---

[1] Since lines 5–8 are now blocked off, the lines that made the doubly starred lines redundant are no longer available. So we erase "**" when the second assumption dies.

```
 *   1      (A ⊃ (F · P))   Valid
     2      (~A ⊃ (S · R))
     3      ~R
         [ ∴ P
     4    ┌ asm: ~P    ⇦
     5    │ ┌ asm: ~A   {break up 1}
     6    │ │ ∴ (S · R)  {from 2 and 5}
     7    │ │ ∴ S   {from 6}
     8    │ └ ∴ R   {from 6}
     9    │ ∴ A   {from 5; 3 contradicts 8}
 *  10    │ ∴ (F · P)  {from 1 and 9}
    11    │ ∴ F   {from 10}
    12    └ ∴ P   {from 10}   ⇦
    13   ∴ P   {from 4; 4 contradicts 12}
```

Study this example carefully. When you understand it well, you're ready to learn the general strategy for doing multiple-assumption proofs.

4.5   Harder proofs

The most difficult part of multiple-assumption proofs is knowing *when* to make another assumption and *what* to assume.

First use the S- and I-rules and RAA to derive everything you can. You may get stuck; this means that you can't derive anything further but yet need to do something to get a proof or refutation. When you get stuck, try to make another assumption. Look for an unstarred complex wff for which you don't already have one side or its negation. This wff will have one of these forms:

$$\sim(A \cdot B) \qquad (A \lor B) \qquad (A \supset B)$$

Assume either side or its negation. Here we could use any of these:

$$\text{asm: A} \qquad \text{asm: } \sim A \qquad \text{asm: B} \qquad \text{asm: } \sim B$$

While any of the four will work, our proof will go differently depending on which we use. Suppose that we want to break up "(A ⊃ B)"; compare what happens if we assume "A" or assume "~A":

| *(immediate gratification)* | (A ⊃ B) asm: A ∴ B | (A ⊃ B) asm: ~A ... | *(delayed gratification)* |

In the first case, we assume "A" and get immediate gratification; we can use an I-rule on "(A ⊃ B)" right away to get "B." In the second case, we assume "~A" and get delayed gratification; we'll be able to use an I-rule on "(A ⊃ B)" only later, after the "~A" assumption dies (if it does) and we derive "A." The "delayed gratification" approach tends to produce shorter proofs; it saves an average of one step, with all the gain coming on invalid arguments. So sometimes a proof is simpler if you assume one thing rather than another.

Follow the same strategy on wffs that are more complicated. To break up "((A · B) ⊃ (C · D))," we could make any of these four assumptions:

asm: (A · B)   asm: ~(A · B)   asm: (C · D)   asm: ~(C · D)

Assume one side or its negation; never assume the denial of a whole line.

Our final proof strategy can prove or refute any propositional argument:

1. START: Block off the conclusion and add "asm:" followed by the conclusion's simpler contradictory.

2. S&I: Go through the unstarred, complex, not-blocked-off wffs and use these to derive whatever new wffs you can using the S- and I-rules. Star (with one star for each not-blocked-off assumption) any wff you simplify using an S-rule, or the longer wff used in an I-rule inference. If you get a contradiction, apply RAA (step 3). If you can derive nothing further and yet have no contradiction, then make another assumption if you can (step 4); otherwise, refute (step 5).

    Note: While you needn't derive wffs again that you already have, you can star wffs that would give you what you already have.

3. RAA: Since you have a contradiction, apply RAA. If all assumptions are now blocked off, you've proved the argument valid. Otherwise, erase star strings having more stars than the number of not-blocked-off assumptions. Then return to step 2.

4. ASSUME: Make another assumption if you have an unstarred, not-blocked-off wff of one of these forms for which you don't already have one side or its negation:

    ~(A · B)   (A ∨ B)   (A ⊃ B)

    Assume one side or its negation – and then return to step 2.

    Note: Don't make an assumption from a wff if you already have one side or its negation. For example, don't make an assumption from "(A ⊃ B)" if you already have "~A" or "B." In this case, the wff is already "broken up."

5. REFUTE: Here all complex, not-blocked-off wffs are either starred or already broken up – and yet you have no contradiction. Draw a box containing any simple wffs (letters or their negation) that aren't blocked off. In the original argument, mark each letter "1" or "0" or "?" depending on whether you have the letter or its negation or neither in the box. These truth conditions should make the premises all true and conclusion false – thus showing the argument to be invalid.

Let's take another example. Consider a proof that begins this way:

```
     1    (A ⊃ (B · C))
     2    (B ⊃ (A · C))
        [ ∴ ((A ∨ B) ⊃ C)
  *  3      asm: ~((A ∨ B) ⊃ C)
     4      ∴ (A ∨ B)  {from 3}
     5      ∴ ~C   {from 3}
```

It's important to use the S- and I-rules as far as we can; make additional assumptions only as a last resort. But now we're stuck; we can't apply the S- or I-rules or RAA, and we don't have enough values to refute the argument. So we break up line 1 by assuming one side or its negation. We decide to assume "A" (line 6). Then we derive further things (using two stars while there are two not-blocked-off assumptions) until we get a contradiction (between 5 and 9):

```
**  1    (A ⊃ (B · C))
    2    (B ⊃ (A · C))
       [ ∴ ((A ∨ B) ⊃ C)
 *  3      asm: ~((A ∨ B) ⊃ C)
    4      ∴ (A ∨ B)  {from 3}
    5      ∴ ~C   {from 3}   ⇐
    6        asm: A   {break up 1}
** 7        ∴ (B · C)  {from 1 and 6}
    8        ∴ B   {from 7}
    9        ∴ C   {from 7}   ⇐
```

Since we have a contradiction, we apply RAA (blocking off lines 6 to 9 and deriving line 10); and we erase each "**" (since now there's only one not-blocked-off assumption):

```
    1    (A ⊃ (B · C))
    2    (B ⊃ (A · C))
       [ ∴ ((A ∨ B) ⊃ C)
 *  3      asm: ~((A ∨ B) ⊃ C)
    4      ∴ (A ∨ B)  {from 3}
    5      ∴ ~C   {from 3}   ⇐
    6      ┌ asm: A   {break up 1}
    7      │ ∴ (B · C)  {from 1 and 6}
    8      │ ∴ B   {from 7}
    9      └ ∴ C   {from 7}   ⇐
   10      ∴ ~A   {from 6; 5 contradicts 9}
```

We continue until we get our second contradiction – which finishes our proof:

```
     1      (A ⊃ (B · C))
  *  2      (B ⊃ (A · C))
        [∴ ((A ∨ B) ⊃ C)
  *  3    ┌ asm: ~((A ∨ B) ⊃ C)
  *  4    │ ∴ (A ∨ B)  {from 3}
     5    │ ∴ ~C  {from 3}
     6    │ ┌ asm: A  {break up 1}
     7    │ │ ∴ (B · C)  {from 1 and 6}
     8    │ │ ∴ B  {from 7}
     9    │ └ ∴ C  {from 7}
    10    │ ∴ ~A  {from 6; 5 contradicts 9}  ⇐
    11    │ ∴ B  {from 4 and 10}
    12    │ ∴ (A · C)  {from 2 and 11}
    13    └ ∴ A  {from 12}  ⇐
    14    ∴ ((A ∨ B) ⊃ C)  {from 3; 10 contradicts 13}
```

4.5a   Exercise – LogiCola GHV

Prove each of these arguments to be valid (all are valid).

```
  *  1      (B ∨ A)   Valid
     2      (B ⊃ A)
        [∴ ~(A ⊃ ~A)
  *  3    ┌ asm: (A ⊃ ~A)
     4    │ ┌ asm: B  {break up 1}
     5    │ │ ∴ A  {from 2 and 4}
     6    │ └ ∴ ~A  {from 3 and 5}
     7    │ ∴ ~B  {from 4; 5 contradicts 6}
     8    │ ∴ A  {from 1 and 7}
     9    └ ∴ ~A  {from 3 and 8}
    10    ∴ ~(A ⊃ ~A)  {from 3; 8 contradicts 9}
```

```
(B ∨ A)
(B ⊃ A)
∴ ~(A ⊃ ~A)
```

1.   (A ⊃ B)
    (A ∨ (A · C))
  ∴ (A · B)

2.   (((A · B) ⊃ C) ⊃ (D ⊃ E))
    D
  ∴ (C ⊃ E)

3.   (B ⊃ A)
    ~(A · C)
    (B ∨ C)
  ∴ (A ≡ B)

4.   (A ∨ (D · E))
    (A ⊃ (B · C))
  ∴ (D ∨ C)

5.   ((A ⊃ B) ⊃ C)
    (C ⊃ (D · E))
  ∴ (B ⊃ D)

6.   (~(A ∨ B) ⊃ (C ⊃ D))
    (~A · ~D)
  ∴ (~B ⊃ ~C)

7.   (~A ≡ B)
  ∴ ~(A ≡ B)

8.   (A ⊃ (B · ~C))
    C
    ((D · ~E) ∨ A)
  ∴ D

4.5b Exercise – LogiCola GHV

First appraise intuitively. Then translate into logic (using the letters given) and prove to be valid (all are valid).

1. If the butler put the tablet into the drink and the tablet was poison, then the butler killed the deceased and the butler is guilty.
   The butler put the tablet into the drink.
   The tablet was poison.
   ∴ The butler is guilty.   [Use P, T, K, and G.]

2. If I'm coming down with a cold and I exercise, then I'll get worse and feel awful.
   If I don't exercise, then I'll suffer exercise deprivation and I'll feel awful.
   ∴ If I'm coming down with a cold, then I'll feel awful.   [Use C, E, W, A, and D.]

3. You'll get an A if and only if you either get a hundred on the final exam or else bribe the teacher.
   You won't get a hundred on the final exam.
   ∴ You'll get an A if and only if you bribe the teacher.   [Use A, H, and B.]

4. If President Nixon knew about the massive Watergate cover-up, then he lied to the American people on national television and he should resign.
   If President Nixon didn't know about the massive Watergate cover-up, then he was incompetently ignorant and he should resign.
   ∴ Nixon should resign.   [Use K, L, R, and I.]

5. Common sense assumes we have moral knowledge.
   There's no disproof of moral knowledge.
   If common sense assumes we have moral knowledge, then if there's no disproof of moral knowledge we should believe that we have moral knowledge.
   Any proof of a moral truth presupposes a more basic moral truth.
   We can't prove moral truths by more basic ones endlessly.
   If any proof of a moral truth presupposes a more basic moral truth and we can't prove moral truths by more basic ones endlessly, then if we should believe that we have moral knowledge we should accept self-evident moral truths.
   ∴ We should accept self-evident moral truths.   [Use C, D, B, P, E, and S; this argument defends ethical intuitionism.]

6. Moral judgments express either truth claims or feelings.
   If moral judgments express truth claims, then "ought" expresses either a concept from sense experience or an objective concept that isn't from sense experience.
   "Ought" doesn't express a concept from sense experience.
   "Ought" doesn't express an objective concept that isn't from sense experience.
   ∴ Moral judgments express feelings and not truth claims.   [Use T, F, S, and O.]

7. If Michigan either won or tied, then Michigan is going to the Rose Bowl and Gensler is happy.
   ∴ If Gensler isn't happy, then Michigan didn't tie.   [Use W, T, R, and H.]

8.   There are moral obligations.
     If there are moral obligations and moral obligations are explainable, then either
     there's an explanation besides God's existence or else God's existence would
     explain moral obligations.
     God's existence wouldn't explain moral obligation.
   ∴ Either moral obligations aren't explainable, or else there's an explanation besides
     God's existence.   [Use M, E, B, and G.]

9.   If determinism is true and Dr Freudlov correctly predicts (using deterministic
     laws) what I'll do, then if she tells me her prediction I'll do something else.
     If Dr Freudlov tells me her prediction and yet I'll do something else, then Dr
     Freudlov doesn't correctly predict (using deterministic laws) what I'll do.
   ∴ If determinism is true, then either Dr Freudlov doesn't correctly predict (using
     deterministic laws) what I'll do or else she won't tell me her prediction.   [Use
     D, P, T, and E.]

10. [The parents told their son that their precondition for financing his graduate
     education was that he leave his girlfriend Suzy. A friend of mine talked the par-
     ents out of their demand by using this argument.]
     If you make this demand on your son and he leaves Suzy, then he'll regret being
     forced to leave her and he'll always resent you.
     If you make this demand on your son and he doesn't leave Suzy, then he'll regret
     not going to graduate school and he'll always resent you.
   ∴ If you make this demand on your son, then he'll always resent you.   [Use D, L,
     F, A, and G; this one is difficult.]

4.6   Harder refutations

Multiple-assumption invalid arguments work much like other invalid arguments – except that we need to make further assumptions before we reach our
refutation. Here's an example:

If the butler was at the party, he	1	$(A^0 \supset (F \cdot P^0)) = 1$	**Invalid**
fixed the drinks and poisoned	** 2	$(\sim A^0 \supset N^1) = 1$	
the deceased.		$[\therefore P^0 = 0$	N, ~A, ~P
If the butler wasn't at the party,	3	asm: ~P	
he was at a neighbor's house.	4	asm: ~A {break up 1}	
∴ The butler poisoned the deceased.	5	∴ N {from 2 and 4}	

We derive all we can and make additional assumptions when needed. But now
we reach no contradiction; instead, we reach a refutation in which the butler
was at a neighbor's house, wasn't at the party, and didn't poison the deceased.
This refutation makes the premises all true and conclusion false.

As we work out our attempted proof, we can follow the five-step proof strategy of the previous section until one of two things happens:

- Every assumption leads to a contradiction. Then we have a proof of validity.
- We can derive nothing further and all complex wffs are either starred or already broken up (we already have one side or its negation). Then the remaining simple wffs will give a refutation that proves invalidity.

In the invalid case, additional assumptions can help to bring us our refutation.
Invalid arguments often need three or more assumptions, as in this example:

$$
\begin{array}{lll}
1 & (A^0 \supset B) = 1 & \text{Invalid} \\
2 & (C^0 \supset D) = 1 & \\
3 & (F^0 \supset (C^0 \cdot D)) = 1 & \boxed{E, \sim A, \sim C, \sim F} \\
& [\therefore (E^1 \supset C^0) = 0 & \\
* \quad 4 & \text{asm: } \sim(E \supset C) & \\
5 & \therefore E \quad \{\text{from 4}\} & \\
6 & \therefore \sim C \quad \{\text{from 4}\} & \\
7 & \text{asm: } \sim A \quad \{\text{break up 1}\} & \\
8 & \text{asm: } \sim F \quad \{\text{break up 3}\} &
\end{array}
$$

We keep going until we can derive nothing further and all complex wffs are either starred (like line 4) or already broken up (like lines 1–3).[1] While our refutation doesn't give us a value for "B" or "D," this is all right, since the refutation still makes the premises all true and conclusion false.

Our proof strategy, if applied correctly, will always give a proof or refutation. How exactly these go may depend on which steps we do first and what we decide to assume; proofs and refutations may differ but still be correct.

4.6a   Exercise – LogiCola GHI

Prove each of these arguments to be invalid (all are invalid).

$$
\begin{array}{l}
(A \lor \sim(B \supset C)) \\
(D \supset (A \supset B)) \\
\therefore (C \supset \sim(D \lor A))
\end{array}
$$

$$
\begin{array}{lll}
1 & (A^1 \lor \sim(B \supset C^1)) = 1 & \text{Invalid} \\
2 & (D^0 \supset (A^1 \supset B)) = 1 & \\
& [\therefore (C^1 \supset \sim(D^0 \lor A^1)) = 0 & \boxed{A, C, \sim D} \\
* \quad 3 & \text{asm: } \sim(C \supset \sim(D \lor A)) & \\
4 & \therefore C \quad \{\text{from 3}\} & \\
5 & \therefore (D \lor A) \quad \{\text{from 3}\} & \\
6 & \text{asm: } A \quad \{\text{break up 1}\} & \\
7 & \text{asm: } \sim D \quad \{\text{break up 2}\} &
\end{array}
$$

[1] If you like, you can star a line when it becomes "broken up" (when you have one side or its negation, but not what is needed to infer something). Then you can continue until all assumptions die (then the argument is valid) or until you can derive nothing further and all complex wffs are starred (then the argument is invalid).

1. ~(A · B)
    ∴ (~A · ~B)

2. (~A ⊃ B)
    ∴ ~(A ⊃ B)

3. ((A · B) ⊃ ~(C · D))
    C
    (E ⊃ B)
    ∴ ~E

4. ~(A · B)
    ∴ ~(A ≡ B)

5. (A ⊃ B)
    (C ⊃ (~D · E))
    ∴ (D ∨ F)

6. (~A ∨ ~B)
    ∴ ~(A ∨ B)

7. (A ⊃ (B · C))
    ((D ⊃ E) ⊃ A)
    ∴ (E ∨ C)

8. (A ⊃ (B ⊃ C))
    (B ∨ ~(C ⊃ D))
    ∴ (D ⊃ ~(A ∨ B))

4.6b   Exercise – LogiCola G (HC & MC)

First appraise intuitively. Then translate into logic (using the letters given) and say whether valid (and give a proof) or invalid (and give a refutation).

1. If the maid prepared the drink, then the butler didn't prepare it.
    The maid didn't prepare the drink.
    If the butler prepared the drink, then the butler poisoned the drink and the butler is guilty.
    ∴ The butler is guilty.   [Use M, B, P, and G.]

2. If you tell your teacher that you like logic, then your teacher will think that you're insincere and you'll be in trouble.
    If you don't tell your teacher that you like logic, then your teacher will think that you dislike logic and you'll be in trouble.
    ∴ You'll be in trouble.   [Use L, I, T, and D.]

3. If we don't get reinforcements, then the enemy will overwhelm us and we won't survive.
    ∴ If we do get reinforcements, then we'll conquer the enemy and we'll survive.
    [Use R, O, S, and C.]

4. If Socrates didn't approve of the laws of Athens, then he would have left Athens or would have tried to change the laws.
    If Socrates didn't leave Athens and didn't try to change the laws, then he agreed to obey the laws.
    Socrates didn't leave Athens.
    ∴ If Socrates didn't try to change the laws, then he approved of the laws and agreed to obey them.   [Use A, L, C, and O. This argument is from Plato's *Crito*, which argued that Socrates shouldn't disobey the law by escaping from jail.]

5. If I hike the Appalachian Trail and go during late spring, then I'll get maximum daylight and maximum mosquitoes.
    If I'll get maximum mosquitoes, then I won't be comfortable.
    If I go right after school, then I'll go during late spring.
    ∴ If I hike the Appalachian Trail and don't go right after school, then I'll be comfortable.   [Use A, L, D, M, C, and S.]

6. [Logical positivism says *"Every genuine truth claim is either experimentally testable or true by definition."* This view, while once popular, is self-refuting and hence not very popular today.]
   If LP (logical positivism) is true and is a genuine truth claim, then it's either experimentally testable or true by definition.
   LP isn't experimentally testable.
   LP isn't true by definition.
   If LP isn't a genuine truth claim, then it isn't true.
   ∴ LP isn't true.   [Use T, G, E, and D.]

7. If you give a test, then students either do well or do poorly.
   If students do well, then you think you made the test too easy and you're frustrated.
   If students do poorly, then you think they didn't learn any logic and you're frustrated.
   ∴ If you give a test, then you're frustrated.   [Use T, W, P, E, F, and L. This is from a class who tried to talk me out of giving a test.]

8. If the world contains moral goodness, then the world contains free creatures and the free creatures sometimes do wrong.
   If the free creatures sometimes do wrong, then the world is imperfect and the creator is imperfect.
   ∴ If the world doesn't contain moral goodness, then the creator is imperfect.   [Use M, F, S, W, and C.]

9. We'll find a cause for your action, if and only if your action has a cause and we look hard enough.
   If all events have causes, then your action has a cause.
   All events have causes.
   ∴ We'll find a cause for your action, if and only if we look hard enough.   [Use F, H, L, and A.]

10. Herman sees that the piece of chalk is white.
    The piece of chalk is the smallest thing on the desk.
    Herman doesn't see that the smallest thing on the desk is white. (He can't see the whole desk and so can't tell that the piece of chalk is the smallest thing on it.)
    If Herman sees a material thing, then if he sees that the piece of chalk is white and the piece of chalk is the smallest thing on the desk then he sees that the smallest thing on the desk is white.
    If Herman doesn't see a material thing, then he sees a sense datum.
    ∴ Herman doesn't see a material thing, but he does see a sense datum.   [Use H, P, H′, M, and S. This argument attacks direct realism – the view that we directly perceive material things and not just sensations or sense data.]

11. If the final loading capacitor in the radio transmitter is arcing, then the SWR (standing wave ratio) is too high and the efficiency is lowered.
    If you hear a cracking sound, then the final loading capacitor in the radio transmitter is arcing.
    ∴ If you don't hear a cracking sound, then the SWR isn't too high.   [Use A, H, L, and C.]

12. If we can know that God exists, then we can know God by experience or we can know God by logical inference from experience.
    If we can't know God empirically, then we can't know God by experience and we can't know God by logical inference from experience.
    If we can know God empirically, then "God exists" is a scientific hypothesis and is empirically falsifiable.
    "God exists" isn't empirically falsifiable.
    ∴ We can't know that God exists.   [Use K, E, L, M, S, and F.]

13. If I perceive, then my perception is either delusive or veridical.
    If my perception is delusive, then I don't directly perceive a material object.
    If my perception is veridical and I directly perceive a material object, then my experience in veridical perception would always differ qualitatively from my experience in delusive perception.
    My experience in veridical perception doesn't always differ qualitatively from my experience in delusive perception.
    If I perceive and I don't directly perceive a material object, then I directly perceive a sensation.
    ∴ If I perceive, then I directly perceive a sensation and I don't directly perceive a material object.   [Use P, D, V, M, Q, and S. This form of the argument from illusion attacks direct realism – the view that we directly perceive material objects and not just sensations or sense data.]

14. If you're romantic and you're Italian, then Juliet will fall in love with you and will want to marry you.
    If you're Italian, then you're romantic.
    ∴ If you're Italian, then Juliet will want to marry you.   [Use R, I, F, and M.]

15. If emotions can rest on factual errors and factual errors can be criticized, then we can criticize emotions.
    If we can criticize emotions and moral judgments are based on emotions, then beliefs about morality can be criticized and morality isn't entirely non-rational.
    ∴ If morality is entirely non-rational, then emotions can't rest on factual errors. [Use E, F, W, M, B, and N.]

16. If you backpack over spring break and don't study logic, then you won't know how to do proofs.
    If you take the test and don't know how to do proofs, then you'll miss many problems and get a low grade.
    ∴ If you backpack over spring break, then you'll get a low grade.   [Use B, S, K, T, M, and L.]

4.7   Other proof methods

The proof method in this book tries to combine the best features of two other methods: traditional proofs and truth trees. These three approaches, while differing in how they do proofs, can prove all the same arguments.

Traditional proofs use a standard set of inference rules and equivalence rules. The nine inference rules are like our S- and I-rules, in that they let us infer whole lines from previous whole lines:

$$
\begin{array}{ll}
(P \cdot Q) \rightarrow P & (P \supset Q), P \rightarrow Q \\
P, Q \rightarrow (P \cdot Q) & (P \supset Q), \sim Q \rightarrow \sim P \\
(P \vee Q), \sim P \rightarrow Q & (P \supset Q), (Q \supset R) \rightarrow (P \supset R) \\
P \rightarrow (P \vee Q) & (P \supset Q) \rightarrow (P \supset (P \cdot Q)) \\
\end{array}
$$

$$((P \supset Q) \cdot (R \supset S)), (P \vee R) \rightarrow (Q \vee S)$$

The sixteen equivalence rules let us replace parts of formulas with equivalent parts (I've dropped outer parentheses here to promote readability):

$$
\begin{array}{ll}
P \equiv \sim\sim P & (P \supset Q) \equiv (\sim P \vee Q) \\
P \equiv (P \cdot P) & (P \cdot (Q \cdot R)) \equiv ((P \cdot Q) \cdot R) \\
P \equiv (P \vee P) & (P \vee (Q \vee R)) \equiv ((P \vee Q) \vee R) \\
(P \cdot Q) \equiv (Q \cdot P) & (P \cdot (Q \vee R)) \equiv ((P \cdot Q) \vee (P \cdot R)) \\
(P \vee Q) \equiv (Q \vee P) & (P \vee (Q \cdot R)) \equiv ((P \vee Q) \cdot (P \vee R)) \\
\sim(P \cdot Q) \equiv (\sim P \vee \sim Q) & (P \equiv Q) \equiv ((P \supset Q) \cdot (Q \supset P)) \\
\sim(P \vee Q) \equiv (\sim P \cdot \sim Q) & (P \equiv Q) \equiv ((P \cdot Q) \vee (\sim P \cdot \sim Q)) \\
(P \supset Q) \equiv (\sim Q \supset \sim P) & ((P \cdot Q) \supset R) \equiv (P \supset (Q \supset R)) \\
\end{array}
$$

Our approach uses a simpler and more understandable set of rules.

Traditional proofs can use **indirect proofs** (where we assume the opposite of the conclusion and then derive a contradiction); but they more often use **direct proofs** (where we just derive things from the premises and eventually derive the desired conclusion) or **conditional proofs** (where we prove "(P ⊃ Q)" by assuming "P" and then deriving "Q"). Here's an argument proved two ways:

Traditional proof	*Our proof*

Traditional proof

1    $((A \supset B) \cdot (C \supset D))$
   $[\therefore ((A \cdot C) \supset (B \vee D))$
2   $\therefore (A \supset B)$ {from 1}
3   $\therefore (\sim A \vee B)$ {from 2}
4   $\therefore ((\sim A \vee B) \vee D)$ {from 3}
5   $\therefore (\sim A \vee (B \vee D))$ {from 4}
6   $\therefore ((\sim A \vee (B \vee D)) \vee \sim C)$ {from 5}
7   $\therefore (\sim C \vee (\sim A \vee (B \vee D)))$ {from 6}
8   $\therefore ((\sim C \vee \sim A) \vee (B \vee D))$ {from 7}
9   $\therefore ((\sim A \vee \sim C) \vee (B \vee D))$ {from 8}
10   $\therefore (\sim(A \cdot C) \vee (B \vee D))$ {from 9}
11   $\therefore ((A \cdot C) \supset (B \vee D))$ {from 10, giving the original conclusion}

Our proof

*   1 $((A \supset B) \cdot (C \supset D))$
    $[\therefore ((A \cdot C) \supset (B \vee D))$
*   2   asm: $\sim((A \cdot C) \supset (B \vee D))$
*   3 $\therefore (A \supset B)$ {from 1}
   4   $\therefore (C \supset D)$ {from 1}
*   5 $\therefore (A \cdot C)$ {from 2}
   6   $\therefore \sim(B \vee D)$ {from 2}
   7   $\therefore A$ {from 5}
   8   $\therefore C$ {from 5}
   9   $\therefore B$ {from 3 and 7}
   10   $\therefore \sim B$ {from 6}
   11   $\therefore ((A \cdot C) \supset (B \vee D))$ {from 2; 9 contradicts 10}

Both proofs have the same number of steps; but this can vary, depending on how we do each proof. Our steps generally use shorter formulas; our proofs tend to simplify larger formulas into smaller ones – while traditional proofs tend to manipulate longer formulas (often by substituting equivalents) to get the desired result. Our proofs are easier to do, since they use an automatic proof-strategy that students learn quickly; traditional proofs require guesswork and intuition. Also, our system refutes invalid arguments; it can separate valid from invalid arguments, prove valid ones to be valid, and refute invalid ones. In contrast, the traditional system is only a proof method; if we try to prove an invalid argument, we'll fail but won't necessarily learn that the argument is invalid.

Another common approach is **truth trees**, which decompose formulas into the cases that make them true. Truth trees use simplifying rules and branching rules. The simplifying rules are like our S-rules, in that they let us simplify a formula into smaller parts and then ignore the original formula. These four simplifying rules (which apply to whole lines) are used:

$$\sim\sim P \rightarrow P$$
$$(P \cdot Q) \rightarrow P, Q$$
$$\sim(P \lor Q) \rightarrow \sim P, \sim Q$$
$$\sim(P \supset Q) \rightarrow P, \sim Q$$

Each form that can't be simplified is branched into the two sub-cases that would make it true; for example, since "$\sim(P \cdot Q)$" is true just if "$\sim P$" is true or "$\sim Q$" is true, it branches into these two formulas. There are five branching rules:

$\sim(P \cdot Q)$	$(P \lor Q)$	$(P \supset Q)$	$(P \equiv Q)$	$\sim(P \equiv Q)$
$\sim P \quad \sim Q$	$P \quad Q$	$\sim P \quad Q$	$P \quad \sim P$ $Q \quad \sim Q$	$P \quad Q$ $\sim Q \quad \sim P$

To test an argument, we write the premises, block off the original conclusion (showing that it is to be ignored in constructing the tree), and add the denial of the conclusion. Then we apply the simplifying and branching rules to each formula, and to each further formula that we get, until every branch either dies (contains a pair of contradictory wffs) or contains only simple wffs (letters or their negation). The argument is valid if and only if every branch dies. Here's an argument proved two ways:

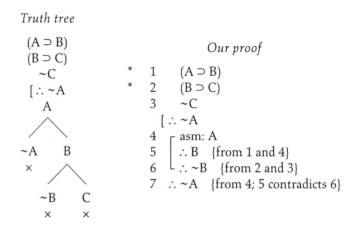

Truth tree

Our proof

In the truth tree, we write the premises, block off the original "∴ A" conclusion (and henceforth ignore it), and add its contradictory "A." Then we branch "(A ⊃ B)" into its two sub-cases: "~A" and "B." The left branch dies, since it contains "A" and "~A"; we indicate this by putting "×" at its bottom. Then we branch "(B ⊃ C)" into its two sub-cases: "~B" and "C." Each branch dies; the left branch has "B" and "~B," while the right has "C" and "~C." Since every branch of the tree dies, no possible truth conditions would make the premises all true and conclusion false, and so the argument is valid.

An argument is invalid if some branch of the tree doesn't die. Then the simple wffs on each live branch give a refutation of the argument – truth conditions making the premises all true and conclusion false.

As compared with traditional proofs, truth trees give a simple and efficient way to decide whether an argument is valid or invalid – a way that uses an automatic strategy instead of guesswork and intuition. But truth trees don't mirror ordinary reasoning very well; they give a mechanical way to test validity instead of a way to help develop reasoning skills. And branching can get messy. Our method avoids these disadvantages but keeps the main advantages of truth trees over traditional proofs.

CHAPTER 5
Basic Quantificational Logic

Quantificational logic studies arguments whose validity depends on "all," "no," "some," and similar notions.[1] This chapter covers the basics, and the next adds relations and identity.

5.1   Easier translations

To help us evaluate quantificational arguments, we'll construct a little quantificational language. Our language builds on propositional logic and includes all the vocabulary, wffs, inference rules, and proofs of the latter. We add two new vocabulary items: small letters and "∃." Here are sample formulas:

Ir	=	Romeo is Italian.
Ix	=	x is Italian.
(x)Ix	=	For all x, x is Italian (all are Italian).
(∃x)Ix	=	For some x, x is Italian (some are Italian).

"Romeo is Italian" is "Ir"; we write the capital letter first. Here "I" is for the general category "Italian" and "r" is for the specific individual "Romeo":

Use capital letters for **general terms** (terms that *describe* or put in a *category*): I = an Italian C = charming R = drives a Rolls Use capitals for "a so and so," adjectives, and verbs.	Use small letters for **singular terms** (terms that pick out a *specific* person or thing): i = the richest Italian c = this child r = Romeo Use small letters for "the so and so," "this so and so," and proper names.

---

[1] While somewhat overlapping with syllogistic logic (Chapter 2), quantificational logic is more powerful and flexible because it also includes propositional logic.

Capital and small letters have various uses in our quantificational language. Capitals can represent statements, general terms, or relations (but we won't study relations until the next chapter):

A capital letter alone (not followed by small letters) represents a *statement*.	S	*It is snowing.*
A capital letter followed by a single small letter represents a *general term*.	Ir	Romeo is *Italian.*
A capital letter followed by two or more small letters represents a *relation*.	Lrj	Romeo *loves* Juliet.

Similarly, small letters can be constants or variables:

A small letter from "a" to "w" is a **constant** – and stands for a specific person or thing.	Ir	*Romeo* is Italian.
A small letter from "x" to "z" is a **variable** – and stands for an unspecified member of a class of things.	Ix	*x* is Italian.

A variable stands for an unspecified person or thing. "Ix" ("x is Italian") is incomplete, and thus not true or false, since we haven't said whom we are talking about; but we can add a quantifier to complete the claim.

A **quantifier** is a sequence of the form "(x)" or "(∃x)" – where any variable may replace "x":

"(x)" is a **universal quantifier**. It claims that the formula that follows is true for *all* values of x.	"(∃x)" is an **existential quantifier**. It claims that the formula that follows is true for *at least one* value of x.
(x)Ix = For all x, x is Italian. = All are Italian.	(∃x)Ix = For some x, x is Italian. = Some are Italian.

Quantifiers express "all" and "some" by saying in how many cases the following formula is true.

As before, a grammatically correct formula is called a *wff*, or *well-formed formula*. For now, wffs are strings that we can construct using the propositional rules plus these two rules:

> 1. The result of writing a capital letter and then a small letter is a wff.
> 2. The result of writing a quantifier and then a wff is a wff.

These rules let us build wffs that we've already mentioned: "Ir," "Ix," "(x)Ix," and "(∃x)Ix." Don't use additional parentheses with these forms:

Right:	Ir	Ix	(x)Ix	(∃x)Ix
Wrong:	(Ir)	(Ix)	(x)(Ix)	(∃x)(Ix)
			((x)Ix)	((∃x)Ix)

Use a pair of parentheses for each quantifier and for each instance of "·," "∨," "⊃," and "≡"; use no other parentheses. Here are some further wffs:

~(x)Ix	=	Not all are Italian.
	=	It is not the case that, for all x, x is Italian.
~(∃x)Ix	=	No one is Italian.
	=	It is not the case that, for some x, x is Italian.
(Ix ⊃ Lx)	=	If x is Italian then x is a lover.
(Ix · Lx)	=	x is Italian and x is a lover.

Translating from English sentences to wffs can be difficult. We'll begin with sentences that translate into wffs starting with a quantifier, or with "~" and then a quantifier. This rule tells where to put what quantifier:

If the English begins with	then begin the wff with
all (every)	(x)
not all (not every)	~(x)
some	(∃x)
no	~(∃x)

Here are basic examples:

All are Italian	=	(x)Ix		Some are Italian	=	(∃x)Ix
Not all are Italian	=	~(x)Ix		No one is Italian	=	~(∃x)Ix

Here are harder examples:

All are rich or Italian	=	(x)(Rx ∨ Ix)
Not everyone is non-Italian	=	~(x)~Ix
Some aren't rich	=	(∃x)~Rx
No one is rich and non-Italian	=	~(∃x)(Rx · ~Ix)

When the English begins with "all," "some," "not all," or "no," the quantifier must go *outside* all parentheses:

Right:	All are rich or Italian	= (x)(Rx ∨ Ix)
Wrong:	All are rich or Italian	= ((x)Rx ∨ Ix)

The *wrong* formula means "Either everyone is rich, or x is Italian" – which isn't what we want to say.

If the English sentence specifies a logical connective (like "or," "and," or "if-then"), then use the corresponding logical symbol. When the English doesn't specify the connective, use these rules:

With "all … is …," use "⊃" for the *middle* connective.	*Otherwise* use "·" for the connective.

"All (every) A is B" uses "⊃," while "Some A is B" and "No A is B" use "·"; here are examples:

All Italians are lovers	=	(x)(Ix ⊃ Lx)
	=	For all x, *if* x is Italian *then* x is a lover.
Some Italians are lovers	=	(∃x)(Ix · Lx)
	=	For some x, x is Italian *and* x is a lover.
No Italians are lovers	=	~(∃x)(Ix · Lx)
	=	It is not the case that, for some x, x is Italian *and* x is a lover.

This next example illustrates both boxed rules:

All rich Italians are lovers	=	(x)((Rx · Ix) ⊃ Lx)
	=	For all x, *if* x is rich *and* Italian, *then* x is a lover.

We use "⊃" as the *middle* connective ("*If* rich Italian, *then* lover") and "·" in the *other* place ("If rich *and* Italian, then lover"). Note carefully the connectives in the next two examples:

Not all Italians are lovers	=	~(x)(Ix ⊃ Lx)
	=	It is not the case that, for all x, *if* x is Italian *then* x is a lover.
All are rich Italians	=	(x)(Rx · Ix)
	=	For all x, x is rich *and* Italian.

In case of doubt, phrase out the symbolic formula to yourself and see if it means the same as the English sentence.

Sentences with a main verb other than "is" should be rephrased to make "is" the main verb – and then translated. Here's an example:

	=	All dogs are cat-haters.
All dogs hate cats	=	For all x, if x is a dog then x is a cat-hater.
	=	(x)(Dx ⊃ Cx)

The **universe of discourse** is the set of entities that words like "all," "some," and "no" range over in a given context. In translating arguments about some one kind of entity (such as persons or statements), we can simplify our formulas by restricting the universe of discourse to that one kind of entity. We did this implicitly when we translated "All are Italian" as "(x)Ix" – instead of as "(x)(Px ⊃ Ix)" ("All persons are Italians"); here our "(x)" really means "For all persons x." We'll often restrict the universe of discourse to persons.

English has many idiomatic expressions; so our translation rules are rough and don't always work. After you symbolize an English sentence, it's wise to read your formula carefully, to make sure it reflects what the English means.

5.1a Exercise – LogiCola H (EM & ET)

Using these equivalences, translate these English sentences into wffs.

Ex	=	x is evil	Cx	=	x is crazy
Lx	=	x is a logician	Rx	=	x runs

Not all logicians run.	~(x)(Lx ⊃ Rx)

1. x isn't evil.
2. x is either crazy or evil.
3. Someone is evil.
4. Someone isn't evil.
5. All are evil.
6. If x is a logician, then x is evil.
7. All logicians are evil.
8. No one is evil.
9. Some logicians are evil.
10. No logician is evil.
11. Some logicians are evil and crazy.
12. No logician who runs is crazy.
13. Not all run.
14. Every logician is crazy or evil.
15. Some who are crazy aren't evil logicians.
16. All crazy logicians are evil.
17. Not all non-logicians are evil.
18. Some logicians who aren't crazy run.
19. No one who is crazy or evil runs.
20. All who aren't logicians are evil.
21. Not everyone is crazy or evil.
22. Not all who are evil or crazy are logicians.

23. All evil people and crazy people are logicians.
24. All are evil logicians.
25. No one who isn't an evil logician is crazy.

5.2 Easier proofs

Quantificational proofs work much like propositional ones, but use four new inference rules for quantifiers.

These two reverse-squiggle (RS) rules hold regardless of what variable replaces "x" and what pair of contradictory wffs replaces "Fx" / "~Fx" (here "→" means we can infer whole lines from left to right):

$$
\begin{array}{c|c}
\text{Reverse} & \text{~(x)Fx} \quad \rightarrow \quad (\exists x)\text{~Fx} \\
\text{squiggle} & \text{~}(\exists x)\text{Fx} \quad \rightarrow \quad (x)\text{~Fx}
\end{array}
$$

So "Not everyone is funny" entails "Someone isn't funny." Similarly, "It is not the case that someone is funny" ("No one is funny") entails "Everyone is non-funny." We can reverse squiggles on more complicated formulas, so long as the whole formula begins with "~" and then a quantifier:

Right:	*Right:*	*Wrong:*
~$(\exists x)$~Gx	~$(x)(Lx \cdot$ ~Mx)	(Ir ⊃ ~(x)Gx)
∴ (x)~~Gx	∴ $(\exists x)$~(Lx $\cdot$ ~Mx)	∴ (Ir ⊃ $(\exists x)$~Gx)

It the first example, it would be simpler to conclude "(x)Gx" (eliminating the double negation). Reverse squiggles whenever you have a wff that begins with "~" and then a quantifier; reversing a squiggle moves the quantifier to the beginning of the formula, so we can later drop it.

We drop quantifiers using the next two rules (which hold regardless of what variable replaces "x" and what wffs replace "Fx" / "Fa" – provided that the two wffs are identical except that wherever the variable occurs freely[1] in the former the same constant occurs in the latter). Here's the drop-existential (DE) rule:

$$
\begin{array}{c|c}
\text{Drop} & (\exists x)\text{Fx} \quad \rightarrow \quad \overset{\downarrow}{\text{Fa,}} \\
\text{existential} & \text{use a } \textit{new} \text{ constant}
\end{array}
$$

---

[1] *Technical footnote:* An instance of a variable occurs "freely" if it doesn't occur as part of a wff that begins with a quantifier using that variable; just the first instance of "x" in "(Fx $\cdot$ (x)Gx)" occurs freely. So we'd go from "$(\exists x)$(Fx $\cdot$ (x)Gx)" to "(Fa $\cdot$ (x)Gx)."

Suppose that *someone* robbed the bank; we can give this person a name – like "Al" – but it must be an *arbitrary name* that we make up. Likewise, when we drop an existential, we'll label this "someone" with a *new constant* – one that hasn't yet occurred in earlier lines of the proof. In proofs, we'll use the next unused letter in alphabetical order – starting with "a," and then "b," and so on:[1]

> (∃x)Mx   Someone is male, someone is female;
> (∃x)Fx   let's call the male "a" and the female "b."
>
> ∴ Ma   ←   "a" is OK since it occurs in no earlier line.
> ∴ Fb   ←   Since "a" has now occurred, we use "b."

We can drop existentials from complicated formulas if the quantifier begins the wff and we replace the variable with the same new constant throughout:

Right:	*Wrong:*	*Wrong:*
(∃x)(Fx · Gx)	((∃x)Fx ⊃ P)	(∃x)(Fx · Gx)
∴ (Fa · Ga)	∴ (Fa ⊃ P)	∴ (Fa · Gb)

The middle formula doesn't *begin* with a quantifier; instead, it begins with a left-hand parenthesis. Drop only *initial* quantifiers.

Here's the drop-universal (DU) rule:

Drop universal	(x)Fx → F↓a, use any constant

If *everyone* is funny, then Al is funny, Bob is funny, and so on. From "(x)Fx" we can derive "Fa," "Fb," and so on – using any constant. As before, the quantifier must begin the wff and we must replace the variable with the same constant throughout:

Right:	*Wrong:*	*Wrong:*
(x)(Fx ⊃ Gx)	((x)Fx ⊃ (x)Gx)	(x)(Fx ⊃ Gx)
∴ (Fa ⊃ Ga)	∴ (Fa ⊃ Ga)	∴ (Fa ⊃ Gb)

The middle inference is wrong because the quantifier doesn't *begin* the formula (a left-hand parenthesis begins it). "((x)Fx ⊃ (x)Gx)" is an if-then and follows

---

[1] *Technical footnote:* This paragraph needs three qualifications. (1) If *someone* robbed the bank, then maybe *more than one* person did; then our name (or constant) will refer to a random *one* of the robbers. (2) Using a new name is consistent with the robber being someone mentioned in the argument so far; different names (like "Jim" and "Smith") might refer to the same individual. (3) Rule DE should be used only when there is at least one not-blocked-off assumption; otherwise, the symbolic version of "Someone is a thief, so Gensler is a thief" would be a two-line proof.

the if-then rules: if we have the first part "(x)Fx" true, we can get the second true; if we have the second part "(x)Gx" false, we can get the first false; and if we get stuck, we need to make another assumption.

Here's an English version of a quantificational proof:

1   All logicians are funny.
2   Someone is a logician.
   [∴ Someone is funny.
3   ┌ Assume: It is not the case that someone is funny.
4   │ ∴ Everyone is non-funny.   {from 3, reverse squiggles}
5   │ ∴ a is a logician.   {from 2, drop existential, call the logician "a"}
6   │ ∴ If a is a logician then a is funny.   {from 1, drop universal}
7   │ ∴ a is funny.   {from 5 and 6}
8   └ ∴ a is non-funny.   {from 4, drop universal}
9   ∴ Someone is funny.   {from 3; 7 contradicts 8}

The steps here should make sense. Our proof strategy is: first reverse squiggles, then drop existentials using new letters, and finally drop universals using the same old letters. Here's the proof in symbols:

```
        1     (x)(Lx ⊃ Fx)   Valid
  *     2     (∃x)Lx
       [∴ (∃x)Fx
  *     3   ┌ asm: ~(∃x)Fx
        4   │ ∴ (x)~Fx   {from 3}
        5   │ ∴ La   {from 2}
  *     6   │ ∴ (La ⊃ Fa)   {from 1}
        7   │ ∴ Fa   {from 5 and 6}
        8   └ ∴ ~Fa   {from 4}
        9   ∴ (∃x)Fx   {from 3; 7 contradicts 8}
```

After making the assumption (line 3), we reverse the squiggle to move the quantifier to the outside (line 4). We drop the existential quantifier using a new constant (line 5). We drop the universal quantifier in line 1 using this same constant – and then use an I-rule (lines 6 and 7). Then we drop the universal in line 4 using this same constant (line 8), which gives us a contradiction. RAA gives us the original conclusion (line 9).

We starred lines 2, 3, and 6; as before, starred lines largely can be ignored in deriving further steps. Here are the new starring rules – with examples:

Star any wff on which you reverse squiggles.	Star any wff from which you drop an existential.
* ~(x)Fx	* (∃x)Fx
∴ (∃x)~Fx	∴ Fa

When we reverse squiggles or drop existentials, the new line has the same information. Don't star when dropping a universal; we can never exhaust an "all" statement by deriving instances – and we may have to derive further things from it later in the proof.

Here's another quantificational proof.

$$
\begin{array}{lll}
& 1 & \text{(x)(Fx} \cdot \text{Gx)} \quad \cdots\cdots\cdots\cdots\cdots\cdots\cdots\cdots\cdots\cdots\cdots\cdots \\
& & [\therefore \text{(x)Fx} \\
* & 2 & \quad \text{asm: } \sim\text{(x)Fx} \quad \cdots \\
* & 3 & \quad \therefore (\exists\text{x})\sim\text{Fx} \cdot \blacktriangleleft\cdots \quad \textit{First reverse squiggles} \\
& 4 & \quad \therefore \sim\text{Fa} \blacktriangleleft\cdots \quad \textit{and drop existentials.} \\
& 5 & \quad \therefore (\text{Fa} \cdot \text{Ga}) \blacktriangleleft\cdots\cdots\cdots \quad \textit{Lastly drop universals.} \\
& 6 & \quad \therefore \text{Fa} \\
& 7 & \therefore \text{(x)Fx} \quad \{\text{from 2; 4 contradicts 6}\}
\end{array}
$$

It would be wrong to switch lines 4 and 5. If we drop the universal first using "a," then we can't drop the existential next using "a" (since "a" would be old).

Our proof strategy works much like before. We first assume the opposite of the conclusion; then we use our four new rules plus the S- and I-rules to derive whatever we can. If we find a contradiction, we apply RAA. If we get stuck and need to break up a wff of the form "$\sim$(A $\cdot$ B)" or "(A $\vee$ B)" or "(A $\supset$ B)," then we make another assumption. If we get no contradiction and yet can't do anything further, then we try to refute the argument.

Reverse squiggles and drop existentials first, drop universals last:

1. FIRST REVERSE SQUIGGLES: For each unstarred, not-blocked-off step that begins with "$\sim$" and then a quantifier, derive a step using the reverse-squiggle rules. Star the original step.

2. AND DROP EXISTENTIALS: For each unstarred, not-blocked-off step that begins with an existential quantifier, derive an instance using the next available *new* constant (unless some such instance already occurs in previous not-blocked-off steps). Star the original step.

   Note: Don't drop an existential if you already have a not-blocked-off instance in previous steps – there's no point in deriving a second instance. So don't drop "($\exists$x)Fx" if you already have "Fc."

3. LASTLY DROP UNIVERSALS: For each not-blocked-off step that begins with a universal quantifier, derive instances using each *old* constant. Don't star the original step; you might have to use it again.

   Note: Drop a universal using a *new* letter only if you've done everything else possible (making further assumptions if needed) and still have no old letters. This is unusual, but happens if we try to prove "(x)$\sim$Fx $\therefore$ $\sim$(x)Fx."

Be sure to drop existentials before universals. Introduce a new letter each time you drop an existential, and use the same old letters when you drop a universal. And drop only *initial* quantifiers.

We won't see invalid quantificational arguments until later.

5.2a Exercise – LogiCola IEV

Prove each of these arguments to be valid (all are valid).

~(∃x)Fx
∴ (x)~(Fx • Gx)

```
*   1    ~(∃x)Fx          Valid
         [ ∴ (x)~(Fx • Gx)
*   2   ┌ asm: ~(x)~(Fx • Gx)
*   3   │ ∴ (∃x)(Fx • Gx)   {from 2}
    4   │ ∴ (x)~Fx  {from 1}
    5   │ ∴ (Fa • Ga)  {from 3}
    6   │ ∴ ~Fa  {from 4}
    7   └ ∴ Fa  {from 5}
    8   ∴ (x)~(Fx • Gx)   {from 2; 6 contradicts 7}
```

1. (x)Fx
    ∴ (x)(Gx ∨ Fx)

2. ~(∃x)(Fx • ~Gx)
    ∴ (x)(Fx ⊃ Gx)

3. ~(∃x)(Fx • Gx)
    (∃x)Fx
    ∴ (∃x)~Gx

4. (x)((Fx ∨ Gx) ⊃ Hx)
    ∴ (x)(~Hx ⊃ ~Fx)

5. (x)(Fx ⊃ Gx)
    (∃x)Fx
    ∴ (∃x)(Fx • Gx)

6. (x)(Fx ∨ Gx)
    ~(x)Fx
    ∴ (∃x)Gx

7. (x)~(Fx ∨ Gx)
    ∴ (x)~Fx

8. (x)(Fx ⊃ Gx)
    (x)(Fx ⊃ ~Gx)
    ∴ (x)~Fx

9. (x)(Fx ⊃ Gx)
    (x)(~Fx ⊃ Hx)
    ∴ (x)(Gx ∨ Hx)

10. (x)(Fx ≡ Gx)
    (∃x)~Gx
    ∴ (∃x)~Fx

5.2b Exercise – LogiCola IEV

First appraise intuitively. Then translate into logic (using the letters given) and prove to be valid (all are valid).

1. All who deliberate about alternatives believe in free will (at least implicitly).
    All deliberate about alternatives.
    ∴ All believe in free will.   [Use Dx and Bx. This argument is from William James.]

2. Everyone makes mistakes.
    ∴ Every logic teacher makes mistakes.   [Use Mx and Lx.]

3. No feeling of pain is publicly observable.
    All chemical processes are publicly observable.
    ∴ No feeling of pain is a chemical process.   [Use Fx, Ox, and Cx. This attacks a form of materialism that identifies mental events with material events. We also could test this argument using syllogistic logic (see Chapter 2).]

4. All (in the electoral college) who do their jobs are useless.
   All (in the electoral college) who don't do their jobs are dangerous.
   ∴ All (in the electoral college) are useless or dangerous. [Use Jx for "x does their job," Ux for "x is useless," and Dx for "x is dangerous." Use the universe of discourse of electoral college members: take "(x)" to mean "for every electoral college member x" and don't translate "in the electoral college."]

5. All that's known is experienced through the senses.
   Nothing that's experienced through the senses is known.
   ∴ Nothing is known. [Use Kx and Ex. Empiricism (premise 1) plus skepticism about the senses (premise 2) yields general skepticism.]

6. No pure water is burnable.
   Some Cuyahoga River water is burnable.
   ∴ Some Cuyahoga River water isn't pure water. [Use Px, Bx, and Cx. The Cuyahoga is a river in Cleveland that used to catch on fire.]

7. Everyone who isn't with me is against me.
   ∴ Everyone who isn't against me is with me. [Use Wx and Ax. These claims from the Gospels are sometimes thought to be incompatible.]

8. All basic laws depend on God's will.
   ∴ All basic laws about morality depend on God's will. [Use Bx, Dx, and Mx.]

9. Some lies in unusual circumstances aren't wrong.
   ∴ Not all lies are wrong. [Use Lx, Ux, and Wx.]

10. Nothing based on sense experience is certain.
    Some logical inferences are certain.
    All certain things are truths of reason.
    ∴ Some truths of reason are certain and aren't based on sense experience. [Use Bx, Cx, Lx, and Rx.]

11. No truth by itself motivates us to action.
    Every categorical imperative would by itself motivate us to action.
    Every categorical imperative would be a truth.
    ∴ There are no categorical imperatives. [Use Tx, Mx, and Cx. Immanuel Kant claimed that commonsense morality accepts categorical imperatives (objectively true moral judgment that command us to act and that we must follow if we are to be rational); but some thinkers argue against the idea.]

12. Every genuine truth claim is either experimentally testable or true by definition.
    No moral judgments are experimentally testable.
    No moral judgments are true by definition.
    ∴ No moral judgments are genuine truth claims. [Use Gx, Ex, Dx, and Mx. This is logical positivism's argument against moral truths.]

13. Everyone who can think clearly would do well in logic.
    Everyone who would do well in logic ought to study logic.
    Everyone who can't think clearly ought to study logic.
    ∴ Everyone ought to study logic. [Use Tx, Wx, and Ox.]

5.3 Easier refutations

Applying our proof strategy to an invalid argument leads to a refutation:

All logicians are funny.
Someone is a logician.
∴ Everyone is funny.

	1	(x)(Lx ⊃ Fx)	**Invalid**
*	2	(∃x)Lx	a, b
		[∴ (x)Fx	
*	3	asm: ~(x)Fx	La, Fa
*	4	∴ (∃x)~Fx {from 3}	~Lb, ~Fb
	5	∴ La {from 2}	
	6	∴ ~Fb {from 4}	
*	7	∴ (La ⊃ Fa) {from 1}	
*	8	∴ (Lb ⊃ Fb) {from 1}	
	9	∴ Fa {from 5 and 7}	
	10	∴ ~Lb {from 6 and 8}	

After making the assumption (line 3), we reverse a squiggle to move a quantifier to the outside (line 4). Then we drop the two existential quantifiers, using a new and different constant each time (lines 5 and 6). We drop the universal quantifier twice, first using "a" and then using "b" (lines 7 and 8). Since we reach no contradiction, we gather the simple pieces to give a refutation. Our refutation is a little possible world with two people, a and b:

> a is a logician. a is funny.
> b isn't a logician. b isn't funny.

Here the premises are true, since all logicians are funny, and someone is a logician. The conclusion is false, since someone isn't funny. Since the premises are all true and conclusion false, our argument is invalid.

If we try to prove an invalid argument, we'll instead be led to a refutation – a little possible world with various individuals (like a and b) and simple truths about these individuals (like La and ~Lb) that would make the premises all true and conclusion false. In evaluating the premises and conclusion, evaluate each wff (or part of a wff) that starts with a quantifier according to these rules:

> An *existential* wff is true if and only if *at least one case* is true.

> A *universal* wff is true if and only if *all cases* are true.

In our world, universal premise "(x)(Lx ⊃ Fx)" is true, since all cases are true:

$$(La \supset Fa) = (1 \supset 1) = 1$$
$$(Lb \supset Fb) = (0 \supset 0) = 1$$

And existential premise "(∃x)Lx" is true, since at least one case is true (we have "La" – "a is a logician"). But universal conclusion "(x)Fx" is false, since at least one case is false (we have "~Fb" – "b isn't funny"). So our possible world makes the premises all true and conclusion false.

Be sure to check that your refutation works. If you don't get premises all 1 and conclusion 0, then you did something wrong – and the source of the problem is likely what you did with the formula that came out wrong.

Here's another example:

```
*   1     ~(∃x)(Fx · Gx)                    Invalid
*   2     (∃x)Fx
         [∴ ~(∃x)Gx                         a, b
*   3     asm: (∃x)Gx                      ┌─────────┐
    4     ∴ (x)~(Fx · Gx)   {from 1}       │ Fa, ~Ga │
    5     ∴ Fa   {from 2}                  │ Gb, ~Fb │
    6     ∴ Gb   {from 3}                  └─────────┘
*   7     ∴ ~(Fa · Ga)   {from 4}
*   8     ∴ ~(Fb · Gb)   {from 4}
    9     ∴ ~Ga   {from 5 and 7}
   10     ∴ ~Fb   {from 6 and 8}
```

In this world, some things are F and some things are G, but nothing is both at once. In evaluating the "~(∃x)(Fx · Gx)" premise, first evaluate the part starting with the quantifier. "(∃x)(Fx · Gx)" is false since no case is true:

$$(Fa · Ga) = (1 · 0) = 0$$
$$(Fb · Gb) = (0 · 1) = 0$$

So the denial "~(∃x)(Fx · Gx)" is true. The "(∃x)Fx" premise is true since at least one case is true (namely, Fa). In evaluating the "~(∃x)Gx" conclusion, first evaluate the part starting with the quantifier. "(∃x)Gx" is true since at least one case is true (namely, Gb); so the denial "~(∃x)Gx" is false. So we get the premises all true and conclusion false.

These two rules are crucial for working out proofs and refutations:

(1)   For each *existential quantifier*, introduce a *new constant*.
(2)   For each *universal quantifier*, derive an instance for each *old constant*.

In our last example, we'd violate (1) if we derived "Ga" in step 6 – since "a" at this point is old; then we'd "prove" the argument to be valid. We'd violate (2) if we didn't derive "~(Fb · Gb)" in line 8. Then our refutation would have no truth value for "Fb"; so "Fb" and premise 1 would both be "?" (unknown truth value) – showing that we had to do something further with premise 1.

Possible worlds for refutations must contain at least one entity. Seldom do we need more than two entities.

5.3a   Exercise – LogiCola IEI

Prove each of these arguments to be invalid (all are invalid).

```
   *   1      ~(x)(Fx ∨ Gx)                          Invalid
               [ ∴ ~(∃x)Gx                             a, b
   *   2      asm: (∃x)Gx
   *   3      ∴ (∃x)~(Fx ∨ Gx)  {from 1}          ~Fa, ~Ga
   *   4      ∴ ~(Fa ∨ Ga)   {from 3}                Gb
       5      ∴ ~Fa   {from 4}
       6      ∴ ~Ga   {from 4}
       7      ∴ Gb   {from 2}
```

~(x)(Fx ∨ Gx)
∴ ~(∃x)Gx

1. (∃x)Fx
    ∴ (x)Fx

2. (∃x)Fx
    (∃x)Gx
    ∴ (∃x)(Fx · Gx)

3. (∃x)(Fx ∨ Gx)
    ~(x)Fx
    ∴ (∃x)Gx

4. (∃x)Fx
    ∴ (∃x)~Fx

5. ~(∃x)(Fx · Gx)
    (x)~Fx
    ∴ (x)Gx

6. (x)(Fx ⊃ Gx)
    ~(x)Gx
    ∴ (x)~(Fx · Gx)

7. (x)((Fx · Gx) ⊃ Hx)
    (∃x)Fx
    (∃x)Gx
    ∴ (∃x)Hx

8. (∃x)(Fx ∨ ~Gx)
    (x)(~Gx ⊃ Hx)
    (∃x)(Fx ⊃ Hx)
    ∴ (∃x)Hx

9. (∃x)~(Fx ∨ Gx)
    (∃x)Hx
    ~(∃x)Fx
    ∴ ~(x)(Hx ⊃ Gx)

10. (∃x)~Fx
    (∃x)~Gx
    ∴ (∃x)(Fx ≡ Gx)

5.3b   Exercise – LogiCola IEC

First appraise intuitively. Then translate into logic (using the letters given) and say whether valid (and give a proof) or invalid (and give a refutation).

1. No pure water is burnable.
    Some Cuyahoga River water isn't burnable.
    ∴ Some Cuyahoga River water is pure water.   [Use Px, Bx, and Cx.]

2. No material thing is infinite.
    Not everything is material.
    ∴ Something is infinite.   [Use Mx and Ix.]

3. Some smoke.
    Not all have clean lungs.
    ∴ Some who smoke don't have clean lungs.   [Use Sx and Cx.]

4. Some Marxists plot violent revolution.
    Some faculty members are Marxists.
    ∴ Some faculty members plot violent revolution.   [Use Mx, Px, and Fx.]

5. All valid arguments that have "ought" in the conclusion also have "ought" in the premises.
    All arguments that seek to deduce an "ought" from an "is" have "ought" in the conclusion but don't have "ought" in the premises.
    ∴ No argument that seeks to deduce an "ought" from an "is" is valid.   [Use Vx for "x is valid," Cx for "x has 'ought' in the conclusion," Px for "x has 'ought' in the premises," Dx for "x seeks to deduce an 'ought' from an 'is,'" and the universe of discourse of arguments. This one is difficult to translate.]

6. Every kick returner who is successful is fast.
    ∴ Every kick returner who is fast is successful.   [Use Kx, Sx, and Fx.]

7. All exceptionless duties are based on the categorical imperative.
    All non-exceptionless duties are based on the categorical imperative.
    ∴ All duties are based on the categorical imperative.   [Use Ex, Bx, and the universe of discourse of duties. This argument is from Kant, who based all duties on his supreme moral principle, called "the categorical imperative."]

8. All who aren't crazy agree with me.
    ∴ No one who is crazy agrees with me.   [Use Cx and Ax.]

9. Everything can be conceived.
    Everything that can be conceived is mental.
    ∴ Everything is mental.   [Use Cx and Mx. This is from George Berkeley, who attacked materialism by arguing that everything is mental and that matter doesn't exist apart from mental sensations; so a chair is just a collection of experiences. Bertrand Russell thought that premise 2 was confused.]

10. All sound arguments are valid.
    ∴ All invalid arguments are unsound.   [Use Sx and Vx and the universe of discourse of arguments.]

11. All trespassers are eaten.
    ∴ Some trespassers are eaten.   [Use Tx and Ex. The premise is from a sign on the Appalachian Trail in northern Virginia. Traditional logic (see Section 2.8) takes "all A is B" to entail "some A is B"; modern logic takes "all A is B" to mean "whatever is A also is B" – which can be true even if there are no A's.]

12. Some necessary being exists.
    All necessary beings are perfect beings.
    ∴ Some perfect being exists.   [Use Nx and Px. Kant claimed that the cosmological argument for God's existence at most proves premise 1; it doesn't prove the existence of God (a perfect being) unless we add premise 2. But premise 2, by the next argument, presupposes the central claim of the ontological argument – that a perfect being necessarily exists. So, Kant claimed, the cosmological argument presupposes the ontological argument.]

13. All necessary beings are perfect beings.
    ∴ Some perfect beings are necessary beings.   [Use Nx and Px. Kant followed traditional logic (see problem 11) in taking "all A is B" to entail "some A is B."]

14.   No one who isn't a logical positivist holds the verifiability criterion of meaning.
∴ All who hold the verifiability criterion of meaning are logical positivists.   [Use
Lx and Hx. The verifiability criterion of meaning says that every genuine truth
claim is either experimentally testable or true by definition.]

5.4   Harder translations

We'll now start using statement letters (like "S" for "It is snowing") and
individual constants (like "r" for "Romeo") in our translations and proofs:

If it's snowing, then Romeo is cold   =   (S ⊃ Cr)

Here "S," since it's a capital letter not followed by a small letter, represents a
whole statement. And "r," since it's a small letter between "a" and "w," is a
constant that stands for a specific person or thing.

We'll also start using multiple and non-initial quantifiers. From now on, use
this expanded rule about what quantifier to use and where to put it:

Wherever the English has	put this in the wff
all (every)	(x)
not all (not every)	~(x)
some	(∃x)
no	~(∃x)

Here's an example:

If all are Italian, then Romeo is Italian   =   ((x)Ix ⊃ Ir)

Since "if" translates as "(," likewise "if all" translates as "((x)." As you translate, mimic the English word order:

all not	=	(x)~	all either	=	(x)(	if all either	= ((x)(
not all	=	~(x)	either all	=	((x)	if either all	= (((x)

Use a separate quantifier for each "all," "some," and "no":

If all are Italian,
then all are lovers   =   ((x)Ix ⊃ (x)Lx)

If not everyone is Italian,
then some aren't lovers.   =   (~(x)Ix ⊃ (∃x)~Lx)

If no Italians are lovers, then
some Italians are not lovers   =   (~(∃x)(Ix · Lx) ⊃ (∃x)(Ix · ~Lx))

"Any" differs in subtle ways from "all." "All" translates into a "(x)" that mirrors where "all" occurs in the English sentence. "Any" is governed by two different but equivalent rules; the easier rule goes as follows:

(1) To translate a sentence with "any," first rephrase it so it means the same thing but doesn't use "any"; then translate the second sentence.

"Not any ..." = "No ...."
"If any ..." = "If some ...."
"Any ..." = "All ...."

Here are examples:

Not anyone is rich
= No one is rich.
= ~(∃x)Rx

Not any Italian is a lover
= No Italian is a lover.
= ~(∃x)(Ix · Lx)

If anyone is just, there will be peace
= If someone is just, there will be peace.
= ((∃x)Jx ⊃ P)

Our second rule usually gives a different formula, but an equivalent one:

(2) To translate a sentence with "any," put a "(x)" at the *beginning* of the wff, regardless of where the "any" occurs in the sentence.

Here are the same examples worked out using the second rule:

Not anyone is rich
= (x)~Rx
= For all x, x isn't rich.

Not any Italian is a lover
= (x)~(Ix · Lx) ← Note the "·" here!
= For all x, x isn't both Italian and a lover.

If anyone is just, there will be peace
= (x)(Jx ⊃ P)
= For all x, if x is just there will be peace.

"Any" at the beginning of a sentence usually just means "all." So "Any Italian is a lover" just means "All Italians are lovers."

5.4a Exercise – LogiCola H (HM & HT)

Using the equivalences below, translate these English sentences into wffs. Recall that our rules are rough guides and sometimes don't work; so read your formula carefully to make sure it reflects what the English means.

Cx = x is crazy
Ex = x is evil
Lx = x is a logician

g = Gensler
R = It will rain

If everyone is evil, then Gensler is evil.

$((x)Ex \supset Eg)$

1. Gensler is either crazy or evil.
2. If Gensler is a logician, then some logicians are evil.
3. If everyone is a logician, then everyone is evil.
4. If all logicians are evil, then some logicians are evil.
5. If someone is evil, it will rain.
6. If everyone is evil, it will rain.
7. If anyone is evil, it will rain.
8. If Gensler is a logician, then someone is a logician.
9. If no one is evil, then no one is an evil logician.
10. If all are evil, then all logicians are evil.
11. If some are logicians, then some are evil.
12. All crazy logicians are evil.
13. Everyone who isn't a logician is evil.
14. Not everyone is evil.
15. Not anyone is evil.
16. If Gensler is a logician, then he's evil.
17. If anyone is a logician, then Gensler is a logician.
18. If someone is a logician, then he or she is evil.
19. Everyone is an evil logician.
20. Not any logician is evil.

5.5 Harder proofs

Now we come to proofs using formulas with multiple or non-initial quantifiers. Such proofs, while they require no new inference rules, often are tricky and require multiple assumptions. As before, drop only initial quantifiers:

$$\frac{((x)Fx \supset (x)Gx)}{\therefore (Fa \supset (x)Gx)}$$ *(both wrong)* $$\frac{((x)Fx \supset (x)Gx)}{\therefore (Fa \supset Ga)}$$

The formula "$((x)Fx \supset (x)Gx)$" is an if-then; to infer with it, we need the first part true or the second part false:

$$\frac{((x)Fx \supset (x)Gx)}{(x)Fx} \quad \therefore (x)Gx$$ *(both right)* $$\frac{((x)Fx \supset (x)Gx)}{\sim(x)Gx} \quad \therefore \sim(x)Fx$$

If we get stuck, we may need to assume one side or its negation.

Here's a proof using a formula with multiple quantifiers:

*	1	$((\exists x)Sx \supset (x)Tx)$ **Valid**
		$[\therefore (St \supset Ti)$
*	2	⌐ asm: $\sim(St \supset Ti)$
	3	∴ St {from 2}
	4	∴ ~Ti {from 2}
	5	⌐ asm: $\sim(\exists x)Sx$ {break up 1}
	6	∴ $(x)\sim Sx$ {from 5}
	7	└ ∴ ~St {from 6}
	8	∴ $(\exists x)Sx$ {from 5; 3 contradicts 7}
	9	∴ $(x)Tx$ {from 1 and 8}
	10	└ ∴ Ti {from 9}
	11	∴ $(St \supset Ti)$ {from 2; 4 contradicts 10}

If some are enslaved, then all have their freedom threatened. ∴ If this person is enslaved, then I have my freedom threatened.

After making the assumption, we apply an S-rule to get lines 3 and 4. Then we're stuck, since we can't drop the non-initial quantifiers in 1. So we make a second assumption in line 5, get a contradiction, and derive 8. We soon get a second contradiction to complete the proof.

Here's a similar invalid argument:

If *all* are enslaved, then all have their freedom threatened. ∴ If this person is enslaved, then I have my freedom threatened.

	1	$((x)Sx \supset (x)Tx)$ **Invalid**
		$[\therefore (St \supset Ti)$
*	2	asm: $\sim(St \supset Ti)$
	3	∴ St {from 2}
	4	∴ ~Ti {from 2}
**	5	asm: $\sim(x)Sx$ {break up 1}
**	6	∴ $(\exists x)\sim Sx$ {from 5}
	7	∴ ~Sa {from 6}

t, i, a

St, ~Ti, ~Sa

In evaluating the premise here, we first evaluate parts starting with quantifiers:

$((x)Sx \supset (x)Tx)$ ←   Our premise. We first evaluate "(x)Sx" and "(x)Tx":
                            "(x)Sx" is false because "Sa" is false.
                            "(x)Tx" is false because "Ti" is false.

$(0 \supset 0)$ ←   So we substitute "0" for "(x)Sx" and "0" for "(x)Tx."
1   ←   So "$((x)Sx \supset (x)Tx)$" is true.

So the premise is true. Since the conclusion is false, the argument is invalid.

5.5a   Exercise – LogiCola I (HC & MC)

Say whether each is valid (and give a proof) or invalid (and give a refutation).

$$
\begin{array}{ll}
1 & (x)(Mx \lor Fx) \qquad\qquad\qquad \text{Invalid} \\
& [\therefore ((x)Mx \lor (x)Fx) \\
*\quad 2 & \text{asm: } \sim((x)Mx \lor (x)Fx) \qquad a, b \\
*\quad 3 & \therefore \sim(x)Mx \quad \{\text{from 2}\} \\
*\quad 4 & \therefore \sim(x)Fx \quad \{\text{from 2}\} \\
*\quad 5 & \therefore (\exists x)\sim Mx \quad \{\text{from 3}\} \\
*\quad 6 & \therefore (\exists x)\sim Fx \quad \{\text{from 4}\} \\
7 & \therefore \sim Ma \quad \{\text{from 5}\} \\
8 & \therefore \sim Fb \quad \{\text{from 6}\} \\
*\quad 9 & \therefore (Ma \lor Fa) \quad \{\text{from 1}\} \\
*\quad 10 & \therefore (Mb \lor Fb) \quad \{\text{from 1}\} \\
11 & \therefore Fa \quad \{\text{from 7 and 9}\} \\
12 & \therefore Mb \quad \{\text{from 8 and 10}\}
\end{array}
$$

(x)(Mx ∨ Fx) / ∴ ((x)Mx ∨ (x)Fx)

Fa, ~Ma / Mb, ~Fb

(This is like arguing that, since everyone is male or female, thus either everyone is male or everyone is female.)

1. (x)(Fx ∨ Gx)
    ~Fa
    ∴ (∃x)Gx

2. (x)(Ex ⊃ R)
    ∴ ((∃x)Ex ⊃ R)

3. ((x)Ex ⊃ R)
    ∴ (x)(Ex ⊃ R)

4. ((∃x)Fx ∨ (∃x)Gx)
    ∴ (∃x)(Fx ∨ Gx)

5. ((∃x)Fx ⊃ (∃x)Gx)
    ∴ (x)(Fx ⊃ Gx)

6. (x)((Fx ∨ Gx) ⊃ Hx)
    Fm
    ∴ Hm

7. Fj
    (∃x)Gx
    (x)((Fx · Gx) ⊃ Hx)
    ∴ (∃x)Hx

8. ((∃x)Fx ⊃ (x)Gx)
    ~Gp
    ∴ ~Fp

9. (∃x)(Fx ∨ Gx)
    ∴ ((x)~Gx ⊃ (∃x)Fx)

10. ~(∃x)(Fx · Gx)
    ~Fd
    ∴ Gd

11. (x)(Ex ⊃ R)
    ∴ ((x)Ex ⊃ R)

12. (x)(Fx · Gx)
    ∴ ((x)Fx · (x)Gx)

13. (R ⊃ (x)Ex)
    ∴ (x)(R ⊃ Ex)

14. ((x)Fx ∨ (x)Gx)
    ∴ (x)(Fx ∨ Gx)

15. ((∃x)Ex ⊃ R)
    ∴ (x)(Ex ⊃ R)

5.5b   Exercise – LogiCola I (HC & MC)

First appraise intuitively. Then translate into logic (using the letters given) and say whether valid (and give a proof) or invalid (and give a refutation).

1. Everything has a cause.
    If the world has a cause, then there is a God.
    ∴ There is a God.   [Use Cx for "x has a cause," w for "the world," and G for "There is a God" (which here we needn't break down into "(∃x)Gx" – "For some x, x is a God"). A student of mine suggested this argument; but the next example shows that premise 1 can as easily lead to the opposite conclusion.]

2. Everything has a cause.
    If there is a God, then something doesn't have a cause (namely, God).
    ∴ There is no God.   [Use Cx and G. The next example qualifies "Everything has a cause" to avoid the problem; some prefer an argument based on "Every *contingent being or set of such beings* has a cause."]

3.   Everything that began to exist has a cause.
     The world began to exist.
     If the world has a cause, then there is a God.
     ∴ There is a God.   [Use Bx, Cx, w, and G. This "kalam argument" is from William
     Craig and James Moreland; they defend premise 2 by appealing to the big-bang
     theory, the law of entropy, and the impossibility of an actual infinite.]

4.   If everyone litters, then the world will be dirty.
     ∴ If you litter, then the world will be dirty.   [Use Lx, D, and u.]

5.   Anything enjoyable is either immoral or fattening.
     ∴ If nothing is immoral, then everything that isn't fattening isn't enjoyable.   [Use
     Ex, Ix, and Fx.]

6.   Anything that can be explained either can be explained as caused by scientific
     laws or can be explained as resulting from a free choice of a rational being.
     The totality of basic scientific laws can't be explained as caused by scientific laws
     (since this would be circular).
     ∴ Either the totality of basic scientific laws can't be explained or else it can be
     explained as resulting from a free choice of a rational being (God).   [Use Ex for
     "x can be explained," Sx for "x can be explained as caused by scientific laws," Fx
     for "x can be explained as resulting from a free choice of a rational being," and t
     for "the totality of scientific laws." This one is from R. G. Swinburne.]

7.   If someone knows the future, then no one has free will.
     ∴ No one who knows the future has free will.   [Use Kx and Fx.]

8.   If everyone teaches philosophy, then everyone will starve.
     ∴ Everyone who teaches philosophy will starve.   [Use Tx and Sx.]

9.   No proposition with empirical content is logically necessary.
     ∴ Either no mathematical proposition has empirical content, or no mathematical
     proposition is logically necessary.   [Use Ex for "x has empirical content," Nx
     for "x is logically necessary," Mx for "x is mathematical," and the universe of
     propositions. This argument is from the logical positivist A. J. Ayer.]

10. Any basic social rule that people would agree to if they were free and rational but
     ignorant of their place in society (whether rich or poor, white or black, male or
     female) is a principle of justice.
     The equal-liberty principle and the difference principle are basic social rules that
     people would agree to if they were free and rational but ignorant of their place
     in society.
     ∴ The equal-liberty principle and the difference principle are principles of justice.
     [Use Ax, Px, e, and d. This argument is from John Rawls. The equal-liberty
     principle says that each person is entitled to the greatest liberty compatible with
     an equal liberty for all others. The difference principle says that wealth is to be
     distributed equally, except for inequalities that serve as incentives that ulti-
     mately benefit everyone and are equally open to all.]

11. If there are no necessary beings, then there are no contingent beings.
   ∴ All contingent beings are necessary beings.   [Use Nx and Cx. Aquinas accepted the premise but not the conclusion.]

12. Anything not disproved that is of practical value to one's life to believe ought to be believed.
   Free will isn't disproved.
   ∴ If free will is of practical value to one's life to believe, then it ought to be believed.   [Use Dx, Vx, Ox, f (for "free will"), and the universe of discourse of beliefs. This argument is from William James.]

13. If the world had no temporal beginning, then some series of moments before the present moment is a completed infinite series.
   There's no completed infinite series.
   ∴ The world had a temporal beginning.   [Use Tx for "x had a temporal beginning," w for "the world," Mx for "x is a series of moments before the present moment," and Ix for "x is a completed infinite series." This one and the next are from Immanuel Kant, who thought our intuitive metaphysical principles lead to conflicting conclusions and thus can't be trusted.]

14. Everything that had a temporal beginning was caused to exist by something previously in existence.
   If the world was caused to exist by something previously in existence, then there was time before the world began.
   If the world had a temporal beginning, then there was no time before the world began.
   ∴ The world didn't have a temporal beginning.   [Use Tx for "x had a temporal beginning," Cx for "x was caused to exist by something previously in existence," w for "the world," and B for "There was time before the world began."]

15. If emotivism is true, then "X is good" means "Hurrah for X!" and all moral judgments are exclamations.
   All exclamations are inherently emotional.
   "This dishonest income tax exemption is wrong" is a moral judgment.
   "This dishonest income tax exemption is wrong" isn't inherently emotional.
   ∴ Emotivism isn't true.   [Use T, H, Mx, Ex, Ix, and t.]

16. If everything is material, then all prime numbers are composed of physical particles.
   Seven is a prime number.
   Seven isn't composed of physical particles.
   ∴ Not everything is material.   [Use Mx, Px, Cx, and s.]

17. If everyone lies, the results will be disastrous.
   ∴ If anyone lies, the results will be disastrous.   [Use Lx and D.]

18.   Everyone makes moral judgments.
      Moral judgments logically presuppose beliefs about God.
      If moral judgments logically presuppose beliefs about God, then everyone who
      makes moral judgments believes (at least implicitly) that there is a God.
   ∴ Everyone believes (at least implicitly) that there is a God.   [Use Mx for "x
      makes moral judgments," L for "Moral judgments logically presuppose beliefs
      about God," and Bx for "x believes (at least implicitly) that there is a God." This
      argument is from the Jesuit theologian Karl Rahner.]

19.   "x=x" is a basic law.
      "x=x" is true in itself, and not true because someone made it true.
      If "x=x" depends on God's will, then "x=x" is true because someone made it
      true.
   ∴ Some basic laws don't depend on God's will.   [Use e (for "x=x"), Bx, Tx, Mx,
      and Dx.]

20.   Nothing that isn't caused can be integrated into the unity of our experience.
      Everything that we could experientially know can be integrated into the unity of
      our experience.
   ∴ Everything that we could experientially know is caused.   [Use Cx, Ix, and Ex.
      This argument is from Immanuel Kant. The conclusion is limited to objects of
      possible experience – since it says "Everything *that we could experientially
      know* is caused"; Kant thought that the unqualified "Everything is caused"
      leads to contradictions (see problems 1 and 2).]

21.   If everyone deliberates about alternatives, then everyone believes (at least
      implicitly) in free will.
   ∴ Everyone who deliberates about alternatives believes (at least implicitly) in free
      will.   [Use Dx and Bx.]

22.   All who are consistent and think that abortion is normally permissible will
      consent to the idea of their having been aborted in normal circumstances.
      You don't consent to the idea of your having been aborted in normal circum-
      stances.
   ∴ If you're consistent, then you won't think that abortion is normally permissible.
      [Use Cx, Px, Ix, and u. See my article in January 1986 *Philosophical Studies* or
      the last chapter of my *Ethics: A Contemporary Introduction* (London and New
      York: Routledge, 1998).]

CHAPTER 6
Relations and Identity

This chapter brings quantificational logic up to full power by adding **identity statements** (like "a=b") and **relational statements** (like "Lrj" for "Romeo loves Juliet"). We'll end with definite descriptions.

6.1 Identity translations

Our rule 3 for forming quantificational wffs introduces "=" ("equals"):

> 3. The result of writing a small letter and then "=" and then a small letter is a wff.

This rule lets us construct wffs like these:

$$
\begin{array}{rcl}
x=y & = & x \text{ equals } y. \\
r=l & = & \text{Romeo is the lover of Juliet.} \\
{\sim}r=l & = & \text{Romeo isn't the lover of Juliet.}
\end{array}
$$

We negate an identity wff by writing "∼" in front. Neither "r=l" nor "∼r=l" use parentheses, since these aren't needed to avoid ambiguity.

The simplest use of "=" is to translate an "is" that goes between singular terms. Recall the difference between general and singular terms:

Use capital letters for **general terms** (terms that *describe* or put in a *category*):
 	
    L = a lover
    C = charming
    R = drives a Rolls
 	
Use capitals for "a so and so," adjectives, and verbs.
	Use small letters for **singular terms** (terms that pick out a *specific* person or thing):
	
	    l = the lover of Juliet
	    c = this child
	    r = Romeo
	
	Use small letters for "the so and so," "this so and so," and proper names.

Compare these two forms:

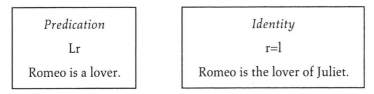

Predication	Identity
Lr	r=l
Romeo is a lover.	Romeo is the lover of Juliet.

Use "=" for "is" if both sides are singular terms (and thus represented by small letters). The "is" of identity can be replaced with "is identical to" or "is the same entity as" – and can be reversed (so if x=y then y=x).

We can translate "other than," "besides," and "alone" using identity:

Someone *other than* Romeo is rich
= Someone *besides* Romeo is rich

= Someone who isn't Romeo is rich.
= For some x, x ≠ Romeo and x is rich.
= (∃x)(~x=r · Rx)

Romeo *alone* is rich

= Romeo is rich and no one besides Romeo is rich.
= (Rr · ~(∃x)(~x=r · Rx))

We also can translate some numerical notions, for example:

At least two are rich

= For some x and some y: x≠y, x is rich, and y is rich.
= (∃x)(∃y)(~x=y · (Rx · Ry))

The pair of quantifiers "(∃x)(∃y)" ("for some x and some y") doesn't say whether x and y are identical; so we need "~x=y" to say that they aren't.

Henceforth we'll often need more variable letters than just "x" to keep references straight. It doesn't matter what letters we use; these two are equivalent:

(∃x)Rx = For some x, x is rich = At least one being is rich.
(∃y)Ry = For some y, y is rich = At least one being is rich.

Here's how we translate "exactly one" and "exactly two":

Exactly one being is rich

= For some x: x is rich and there's no y such that y≠x and y is rich.
= (∃x)(Rx · ~(∃y)(~y=x · Ry))

Exactly two beings are rich

= For some x and some y: x is rich and y is rich and x≠y and there's no z such that z≠x and z≠y and z is rich.
= (∃x)(∃y)(((Rx · Ry) · ~x=y) · ~(∃z)((~z=x · ~z=y) · Rz))

So our notation can express "There are exactly n F's" for any specific whole number n.

We also can express addition. Here's an English paraphrase of "1+1=2" and the corresponding formula:

If exactly one being is F	$((((\exists x)(Fx \cdot \sim(\exists y)(\sim y=x \cdot Fy))$
and exactly one being is G	$\cdot (\exists x)(Gx \cdot \sim(\exists y)(\sim y=x \cdot Gy)))$
and nothing is F-and-G,	$\cdot \sim(\exists x)(Fx \cdot Gx)) \supset$
then exactly two beings	$(\exists x)(\exists y)(((Fx \vee Gx) \cdot (Fy \vee Gy)) \cdot (\sim x=y$
are F-or-G.	$\cdot \sim(\exists z)((\sim z=x \cdot \sim z=y) \cdot (Fz \vee Gz)))))$

We could prove our "1+1=2" formula by assuming its denial and deriving a contradiction. While we won't do this, it's interesting that it could be done. In principle, we could prove "2+2=4" and "5+7=12" – and the additions on your income tax form. Some mean logic teachers assign such things for homework.

6.1a Exercise – LogiCola H (IM & IT)

Translate these English sentences into wffs.

Jim is the goalie and is a student.	$(j=g \cdot Sj)$

1. Aristotle is a logician.
2. Aristotle is the greatest logician.
3. Aristotle isn't Plato.
4. Someone besides Aristotle is a logician.
5. There are at least two logicians.
6. Aristotle alone is a logician.
7. All logicians other than Aristotle are evil.
8. No one besides Aristotle is evil.
9. The philosopher is Aristotle.
10. There's exactly one logician.
11. There's exactly one evil logician.
12. Everyone besides Aristotle and Plato is evil.
13. If the thief is intelligent, then you aren't the thief.
14. Carol is my only sister.
15. Alice runs but isn't the fastest runner.
16. There's at most one king.
17. The king is bald.
18. There's exactly one king and he is bald.

6.2 Identity proofs

We need two new rules for identity. This self-identity (SI) rule holds regardless of what constant replaces "a":

Self-identity $\quad\boxed{\rightarrow \quad \text{a=a}}$

This is an **axiom** – a basic assertion that isn't proved but can be used to prove other things. Rule SI says that we may assert a self-identity as a "derived step" anywhere in a proof, no matter what the earlier lines are. Adding "a=a" can be useful if this gives us a contradiction (since we already have "~a=a") or lets us apply an I-rule (since we already have "(a=a ⊃ Gb)").

The equals-may-substitute-for-equals (SE) rule is based on the idea that identicals are interchangeable: if a=b, then whatever is true of a also is true of b, and vice versa. This rule holds regardless of what constants replace "a" and "b" and what wffs replace "Fa" and "Fb" – provided that the two wffs are alike except that the constants are interchanged in one or more occurrences:

Substitute $\quad\boxed{\text{Fa, a=b} \quad \rightarrow \quad \text{Fb}}$
equals

Here's a simple identity proof:

1	Wi	**Valid**
2	~Wm	

I weigh 180 pounds.
My mind doesn't weigh 180
    pounds.
∴ I'm not identical to my mind.

1   Wi   **Valid**
2   ~Wm
   [∴ ~i=m
3   ⌐ asm: i=m
4   L ∴ Wm {from 1 and 3}
5 ∴ ~i=m {from 3; 2 contradicts 4}

Line 4 follows by substituting equals; if i and m are identical, then whatever is true of one is true of the other.

Here's a simple invalid argument and its refutation:

The bankrobber wears size-
    twelve shoes.
You wear size-twelve shoes.
∴ You're the bankrobber.

1   Wb   **Invalid** b, u
2   Wu
   [∴ u=b $\boxed{\text{Wb, Wu, ~u=b}}$
3   asm: ~u=b

Since we can't infer anything (we can't do much with "~u=b"), we set up a possible world to refute the argument. This world contains two distinct persons, the bankrobber and you, each wearing size-twelve shoes. Since the premises are all true and conclusion false in this world, our argument is invalid.

Our next example involves *pluralism* and *monism*:

Pluralism	*Monism*
There's more than one being.	There's exactly one being.
(∃x)(∃y)~x=y	(∃x)(y)y=x
For some x and some y: x≠y.	For some x, every y is identical to x.

Here's a proof that pluralism entails the falsity of monism:

```
                        *  1    (∃x)(∃y)~x=y   Valid
                           [ ∴ ~(∃x)(y)y=x
                        *  2  ┌ asm: (∃x)(y)y=x
There's more than       *  3  │ ∴ (∃y)~a=y   {from 1}
   one being.              4  │ ∴ ~a=b   {from 3}
∴ It's false that there's    5  │ ∴ (y)y=c   {from 2}
   exactly one being.        6  │ ∴ a=c   {from 5}
                          7  │ ∴ b=c   {from 5}
                          8  └ ∴ a=b   {from 6 and 7}
                          9  ∴ ~(∃x)(y)y=x   {from 2; 4 contradicts 8}
```

Lines 1 and 2 have back-to-back quantifiers. We can drop only quantifiers that are initial and hence outermost; so we have to drop the quantifiers one at a time, starting from the outside. After dropping quantifiers, we substitute equals to get line 8. Our "b=c" premise lets us take "a=c" and substitute "b" for the "c," thus getting "a=b."

We didn't bother to derive "c=c" from "(y)y=c" in line 5. From now on, it'll often be too tedious to drop universal quantifiers using *every* old constant. So we'll just derive instances likely to be useful for our proof or refutation.

Our substitute-equals rule seems to hold universally in arguments about matter or mathematics. But the rule can fail with mental phenomena. Consider this argument (where "Bx" stands for "Jones believes that x is on the penny"):

Jones believes that Lincoln is on the penny.   Bl
Lincoln is the first Republican US president.   l=r
∴ Jones believes that the first Republican US   ∴ Br
   president is on the penny.

If Jones is unaware that Lincoln was the first Republican president, the premises could be true while the conclusion is false. So the argument is invalid. But yet we can derive the conclusion from the premises using our substitute-equals rule. So something is wrong here.

To avoid the problem, we'll disallow translating into quantificational logic any predicates or relations that violate the substitute-equals rule. So we won't let "Bx" stand for "Jones believes that x is on the penny." Statements about beliefs and other mental phenomena often violate this rule; so we have to be careful translating such statements into quantificational logic.[1]

So the mental seems to follow different logical patterns from the physical. Does this refute the materialist project of reducing the mental to the physical? Philosophers dispute this question.

---

[1] Chapter 10 will develop special ways to symbolize belief formulas and will explicitly restrict the use of the substitute-equals rule with such formulas (see Section 10.2).

6.2a   Exercise – LogiCola IDC

Say whether each is valid (and give a proof) or invalid (and give a refutation).

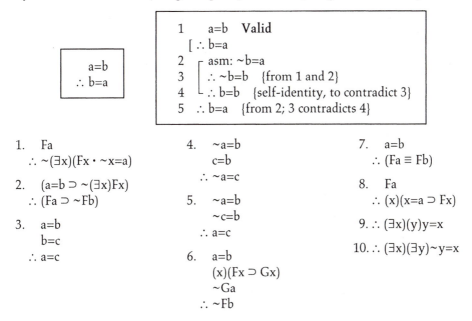

1. Fa
    ∴ ~(∃x)(Fx · ~x=a)

2. (a=b ⊃ ~(∃x)Fx)
    ∴ (Fa ⊃ ~Fb)

3. a=b
    b=c
    ∴ a=c

4. ~a=b
    c=b
    ∴ ~a=c

5. ~a=b
    ~c=b
    ∴ a=c

6. a=b
    (x)(Fx ⊃ Gx)
    ~Ga
    ∴ ~Fb

7. a=b
    ∴ (Fa ≡ Fb)

8. Fa
    ∴ (x)(x=a ⊃ Fx)

9. ∴ (∃x)(y)y=x

10. ∴ (∃x)(∃y)~y=x

6.2b   Exercise – LogiCola IDC

First appraise intuitively. Then translate into logic and say whether valid (and give a proof) or invalid (and give a refutation). You'll have to figure out what letters to use; be careful about deciding between small and capital letters.

1. Keith is my only nephew.
    My only nephew knows more about BASIC than I do.
    Keith is a ten-year-old.
    ∴ Some ten-year-olds know more about BASIC than I do.   [I wrote this argument many years ago; now Keith is older and I have two nephews.]

2. Some are logicians.
    Some aren't logicians.
    ∴ There's more than one being.

3. This chemical process is publicly observable.
    This pain isn't publicly observable.
    ∴ This pain isn't identical to this chemical process.   [This attacks the identity theory of the mind, which identifies mental events with chemical processes.]

4. The person who left a lighter is the murderer.
    The person who left a lighter is a smoker.
    No smokers are backpackers.
    ∴ The murderer isn't a backpacker.

5.   The murderer isn't a backpacker.
      You aren't a backpacker.
      ∴ You're the murderer.

6.   If Speedy Jones looks back to the quarterback just before the hike, then Speedy
         Jones is the primary receiver.
      The primary receiver is the receiver you should try to cover.
      ∴ If Speedy Jones looks back to the quarterback just before the hike, then Speedy
         Jones is the receiver you should try to cover.

7.   Judy isn't the world's best cook.
      The world's best cook lives in Detroit.
      ∴ Judy doesn't live in Detroit.

8.   Patricia lives in North Dakota.
      Blondie lives in North Dakota.
      ∴ At least two people live in North Dakota.

9.   Your grade is the average of your tests.
      The average of your tests is B.
      ∴ Your grade is B.

10.   Either you knew where the money was, or the thief knew where it was.
      You didn't know where the money was.
      ∴ You aren't the thief.

11.   The man of Suzy's dreams is either rich or handsome.
      You aren't rich.
      ∴ If you're handsome, then you're the man of Suzy's dreams.

12.   If someone confesses, then someone goes to jail.
      I confess.
      I don't go to jail.
      ∴ Someone besides me goes to jail.

13.   David stole money.
      The nastiest person at the party stole money.
      David isn't the nastiest person at the party.
      ∴ At least two people stole money.   [See problem 4 of Section 2.3b.]

14.   No one besides Carol and the detective had a key.
      Someone who had a key stole money.
      ∴ Either Carol or the detective stole money.

15.   Exactly one person lives in North Dakota.
      Paul lives in North Dakota.
      Paul is a farmer.
      ∴ Everyone who lives in North Dakota is a farmer.

16.   The wildcard team with the best record goes to the playoffs.
      Cleveland isn't the wildcard team with the best record.
      ∴ Cleveland doesn't go to the playoffs.

6.3 Relational translations

Our last rule for forming quantificational wffs introduces relations:

> 4. The result of writing a capital letter and then two or more small letters is a wff.

$$\begin{aligned} \text{Lrj} &= \text{Romeo loves Juliet.} \\ \text{Gxyz} &= \text{x gave y to z.} \end{aligned}$$

Translating relational sentences into logic can be difficult, since there are few rules to help us. We mostly have to study examples and catch the patterns.

Here are further examples without quantifiers:

Juliet loves Romeo	=	Ljr
Juliet loves herself	=	Juliet loves Juliet.
	=	Ljj
Juliet loves Romeo and Antonio	=	Juliet loves Romeo and Juliet loves Antonio.
	=	(Ljr • Lja)

These use single quantifiers:

Everyone loves Juliet	=	For all x, x loves Juliet.
	=	(x)Lxj
Someone loves Juliet = Juliet is loved	=	For some x, x loves Juliet.
	=	(∃x)Lxj
Everyone is loved by Juliet	=	For all x, Juliet loves x.
	=	(x)Ljx

These are similar, but more difficult:

All Italians love Juliet	=	For all x, if x is Italian then x loves Juliet.
	=	(x)(Ix ⊃ Lxj)
Some Italians love Juliet	=	For some x, x is Italian and x loves Juliet.
	=	(∃x)(Ix • Lxj)

If the English has a quantifier just after "loves," put the quantifier first:

"Juliet loves everyone (someone, no one)."	means	"For all (some, no) x, Juliet loves x."

| Juliet loves everyone | = | For all x, Juliet loves x. |
| | = | (x)Ljx |

| Juliet loves someone | = | For some x, Juliet loves x. |
| = Juliet is a lover | = | (∃x)Ljx |

| Juliet loves no one | = | It is not the case that, for some x, Juliet loves x. |
| | = | ~(∃x)Ljx |

These are similar, but more difficult:

| Juliet loves every Italian | = | For all x, if x is Italian then Juliet loves x. |
| | = | (x)(Ix ⊃ Ljx) |

| Juliet loves some Italian | = | For some x, x is Italian and Juliet loves x. |
| | = | (∃x)(Ix · Ljx) |

	=	It is not the case that, for some x, x is Italian
Juliet loves no Italian		and Juliet loves x.
	=	~(∃x)(Ix · Ljx)

Here are sentences with two quantifiers:

| Everyone loves everyone | = | For all x and for all y, x loves y. |
| | = | (x)(y)Lxy |

| Someone loves someone | = | For some x and for some y, x loves y. |
| | = | (∃x)(∃y)Lxy |

In the second case, the "someone" who loves may or may not be the same "someone" who is loved. Compare these two:

| Some love themselves | = | For some x, x loves x. |
| | = | (∃x)Lxx |

| Some love others | = | For some x and some y, x≠y and x loves y. |
| | = | (∃x)(∃y)(~x=y · Lxy) |

Study carefully this next pair – which differs only in the order of the quantifiers:

Everyone loves someone.	There's someone that everyone loves.
= Everyone loves at least one person.	= There's some one specific person that everyone loves.
= (x)(∃y)Lxy	= (∃y)(x)Lxy
= For all x there's some y, such that x loves y.	= There's some y such that, for all x, x loves y.

In the first case, we might love *different* people. In the second, we love the *same* person; perhaps we all love God. These pairs emphasize the difference:

Everyone loves someone	≠	There's someone that everyone loves.
Everyone lives in some house	≠	There's some house where everyone lives.
Everyone makes some error	≠	There's some error that everyone makes.

The sentences on the right make the stronger claim.

With back-to-back quantifiers, the order doesn't matter if both quantifiers are of the same type; but the order matters if the quantifiers are mixed:

$$(x)(y) = (y)(x) \qquad (\exists x)(\exists y) = (\exists y)(\exists x) \qquad (x)(\exists y) \neq (\exists y)(x)$$

Also, it doesn't matter what variable letters we use, so long as the reference pattern is the same. These three are equivalent:

$$(x)(\exists y)Lyx \qquad (y)(\exists x)Lxy \qquad (z)(\exists x)Lxz$$

Each has a universal, then an existential, then "L," then the variable used in the existential, and finally the variable used in the universal.

Many relations have special properties, such as reflexivity or symmetry. Here are examples:

"Is identical to" is *reflexive*. (Identity is a relation but uses a
  special symbol.)
= Everything is identical to itself.
= (x)x=x

"Taller than" is *irreflexive*.
= Nothing is taller than itself.
= (x)~Txx

"Being a relative of" is *symmetrical*.
= In all cases, if x is a relative of y, then y is a relative of x.
= (x)(y)(Rxy ⊃ Ryx)

"Being a parent of" is *asymmetrical*.
= In all cases, if x is a parent of y then y isn't a parent of x.
= (x)(y)(Pxy ⊃ ~Pyx)

"Being taller than" is *transitive*.
= In all cases, if x is taller than y and y is taller than z,
  then x is taller than z.
= (x)(y)(z)((Txy · Tyz) ⊃ Txz)

"Being a foot taller than" is *intransitive*.
= In all cases, if x is a foot taller than y and y is a foot
  taller than z, then x isn't a foot taller than z.
= (x)(y)(z)((Txy · Tyz) ⊃ ~Txz)

Love fits none of these six categories. Love is neither reflexive nor irreflexive: sometimes people love themselves and sometimes they don't. Love is neither symmetrical nor asymmetrical: if x loves y, then sometimes y loves x in return and sometimes not. Love is neither transitive nor intransitive: if x loves y and y loves z, then sometimes x loves z and sometimes not.

These examples are difficult:

> Every Italian loves someone.
> = For all x, if x is Italian then there's some y such that x loves y.
> = $(x)(Ix \supset (\exists y)Lxy)$
>
> Everyone loves some Italian.
> = For all x there's some y such that y is Italian and x loves y.
> = $(x)(\exists y)(Iy \cdot Lxy)$
>
> Everyone loves a lover.
> = For all x, if x loves someone then everyone loves x.
> = $(x)((\exists y)Lxy \supset (z)Lzx)$
>
> Juliet loves everyone besides herself.
> = For all x, if x ≠ Juliet then Juliet loves x.
> = $(x)(\sim x{=}j \supset Ljx)$
>
> Romeo loves all and only those who don't love themselves.
> = For all x, Romeo loves x if and only if x doesn't love x.
> = $(x)(Lrx \equiv \sim Lxx)$

Study these and the other examples carefully, focusing on how to paraphrase the English sentences.

I have no tidy rules for translating relational sentences into formulas. But you might find these steps helpful if you get confused:

- Put a different variable letter after each quantifier word in English, and rephrase according to how logic expresses things.
- Replace each quantifier word in English by a symbolic quantifier, and keep rephrasing, until the whole sentence is translated.

Here are three examples:

> Every Italian loves some Italian.
> = Every x who is Italian loves some y who is Italian.
> = $(x)(x$ is Italian $\supset (\exists y)(y$ is Italian $\cdot x$ loves y$))$
> = $(x)(Ix \supset (\exists y)(Iy \cdot Lxy))$
>
> There's an unloved lover.
> = For some x, no one loves x and x loves someone.
> = $(\exists x)($no y loves x $\cdot$ x loves some z$)$
> = $(\exists x)(\sim(\exists y)Lyx \cdot (\exists z)Lxz)$

Some Italian besides Romeo loves Juliet.
= Some x who is Italian and not Romeo loves Juliet.
= (∃x)(x is Italian · x isn't Romeo · x loves Juliet)
= (∃x)((Ix · ~x=r) · Lxj)

Paraphrase the English bit by bit, following the quantificational idiom.

6.3a Exercise – LogiCola H (RM & RT)

Using these equivalences, translate these English sentences into wffs.

| Cxy | = | x caused y | Ex | = | x is evil | g | = | God |
| Gxy | = | x is greater than y | a | = | Aristotle | w | = | the world |

Aristotle caused nothing that is evil.	~(∃x)(Ex · Cax)

1. God caused the world.
2. The world caused God.
3. Nothing is greater than itself.
4. Aristotle is greater than anything else.
5. Aristotle is greater than some evil beings.
6. It is always true that if a first thing is evil and a second thing isn't evil then the first is greater than the second.
7. If God caused the world, then God is greater than the world.
8. It is not always true that if a first thing caused a second then the first is greater than the second.
9. Every entity is greater than some entity.
10. There's something than which nothing is greater.
11. God had no cause.
12. If God had no cause, then the world had no cause.
13. Nothing caused itself.
14. In all cases, if a first thing is greater than a second, then the second isn't greater than the first.
15. Everything is caused by something.
16. There's something that caused everything.
17. Something evil caused all evil things.
18. God caused everything besides himself.
19. In all cases, if a first thing caused a second and the second caused a third, then the first caused the third.
20. There's a first cause (there's some x that caused something but nothing caused x).

6.4 Relational proofs

In relational proofs, as before, we'll reverse squiggles, drop existentials (using new constants), and lastly drop universals. But now back-to-back quantifiers will be common (as in line 3 of this next proof); we'll drop such quantifiers one at a time, starting at the outside, since we can drop only an *initial* quantifier:

	1	Lrj	**Valid**
	2	~Ljr	
		[∴ ~(x)(y)(Lxy ⊃ Lyx)	
	3	┌ asm: (x)(y)(Lxy ⊃ Lyx)	
	4	│ ∴ (y)(Lry ⊃ Lyr) {from 3}	
*	5	│ ∴ (Lrj ⊃ Ljr) {from 4}	
	6	└ ∴ Ljr {from 1 and 5}	
	7	∴ ~(x)(y)(Lxy ⊃ Lyx) {from 3; 2 contradicts 6}	

Romeo loves Juliet.
Juliet doesn't love Romeo.
∴ It's not always true that if a first person loves a second then the second loves the first.

Our older proof strategy would have us drop each initial universal quantifier twice, once using "r" and once using "j." But now this would be tedious; so we instead derive only what is likely to be useful for our proof or refutation.

Here's another relational proof:

*	1	(∃y)(x)Lxy **Valid**	
		[∴ (x)(∃y)Lxy	
*	2	┌ asm: ~(x)(∃y)Lxy	
*	3	│ ∴ (∃x)~(∃y)Lxy {from 2}	
*	4	│ ∴ ~(∃y)Lay {from 3}	
	5	│ ∴ (y)~Lay {from 4}	
	6	│ ∴ (x)Lxb {from 1}	
	7	│ ∴ Lab {from 6}	
	8	└ ∴ ~Lab {from 5}	
	9	∴ (x)(∃y)Lxy {from 2; 7 contradicts 8}	

There's someone that everyone loves.
∴ Everyone loves some- one.

This should be valid intuitively – since if there's one specific person (God, for example) that everyone loves, then everyone loves at least one person.

Relational proofs raise interesting problems. With quantificational argu- ments that lack relations and identity:

1. there are mechanical strategies (like that of Section 5.2) that in every case will give a proof or refutation in a finite number of steps; and
2. a refutation never requires an infinite number of entities – and at most requires 2^n entities (where *n* is the number of distinct predicates).

Neither feature holds for relational arguments. Against 1, there's no possible mechanical strategy that always will give us a proof or refutation of a relational argument. This result is called **Church's theorem**, after Alonzo Church. As a result, working out relational arguments sometimes requires ingenuity and not just mechanical methods; the defect with our proof strategy, we'll see, is that it can lead into endless loops. Against 2, refuting invalid relational arguments sometimes requires a possible world with an infinite number of entities.

Instructions lead into an **endless loop** if they command the same sequence of actions over and over, endlessly. I've written computer programs with endless loops by mistake. I put an endless loop into the glossary on purpose:

Endless loop See loop, endless.	**Loop, endless** See endless loop.

Our quantificational proof strategy can lead into such a loop. If you see this coming, quit the strategy and improvise your own refutation.

Trying to prove "$\sim(x)(\exists y)x=y$" ("Not everything is identical to something") leads into an endless loop:

		[$\therefore \sim(x)(\exists y)x=y$ **Invalid**
Asm: Everything is identical to something.	1	asm: $(x)(\exists y)x=y$
$\therefore$ a is identical to something.	2	$\therefore (\exists y)a=y$ {from 1}
$\therefore$ a is identical to b.	3	$\therefore a=b$ {from 2}
$\therefore$ b is identical to something.	4	$\therefore (\exists y)b=y$ {from 1}
$\therefore$ b is identical to c.	5	$\therefore b=c$ {from 4}
$\therefore$ c is identical to something....	6	$\therefore (\exists y)c=y$ {from 1} ...

We drop the universal quantifier in 1, using a new constant "a" (since there are no old constants) to get 2; a step later, we get new constant "b." We drop the universal in 1 using "b" to get 4; a step later, we get new constant "c." And so on endlessly. To refute the argument, we can use a world with a single entity, a, that is identical to itself:

$$a \quad \boxed{a=a}$$

In this world, everything is identical to at least one thing – and hence the conclusion is false. We have to think up this world for ourselves. The strategy doesn't provide it automatically; instead, it leads into an endless loop.

Wffs that begin with a universal/existential quantifier combination, like "$(x)(\exists y)$," often lead into an endless loop. Here's another example:[1]

Everyone loves someone.	$(x)(\exists y)Lxy$ **Invalid**
$\therefore$ There's someone that everyone loves.	$\therefore (\exists y)(x)Lxy$

---

[1] This example is like arguing "Everyone lives in some house, so there must be some (one) house that everyone lives in." Some great minds have committed this fallacy. Aristotle argued "Every agent acts for an end, so there must be some (one) end for which every agent acts." St Thomas Aquinas argued "If everything at some time fails to exist, then there must be some (one) time at which everything fails to exist." And John Locke argued "Everything is caused by something, so there must be some (one) thing that caused everything."

Here the premise by itself leads into an endless loop:

Everyone loves someone.	$(x)(\exists y)Lxy$
$\therefore$ a loves someone.	$\therefore (\exists y)Lay$
$\therefore$ a loves b.	$\therefore Lab$
$\therefore$ b loves someone.	$\therefore (\exists y)Lby$
$\therefore$ b loves c.	$\therefore Lbc$
$\therefore$ c loves someone....	$\therefore (\exists y)Lcy \ ...$

Again we must improvise, since our strategy doesn't automatically give us a proof or refutation. With some ingenuity, we can construct this possible world, with beings a and b, that makes the premise true and conclusion false:

$$a, b \quad \boxed{\begin{array}{l} Laa, \sim Lab \\ Lbb, \sim Lba \end{array}} \quad \text{(egoistic world)}$$

Here all love themselves, and only themselves. This makes "Everyone loves someone" true but "There's someone that everyone loves" false. Here's another refutation:

$$a, b \quad \boxed{\begin{array}{l} Lab, \sim Laa \\ Lba, \sim Lbb \end{array}} \quad \text{(altruistic world)}$$

Here all love the other but not themselves; this again makes the premise true and conclusion false.

We don't automatically get a refutation with invalid arguments that lead into an endless loop. Instead, we have to think out the refutation by ourselves. While there's no strategy that always works, I'd suggest that you:

1. try breaking out of the loop before introducing your third constant (often it suffices to use two beings, a and b; don't multiply entities unnecessarily),
2. begin your refutation with values you already have (maybe, for example, you already have "Lab" and "Laa"), and
3. experiment with adding other wffs to make the premises true and conclusion false (if you already have "Lab" and "Laa," then try adding "Lba" or "~Lba" – and "Lbb" or "~Lbb" – until you get a refutation).

We have to fiddle with the values until we find a refutation that works.

Refuting a relational argument sometimes requires a universe with an infinite number of entities. Here's an example:

In all cases, if x is greater than y and y is
   greater than z then x is greater than z.
In all cases, if x is greater than y then y
   isn't greater than x.
   b is greater than a.
∴ There's something than which nothing
   is greater.

(x)(y)(z)((Gxy · Gyz) ⊃ Gxz)
(x)(y)(Gxy ⊃ ~Gyx)
Gba
∴ (∃x)~(∃y)Gyx

Given these premises, every world with a finite number of beings must have
some being unsurpassed in greatness (making the conclusion true). But we can
imagine a world with an infinity of beings – in which each being is surpassed in
greatness by another. So the argument is invalid.

We can refute the argument by giving another of the same form with true
premises and a false conclusion. Let's take the natural numbers (0, 1, 2, …) as
the universe of discourse. Let "a" refer to 0 and "b" refer to 1 and "Gxy" mean
"x > y." On this interpretation, the premises are all true. But the conclusion,
which says "There's a number than which no number is greater," is false. This
shows that the form is invalid.

So relational arguments raise problems about infinity (endless loops and
infinite worlds) that other kinds of arguments we've studied don't raise.

6.4a Exercise – LogiCola I (RC & BC)

Say whether each is valid (and give a proof) or invalid (and give a refutation).

$$(\exists x)(\exists y)Lxy$$
$$\therefore (\exists y)(\exists x)Lxy$$

```
 *  1      (∃x)(∃y)Lxy   Valid
        [ ∴ (∃y)(∃x)Lxy
 *  2    ┌ asm: ~(∃y)(∃x)Lxy
    3    │ ∴ (y)~(∃x)Lxy   {from 2}
 *  4    │ ∴ (∃y)Lay   {from 1}
    5    │ ∴ Lab   {from 4}
 *  6    │ ∴ ~(∃x)Lxb   {from 3}
    7    │ ∴ (x)~Lxb   {from 6}
    8    └ ∴ ~Lab   {from 7}
    9   ∴ (∃y)(∃x)Lxy   {from 2; 5 contradicts 8}
```

1. (x)Lxa
  ∴ (x)Lax

2. (∃x)(y)Lxy
  ∴ (∃x)Lxa

3. (x)(y)(Lxy ⊃ x=y)
  ∴ (x)Lxx

4. (x)(∃y)Lxy
  ∴ Laa

5. (x)(y)Lxy
  ∴ (x)(y)((Fx · Gy) ⊃ Lxy)

6. (x)(y)(Uxy ⊃ Lxy)
  (x)(∃y)Uxy
  ∴ (x)(∃y)Lxy

7. (x)Lxx
  ∴ (∃x)(y)Lxy

8. (x)Gaxb
    ∴ (∃x)(∃y)Gxcy

9. (x)(y)Lxy
    ∴ (∃x)Lax

10. Lab
    Lbc
    ∴ (∃x)(Lax · Lxc)

11. (x)Lxx
    ∴ (x)(y)(Lxy ⊃ x=y)

12. (∃x)Lxa
    ~Laa
    ∴ (∃x)(~a=x · Lxa)

13. (x)(y)(z)((Lxy · Lyz) ⊃ Lxz)
    (x)(y)(Kxy ⊃ Lyx)
    ∴ (x)Lxx

14. (x)Lxa
    (x)(Lax ⊃ x=b)
    ∴ (x)Lxb

15. (x)(y)(Lxy ⊃ (Fx · ~Fy))
    ∴ (x)(y)(Lxy ⊃ ~Lyx)

6.4b   Exercise – LogiCola I (RC & BC)

First appraise intuitively. Then translate into logic and say whether valid (and give a proof) or invalid (and give a refutation).

1. Juliet loves everyone.
    ∴ Someone loves you.   [Use Lxy, j, and u.]

2. Nothing caused itself.
    ∴ There's nothing that caused everything.   [Use Cxy.]

3. Alice is older than Betty.
    ∴ Betty isn't older than Alice.   [Use Oxy, a, and b. What premise implicit would make this valid?]

4. There's something that everything depends on.
    ∴ Everything depends on something.   [Use Dxy.]

5. Everything depends on something.
    ∴ There's something that everything depends on.   [Use Dxy.]

6. Romeo loves all females.
    No females love Romeo.
    Juliet is female.
    ∴ Romeo loves someone who doesn't love him.   [Use Lxy, r, Fx, and j.]

7. In all cases, if a first thing caused a second then the first exists before the second.
    Nothing exists before it exists.
    ∴ Nothing caused itself.   [Use Cxy and Bxy (for "x exists before y exists").]

8. Everyone hates my enemy.
    My enemy doesn't hate anyone besides me.
    ∴ My enemy is me.   [Use Hxy, e, and m.]

9. Not everyone loves everyone.
    ∴ Not everyone loves you.   [Use Lxy and u.]

10. There's someone that everyone loves.
    ∴ Some love themselves. [Use Lxy.]

11. Andy shaves all and only those who don't shave themselves.
    ∴ It is raining. [Use Sxy, a, and R.]

12. No one hates themselves.
    I hate all logicians.
    ∴ I am not a logician. [Use Hxy, i, and Lx.]

13. Juliet loves everyone besides herself.
    Juliet is Italian.
    Romeo is my logic teacher.
    My logic teacher isn't Italian.
    ∴ Juliet loves Romeo. [Use j, Lxy, Ix, r, and m.]

14. Romeo loves either Lisa or Colleen.
    Romeo doesn't love anyone who isn't Italian.
    Colleen isn't Italian.
    ∴ Romeo loves Lisa. [Use Lxy, r, l, and c.]

15. Everyone loves all lovers.
    Romeo loves Juliet.
    ∴ I love you. [Use Lxy, r, j, i, and u. This one is difficult.]

16. Everyone loves someone.
    ∴ Some love themselves. [Use Lxy.]

17. Nothing caused itself.
    This chemical brain process caused this pain.
    ∴ This chemical brain process isn't identical to this pain. [Use Cxy, b, and p.]

18. For every positive contingent truth, something explains why it's true.
    The existence of the world is a positive contingent truth.
    If something explains the existence of the world, then some necessary being explains the existence of the world.
    ∴ Some necessary being explains the existence of the world. [Cx, Exy, e, and Nx. This argument for the existence of God is from Richard Taylor.]

19. That girl is Miss Novak.
    ∴ If you don't like Miss Novak, then you don't like that girl. [Use t, m, u, and Lxy. This is from the movie, *The Little Shop around the Corner*: "If you don't like Miss Novak, I can tell you right now that you won't like that girl. Why? Because it is Miss Novak."]

20. Everyone who is wholly good prevents every evil that he can prevent.
    Everyone who is omnipotent can prevent every evil.
    If someone prevents every evil, then there's no evil.
    There's evil.
    ∴ Either God isn't omnipotent, or God isn't wholly good. [Use Gx, Ex, Cxy (for "x can prevent y"), Pxy (for "x prevents y"), Ox, and g. This argument is from J. L. Mackie.]

21.   Your friend is wholly good.
Your knee pain is evil.
Your friend can prevent your knee pain.
Your friend doesn't prevent your knee pain (since he could prevent it only by amputating your leg – which would bring about a worse situation).
∴ "Everyone who is wholly good prevents every evil that he can prevent" is false. [Use f, Gx, k, Ex, Cxy, and Pxy. Alvin Plantinga thus attacked premise 1 of the previous argument; he proposed instead roughly this: "Everyone who is wholly good prevents every evil that he knows about if he can do so without thereby eliminating a greater good or bringing about a greater evil."]

22.   For everything contingent, there's some time at which it fails to exist.
∴ If everything is contingent, then there's some time at which everything fails to exist.   [Use Cx for "x is contingent"; Ext for "x exists at time t"; t for a time variable; and t′, t″, t‴, … for time constants. This is a critical step in St Thomas Aquinas's third argument for the existence of God.]

23.   If everything is contingent, then there's some time at which everything fails to exist.
If there's some time at which everything fails to exist, then there's nothing in existence now.
There's something in existence now.
Everything that isn't contingent is necessary.
∴ There's a necessary being.   [Besides the letters for the previous argument, use Nx for "x is necessary" and n for "now." This continues St Thomas's argument; here premise 1 is from the previous argument.]

24.   [The great logician Gottlob Frege tried to systematize mathematics. One of his axioms said that *every sentence with a free variable*[1] *determines a set.* So then "x is blue" determines a set: there's a set y containing all and only blue things. While this seems sensible, Bertrand Russell showed that Frege's axiom entails that "x doesn't contain x" determines a set – so there's a set y containing all and only those things that don't contain themselves – and this leads to the self-contradiction "y contains y if and only if y doesn't contain y." The foundations of mathematics haven't been the same since "Russell's paradox."]
If every sentence with a free variable determines a set, then there's a set y such that, for all x, y contains x if and only if x doesn't contain x.
∴ Not every sentence with a free variable determines a set.   [Use D for "Every sentence with a free variable determines a set," Sx for "x is a set," and Cyx for "y contains x."]

25.   All dogs are animals.
∴ All heads of dogs are heads of animals.   [Use Dx, Ax, and Hxy (for "x is a head of y"). Translate "x is a head of a dog" as "for some y, y is a dog and x is a head of y." Augustus DeMorgan in the nineteenth century claimed that this was a valid argument that traditional logic couldn't validate.]

---

[1] An instance of a variable is "free" in a wff if it doesn't occur as part of a wff that begins with a quantifier using that variable; each instance of "x" is free in "Fx" but not in "(x)Fx."

6.5   Definite descriptions

Phrases of the form "the so and so" are called **definite descriptions**, since they're meant to pick out a definite (single) person or thing. This final section sketches Bertrand Russell's influential ideas on definite descriptions. While philosophical discussions about these and about proper names can get complex and controversial, I'll try to keep things fairly simple.

Consider these two sentences and how we've been symbolizing them:

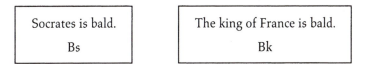

Socrates is bald.	The king of France is bald.
Bs	Bk

The first sentence has a proper name ("Socrates") while the second has a definite description ("the king of France"); both seem to ascribe a *property* (baldness) to a particular *object* or entity. Russell argued that this object-property analysis is misleading in the second case;[1] sentences with definite descriptions (like "the king of France") were in reality more complicated and should be analyzed in terms of a complex of predicates and quantifiers:

> The king of France is bald.
> $=$ There's exactly one king of France, and he is bald.
> $=$ For some x: x is king of France, there's no y such
>   that $y \neq x$ and y is king of France, and x is bald.
> $=$ $(\exists x)((Kx \cdot \sim(\exists y)(\sim y=x \cdot Ky)) \cdot Bx)$

Russell saw his analysis as having several advantages; I'll mention two.

First, "The king of France is bald" might be false for any of three reasons:

1. There's no king of France;
2. there's more than one king of France; or
3. there's exactly one king of France, and he has hair on his head.

In fact, "The king of France is bald" is false for reason 1: France is a republic and has no king. This accords well with Russell's analysis. By contrast, the object-property analysis suggests that if "The king of France is bald" is false, then "The king of France isn't bald" would have to be true[2] – and so the king of France would have to have hair! So Russell's analysis seems to express better the logical complexity of definite descriptions.

---

[1] He also thought the analysis misleading in the first case; but I don't want to discuss this now.
[2] On Russell's analysis, "The king of France isn't bald" is false too – since it means "There's exactly one king of France, and he isn't bald."

Second, the object-property analysis of definite descriptions can lead us into metaphysical errors, like positing existing things that aren't real. The philosopher Alexius Meinong argued roughly as follows:

> "The round square does not exist" is a true
> statement about the round square.
> If there's a true statement about something,
> then that something has to exist.
> ∴ The round square exists.
> But the round square isn't a real thing.
> ∴ Some things that exist aren't real things.

For a time, Russell accepted this argument. Later he came to see the belief in non-real existing things as foolish; he rejected Meinong's first premise and appealed to the theory of descriptions to clear up the confusion.

According to Russell, Meinong's error comes from his naïve object-property understanding of the following statement:

> The round square does not exist.

This, Russell contended, isn't a true statement ascribing non-existence to some object called "the round square." If it were a true statement about the round square, then the round square would have to exist – which the statement denies. Instead, the statement just denies that there's exactly one round square. So Russell's analysis keeps us from having to accept that there are existing things that aren't real.

CHAPTER 7
Basic Modal Logic

Modal logic studies arguments whose validity depends on "necessary," "possible," and similar notions. This chapter covers the basics, and the next gets into further modal systems.

7.1 Translations

To help us evaluate modal arguments, we'll construct a little modal language. For now, our language will build on propositional logic, and thus include all the vocabulary, wffs, inference rules, and proofs of the latter. Our language adds two new vocabulary items: "◇" and "□" (diamond and box):

◇A	=	It's possible that A	=	A is true in some possible world.
A	=	It's true that A	=	A is true in the actual world.
□A	=	It's necessary that A	=	A is true in all possible worlds.

Calling something *possible* is a weak claim – weaker than calling it *true*. Calling something *necessary* is a strong claim; it says, not just that the thing is true, but that it *has* to be true – it *couldn't* be false.

"Possible" here means *logically possible* (*not self-contradictory*). "I run a mile in two minutes" may be physically impossible; but there's no self-contradiction in the idea, so it's logically possible. Likewise, "necessary" means *logically necessary* (*self-contradictory to deny*). "2+2=4" and "All bachelors are unmarried" are examples of **necessary truths**; such truths are based on logic, the meaning of concepts, or necessary connections between properties.

We can rephrase "possible" as *true in some possible world* – and "necessary" as *true in all possible worlds*. A **possible world** is a consistent and complete[1] description of how things might have been or might in fact be. Picture a possible world as a *consistent story* (or novel). The story is *consistent*, in that its statements don't entail self-contradictions; it describes a set of possible situations that are all possible together. The story may or may not be true. The **actual world** is the story that's true – the description of how things in fact are.

---

[1] Since we are finite beings, we will in practice only give partial (not "complete") descriptions.

As before, a grammatically correct formula is called a *wff*, or *well-formed formula*. For now, wffs are strings that we can construct using the propositional rules plus this additional rule:

> 1. The result of writing "◇" or "□," and then a wff, is a wff.

Don't use parentheses with "◇A" and "□A":

Right:	◇A	□A
Wrong:	◇(A)	□(A)
	(◇A)	(□A)

Parentheses here would serve no purpose.

Now we'll focus on how to translate English sentences into modal logic. Here are some simpler examples:

A is possible (consistent, could be true)   =   ◇A

A is necessary (must be true, has to be true)   =   □A

A is impossible (self-contradictory)   =   ~◇A   =   A couldn't be true.

                         =   □~A   =   A has to be false.

An impossible statement (like "2≠2") is one that's false in every possible world.

These examples are more complicated:

A is consistent (compatible) with B   =   It's possible that A and B are both true.

                         =   ◇(A · B)

A entails B   =   It's necessary that if A then B.

              =   □(A ⊃ B)

"Entails" makes a stronger claim than plain "if-then." Compare these two:

"There's rain" entails "There's precipitation"   =   □(R ⊃ P)

If it's Saturday, then I don't teach class   =   (S ⊃ ~T)

The first if-then is logically necessary; every conceivable situation with rain also has precipitation. The second if-then just happens to be true; we can consistently imagine me teaching on Saturday – even if in fact I never do.

These common forms negate the whole wff:

A is inconsistent with B   =   It's not possible that A and B are both true.

                    =   ~◇(A · B)

A doesn't entail B   =   It's not necessary that if A then B.

             =   ~□(A ⊃ B)

Here is how we translate "contingent":

A is a contingent statement	=	A is possible and not-A is possible.
	=	$(\Diamond A \cdot \Diamond {\sim} A)$
A is a contingent truth	=	A is true but could have been false.
	=	$(A \cdot \Diamond {\sim} A)$

Statements are necessary, impossible, or contingent. But truths are only necessary or contingent (since impossible statements are false).

When translating, it's usually good to mimic the English word order:

necessary not	=	$\Box{\sim}$	necessary if	=	$\Box($
not necessary	=	${\sim}\Box$	if necessary	=	$(\Box$

Use a separate box or diamond for each "necessary" or "possible":

If A is necessary and B is possible, then C is possible $= ((\Box A \cdot \Diamond B) \supset \Diamond C)$

The following tricky English forms are ambiguous; translate these into two modal wffs, and say that the English could mean one or the other:

"If A is true, then it's necessary (must be) that B" could mean *"(A ⊃ □B)"* or *"□(A ⊃ B)."*	*"If A is true, then it's impossible (couldn't be) that B"* could mean *"(A ⊃ □~B)"* or *"□(A ⊃ ~B)."*

So this next sentence could have either of the following two meanings:

"If you're a bachelor, then you must be unmarried."

	=	"If you're a bachelor, then you're *inherently unmarriable* (in no
$(B \supset \Box U)$		possible world would anyone ever marry you)."
	=	If B, then U (by itself) is necessary.
	=	"It's necessary that *if* you're a bachelor *then* you're unmarried."
$\Box(B \supset U)$	=	It's necessary that if B then U.

The box-inside "$(B \supset \Box U)$" posits an *inherent necessity*: given that the antecedent is true, "You're unmarried" is inherently necessary. This version is insulting and presumably false. The box-outside "$\Box(B \supset U)$" posits a *relative necessity*: what is necessary is, not "You're a bachelor" or "You're unmarried" by itself, but only the connection between the two. This version is trivially true because "bachelor" means *unmarried man*.

The medievals called the box-inside form the "necessity of the *consequent*" (the second part being necessary); they called the box-outside form the "necessity of the *consequence*" (the whole if-then being necessary). The ambiguity is important philosophically; several intriguing but fallacious philosophical arguments depend on the ambiguity for their plausibility.

It's not ambiguous if you say the second part "by itself" is necessary or impossible – or if you use "entails" or start with "necessary." These forms aren't ambiguous:

If A, then B (by itself) is necessary	=	(A ⊃ □B)
A entails B	=	□(A ⊃ B)
Necessarily, if A then B	=	□(A ⊃ B)
It's necessary that if A then B	=	□(A ⊃ B)
"If A then B" is a necessary truth	=	□(A ⊃ B)

The ambiguous forms have if-then with a strong modal term (like "necessary," "must," "impossible," or "can't") in the then-part, like these:[1]

If A, then it's necessary that B.	If A, then it's impossible that B.
If A, then it must be that B.	If A, then it can't be that B.

When you translate an ambiguous English sentence, say that it's ambiguous and give both translations. When you do an English argument with an ambiguous statement, give both translations and work out both arguments.

7.1a   Exercise – LogiCola J (BM & BT)

Using these equivalences, translate these English sentences into wffs. Be sure to translate ambiguous forms both ways.

G	=	There's a God (God exists)
E	=	There's evil (Evil exists)
M	=	There's matter (Matter exists)

R	=	There's rain
P	=	There's precipitation

"God exists and evil doesn't exist" entails "There's no matter."	□((G · ~E) ⊃ ~M)

1. It's necessary that God exists.
2. "There's a God" is self-contradictory.
3. It isn't necessary that there's matter.
4. It's necessary that there's no matter.
5. "There's rain" entails "There's precipitation."
6. "There's precipitation" doesn't entail "There's rain."
7. "There's no precipitation" entails "There's no rain."
8. If rain is possible, then precipitation is possible.

---

[1] There's an exception to this rule: if the if-part is a claim about necessity or possibility, then just use the box-inside form. So "If A is necessary then B is necessary" is just "(□A ⊃ □B)" – and "If A is possible then B is impossible" is just "(◇A ⊃ ~◇B)."

9. God exists.
10. If there's rain, then there must be rain.
11. It isn't possible that there's evil.
12. It's possible that there's no evil.
13. If there's rain, then it's possible that there's rain.
14. "There's matter" is compatible with "There's evil."
15. "There's a God" is inconsistent with "There's evil."
16. Necessarily, if there's a God then there's no evil.
17. If there's a God, then there can't be evil.
18. If there must be matter, then there's evil.
19. Necessarily, if there's a God then "There's evil" (by itself) is self-contradictory.
20. It's necessary that either there's a God or there's matter.
21. Either it's necessary that there's a God or it's necessary that there's matter.
22. "There's rain" is a contingent statement.
23. "There's rain" is a contingent truth.
24. "If there's rain, then there's evil" is a necessary truth.
25. If there's rain, then "There's evil" (by itself) is logically necessary.
26. If there's rain, then it's necessary that there's evil.
27. It's necessary that it's possible that there's matter.
28. "There's a God" isn't a contingent truth.
29. If there's a God, then it must be that there's a God.
30. It's necessary that if there's a God then "There's a God" (by itself) is necessary.

7.2 Proofs

Modal proofs work much like propositional proofs; but we need to add possible worlds and four new inference rules.

A **world prefix** is a string of zero or more instances of "W." So " " (zero instances), "W," "WW," and so on are world prefixes; these represent possible worlds, with the blank world prefix (" ") representing the actual world. A *derived step* is now a line consisting of a world prefix and then "∴" and then a wff. And an *assumption* is now a line consisting of a world prefix and then "asm:" and then a wff. Here are examples of derived steps and assumptions:

∴ A	(So A is true in the actual world.)	asm: A	(Assume A is true in the actual world.)
W ∴ A	(So A is true in world W.)	W asm: A	(Assume A is true in world W.)
WW ∴ A	(So A is true in world WW.)	WW asm: A	(Assume A is true in world WW.)

Seldom do we need to assume something in another world.

We'll still use the S- and I-rules and RAA in modal proofs. Unless otherwise specified, we can use an inference rule only within a given world; so if we have

"(A ⊃ B)" and "A" in the same world, then we can infer "B" in this same world. RAA needs additional wording (*italicized below*) for world prefixes:

> RAA: Suppose that some pair of not-blocked-off lines *using the same world prefix* have contradictory wffs. Then block off all the lines from the last not-blocked-off assumption on down and infer a step consisting in *this assumption's world prefix followed by* "∴" followed by a contradictory of that assumption.

To apply RAA, lines with the same world prefix must have contradictory wffs. Having "W ∴ A" and "WW ∴ ~A" isn't enough; "A" may well be true in one world but false in another. But "WW ∴ A" and "WW ∴ ~A" provide a genuine contradiction. The line derived using RAA must have the same world prefix as the assumption; if "W asm: A" leads to a contradiction in any world, then RAA lets us derive "W ∴ ~A."

Modal proofs use four new inference rules. These two reverse-squiggle (RS) rules hold regardless of what pair of contradictory wffs replaces "A" / "~A" (here "→" means we can infer whole lines from left to right):

Reverse squiggle	~□A → ◇~A
	~◇A → □~A

These let us go from "not necessary" to "possibly false" – and from "not possible" to "necessarily false." Use these rules only within the same world. We can reverse squiggles on complicated formulas, so long as the whole formula begins with "~□" or "~◇":

Right:	*Right:*	*Wrong:*
~◇~B	~□(C · ~D)	(P ⊃ ~□Q)
∴ □~~B	∴ ◇~(C · ~D)	∴ (P ⊃ ◇~Q)

In the first example, it would be simpler to conclude "□B" (eliminating the double negation). Reverse squiggles whenever you have a wff that begins with "~" and then a modal operator; reversing a squiggle moves the modal operator to the beginning of the formula, so we can later drop it.

We drop modal operators using the next two rules (which hold regardless of what wff replaces "A"). Here's the drop-diamond (DD) rule:

Drop diamond	◇A → W ∴ A, use a *new* string of W's

Here the line with "◇A" can use any world prefix – and the line with "∴ A" must use a *new* string (one not occurring in earlier lines) of one or more W's. If "A" is possible, then "A" is thereby true in *some* possible world; we can give this world a name – but a *new* name, since "A" needn't be true in any of the worlds used in the proof so far. In proofs, we'll use "W" for the first diamond we drop, "WW" for the second, and so forth. So if we drop two diamonds, then we must introduce two worlds:

◇H	Heads is possible, tails is possible; call an imagined
◇T	world with heads "W," and one with tails "WW."
W ∴ H	← "W" is OK because it occurs in no earlier line.
WW ∴ T	← Since "W" has now occurred, we use "WW."

We can drop diamonds from complicated formulas, so long as the diamond *begins* the wff:

Right:	*Wrong:*	*Wrong:*
◇(A · B)	(◇A ⊃ B)	(◇A · ◇B)
W ∴ (A · B)	W ∴ (A ⊃ B)	W ∴ (A · B)

The last two formulas don't *begin* with a diamond; instead, they begin with "(." Drop only *initial* diamonds – and introduce a new and different world prefix whenever you drop a diamond.

Here's the drop-box (DB) rule:

Drop box	□A → W ∴ A, use any world prefix

Here the line with "□A" can use any world prefix – and the line with "∴ A" can use any world prefix too (including the blank one). If "A" is necessary, then "A" is true in *all* possible worlds, and so we can put "A" in any world we like. However, it's bad strategy to drop a box using a new world; instead, stay in old worlds. As before, we can drop boxes from complicated formulas, so long as the box *begins* the wff:

Right:	*Wrong:*	*Wrong:*
□(A ⊃ B)	(□A ⊃ B)	(□A ⊃ □B)
W ∴ (A ⊃ B)	W ∴ (A ⊃ B)	W ∴ (A ⊃ B)

The last two formulas begin, not with a box, but with a left-hand parenthesis. "(□A ⊃ B)" and "(□A ⊃ □B)" are if-then forms and follow the if-then rules: if we have the first part true, we can get the second true; if we have the second part false, we can get the first false; and if we get stuck, we need to make another assumption.

Here's an English version of a modal proof:

1   Necessarily, if there's rain then there's precipitation.
2   It's possible that there's rain.
  [∴ It's possible that there's precipitation.
3 ┌ Assume: It's not possible that there's precipitation.
4 │ ∴ It's necessary that there's no precipitation.   {from 3, reverse squiggle}
5 │ ∴ In world W: There's rain.   {from 2, drop diamond, call the world "W"}
6 │ ∴ In world W: If there's rain then there's precipitation.   {from 1, drop box}
7 │ ∴ In world W: There's precipitation.   {from 5 and 6}
8 └ ∴ In world W: There's no precipitation.   {from 4, drop box}
9   ∴ It's possible that there's precipitation.   {from 3; 7 contradicts 8}

The steps here should make sense. Our proof strategy is: first reverse squiggles, then drop diamonds into new worlds, and finally drop boxes into the same old worlds. Here's the proof in symbols:

       1   □(R ⊃ P)   **Valid**
   *   2   ◇R
         [∴ ◇P
   *   3 ┌ asm: ~◇P
       4 │ ∴ □~P   {from 3}
       5 │ W ∴ R   {from 2}
   *   6 │ W ∴ (R ⊃ P)   {from 1}
       7 │ W ∴ P   {from 5 and 6}
       8 └ W ∴ ~P   {from 4}
       9   ∴ ◇P   {from 3; 7 contradicts 8}

After making the assumption (line 3), we reverse the squiggle to move the modal operator to the outside (line 4). We drop the diamond using a new world (line 5). We drop the box in line 1 using this same world – and use an I-rule to get "P" in world W (lines 6 and 7). Then we drop the box in line 4 using this same world, to get "~P" in world W (line 8). Since we have a contradiction, we use RAA to give us the original conclusion.

We starred lines 2, 3, and 6; as before, starred lines largely can be ignored in deriving further steps. Here are two new starring rules – with examples:

Star any wff on which you reverse squiggles.	Star any wff from which you drop a diamond.
* ~□A	* ◇A
————	————
∴ ◇~A	W ∴ A

When we reverse squiggles or drop diamonds, the new line has the same information. Don't star when dropping a box; we can never exhaust a "necessary" statement – and we may have to use it again later in the proof.

Here's another modal proof:

```
   1      □(A · B) ·······························
          [∴ □A                                :
*  2    ┌ asm: ~□A ···:                         :
*  3    │ ∴ ◇~A      ◀··: First reverse squiggles :
   4    │ W ∴ ~A     ◀··: and drop diamonds.      :
   5    │ W ∴ (A · B) ◀·· Lastly drop boxes. ·····
   6    └ W ∴ A
   7    ∴ □A   {from 2; 4 contradicts 6}
```

Here it would be useless and bad strategy to drop the box into the actual world – to go from "□(A · B)" in line 1 to "∴ (A · B)" with no initial W's.

Drop a box into the actual world in only two cases:

> Drop a box into the actual world just if:
>
> • the original premises or conclusion have an unmodalized instance of a letter, or
> • you've done everything else possible (including further assumptions if needed) and still have no other worlds.

These examples illustrate the two cases:

```
1      □(A · B) ·············           1      □~A
       [∴ A  ← unmodalized :                  [∴ ~□A              no other
2    ┌ asm: ~A             :           2    ┌ asm: □A ·········,  worlds
3    │ ∴ (A · B)  {from 1} ◀·           3    │ ∴ A  {from 2} ◀·:
4    └ ∴ A  {from 3}                    4    └ ∴ ~A  {from 1}
5    ∴ A  {from 2; 2 contradicts 4}     5    ∴ ~□A  {from 2; 3 contradicts 4}
```

In the first argument, "A" in the conclusion is *unmodalized* – which means that it doesn't occur as part of a larger wff beginning with a box or diamond. Whenever our original premises or conclusion have an unmodalized instance of a letter, our standard strategy will be to drop all boxes into the actual world.[1]

In the second argument, we drop boxes into the actual world because there are no other old worlds to use (because there was no "◇" to drop) and we've done everything else that we can do. This second case is fairly unusual – while the first is quite common.

---

[1] In "(A · ◇B)," the first letter is unmodalized. If this formula was a premise or conclusion, then our standard strategy would say to drop all boxes into the actual world.

Our proof strategy works much like before. We first assume the opposite of the conclusion; then we use our four new rules plus the S- and I-rules to derive whatever we can. If we find a contradiction, we apply RAA. If we get stuck and need to break up a wff of the form "~(A • B)" or "(A ∨ B)" or "(A ⊃ B)," then we make another assumption. If we get no contradiction and yet can't do anything further, then we try to refute the argument.

Reverse squiggles and drop diamonds first, drop boxes last:

1. FIRST REVERSE SQUIGGLES: For each unstarred, not-blocked-off step that begins with "~" and then a box or diamond, derive a step using the reverse-squiggle rules. Star the original step.

2. AND DROP DIAMONDS: For each unstarred, not-blocked-off step that begins with a diamond, derive an instance using the next available *new* world prefix (unless some such instance already occurs in previous not-blocked-off steps). Star the original step.

    Note: Don't drop a diamond if you already have a not-blocked-off instance in previous steps – there's no point in deriving a second instance. For example, don't drop "◇A" if you already have "W ∴ A."

3. LASTLY DROP BOXES: For each not-blocked-off step that begins with a box, derive instances using each *old* world. Don't star the original step; you might have to use it again.

    Note: Drop a box into the actual world just if (a) the premises or conclusion have an unmodalized instance of a letter, or (b) you've done everything else (including further assumptions if needed) and still have no other worlds.

Be sure to drop diamonds before boxes. Introduce a new world each time you drop a diamond, and use the same old worlds when you drop a box. And drop only *initial* diamonds and boxes.

We won't see invalid modal arguments until later.

7.2a   Exercise – LogiCola KV

Prove each of these arguments to be valid (all are valid).

$$\begin{array}{c} \Box(A \supset B) \\ \Diamond\sim B \\ \hline \therefore \Diamond\sim A \end{array}$$

```
        1      □(A ⊃ B)   Valid
   *    2      ◇~B
               [ ∴ ◇~A
   *    3    ┌ asm: ~◇~A
        4    │ ∴ □A   {from 3}
        5    │ W ∴ ~B   {from 2}
   *    6    │ W ∴ (A ⊃ B)   {from 1}
        7    │ W ∴ A   {from 4}
        8    └ W ∴ B   {from 6 and 7}
        9      ∴ ◇~A   {from 3; 5 contradicts 8}
```

1. ◇(A · B)
    ∴ ◇A

2. A
    ∴ ◇A

3. ~◇(A · ~B)
    ∴ □(A ⊃ B)

4. □(A ∨ ~B)
    ~□A
    ∴ ◇~B

5. (◇A ∨ ◇B)
    ∴ ◇(A ∨ B)

6. (A ⊃ □B)
    ◇~B
    ∴ ◇~A

7. ~◇(A · B)
    ◇A
    ∴ ~□B

8. □A
    ∴ ◇A

9. □A
    ~□B
    ∴ ~□(A ⊃ B)

10. □(A ⊃ B)
    ∴ (□A ⊃ □B)

7.2b   Exercises – LogiCola KV

First appraise intuitively. Then translate into logic (using the letters given) and prove
to be valid (all are valid).

1. "You knowingly testify falsely because of threats to your life" entails "You lie."
    It's possible that you knowingly testify falsely because of threats to your life but
    don't intend to deceive. (Maybe you hope no one will believe you.)
    ∴ "You lie" is consistent with "You don't intend to deceive."   [Use T, L, and I.
    This argument is from Tom Carson, who writes on the morality of lying.]

2. Necessarily, if you don't decide then you decide not to decide.
    Necessarily, if you decide not to decide then you decide.
    ∴ Necessarily, if you don't decide then you decide.   [Use D for "You decide" and
    N for "You decide not to decide." This is adapted from Jean-Paul Sartre.]

3. If truth is a correspondence with the mind, then "There are truths" entails
    "There are minds."
    "There are minds" isn't logically necessary.
    Necessarily, if there are no truths then it is not true that there are no truths.
    ∴ Truth isn't a correspondence with the mind.   [Use C, T, and M.]

4. There's a perfect God.
    There's evil in the world.
    ∴ "There's a perfect God" is logically compatible with "There's evil in the world."
    [Use G and E. Most who doubt the conclusion would also doubt premise 1.]

5. "There's a perfect God" is logically compatible with T.
    T logically entails "There's evil in the world."
    ∴ "There's a perfect God" is logically compatible with "There's evil in the world."
    [Use G, T, and E. Here T (for "theodicy") is a possible explanation of why God
    permits evil that's consistent with God's perfection and entails the existence of
    evil. T might say: "The world has evil because God, who is perfect, wants us to
    make significant free choices to struggle to bring a half-completed world toward
    its fulfillment; moral evil comes from the abuse of human freedom and physical
    evil from the half-completed state of the world." The basic argument (but not
    the specific T) is from Alvin Plantinga.]

6. "There's a perfect God and there's evil in the world and God has some reason for permitting the evil" is logically consistent.

∴ "There's a perfect God and there's evil in the world" is logically consistent. [Use G, E, and R. This is Ravi Zacharias's version of Plantinga's argument.]

7. God is omnipotent.
"You freely always do the right thing" is logically possible.
If "You freely always do the right thing" is logically possible and God is omnipotent, then it's possible for God to bring it about that you freely always do the right thing.

∴ It's possible for God to bring it about that you freely always do the right thing. [Use O, F, and B. This argument is from J. L. Mackie. He thought God had a third option besides making robots who always act rightly and free beings who sometimes act wrongly: he could make free beings who always act rightly.]

8. "God brings it about that you do A" is inconsistent with "You freely do A."
"God brings it about that you freely do A" entails "God brings it about that you do A."
"God brings it about that you freely do A" entails "You freely do A."

∴ It's impossible for God to bring it about that you freely do A. [Use B, F, and G. This attacks the conclusion of the previous argument.]

9. "This is a square" entails "This is composed of straight lines."
"This is a circle" entails "This isn't composed of straight lines."

∴ "This is a square and also a circle" is self-contradictory. [Use S, L, and C.]

10. "This is red and there's a blue light that makes red things look violet to normal observers" entails "Normal observers won't sense redness."
"This is red and there's a blue light that makes red things look violet to normal observers" is logically consistent.

∴ "This is red" doesn't entail "Normal observers will sense redness." [Use R, B, and N. This argument is from Roderick Chisholm.]

11. "All brown dogs are brown" is a necessary truth.
"Some dog is brown" isn't a necessary truth.
"Some brown dog is brown" entails "Some dog is brown."

∴ "All brown dogs are brown" doesn't entail "Some brown dog is brown." [Use A for "All brown dogs are brown," X for "Some dog is brown," and S for "Some brown dog is brown." This attacks a doctrine of traditional logic (see Section 2.8), that "all A is B" entails "some A is B."]

12. It's necessary that, if God exists as a possibility and not in reality, then there could be a being greater than God (namely, a similar being that also exists in reality).
"There could be a being greater than God" is self-contradictory (since "God" is defined as "a being than which no greater could be").
It's necessary that God exists as a possibility.

∴ It's necessary that God exists in reality. [Use P for "God exists as a possibility," R for "God exists in reality," and C for "There could be a being greater than God." This is a modal version of St Anselm's ontological argument.]

13. If "X is good" and "I like X" are interchangeable, then "I like hurting people"
     logically entails "Hurting people is good."
     "I like hurting people but hurting people isn't good" is consistent.
     ∴ "X is good" and "I like X" aren't interchangeable.   [Use I, L, and G. This argu-
     ment attacks subjectivism.]

14. "You sin" entails "You know what you ought to do and you're able to do it and
     you don't do it."
     It's necessary that if you know what you ought to do then you want to do it.
     It's necessary that if you want to do it and you're able to do it then you do it.
     ∴ It's impossible for you to sin.   [Use S, K, A, D, and W.]

15. Necessarily, if it is true that there are no truths then there are truths.
     ∴ It is necessary that there are truths.   [Use T for "There are truths."]

7.3   Refutations

Applying our proof strategy to an invalid argument leads to a refutation:

*	1	◇~H	Invalid		
	2	□(H ∨ T)			
		[∴ □T		W	H, ~T
*	3	asm: ~□T		WW	T, ~H
*	4	∴ ◇~T {from 3}			
	5	W ∴ ~T {from 4}			
	6	WW ∴ ~H {from 1}			
*	7	W ∴ (H ∨ T) {from 2}			
*	8	WW ∴ (H ∨ T) {from 2}			
	9	W ∴ H {from 5 and 7}			
	10	WW ∴ T {from 6 and 8}			

It's possible that it's not heads.
It's necessary that it's heads or tails.
∴ It's necessary that it's tails.

After making the assumption (line 3), we reverse a squiggle to move the modal
operator to the outside (line 4). Then we drop the two diamonds, using a new
and different world each time (lines 5 and 6). We drop the box twice, using first
world W and then world WW (lines 7 and 8). Since we reach no contradiction,
we gather the simple pieces to give a refutation. Here our refutation has two
possible worlds: one with heads-and-not-tails and another with tails-and-not-
heads. Presumably, our refutation will make premises true and conclusion false,
and thus show the argument to be invalid. But how are we to calculate the truth
value of the premises and conclusion?

In evaluating the premises and conclusion, evaluate each wff (or part of a
wff) that starts with a diamond or box according to these rules:

> "◇A" is true if and only if *at least one world* has "A" true.

> "□A" is true if and only if *all worlds* have "A" true.

Recall the galaxy of possible worlds that we reached for our last argument:

W	H, ~T
WW	T, ~H

This galaxy makes our premises true and conclusion false. Here's how we'd evaluate each wff:

◇~H   ←   First premise: by our rule, this is true if and only if *at least one world* has "~H" true. But world WW has "~H" true.

1   ←   So "◇~H" is true.

□(H ∨ T)   ←   Second premise: by our rule, this is true if and only if *all worlds* have "(H ∨ T)" true. In world W: (H ∨ T) = (1 ∨ 0) = 1. In world WW: (H ∨ T) = (0 ∨ 1) = 1.

1   ←   So "□(H ∨ T)" is true.

□T   ←   Conclusion: by our rule, this is true if and only if *all worlds* have T true. But world W has T false.

0   ←   So "□T" is false.

So this galaxy of possible worlds shows our argument to be invalid.

If our refutation had neither "H" nor "~H" in world W, then the value of H in world W would be "?" (unknown). This would happen in our example if we neglected to go from "□(H ∨ T)" to "W ∴ (H ∨ T)."

As before, it's important to check that our refutation works. If we don't get premises all true and conclusion false, then we did something wrong – and we should check what we did with the formula that didn't come out right.

So far we've evaluated formulas that begin with a diamond or box, like "◇~H" or "□(H ∨ T)." But some formulas, like "(◇H ⊃ □T)," have the diamond or box further inside. In these cases, we'd first evaluate parts of the wff that begin with a diamond or box, and then substitute "1" or "0" for these parts. With "(◇H ⊃ □T)," we'd first evaluate "◇H" and "□T" to see whether these are "1" or "0"; then we'd substitute "1" or "0" for these parts and determine the truth value of the whole formula.

I'll give examples to show how this works. Let's assume the same galaxy:

W	H, ~T
WW	T, ~H

Now let's evaluate three sample wffs:

~□H   ←   Here we'd first evaluate "□H." This is true if and only if *all worlds* have H true.
Since world WW has H false, "□H" is false.

~0   ←   So we substitute "0" for "□H."

1   ←   So "~□H" is true.

(◊H ⊃ □T)   ←   Here we'd first evaluate "◊H" and "□T."
"◊H" is true if and only if *at least one world* has H true. Since world W has H true, "◊H" is true.
"□T" is true if and only if *all worlds* have T true. Since world W has T false, "□T" is false.

(1 ⊃ 0)   ←   So we substitute "1" for "◊H" and "0" for "□T."

0   ←   So "(◊H ⊃ □T)" is false.

~□(H ⊃ ~T)   ←   Here we'd first evaluate "□(H ⊃ ~T)." This is true if and only if *all worlds* have "(H ⊃ ~T)" true.
In world W: (H ⊃ ~T) = (1 ⊃ ~0) = (1 ⊃ 1) = 1.
In world WW: (H ⊃ ~T) = (0 ⊃ ~1) = (0 ⊃ 0) = 1.

~1   ←   So "□(H ⊃ ~T)" is true; so we substitute "1" for it.

0   ←   So "~□(H ⊃ ~T)" is false.

The key thing is to evaluate each part starting with a diamond or box, and then substitute "1" or "0" for it.

In working out English modal arguments, you'll sometimes find an ambiguous premise. Premise 1 is ambiguous in the following argument:

> If you're a bachelor, then you must be unmarried.
> You're a bachelor.
> ∴ It's logically necessary that you're unmarried.

Premise 1 could have either of these two meanings:

(B ⊃ □U)   "If you're a bachelor, then you're *inherently unmarriable* – in no possible world would anyone ever marry you." (We hope this is false.)

□(B ⊃ U)   "It's necessary that *if* you're a bachelor *then* you're unmarried." (This is trivially true because "bachelor" means *unmarried man*.)

In such cases, say that the argument is ambiguous and work out both versions:

	Box-inside version:		*Box-outside version:*

		Box-inside version:			*Box-outside version:*
*	1	(B ⊃ □U) **Valid**		1	□(B ⊃ U) **Invalid**
	2	B		2	B
		[∴ □U			[∴ □U
	3	┌ asm: ~□U	*	3	asm: ~□U
	4	└ ∴ □U {from 1 and 2}	*	4	∴ ◇~U {from 3}
	5	∴ □U {from 3; 3 contradicts 4}		5	W ∴ ~U {from 4}
			*	6	W ∴ (B ⊃ U) {from 1}
		(While this is valid,	*	7	∴ (B ⊃ U) {from 1}
		premise 1 is false.)		8	W ∴ ~B {from 5 and 6}
				9	∴ U {from 2 and 7}

Box-outside version refutation box:

$$W \quad \boxed{\begin{array}{c} B, U \\ \hline \sim B, \sim U \end{array}}$$

Both versions are flawed; the first has a false premise, while the second is invalid. So the proof that you're inherently unmarriable ("□U" – "It's logically necessary that you're unmarried") fails.

In the second version, the refutation uses an actual world and a possible world W. An unmodalized instance of a letter, like B in premise 2, should be evaluated according to the actual world; so here B is true. Premise 1 "□(B ⊃ U)" also comes out true, since "(B ⊃ U)" is true in both worlds:

$$\begin{array}{ll} \text{In the actual world:} & (B \supset U) = (1 \supset 1) = 1 \\ \text{In world W:} & (B \supset U) = (0 \supset 0) = 1 \end{array}$$

And conclusion "□U" is false, since "U" is false in world W. So the galaxy makes the premises all true and conclusion false, establishing invalidity.

Arguments with a modal ambiguity, like this one, often have one interpretation that has a false premise and another that is invalid. Such arguments often seem sound until we focus on the ambiguity.

7.3a   Exercise – LogiCola KI

Prove each of these arguments to be invalid (all are invalid).

$$\begin{array}{l} □(A \supset B) \\ ◇A \\ \hline ∴ □B \end{array}$$

	1	□(A ⊃ B) **Invalid**
*	2	◇A
		[∴ □B
*	3	asm: ~□B
*	4	∴ ◇~B {from 3}
	5	W ∴ ~B {from 4}
	6	WW ∴ A {from 2}
*	7	W ∴ (A ⊃ B) {from 1}
*	8	WW ∴ (A ⊃ B) {from 1}
	9	W ∴ ~A {from 5 and 7}
	10	WW ∴ B {from 6 and 8}

Refutation box:

$$\begin{array}{ll} W & \sim A, \sim B \\ WW & A, B \end{array}$$

1. ◇A
    ∴ □A

2. A
    ∴ □A

3. ◇A
    ◇B
    ∴ ◇(A · B)

4. □(A ⊃ ~B)
    B
    ∴ □~A

5. (□A ⊃ □B)
    ∴ □(A ⊃ B)

6. ◇A
    ~□B
    ∴ ~□(A ⊃ B)

7. □(C ⊃ (A ∨ B))
    (~A · ◇~B)
    ∴ ◇~C

8. ◇A
    ~□B
    ∴ ~□(A ⊃ B)

9. □((A · B) ⊃ C)
    ◇A
    ◇B
    ∴ ◇C

10. ~□A
     □(B ≡ A)
     ∴ ~◇B

7.3b   Exercise – LogiCola KC

First appraise intuitively. Then translate into logic (using the letters given) and say whether valid (and give a proof) or invalid (and give a refutation). Translate ambiguous English arguments both ways and work out each symbolization separately.

1. If the pragmatist view of truth is right, then "A is true" entails "A is useful to believe."
    "A is true but not useful to believe" is consistent.
    ∴ The pragmatist view of truth isn't right.   [Use P, T, and B.]

2. You know.
    "You're mistaken" is logically possible.
    ∴ "You know and are mistaken" is logically possible.   [Use K and M.]

3. Necessarily, if this will be then this will be.
    ∴ If this will be, then it's necessary (in itself) that this will be.   [Use B. This illustrates two senses of "Que será será" – "Whatever will be will be." The first sense is a truth of logic while the second is a form of fatalism.]

4. If I'm still, then it's necessary that I'm not moving.
    I'm still.
    ∴ "I'm not moving" is a logically necessary truth. (In other words, I'm logically incapable of moving.)   [Use S and M. This is adapted from the medieval thinker Boethius, who used a similar example to explain the box-inside / box-outside distinction.]

5. It's necessarily true that if you're morally responsible for your actions then you're free.
    It's necessarily true that if your actions are uncaused then you aren't morally responsible for your actions.
    ∴ "You're free" doesn't entail "Your actions are uncaused."   [Use R, F, and U. This argument is from A. J. Ayer.]

6. If "One's conscious life won't continue forever" entails "Life is meaningless," then a finite span of life is meaningless.
    If a finite span of life is meaningless, then an infinite span of life is meaningless.
    If an infinite span of life is meaningless, then "One's conscious life will continue forever" entails "Life is meaningless."
    ∴ If it's possible that life is not meaningless, then "One's conscious life won't continue forever" doesn't entail "Life is meaningless."   [Use C, L, F, and I.]

7. If you have money, then you couldn't be broke.
    You could be broke.
    ∴ You don't have money.   [Use M and B. Is this argument just a valid instance of *modus tollens*: "(P ⊃ Q), ~Q ∴ ~P"?]

8. If you know, then you couldn't be mistaken.
    You could be mistaken.
    ∴ You don't know.   [Use K and M. Since we could repeat this reasoning for any alleged item of knowledge, the argument seems to show that genuine knowledge is impossible.]

9. It's necessary that if there's a necessary being then "There's a necessary being" (by itself) is necessary.
    "There's a necessary being" is logically possible.
    ∴ "There's a necessary being" is logically necessary.   [Use N for "There's a necessary being" or "There's a being that exists of logical necessity"; this being is often identified with God. This argument is from Charles Hartshorne and St Anselm; it's sometimes called "Anselm's second ontological argument." The proof raises logical issues that we'll deal with in the next chapter.]

10. It's necessary that either I'll do it or I won't do it.
    ∴ Either it's necessary that I'll do it, or it's necessary that I won't do it.   [Use D for "I'll do it." Aristotle and the stoic Chrysippus discussed this argument for fatalism (which claims that every event happens of inherent necessity). Chrysippus thought this argument was fallacious and was like arguing "Everything is either A or non-A; hence either everything is A or everything is non-A."]

11. "This agent's actions were all determined" is consistent with "I describe this agent's character in an approving way."
    "I describe this agent's character in an approving way" is consistent with "I praise this agent."
    ∴ "This agent's actions were all determined" is consistent with "I praise this agent."   [Use D, A, and P.]

12. If thinking is just a chemical brain process, then "I think" entails "There's a chemical process in my brain."
    "There's a chemical process in my brain" entails "I have a body."
    "I think but I don't have a body" is logically consistent.
    ∴ Thinking isn't just a chemical brain process.   [Use J, T, C, and B. This argument attacks a form of materialism.]

13. If "I did that on purpose" entails "I made a prior purposeful decision to do that," then there's an infinite chain of previous decisions to decide.
It's impossible for there to be an infinite chain of previous decisions to decide.
∴ "I did that on purpose" is consistent with "I didn't make a prior purposeful decision to do that." [Use D, P, and I. This argument is from Gilbert Ryle.]

14. God knew that you'd do it.
If God knew that you'd do it, then it was necessary that you'd do it.
If it was necessary that you'd do it, then you weren't free.
∴ You weren't free. [Use K, D, and F. This argument is the focus of an ancient controversy. Would divine foreknowledge preclude human freedom? If it would, then should we reject human freedom (as did Luther) or divine foreknowledge (as did Charles Hartshorne)? Or perhaps (as the medieval thinkers Boethius, Aquinas, and Ockham claimed) is the argument that divine foreknowledge precludes human freedom itself fallacious?]

15. If "good" means "socially approved," then "Racism is socially approved" logically entails "Racism is good."
"Racism is socially approved but not good" is consistent.
∴ "Good" doesn't mean "socially approved." [Use M, S, and G. This argument attacks cultural relativism.]

16. Necessarily, if God brings it about that A is true, then A is true.
A is a self-contradiction.
∴ It's impossible for God to bring it about that A is true. [Use B and A, where B is for "God brings it about that A is true."]

17. If this is experienced, then this must be thought about.
"This is thought about" entails "This is put into the categories of judgments."
∴ If it's possible for this to be experienced, then it's possible for this to be put into the categories of judgments. [Use E, T, and C. This argument is from Immanuel Kant, who argued that our mental categories apply, not necessarily to everything that exists, but rather to everything that we could experience.]

18. Necessarily, if formula B has an all-1 truth table then B is true.
∴ If formula B has an all-1 truth table, then B (taken by itself) is necessary. [Use A and B. This illustrates the box-outside versus box-inside distinction.]

19. Necessarily, if you mistakenly think that you exist then you don't exist.
Necessarily, if you mistakenly think that you exist then you exist.
∴ "You mistakenly think that you exist" is impossible. [Use M and E. This relates to Descartes's "I think, therefore I am" ("Cogito ergo sum").]

20. If "good" means "desired by God," then "This is good" entails "There's a God."
"There's no God, but this is good" is consistent.
∴ "Good" doesn't mean "desired by God." [Use M, A, and B. This attacks one form of the divine command theory of ethics. Some (see problem 9 of this section and problem 14 of Section 7.2b) would dispute premise 2 and say that "There's no God" is logically impossible.]

21. If Plato is right, then it's necessary that ideas are superior to material things.
    It's possible that ideas aren't superior to material things.
    ∴ Plato isn't right.   [Use P and S.]

22. "I seem to see a chair" doesn't entail "There's some actual chair that I seem to see."
    If we directly perceive material objects, then "I seem to see a chair and there's some actual chair that I seem to see" is consistent.
    ∴ We don't directly perceive material objects.   [Use S, A, and D.]

23. "There's a God" is logically incompatible with "There's evil in the world."
    There's evil in the world.
    ∴ "There's a God" is self-contradictory.   [Use G and E.]

24. If you do all your homework right, then it's impossible that you get this problem wrong.
    It's possible that you get this problem wrong.
    ∴ You don't do all your homework right.   [Use R and W.]

25. "You do what you want" is compatible with "Your act is determined."
    "You do what you want" entails "Your act is free."
    ∴ "Your act is free" is compatible with "Your act is determined."   [Use W, D, and F.]

26. It's necessarily true that if God doesn't exist in reality then there's a being greater than God.
    It's not possible that there's a being greater than God (since "God" is defined as "a being than which no being could be greater").
    ∴ It's necessary that God exists in reality.   [Use R and B. This is a simplified modal form of St Anselm's ontological argument.]

27. It was always true that you'd do it.
    If it was always true that you'd do it, then it was necessary that you'd do it.
    If it was necessary that you'd do it, then you weren't free.
    ∴ You weren't free.   [Use A (for "It was always true that you'd do it" – don't use a box here), D, and F. This argument is much like problem 14. Are statements about future contingencies (for example, "I'll brush my teeth tomorrow") true or false before they happen? Should we do truth tables for such statements in the normal way, assigning them "1" or "0"? Does this preclude human freedom? If so, should we then reject human freedom? Or should we claim that statements about future contingencies aren't "1" or "0" but must instead have some third truth value (maybe "½")? Or is the argument fallacious?]

CHAPTER 8
Further Modal Systems

Modal logic studies arguments whose validity depends on "necessary," "possible," and similar notions. The previous chapter presented a basic system that builds on propositional logic. This present chapter will consider alternative systems of propositional and quantified modal logic.

8.1 Galactic travel

While logicians usually agree on which arguments are valid, there are some disagreements about modal arguments. Many of the disputes involve arguments in which one modal operator occurs within the scope of another – like "◇◇A ∴ ◇A" and "□(A ⊃ □B), ◇A ∴ B."

These disputes reflect differences in how to formulate the box-dropping rule. So far, we've been assuming a system called "S5," which lets us go from any world to any world when we drop a box (see Section 7.2):

<table>
<tr><td>Drop
box</td><td>□A → W̊ ∴ A,
use any world prefix</td><td>Here the line with "□A" can use any world prefix – and so can the line with "∴ A."</td></tr>
</table>

This assumes that whatever is necessary in *any* world is thereby true in *all* worlds without restriction. A further implication is that whatever is necessary in one world is thereby necessary in all worlds.

Some weaker views reject these ideas. On these views, what is necessary only has to be true in all "suitably related" worlds; so these views put restrictions on the drop-box rule. All the views in question let us go from "□A" in a world to "A" in the *same* world. But we can't always go from "□A" in one world to "A" in *another* world; traveling between worlds requires a suitable "travel ticket."

We get travel tickets when we drop diamonds. Let "W1" and "W2" stand for world prefixes. Suppose we go from "◇A" in world W1 to "A" in new world W2. Then we get a travel ticket from W1 to W2, and we'll write "W1 ⇒ W2":

<table>
<tr><td>W1 ⇒ W2</td><td>We have a ticket to move from world W1 to world W2.</td></tr>
</table>

Here's an example. Suppose we are doing a proof with wffs "◇◇A" and "◇B." We'd get these travel tickets when we drop diamonds (here "#" stands for the actual world):

Dropping a diamond gives us a travel ticket from the world in the "from" step to the world in the "to" step. So in line 11 we get ticket "# ⇒ W" – because we moved from "◇◇A" in the actual world ("#") to "◇A" in world W.

Tickets are reusable; we can use "W1 ⇒ W2" any number of times. The rules for using tickets vary. Some systems let us combine tickets or use them in both directions; but the weakest system T lets us use only one ticket at a time – and only in the direction of the arrow. Suppose that we have "□A" in world W1; then we may put "A" in world W2 provided that:

System T	*System B*	*System S4*
we have a ticket *from* W1 *to* W2	we have a ticket (in either direction) *between* W1 *and* W2	we have a ticket or series of tickets *from* W1 *to* W2

Suppose we have three travel tickets:

$$\# \Rightarrow W \qquad W \Rightarrow WW \qquad \# \Rightarrow WWW$$

System T (the minimal TICKET system) would let us, when we drop boxes, go from # to W, from W to WW, and from # to WWW. The other systems allow these and more. System B (BOTH directions) lets us use single tickets in either direction; so we also can go from W to #, from WW to W, and from WWW to #. System S4 (SERIES) lets us use a series of tickets in the direction of the arrow; this lets us go from # to WW. In contrast, system S5 lets us go from any world to any world; this is equivalent to letting us use any ticket or series of tickets in either direction.

S5 is the most liberal system and accepts the most valid arguments; so S5 is the strongest system. T is the weakest system, allowing the fewest proofs. B and S4 are intermediate, each allowing some proofs that the other doesn't.

The four systems give the same result for most arguments. But some arguments are valid in one system but invalid in another; these arguments use wffs that apply a modal operator to a wff already containing a modal operator.

This argument is valid in S4 or S5 but invalid in T or B:

```
    1    □A          Valid
       [∴ □□A
*   2   ┌ asm: ~□□A
*   3   │ ∴ ◇~□A    {from 2}
*   4   │ W ∴ ~□A   {from 3}              # ⇒ W
*   5   │ W ∴ ◇~A   {from 4}
    6   │ WW ∴ ~A   {from 5}              W ⇒ WW
    7   └ WW ∴ A    {from 1}           Need S4 or S5
    8    ∴ □□A   {from 2; 6 contradicts 7}
```

Step 7 requires that we combine a series of tickets in the direction of the arrow. Tickets "# ⇒ W" and "W ⇒ WW" then let us go from "□A" in actual world # to "A" in world WW. So step 7 requires systems S4 or S5.

This next one is valid in B or S5 but invalid in T or S4:

```
    1    A           Valid
       [∴ □◇A
*   2   ┌ asm: ~□◇A
*   3   │ ∴ ◇~◇A    {from 2}
*   4   │ W ∴ ~◇A   {from 3}              # ⇒ W
    5   │ W ∴ □~A   {from 4}
    6   └ ∴ ~A      {from 5}            Need B or S5
    7    ∴ □◇A   {from 2; 1 contradicts 6}
```

Step 6 requires using ticket "# ⇒ W" in the opposite direction, to go from "□~A" in world W to "~A" in actual world #. This requires systems B or S5.

This last one is valid in S5 but invalid in T or B or S4:

```
*   1    ◇A          Valid
       [∴ □◇A
*   2   ┌ asm: ~□◇A
*   3   │ ∴ ◇~◇A    {from 2}
*   4   │ W ∴ ~◇A   {from 3}              # ⇒ W
    5   │ W ∴ □~A   {from 4}
    6   │ WW ∴ A    {from 1}              # ⇒ WW
    7   └ WW ∴ ~A   {from 5}             Need S5
    8    ∴ □◇A   {from 2; 6 contradicts 7}
```

Step 7 requires combining a series of tickets and using them in both directions. Tickets "# ⇒ W" and "# ⇒ WW" then let us go from "□~A" in W to "~A" in WW. So step 7 requires system S5.

S5 is the simplest system in several ways:

1. We can formulate S5 more simply. The box-dropping rule doesn't have to mention travel tickets; we need only say that, if we have "□A" in any world, then we can put "A" in any world (the same or a different one).

2. S5 expresses simple intuitions about necessity and possibility: what is *necessary* is what is true in *all* worlds, what is *possible* is what is true in *some* worlds, and what is necessary or possible doesn't vary between worlds.

3. On S5, any string of boxes and diamonds simplifies to the last element of the string. So "□□" and "◇□" simplify to "□" – and "◇◇" and "□◇" simplify to "◇."

Which is the best system? This depends on what we take the box and diamond to mean. If we take them to be about the logical necessity and possibility of *ideas*, then S5 is the best system. If an idea (for example, the claim that 2=2) is logically necessary, then it couldn't have been other than logically necessary. So if A is logically necessary, then it's logically necessary that A is logically necessary ["(□A ⊃ □□A)"]. Similarly, if an idea is logically possible, then it's logically necessary that it's logically possible ["(◇A ⊃ □◇A)"]. Of the four systems, only S5 accepts both these formulas. All this presupposes that we use the box to talk about the logical necessity of *ideas*.

Alternatively, we could take the box to be about the logical necessity of *sentences*. Now the *sentence* "2=2" just happens to express a necessary truth; it wouldn't have expressed one if English had used "=" to mean "≠." So the *sentence* is necessary, but it isn't necessary that it's necessary; this makes "(□A ⊃ □□A)" false. But the *idea* that "2=2" now expresses is both necessary and necessarily necessary – and a change in how we use language wouldn't make this *idea* false. So whether S5 is the best system can depend on whether we take the box to be about the necessity of *ideas* or of *sentences*.

There are still other ways to take "necessary." In a given context, calling something "necessary" might mean that it's "physically necessary" or "proven" or "known" or "obligatory." Some logicians like the weak system T because it holds for various senses of "necessary"; such logicians might still use S5 for arguments about the logical necessity of *ideas*. While I have sympathy with this view, most of the modal arguments that I'm interested in are about the logical necessity of ideas. So I use S5 as the standard system of modal logic but feel free to switch to weaker systems for arguments about other sorts of necessity.

Here we've considered the four main modal systems. We could invent other systems – for example, ones in which we can combine travel tickets only in groups of three. Logicians develop such systems, not to help us in analyzing real arguments, but rather to explore interesting formal structures.[1]

---

[1] For more on alternative modal systems, consult G. E. Hughes and M. J. Cresswell, *An Introduction to Modal Logic* (London: Methuen, 1968).

8.1a Exercise – LogiCola KG

Using system S5, prove each of these arguments to be valid (all are valid in S5). Also say in which systems the argument is valid: T, B, S4, or S5.

$$\begin{array}{c} \sim\Box A \\ \hline \therefore \Box\sim\Box A \end{array}$$

Step 7 combines a series of tickets and uses them in both directions. This requires S5.

```
*  1    ~□A   Valid
       [∴ □~□A
*  2    ┌ asm: ~□~□A
*  3    │ ∴ ◇□A    {from 2}
*  4    │ ∴ ◇~A    {from 1}
   5    │ W ∴ □A    {from 3}        # ⇒ W
   6    │ WW ∴ ~A   {from 4}        # ⇒ WW
   7    └ WW ∴ A    {from 5}        Need S5
   8    ∴ □~□A    {from 2; 6 contradicts 7}
```

1. ◇□A
   ∴ A

2. ◇A
   ∴ ◇◇A

3. ◇◇A
   ∴ ◇A

4. ◇□A
   ∴ □A

5. (□A ⊃ □B)
   ∴ □(□A ⊃ □B)

6. □(A ⊃ B)
   ∴ □(□A ⊃ □B)

7. (◇A ⊃ □B)
   ∴ □(A ⊃ □B)

8. □(A ⊃ □B)
   ∴ (◇A ⊃ □B)

9. ◇□◇A
   ∴ ◇A

10. ◇A
    ∴ ◇□◇A

11. □A
    ∴ □(B ⊃ □A)

12. □◇□◇A
    ∴ □◇A

13. □◇A
    ∴ □◇□◇A

14. □(A ⊃ □B)
    ◇A
    ∴ □B

15. □A
    ∴ □□□A

8.1b Exercise – LogiCola KG

First appraise intuitively. Then translate into logic (using the letters given) and prove to be valid in system S5 (all are valid in S5). Also say in which systems the argument is valid: T, B, S4, or S5.

1. It's necessary that if there's a necessary being then "There's a necessary being" (by itself) is necessary.
   "There's a necessary being" is logically possible.
   ∴ "There's a necessary being" is logically necessary. [Use N for "There's a necessary being" or "There's a being that exists of logical necessity"; this being is often identified with God. This argument (which we saw before in Section 7.3b) is from Charles Hartshorne and St Anselm. Its validity depends on which system of modal logic is correct. Some philosophers defend the argument, often after defending a modal system needed to make it valid. Others argue that the argument is invalid, and so any modal system that would make it valid must be wrong. Still others deny the theological import of the conclusion; they say that a necessary being could be a prime number or the world and needn't be God.]

2. "There's a necessary being" isn't a contingent statement.
    "There's a necessary being" is logically possible.
    ∴ There's a necessary being.   [Use N. This version of the Anselm-Hartshorne argument is more clearly valid.]

3. Prove that the first premise of argument 1 is logically equivalent to the first premise of argument 2. (You can prove that two statements are logically equivalent by first deducing the second from the first, and then deducing the first from the second.) In which systems does this equivalence hold?

4. It's necessary that if there's a necessary being then "There's a necessary being" (by itself) is necessary.
    "There's no necessary being" is logically possible.
    ∴ There's no necessary being.   [Use N. Some object that the first premise of the Anselm-Hartshorne argument just as easily leads to the opposite conclusion.]

5. It's necessary that 2+2=4.
    It's possible that no language ever existed.
    If all necessary truths hold because of language conventions, then "It's necessary that 2+2=4" entails "Some language has sometime existed."
    ∴ Not all necessary truths hold because of language conventions.   [Use T, L, and N. This attacks the linguistic theory of logical necessity.]

8.2   Quantified translations

We'll now develop a system of quantified modal logic that combines our quantificational and modal systems. We'll call this our "naïve" system, since it ignores certain problems; later we'll add refinements.[1]

Many quantified modal translations follow familiar patterns. For example, "everyone" translate into a universal quantifier that follows the English word order – while "anyone," regardless of where it occurs, translates into a universal quantifier at the beginning of the wff:

> It's possible for *everyone* to be above average. (FALSE)
> = ◇(x)Ax
> = It's possible that, for all x, x is above average.

> It's possible for *anyone* to be above average. (PERHAPS TRUE)
> = (x)◇Ax
> = For all x, it's possible that x is above average.

---

[1] My basic understanding of quantified modal logic follows that of Alvin Plantinga's *The Nature of Necessity* (London: Oxford University Press, 1974). For related discussions, see A. N. Prior's article on "Logic, Modal" in the *Encyclopedia of Philosophy* (edited by Paul Edwards, London and New York: Macmillan and the Free Press, 1967) and Kenneth Konyndyk's *Introductory Modal Logic* (Notre Dame, Indiana: Notre Dame Press, 1986).

Quantified modal logic can express the difference between necessary and contingent properties. Numbers seem to have both kinds of property. The number 8, for example, has the necessary properties of being even and of being one greater than seven; 8 couldn't have lacked these properties. But 8 also has contingent properties, ones it could have lacked, such as being my favorite number and being less than the number of chapters in this book. We can symbolize "necessary property" and "contingent property" as follows:

$$\Box Fx \quad \begin{array}{ll} = & \text{F is a necessary (essential) property of x.} \\ = & \text{x has the necessary property of being F.} \\ = & \text{x is necessarily F.} \\ = & \text{In all possible worlds, x would be F.} \end{array}$$

$$(Fx \cdot \Diamond {\sim} Fx) \quad \begin{array}{ll} = & \text{F is a contingent (accidental) property of x.} \\ = & \text{x is F but could have lacked F.} \\ = & \text{x is contingently F.} \\ = & \text{In the actual world x is F; but in some possible} \\ & \text{world x isn't F.} \end{array}$$

Humans have mostly contingent properties. Socrates had contingent properties like having a beard and being a philosopher; these are contingent, because he could (without self-contradiction) have been a clean-shaven non-philosopher. But Socrates also had necessary properties, like being self-identical and not being a square circle; every being has these properties of necessity.

Aristotelian essentialism is the controversial view that there are properties that some beings have of necessity and some other beings totally lack. Plantinga, in support of this view, suggests that Socrates had these properties (that some other beings totally lack) of necessity: not being a prime number, being snubnosed in W (a specific possible world), being a person (capable of conscious rational activity), and being identical with Socrates. The last property differs from that of being named "Socrates."

Plantinga explains "necessary property" as follows. Suppose that "a" names a being and "F" names a property. Then the entity named by "a" has the property named by "F" necessarily, if and only if the proposition expressed by "a is non-F" is logically impossible. Then to say that Socrates necessarily has the property of not being a prime number is to say that the proposition "Socrates is a prime number" (with the name "Socrates" referring to the person Socrates) is logically impossible. We must use names (like "Socrates") here and not definite descriptions (like "the entity I'm thinking about").

We've talked previously about the ambiguity between box-inside and box-outside forms. This quantified modal sentence has a similar ambiguity:

"All persons are necessarily persons."

This sentence could mean either of these:

$$(x)(Px \supset \Box Px) \quad = \quad \text{Everyone who in fact is a person has the necessary property of being a person.}$$

$$\Box(x)(Px \supset Px) \quad = \quad \text{It's necessary that all persons are persons.}$$

The controversial box-inside "$(x)(Px \supset \Box Px)$" attributes to each person the necessary property of being a person; the medievals called this *de re* ("of the thing") **necessity**. If this first form is true, then you couldn't have been a non-person – the idea of you existing as a non-person is self-contradictory; this would exclude, for example, the possibility of your being reincarnated as an unconscious doorknob. In contrast, the box-outside "$\Box(x)(Px \supset Px)$" is trivially true and attributes necessity to the proposition (or saying) "All persons are persons"; the medievals called this *de dicto* ("of the saying") **necessity**.

Watch for this ambiguous form:

"All A's are necessarily B's."

When you translate it, say that it could mean either of these:

$$(x)(Ax \supset \Box Bx) \quad = \quad \text{All A's have the necessary property of being B's.}$$

$$\Box(x)(Ax \supset Bx) \quad = \quad \text{It's necessary that all A's are B's.}$$

When you have an English argument with an ambiguous premise, give both translations and work out both symbolizations. As before, various philosophical fallacies result from confusing the forms.

8.2a   Exercise – LogiCola J (QM & QT)

Translate these English sentences into wffs; translate ambiguous forms both ways.

It's necessary that all mathematicians have the necessary property of being rational.	$\Box(x)(Mx \supset \Box Rx)$

Here the first box symbolizes *de dicto* necessity ("It's necessary that ..."), while the second symbolizes *de re* necessity ("have the necessary property of being rational").

1. It's possible for anyone to be unsurpassed in greatness.
2. It's possible for everyone to be unsurpassed in greatness.
3. John has the necessary property of being unmarried.
4. All bachelors are necessarily unmarried.
5. Being named "Socrates" is a contingent property of Socrates.
6. All mathematicians are necessarily rational.
7. All mathematicians are contingently two-legged.
8. John is necessarily sitting.
9. Everyone that we observe to be sitting is necessarily sitting.
10. All numbers have the necessary property of being abstract entities.

11. It's necessary that all living beings in this room are persons.
12. All living beings in this room have the necessary property of being persons.
13. All living beings in this room have the contingent property of being persons.
14. Any contingent claim could be true. [Use Cx for "x is a contingent claim" and Tx for "x is true."]
15. "All contingent claims are true" is possible.
16. It's necessary that everything is self-identical.
17. Everything is such that it has the necessary property of being self-identical.
18. All mathematical statements that are true are necessarily true. [Use Mx and Tx.]
19. It's possible that God has the necessary property of being unsurpassed in greatness.
20. Some being has the necessary property of being unsurpassed in greatness.

8.3 Quantified proofs

Proofs use the same quantificational and modal inference rules as before. Here's an example of a quantified modal proof:

It's necessary that everything is self-identical.
∴ Every entity has the necessary property of being
self-identical.

```
             1      □(x)x=x   Valid
             [∴ (x)□x=x
      *      2    ┌ asm: ~(x)□x=x
      *      3    │ ∴ (∃x)~□x=x   {from 2}
      *      4    │ ∴ ~□a=a   {from 3}
      *      5    │ ∴ ◇~a=a   {from 4}
             6    │ W ∴ ~a=a   {from 5}
             7    │ W ∴ (x)x=x   {from 1}
             8    └ W ∴ a=a   {from 7}
             9    ∴ (x)□x=x   {from 2; 6 contradicts 8}
```

In working out English modal arguments, you'll sometimes find an ambiguous premise. Premise 1 is ambiguous in the following argument:

All bachelors are necessarily unmarried.
You're a bachelor.
∴ "You're unmarried" is logically necessary.

Premise 1 could have either of these two meanings:

(x)(Bx ⊃ □Ux)   "All bachelors are *inherently unmarriable* – in no possible world would anyone ever marry them." (We hope this is false.)

□(x)(Bx ⊃ Ux)   "It's necessarily true that all bachelors are unmarried." (This is trivially true because "bachelor" means *unmarried man*.)

In such cases, say that the argument is ambiguous and work out both versions:

Box-inside version:

1   (x)(Bx ⊃ □Ux)   **Valid**
2   Bu
  [∴ □Uu
3   ┌ asm: ~□Uu
* 4 │ ∴ (Bu ⊃ □Uu) {from 1}
5   └ ∴ □Uu {from 4 and 2}
6   ∴ □Uu {from 3; 3 contra-
      dicts 5}

(While this is valid,
premise 1 is false.)

Box-outside version:

1   □(x)(Bx ⊃ Ux)   **Invalid**
2   Bu
  [∴ □Uu

W	Bu, Uu
	~Bu, ~Uu

* 3   asm: ~□Uu
* 4   ∴ ◇~Uu {from 3}
5   W ∴ ~Uu {from 4}
6   W ∴ (x)(Bx ⊃ Ux) {from 1}
7   ∴ (x)(Bx ⊃ Ux) {from 1}
* 8   W ∴ (Bu ⊃ Uu) {from 6}
* 9   ∴ (Bu ⊃ Uu) {from 7}
10   W ∴ ~Bu {from 5 and 8}
11   ∴ Uu {from 2 and 9}

Both versions are flawed; the first has a false premise while the second is invalid. So the proof that you're inherently unmarriable fails.

Our refutation has two possible worlds, each with only one entity – you. In the actual world, you're a bachelor and unmarried; in world W, you're not a bachelor and not unmarried. In this galaxy, the premises are true (since in both worlds all bachelors are unmarried – and in the actual world you're a bachelor) but the conclusion is false (since in world W you're not unmarried).

Arguments with a modal ambiguity, like this one, often have one interpretation that has a false premise and another that is invalid. Such arguments often seem sound until we focus on the ambiguity.

As with relational arguments, applying our proof strategy mechanically will sometimes lead into an endless loop. In the following case, we keep getting new letters and new worlds, endlessly:

It's possible for anyone to be
   above average.
∴ It's possible for everyone to be
   above average.

1   (x)◇Ax
  [∴ ◇(x)Ax
* 2   asm: ~◇(x)Ax
3   ∴ □~(x)Ax {from 2}

New letter ➔ * 4   ∴ ◇Aa {from 1}
New world ➔ 5   W ∴ Aa {from 4}
* 6   W ∴ ~(x)Ax {from 3}
* 7   W ∴ (∃x)~Ax {from 6}
New letter ➔ 8   W ∴ ~Ab {from 7}
* 9   ∴ ◇Ab {from 1}
New world ➔ 10   WW ∴ Ab {from 9}
* 11   WW ∴ ~(x)Ax {from 3}
* 12   WW ∴ (∃x)~Ax {from 11}
New letter ➔ 13   WW ∴ ~Ac {from 12}
   ... 14   ∴ ◇Ac {from 1} ...

Using ingenuity, we can devise a refutation with two entities and two worlds:

a, b

W	Aa, ~Ab
WW	Ab, ~Aa

Here each person is above average in some world or other – but in no world is every person above average. For now, we'll assume in our refutations that every world contains the same entities (and at least one such entity).

8.3a   Exercise – LogiCola KQ

Say whether valid (and give a proof) or invalid (and give a refutation).

```
              1    (x)□Fx   Valid
            [ ∴ □(x)Fx
      *     2   ┌ asm: ~□(x)Fx
      *     3   │ ∴ ◇~(x)Fx  {from 2}
      *     4   │ W ∴ ~(x)Fx  {from 3}
      *     5   │ W ∴ (∃x)~Fx  {from 4}
            6   │ W ∴ ~Fa   {from 5}
            7   │ ∴ □Fa   {from 1}
            8   └ W ∴ Fa   {from 7}
            9    ∴ □(x)Fx   {from 2; 6 contradicts 8}
```

This is called the "Barcan inference," after Ruth Barcan Marcus. It's doubtful that our naïve quantified modal logic gives the right results for this argument and for several others. We'll discuss this argument again in Section 8.4.

1. (∃x)□Fx
    ∴ □(∃x)Fx

2. a=b
    ∴ (□Fa ⊃ □Fb)

3. ∴ □(∃x)x=a

4. ∴ (∃x)□x=a

5. ◇(x)Fx
    ∴ (x)◇Fx

6. ∴ (x)□x=x

7. ∴ □(x)x=x

8. □(x)(Fx ⊃ Gx)
    ∴ (x)(Fx ⊃ □Gx)

9. ◇(∃x)Fx
    ∴ (∃x)◇Fx

10. (∃x)◇Fx
     ∴ ◇(∃x)Fx

11. (◇(x)Fx ⊃ (x)◇Fx)
     ∴ ((∃x)~Fx ⊃ □(∃x)~Fx)

12. ∴ (x)(y)(x=y ⊃ □x=y)

13. □(x)(Fx ⊃ Gx)
     □Fa
     ∴ □Ga

14. ~a=b
     ∴ □~a=b

8.3b   Exercise – LogiCola KQ

First appraise intuitively. Then translate into logic (using the letters given) and say whether valid (and give a proof) or invalid (and give a refutation). Translate ambiguous English arguments both ways and work out each symbolization separately.

1.   I have a beard.
∴ "Whoever doesn't have a beard isn't me" is a necessary truth.   [Use Bx and i.
G. E. Moore criticized such reasoning, which he saw as essential to the idealistic
metaphysics of his day and its claim that every property of a thing is necessary.
The conclusion entails that "I have a beard" is logically necessary.]

2.   "Whoever doesn't have a beard isn't me" is a necessary truth.
∴ "I have a beard" is logically necessary.   [Use Bx and i.]

3.   Aristotle isn't identical to Plato.
If some being has the property of being necessarily identical to Plato but not all
beings have the property of being necessarily identical to Plato, then some
beings have necessary properties that other beings lack.
∴ Some beings have necessary properties that other beings lack.   [Use a, p, and S
(for "Some beings have necessary properties that other beings lack"). This
defense of Aristotelian essentialism is essentially from Alvin Plantinga.]

4.   All mathematicians are necessarily rational.
Paul is a mathematician.
∴ Paul is necessarily rational.   [Use Mx, Rx, and p.]

5.   Necessarily there exists something unsurpassed in greatness.
∴ There exists something that necessarily is unsurpassed in greatness.   [Use Ux.]

6.   The number that I'm thinking of isn't necessarily even.
8 = the number that I'm thinking of.
∴ 8 isn't necessarily even.   [Use n, E, and e. Does our naïve quantified modal logic
correctly decide whether this argument is valid?]

7.   "I'm a thinking being, and there are no material objects" is logically possible.
Every material object has the necessary property of being a material object.
∴ I'm not a material object.   [Use Tx, Mx, and i. This is from Alvin Plantinga.]

8.   All humans are necessarily rational.
All living beings in this room are human.
∴ All living beings in this room are necessarily rational.   [Use Hx, Rx, and Lx.
This is from Aristotle, who was the first logician and the first to combine quan-
tification with modality.]

9.   It isn't necessary that all cyclists are rational.
Paul is a cyclist.
Paul is rational.
∴ Paul is contingently rational.   [Use Cx, Rx, and r.]

10.   "Socrates has a pain in his toe but doesn't show pain behavior" is consistent.
It's necessary that everyone who has a pain in his toe has pain.
∴ "All who have pain show pain behavior" isn't a necessary truth.   [Use s, Tx for
"x has a pain in his toe," Bx for "x shows pain behavior," and Px for "x is in
pain." This attacks a behaviorist analysis of the concept of "pain."]

11.   If Q (the question "Why is there something and not nothing?") is a meaningful question, then it's possible that there's an answer to Q.
      Necessarily, every answer to Q refers to an existent that explains the existence of other things.
      Necessarily, nothing that refers to an existent that explains the existence of other things is an answer to Q.
   ∴ Q isn't a meaningful question.   [Use M, Ax, and Rx.]

12.   The number of apostles is 12.
      12 is necessarily greater than 8.
   ∴ The number of apostles is necessarily greater than 8.   [Use n, t, e, and Gxy. Does our naïve system correctly decide whether this argument is valid?]

13.   All (well-formed) cyclists are necessarily two legged.
      Paul is a (well-formed) cyclist.
   ∴ Paul is necessarily two legged.   [Use Cx, Tx, and p.]

14.   Something exists in the understanding than which nothing could be greater. (In other words, there's some x such that x exists in the understanding and it isn't possible that there be something greater that x.)
      Anything that exists in reality is greater than anything that doesn't exist in reality.
      Socrates exists in reality.
   ∴ Something exists in reality than which nothing could be greater. (In other words, there's some x such that x exists in reality and it isn't possible that there be something greater than x.)   [Use Ux for "x exists in the understanding," Rx for "x exists in reality," Gxy for "x is greater than y," and s for "Socrates." Use a universe of discourse of *possible beings* – including fictional beings like Santa Claus in addition to actual beings. (Is this legitimate?) This is a form of St Anselm's first ontological argument for the existence of God.]

15.   "Someone is unsurpassably great" is logically possible.
      "Everyone who is unsurpassably great is, in every possible world, omnipotent, omniscient, and morally perfect" is necessarily true.
   ∴ Someone is omnipotent, omniscient, and morally perfect.   [Use Ux and Ox. This is a simplified form of Alvin Plantinga's ontological argument for the existence of God. Plantinga regards the second premise as true by definition; he sees the first premise as controversial but reasonable.]

8.4   A sophisticated system

Our naïve quantified modal logic has two problems. First, it mishandles definite descriptions (terms of the form "the so and so"). So far, we've translated these using small letters; but this can cause problems in modal contexts. To solve the problems, we'll use Russell's analysis of definite descriptions (Section 6.5).

Consider how we've been translating this English sentence:

> *The number I'm thinking of is necessarily odd* = □On

This sentence is ambiguous; it could mean either of two things (where "Tx" means "I'm thinking of number x"):

This is necessary: "I'm thinking of just one number and it is odd."	I'm thinking of just one number, and it has the necessary property of being odd.
□(∃x)((Tx • ~(∃y)(~x=y • Ty)) • Ox)	(∃x)((Tx • ~(∃y)(~x=y • Ty)) • □Ox)

The first form is false, since I might be thinking of no number, or more than one, or an even number. But the second form might be true. Suppose I'm thinking of just the number 7. Now 7 is odd – but it doesn't just happen to be odd; being odd is a necessary property of 7. So if 7 is the number that I'm thinking of, then the second form is true.

So our naïve way to translate "the so and so" is ambiguous. To fix this problem, our sophisticated system will require that we symbolize "the so and so" using Russell's "there is just one ..." analysis. This analysis also blocks the proof of invalid arguments like this one:

8 is the number I'm thinking of. It's necessary that 8 is 8. ∴ It's necessary that 8 is the number I'm thinking of.	e=n □e=e ∴ □e=n

This is invalid – since the premises could be true while the conclusion is false. This argument is provable in naïve quantified modal logic, since the conclusion follows from the premises by the substitute-equals rule (Section 6.2). Our sophisticated system avoids the problem by requiring the longer analysis of "the number I'm thinking of"; so "8 is the number I'm thinking of" gets changed into "I'm thinking of just one number and it is 8" – and the above argument becomes this:

I'm thinking of just one number and it is 8. It's necessary that 8 is 8. ∴ This is necessary: "I'm thinking of just one number and it is 8."	(∃x)((Tx • ~(∃y)(~x=y • Ty)) • x=e) □e=e ∴ □(∃x)((Tx • ~(∃y)(~x=y • Ty)) • x=e) **Invalid**

So translated, the argument becomes invalid and not provable.

The second problem is that our naïve system assumes that the same entities exist in all possible worlds. This leads to implausible results; for example, it makes Gensler (and everyone else) into a logically necessary being:

$$[\therefore \Box(\exists x)x{=}g \qquad \text{Valid ???}$$

*	1	⌐ asm: ~$\Box(\exists x)x{=}g$	
*	2	$\therefore \Diamond{\sim}(\exists x)x{=}g$ {from 1}	
*	3	W $\therefore {\sim}(\exists x)x{=}g$ {from 2}	
	4	W $\therefore (x){\sim}x{=}g$ {from 3}	
	5	W $\therefore {\sim}g{=}g$ {from 4} ← ???	
	6	⌊ W $\therefore g{=}g$ {self-identity rule}	
	7	$\therefore \Box(\exists x)x{=}g$ {from 1; 5 contradicts 6}	

∴ In every possible world, there exists a being who is Gensler.

But Gensler isn't a logically necessary being – since there are impoverished possible worlds without me. So something is wrong here.

There are two ways out of the problem. One way is to change how we take "$(\exists x)$." The provable "$\Box(\exists x)x{=}g$" is false if we take "$(\exists x)$" to mean "for some *existing being* x." But we might take "$(\exists x)$" to mean "for some *possible being* x"; then "$\Box(\exists x)x{=}g$" would mean the more plausible: "In every possible world, there's a *possible being* who is Gensler." Perhaps there is a possible being Gensler in every world; in some of these worlds Gensler exists, and in others he doesn't. This view would need an existence predicate "Ex" to distinguish between possible beings that exist and those that don't; we could use the formula "$(\exists x){\sim}Ex$" to say that there are possible beings that don't exist.

This view is paradoxical, since it posits non-existent beings. Alvin Plantinga defends the opposite view, which he calls "actualism." **Actualism** holds that to be a being and to exist is the same thing; there neither are nor could have been non-existent beings. Of course there could have been beings other than those that now exist. But this doesn't mean that there *now* are beings that don't exist. Actualism denies the latter claim.

Since I favor actualism, I won't posit non-existent beings and I'll continue to take "$(\exists x)$" to mean "for some existing being." On this reading, "$\Box(\exists x)x{=}g$" means "It's necessary that there's an existing being who is Gensler." This is false, since I might not have existed. So we must reject some step of the above proof.

The faulty step seems to be the derivation of 5 from 4:

In W, every existing being is distinct from Gensler.

∴ In W, Gensler is distinct from Gensler.

4 W $\therefore (x){\sim}x{=}g$
5 W $\therefore {\sim}g{=}g$ {from 4}

This inference shouldn't be valid – unless we presuppose the additional premise "W $\therefore (\exists x)x{=}g$" – that Gensler is an existing being in world W.

Rejecting this step requires moving to a **free logic** – one that is free of the assumption that individual constants like "g" always refer to existing beings. Recall our drop-universal rule DU of Section 5.2:

DU
$$\boxed{\begin{array}{c} \text{(x)Fx} \;\;\rightarrow\;\; \text{Fa,} \\ \text{if "a" is } \textit{any} \text{ constant} \end{array}}$$
Every existing being is F.
∴ a is F.

Suppose that every existing being is F; "a" might not denote an existing being, and so "a is F" might not be true. So we need to modify the rule to require a premise that says that "a" denotes an existing being:

DU*
$$\boxed{\begin{array}{c} \text{(x)Fx, (∃x)x=a} \;\;\rightarrow\;\; \text{Fa,} \\ \text{if "a" is } \textit{any} \text{ constant} \end{array}}$$
Every existing being is F.
∴ a is an existing being.
∴ a is F.

Here we symbolize "a is an existing being" by "(∃x)x=a" ("For some existing being x, x is identical to a"). With this change, "□(∃x)x=g" ("Gensler is a necessary being") is no longer provable.

If we weaken DU, we should strengthen our drop-existential rule DE:

DE*
$$\boxed{\begin{array}{c} \text{(∃x)Fx} \;\;\rightarrow\;\; \text{Fa, (∃x)x=a,} \\ \text{if "a" is a } \textit{new} \text{ constant} \end{array}}$$
Some existing being is F.
∴ a is F.
∴ a is an existing being.

When we drop an existential using DE*, we get an existence claim (like "(∃x)x=a") that we can use in dropping universals with DU*. The resulting system can prove almost everything we could prove before – except that the proofs are now a few steps longer. The main effect is to block a few proofs; we can no longer prove that Gensler exists in all possible worlds.

Our free-logic system also blocks the proof of this Barcan inference:

Every existing being has the necessary property of being F. ∴ In every possible world, every existing being is F.	1 (x)□Fx
	   [∴ □(x)Fx
	* 2 asm: ~□(x)Fx
	* 3 ∴ ◇~(x)Fx {from 2}
	* 4 W ∴ ~(x)Fx {from 3}
	* 5 W ∴ (∃x)~Fx {from 4}
	  6 W ∴ ~Fa {from 5}
	  7 W ∴ (∃x)x=a {from 5}
		Invalid
		
		b exists
		a doesn't
		Fb, ~Fa
		--- 	
		a & b exist
		Fb, ~Fa

Our new rule for dropping "(∃x)" tells us that "a" denotes an existing being in world W (line 7). But we don't know if "a" denotes an existing being in the actual world; so we can't conclude "□Fa" from "(x)□Fx" in line 1. With our naïve system, we could conclude "□Fa" – and then put "Fa" in world W to contradict line 6; but now the step is blocked, and the proof fails.

While we don't automatically get a refutation, we can invent one on our own. Our refutation lists which entities exist in which worlds; it uses "a exists" for "(∃x)x=a." Here "Every existing being has the necessary property of being

F" is true – since entity-b is the only existing being and in every world it is F. But "In every possible world, every existing being is F" is false – since in world W there is an existing being, a, that isn't F.

Here's another objection to the argument. Suppose only abstract objects existed (numbers, sets, etc.) and all these had the necessary property of being abstract. Then "Every existing being has the necessary property of being abstract" would be true. But "In every possible world, every existing being is abstract" could still be false – if other possible worlds had concrete entities.[1]

Our new approach allows different worlds to have different existing entities. Gensler might exist in one world but not another. We shouldn't picture existing in different worlds as anything spooky; it's just a way of talking about different possibilities. I might not have existed. We can tell consistent stories where my parents didn't meet and where I never came into existence. If these stories had been true, then I wouldn't have existed. So I don't exist in these stories (although I might exist in other stories). Existing in a possible world is much like existing in a story. (A "possible world" is a technical analogue of a "consistent story.") "I exist in world W" just means "If world W had been actual, then I would have existed."

We also can allow possible worlds with no entities. In such worlds, all wffs starting with existential quantifiers are false and all those starting with universal quantifiers are true.

Should we allow this as a possible world when we do our refutations?

$$\text{W} \quad \boxed{\text{a doesn't exist, Fa}}$$

It seems incoherent to claim that "a has property F" is true while a doesn't exist. It seems that only existing beings have positive properties; in a consistent story where Gensler doesn't exist, Gensler couldn't be a logician or a backpacker. So if "a exists" isn't true in a possible world, then "a has property F" isn't true in that world either. We can put this idea into an inference rule PE* (for "property existence"):

$$\text{PE*} \quad \boxed{\text{Fa} \;\rightarrow\; (\exists x)x{=}a} \qquad \begin{array}{l} \text{a has property F.} \\ \therefore \text{ a is an existing being.} \end{array}$$

Rule PE* holds regardless of what constant replaces "a," what variable replaces "x," and what wff containing only a capital letter and "a" and perhaps other small letters (but nothing else) replaces "Fa." By PE*, "Descartes thinks" entails "Descartes exists." Conversely, the falsity of "Descartes exists" entails

---

[1] Or suppose God created nothing and all uncreated beings had the necessary property of being uncreated. Then "Every existing being has the necessary property of being uncreated" would be true. But "In every possible world, every existing being is uncreated" could still be false – since God might conceive of possible worlds with created beings.

the falsity of "Descartes thinks." Rule PE* expresses that it's a necessary truth that only existing objects have properties. Plantinga calls this view "serious actualism"; actualists who reject PE* are deemed frivolous.

The first example below isn't an instance of PE* (since the wff substituted for "Fa" in PE* can't contain "~"):

Wrong:		*Right:*	
~Fa	a isn't F	Fa	a is F
∴ (∃x)x=a	∴ a exists	∴ (∃x)x=a	∴ a exists

This point is confusing because "a isn't F" in English can have two different senses. "Descartes doesn't think" could mean either of these:

$$\text{Descartes is an existing being who doesn't think} \quad = \quad (\exists x)(x{=}d \cdot {\sim}Td)$$
$$\text{It's false that Descartes is an existing being who thinks} \quad = \quad {\sim}(\exists x)(x{=}d \cdot Td)$$

The first form is *de re* (about the thing); it affirms the property of being a non-thinker of the entity Descartes. Taken this first way, "Descartes doesn't think" entails "Descartes exists." The second form is *de dicto* (about the saying); it denies the statement "Descartes thinks" (which may be false either because Descartes is a non-thinking entity or because Descartes doesn't exist). Taken this second way, "Descartes doesn't think" doesn't entail "Descartes exists."

One might object to PE* on the grounds that Santa Claus has properties (such as being fat) but doesn't exist. But various stories predicate conflicting properties to Santa; they differ, for example, on what day he delivers presents. Does Santa have contradictory properties? Or is one Santa story uniquely "true"? What would that mean? When we say "Santa is fat," we mean that in such and such a story (or possible world) there's a being called Santa who is fat. We shouldn't think of Santa as a non-existing being in our actual world who has properties such as being fat. Rather, what exists in our actual world is stories about there being someone with certain properties – and children who believe these stories. So Santa needn't make us give up PE*.

We need to modify our current definition of "necessary property":

$$\text{F is a necessary property of a} \quad \begin{array}{l} = \quad \Box Fa \\ = \quad \text{In all possible worlds, a is F.} \end{array}$$

Let's grant that Socrates has properties only in worlds where he exists – and that there are worlds where he doesn't exist. Then there are worlds where Socrates has no properties – and so there aren't any properties that Socrates has in all worlds. By our definition, Socrates would have no necessary properties.

Socrates still might have some necessary *combinations* of properties. Perhaps it's true in all worlds that if Socrates exists then Socrates is a person. This suggests a looser definition of "necessary property":

$$
\begin{array}{rl}
\text{F is a necessary property of a} \quad = & \Box((\exists x)x{=}a \supset Fa) \\
= & \text{In all possible worlds where} \\
& \text{a exists, a is F.}
\end{array}
$$

This looser definition reflects more clearly what philosophers mean when they speak of "necessary properties." It also lets us claim that Socrates has the necessary property of being a person. This would mean that Socrates is a person in every possible world where he exists; equivalently, in no possible world does Socrates exist as anything other than a person. Here's an analogous definition of "contingent property":

$$
\begin{array}{rl}
\text{F is a contingent property of a} \quad = & (Fa \cdot \Diamond((\exists x)x{=}a \cdot {\sim}Fa)) \\
= & \text{a is F; but in some possible world} \\
& \text{where a exists, a isn't F.}
\end{array}
$$

These refinements would overcome problems but make our system much harder to use. We seldom need the refinements. So we'll keep the naïve system of earlier sections as our "official system" and build on it in the following chapters. But we'll be conscious that this system is oversimplified in various ways. If and when the naïve system gives questionable results, we can appeal to the sophisticated system to clear things up.

CHAPTER 9
Deontic and Imperative Logic

Deontic logic studies arguments whose validity depends on "ought," "permissible," and similar notions. **Imperative logic**, by contrast, studies arguments with imperatives, like "Do this." We'll take imperative logic first, and then build deontic logic on it.[1]

9.1 Imperative translations

Imperative logic builds on previous systems and adds two ways to form wffs:

> 1. Any underlined capital letter is a wff.
> 2. The result of writing a capital letter and then one or more small letters, one small letter of which is underlined, is a wff.

Underlining turns indicatives into imperatives:

Indicative (You're doing A.)	Imperative (Do A.)
A	$\underline{A}$
Au	A$\underline{u}$

Here are some further translations:

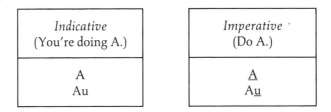

$$
\begin{aligned}
\text{Don't do A} &= \text{~}\underline{A} \\
\text{Do A and B} &= (\underline{A} \cdot \underline{B}) \\
\text{Do A or B} &= (\underline{A} \vee \underline{B}) \\
\text{Don't do either A or B} &= \text{~}(\underline{A} \vee \underline{B})
\end{aligned}
$$

[1] We'll mostly follow Hector-Neri Castañeda's approach. See his "Imperative reasonings," *Philosophy and Phenomenological Research* 21 (1960): pages 21–49; "Outline of a theory on the general logical structure of the language of action," *Theoria* 26 (1960): pages 151–82; "Actions, imperatives, and obligations," *Proceedings of the Aristotelian Society* 68 (1967–68): pages 25–48; and "On the semantics of the ought-to-do," *Synthese* 21 (1970): pages 448–68.

$$
\begin{array}{rcl}
\text{Don't both do A and do B} & = & \\
\text{Don't combine doing A with doing B} & = & \sim(\underline{A} \cdot \underline{B}) \\
\\
\text{Don't combine doing A with not doing B} & = & \\
\text{Don't do A without doing B} & = & \sim(\underline{A} \cdot \sim\underline{B})
\end{array}
$$

Underline imperative parts but not factual ones:

$$
\begin{array}{rcl}
\text{You're doing A and you're doing B} & = & (A \cdot B) \\
\text{You're doing A, but do B} & = & (A \cdot \underline{B}) \\
\text{Do A and B} & = & (\underline{A} \cdot \underline{B}) \\
\\
\text{If you're doing A, then you're doing B} & = & (A \supset B) \\
\text{If you (in fact) are doing A, then do B} & = & (A \supset \underline{B}) \\
\text{Do A, only if you (in fact) are doing B} & = & (\underline{A} \supset B)
\end{array}
$$

Since English doesn't put an imperative after "if," we can't read "$(\underline{A} \supset B)$" as "If do A, then you're doing B." But we can read it as the equivalent "Do A, only if you're doing B." This means the same as "$(\sim B \supset \sim\underline{A})$" – "If you aren't doing B, then don't do A."

There's a subtle difference between these two:

$$
\begin{array}{rcl}
\text{If you (in fact) are doing A, then don't do B} & = & (A \supset \sim\underline{B}) \\
\text{Don't combine doing A with doing B} & = & \sim(\underline{A} \cdot \underline{B})
\end{array}
$$

"A" is underlined in the second but not the first; otherwise, the two wffs would be equivalent. The if-then "$(A \supset \sim\underline{B})$" says that if A is done then you aren't to do B. But the don't-combine "$\sim(\underline{A} \cdot \underline{B})$" just forbids a combination – doing A and B together. If you're doing A, it doesn't follow that you aren't to do B; you could instead do B and stop doing A. We'll see more on this distinction later.

These examples underline the letter for the agent:

$$
\begin{array}{rcl}
\text{X, do (or be) A} & = & A\underline{x} \\
\text{X, do A to Y} & = & A\underline{x}y
\end{array}
$$

These use quantifiers:

$$
\begin{array}{rcl}
\text{Everyone does A} & = & (x)Ax \\
\text{Let everyone do A} & = & (x)A\underline{x} \\
\\
\text{Let everyone who (in fact) is doing A do B} & = & (x)(Ax \supset B\underline{x}) \\
\\
\text{Let someone who (in fact) is doing A do B} & = & (\exists x)(Ax \cdot B\underline{x}) \\
\text{Let someone both do A and do B} & = & (\exists x)(A\underline{x} \cdot B\underline{x})
\end{array}
$$

Notice which letters are underlined.

9.1a   Exercise – LogiCola L (IM & IT)

Translate these English sentences into wffs; take each "you" as a singular "you."

| If the cocoa is about to boil, remove it from the heat | $(B \supset \underline{R})$ |

Our sentence also could translate as "$(B \supset R\underline{u})$" or "$(Bc \supset R\underline{uc})$."

1. Leave or shut up.
2. If you don't leave, then shut up.
3. Do A, only if you want to do A.   [Use A and W.]
4. Do A, only if you want to do A.   [This time use Au and Wu.]
5. Don't combine accelerating with braking.
6. If you accelerate, then don't brake.
7. If you brake, then don't accelerate.
8. If you believe that you ought to do A, then do A.   [Use B for "You believe that you ought to do A" and A for "You do A."]
9. Don't combine believing that you ought to do A with not doing A.
10. If everyone does A, then do A yourself.
11. If you have a cold, then take Dristan.   [Use Cx, Dx, and u.]
12. Let everyone who has a cold take Dristan.
13. Gensler, rob Jones.   [Use Rxy, g, and j.]
14. If Jones hits you, then hit Jones.   [Use Hxy, j, and u.]
15. If you believe that A is wrong, then don't do A.   [Use B for "You believe that A is wrong" and A for "You do A."]
16. If you do A, then don't believe that A is wrong.
17. Don't combine believing that A is wrong with doing A.
18. Would that someone be sick and also be well.   [Use Sx and Wx.]
19. Would that someone who is sick be well.
20. Would that someone be sick who is well.
21. Be with someone you love.   [Use Wxy, Lxy, and u.]
22. Love someone you're with.

9.2   Imperative proofs

Imperative proofs work much like indicative ones and require no new inference rules. But we must treat "A" and "$\underline{A}$" as different wffs. "A" and "$\sim\underline{A}$" aren't contradictories; it's consistent to say "You're now doing A, but don't."

Here's an imperative argument that follows an I-rule inference:

If you're accelerating, then don't brake.	$(A \supset \sim\underline{B})$	**Valid**
You're accelerating.	A	
∴ Don't brake.	∴ $\sim\underline{B}$	

While this seems intuitively valid, there's a problem with calling it "valid" – since we defined "valid" using "true" and "false" (Section 1.2):

> An argument is *valid* if it would be contradictory to have the premises all *true* and conclusion *false*.

"Don't brake" and other imperatives aren't true or false. So how can the valid/invalid distinction apply to imperative arguments?

We need a broader definition of "valid" that applies equally to indicative and imperative arguments. This one (which avoids "true" and "false") does the job:

> An argument is *valid* if the conjunction of its premises with the contradictory of its conclusion is inconsistent.

To say that our argument is *valid* means that this combination is inconsistent:

"If you're accelerating, then don't brake; you're accelerating; brake."

The combination *is* inconsistent. So our argument is *valid* in this new sense.[1]

This next argument is just like the first one except that it uses a don't-combine premise – which makes it invalid:

Don't combine accelerating with braking.	$\sim(\underline{A} \cdot \underline{B})$	Invalid
You're accelerating.	A	
∴ Don't brake.	∴ $\sim\underline{B}$	

The first premise forbids us to accelerate and brake together. Suppose that we're accelerating. It doesn't follow that we shouldn't brake; maybe, to avoid hitting a car, we should brake and stop accelerating. So the argument is invalid. It's consistent to conjoin the premises with the contradictory of the conclusion:

> Don't combine accelerating with braking – never do both together; you in fact are accelerating right now; but you'll hit a car unless you slow down; so stop accelerating right away – and brake immediately.

Here it makes good consistent sense to endorse the premises while also adding the denial of the conclusion ("Brake").

---

[1] We could equivalently define a *valid argument* as one in which every set of imperatives and indicatives that is consistent with the premises also is consistent with the conclusion.

We'd work out the symbolic argument this way (being careful to treat "A" and "$\underline{A}$" as different wffs – almost as if they were different letters):

*	1	$\sim(\underline{A}^{\circ} \cdot \underline{B}^1) = 1$	**Invalid**
	2	$\underline{A}^1 = 1$	
		$[\therefore \sim\underline{B}^1 = 0$	$\boxed{A, \sim\underline{A}, \underline{B}}$
	3	asm: $\underline{B}$	
	4	$\therefore \sim\underline{A}$ {from 1 and 3}	

On our refutation:

$$A = 1$$
$$\underline{A} = 0$$
$$\underline{B} = 1$$

We quickly get a refutation – a set of assignments of 1 and 0 to the letters that make the premises 1 but conclusion 0. Our refutation says this:

> You're accelerating; don't accelerate; instead, brake.

But there's a problem here. Our refutation assigns *false* to the imperative "Accelerate" – even though imperatives aren't true or false. So what does "$\underline{A} = 0$" mean?

We can generically read "1" as "correct" and "0" as "incorrect." Applied to indicatives, these mean "true" or "false." Applied to imperatives, these mean that the prescribed action is "correct" or "incorrect" relative to some standard that divides actions prescribed by the imperative letters into *correct* and *incorrect* actions. The standard could be of different sorts, based on things like morality, law, or traffic safety goals; generally we won't specify the standard.

Suppose we have an argument with just indicative and imperative letters, "$\sim$," and propositional connectives. The argument is *valid* if and only if, relative to every assignment of "1" or "0" to the indicative and imperative letters, if the premises are "1," then so is the conclusion. Equivalently, the argument is *valid* if and only if, relative to any possible facts and any possible standards for correct actions, if all the premises are correct then so is the conclusion.

So our refutation amounts to this – where we imagine a certain combination of facts being true and actions being correct or incorrect:

$A = 1$	"You're accelerating" is true.
$\underline{A} = 0$	Accelerating is incorrect.
$\underline{B} = 1$	Braking is correct.

Our argument could have all the premises correct but not the conclusion.
Compare the two imperative arguments that we've considered:

If you're accelerating, then don't brake.	$(A \supset \sim\underline{B})$	**Valid**
You're accelerating.	A	
$\therefore$ Don't brake.	$\therefore \sim\underline{B}$	

Don't combine accelerating with braking.	$\sim(\underline{A} \cdot \underline{B})$	**Invalid**
You're accelerating.	A	
$\therefore$ Don't brake.	$\therefore \sim\underline{B}$	

Both arguments are the same, except that the first uses an if-then "(A ⊃ ~B),"
while the second uses a don't-combine "~(A · B)." Since one argument is valid
and the other isn't, the two wffs aren't equivalent.

Consider these three forms:

(A ⊃ ~B)	=	If you're accelerating, then don't brake.
(B ⊃ ~A)	=	If you're braking, then don't accelerate.
~(A · B)	=	Don't combine accelerating with braking.

The first two mix indicatives and imperatives; they tell you exactly what to do
under specified conditions. The last is a pure imperative of the don't-combine
form; it just tells you to avoid a certain combination of actions – it tells you not
to do certain things together.

Imagine that you find yourself accelerating and braking (making "A" and
"B" both true) – thus wearing down your brakes and wasting gasoline. Then
you violate all three imperatives. But the three differ on what to do next. The
first tells you not to brake; the second tells you not to accelerate. But the third
leaves it open whether you're to stop accelerating or stop braking. Maybe you
need to brake (and stop accelerating) to avoid hitting another car; or maybe you
need to accelerate (and stop braking) to pass another car. The don't-combine
form doesn't tell a person in this forbidden combination exactly what to do.

This if-then/don't-combine distinction is crucial for consistency imperatives.
Consider these three forms (using A for "You do A" and B for "You believe
that A is wrong"):

(B ⊃ ~A)	=	If you believe that A is wrong, then don't do A.
(A ⊃ ~B)	=	If you do A, then don't believe that A is wrong.
~(A · B)	=	Don't combine believing that A is wrong with doing A.

Imagine that you believe that A is wrong and yet you do A. Then you violate
all three imperatives; but the three differ on what to do next. The first tells you
to stop doing A; the second tells you to stop believing that A is wrong. Which
of these is better advice depends on the situation. Maybe your belief in the
wrongness of A is correct and well-founded, and you need to stop doing A; then
the second form is faulty, since it tells you to change your belief. Or maybe
your action is fine but your belief is faulty (maybe you treat dark-skinned
people fairly but think this is wrong); then the first form is faulty, since it tells
you to change your action. So the two if-then forms can give bad advise.

The third form is a don't-combine imperative forbidding this combination:

believing that A is wrong	+	doing A

This combination always has a faulty element. If your believing is correct, then
your doing is faulty; if your doing is correct, then your believing is faulty. If

you believe that A is wrong and yet do A, then your belief clashes with your action. How should you regain consistency? We saw that this depends on the situation; sometimes it's better to change your belief and sometimes it's better to change your action. The don't-combine form forbids an inconsistency, but it doesn't tell a person in this forbidden combination exactly what to do.

Here's an analogous pair:

$$(B \supset \underline{A}) \quad = \quad \text{If you believe that you ought to do A, then do A.}$$
$$\sim(\underline{B} \cdot \sim\underline{A}) \quad = \quad \text{Don't combine believing that you ought to do A}$$
$$\text{with not doing A.}$$

"Follow your conscience" is often seen as equivalent to the first form; but this form can tell you to do evil things when you have faulty beliefs (see example 6 of section 9.2b). The don't-combine form is better; it just forbids an inconsistent belief-action combination. If your beliefs conflict with you actions, you have to change one or the other; either may be defective.

Before leaving this section, let me point out problems in two alternative ways to understand imperative logic. Consider this argument:

If you get 100 percent, then celebrate.	$(G \supset \underline{C})$	Invalid
Get 100 percent.	$\underline{G}$	
∴ Celebrate.	∴ $\underline{C}$	$\underline{G}, \sim G, \sim\underline{C}$

This is intuitively invalid. Don't celebrate yet – maybe you'll flunk. To derive the conclusion, we need, not an imperative second premise, but rather a factual one saying that you *did* get 100 percent.

Two proposed ways of understanding imperative logic would wrongly judge this argument to be valid. The *obedience view* says that an imperative argument is valid if doing what the premises prescribe necessarily involves doing what the conclusion prescribes. This is fulfilled in the present case; if you do what both premises say, you'll get 100 percent and celebrate. So the obedience view says that our argument is valid. So the obedience view is wrong.

The *threat view* analyzes the imperative "Do A" as "Either you will do A or else S will happen" – where sanction "S" is some unspecified bad thing. So "$\underline{A}$" is taken to mean "(A ∨ S)." But if we replace "$\underline{C}$" with "(C ∨ S)" and "$\underline{G}$" with "(G ∨ S)," and then our argument becomes valid. So the threat view says that our argument is valid. So the threat view is wrong.

9.2a   Exercise – LogiCola MI

Say whether valid (and give a proof) or invalid (and give a refutation).

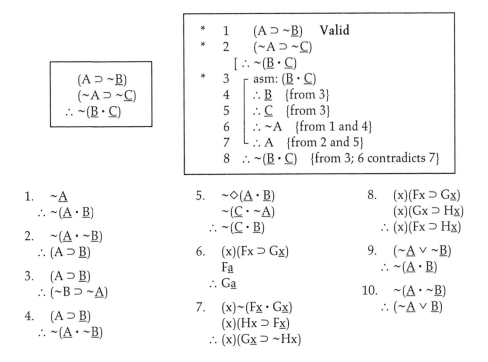

*	1	(A ⊃ ~B) Valid
*	2	(~A ⊃ ~C)
		[∴ ~(B · C)
*	3	┌ asm: (B · C)
	4	│ ∴ B {from 3}
	5	│ ∴ C {from 3}
	6	│ ∴ ~A {from 1 and 4}
	7	└ ∴ A {from 2 and 5}
	8	∴ ~(B · C) {from 3; 6 contradicts 7}

(A ⊃ ~B)
(~A ⊃ ~C)
∴ ~(B · C)

1.   ~A
∴ ~(A · B)

2.   ~(A · ~B)
∴ (A ⊃ B)

3.   (A ⊃ B)
∴ (~B ⊃ ~A)

4.   (A ⊃ B)
∴ ~(A · ~B)

5.   ~◇(A · B)
~(C · ~A)
∴ ~(C · B)

6.   (x)(Fx ⊃ Gx)
Fa
∴ Ga

7.   (x)~(Fx · Gx)
(x)(Hx ⊃ Fx)
∴ (x)(Gx ⊃ ~Hx)

8.   (x)(Fx ⊃ Gx)
(x)(Gx ⊃ Hx)
∴ (x)(Fx ⊃ Hx)

9.   (~A ∨ ~B)
∴ ~(A · B)

10.   ~(A · ~B)
∴ (~A ∨ B)

9.2b   Exercise – LogiCola MI

First appraise intuitively. Then translate into logic (using the letters given) and say whether valid (and give a proof) or invalid (and give a refutation).

1.   Make chicken for dinner or make eggplant for dinner.
Peter is a vegetarian.
If Peter is a vegetarian, then don't make chicken for dinner.
∴ Make eggplant for dinner.   [Use C, E, and V. This one is from Peter Singer.]

2.   Don't eat cake.
If you don't eat cake, then give yourself a gold star.
∴ Give yourself a gold star.   [Use E and G.]

3.   Don't both drive and watch the scenery.
Drive.
∴ Don't watch the scenery.   [Use D and W.]

4.   If you're shifting, then pedal.
You're shifting.
∴ Pedal.   [Use S and P. Shifting without pedaling is bad for many older bicycles.]

5.   Don't combine shifting with not pedaling.
You're shifting.
∴ Pedal.   [Use S and P.]

6. If you believe that you ought to commit mass murder, then commit mass murder.
   You believe that you ought to commit mass murder.
   ∴ Commit mass murder.   [Use B and C. Suppose we take "Follow your conscience" to mean "If you believe that you ought to do A, then do A." Then this principle can tell us to do evil things. Would the corresponding don't-combine form also tell us to do evil things? See the next example.]

7. Don't combine believing that you ought to commit mass murder with not committing murder.
   You believe that you ought to commit mass murder.
   ∴ Commit mass murder.   [Use B and C.]

8. Don't combine having this end with not taking this means.
   Don't take this means.
   ∴ Don't have this end.   [Use E and M.]

9. Lie to your friend only if you want people to lie to you under such circumstances.
   You don't want people to lie to you under such circumstances.
   ∴ Don't lie to your friend.   [Use L and W. Premise 1 is based on a simplified version of Immanuel Kant's formula of universal law; we'll see a more sophisticated version in Chapter 11.]

10. Studying is needed to become a teacher.
    "Become a teacher" entails "Do what is needed to become a teacher."
    "Do what is needed to become a teacher" entails "If studying is needed to become a teacher, then study."
    ∴ Either study or don't become a teacher.   [Use N for "Studying is needed to become a teacher," B for "You become a teacher," D for "You do what is needed to become a teacher," and S for "You study." This example shows that we can deduce some complex imperatives from purely descriptive premises.]

11. Winn Dixie is the largest grocer in Big Pine Key.
    ∴ Either go to Winn Dixie or don't go to the largest grocer in Big Pine Key.   [Use w, l, Gxy, and u.]

12. Drink something that is available.
    The only things available are juice and soda.
    ∴ Drink some juice or soda.   [Use Dxy, u, Ax, Jx, and Sx.]

13. If the cocoa is about to boil, remove it from the heat.
    If the cocoa is steaming, it's about to boil.
    ∴ If the cocoa is steaming, remove it from the heat.   [Use B, R, and S.]

14. Don't shift.
    ∴ Don't combine shifting with not pedaling.   [Use S and P.]

15. If he's in the street, wear your gun.
    Don't wear your gun.
    ∴ He isn't in the street.   [Use S and G. This imperative argument, from Hector-Neri Castañeda, has a factual conclusion; calling it "valid" means that it's inconsistent to conjoin the premises with the denial of the conclusion.]

16.   Back up all your floppy disks.
      This is one of your floppy disks.
      ∴ Back this up.   [Use Bxy, Dx, u, and t.]

17.   If you take logic, then you'll make logic mistakes.
      Take logic.
      ∴ Make logic mistakes.   [Use T and M.]

18.   Get a soda.
      If you get a soda, then pay a dollar.
      ∴ Pay a dollar.   [Use G and P.]

19. ∴ Either do A or don't do A.   [This (vacuous) imperative tautology is analogous to
      the logical truth "You're doing A or you aren't doing A."]

20.   Don't combine believing that A is wrong with doing A.
      ∴ Either don't believe that A is wrong, or don't do A.   [Use B and A.]

21.   Mail this letter.
      ∴ Mail this letter or burn it.   [Use M and B. This one has been used to discredit
      imperative logic. The argument is valid, since this is inconsistent: "Mail this
      letter; don't either mail this letter or burn it." Note that "Mail this letter or
      burn it" doesn't entail "You may burn it"; it's consistent to follow "Mail this
      letter or burn it" with "Don't burn it."]

22.   Let every incumbent who will be honest be endorsed.
      ∴ Let every incumbent who won't be endorsed not be honest.   [Use Hx, Ex, and
      the universe of discourse of incumbents.]

9.3   Deontic translations

Deontic logic adds two operators: "O" (for "ought") and "R" (for "all right" or
"permissible"); these attach to imperatives to form deontic wffs:

O$\underline{A}$	=	It's obligatory that A.	R$\underline{A}$	=	It's permissible that A.
OA$\underline{x}$	=	X ought to do A.	RA$\underline{x}$	=	It's all right for X to do A.
OA$\underline{x}$y	=	X ought to do A to Y.	RA$\underline{x}$y	=	It's all right for X to do A to Y.

"O" / "□" (moral / logical necessity) are somewhat analogous, as are "R" / "◇"
(moral / logical possibility).

"Ought" here is intended in the all-things-considered, normative sense that
we often use in discussing moral issues. This sense of "ought" differs from at
least two other senses that may follow different logical patterns:

- *Prima facie* senses of "ought" (which give a moral consideration that may
  be overridden in a given context): "Insofar as I promised to go with you to
  the movies, I ought to do this [*prima facie* duty]; but insofar as my wife

needs me to drive her to the hospital, I ought to do this instead [*prima facie* duty]. Since my duty to my wife is more urgent, in the last analysis I ought to drive my wife to the hospital [all-things-considered duty]."

- Descriptive senses of "ought" (which state what is required by conventional social rules but needn't express one's own positive or negative evaluation): "You ought [by company regulations] to wear a tie to the office."

I'll be concerned with logical connections between ought judgments, where "ought" is taken in this all-things-considered, normative sense.[1] I'll mostly avoid metaethical issues, like how to further analyze "ought," whether moral judgments are objectively true or false, and how to justify ethical principles.[2] I'll sometimes call ought judgments *true* or *false* (since I believe that they are); but someone who thinks otherwise could rephrase my remarks to avoid this.

Here are some further translations:

$$\text{Act A is obligatory (required, a duty)} \quad = \quad O\underline{A}$$
$$\text{Act A is all right (right, permissible, OK)} \quad = \quad R\underline{A}$$

$$\text{Act A is wrong} \quad
\begin{array}{lll}
= & \sim\!R\underline{A} & = \quad \text{Act A isn't all right.} \\
= & O\!\sim\!\underline{A} & = \quad \text{Act A ought not to be done.}
\end{array}$$

$$\text{It ought to be that A and B} \quad = \quad O(\underline{A} \cdot \underline{B})$$
$$\text{It's all right that A or B} \quad = \quad R(\underline{A} \vee \underline{B})$$

$$\text{If you do A, then you ought not to do B} \quad = \quad (A \supset O\!\sim\!\underline{B})$$
$$\text{You ought not to combine doing A with doing B} \quad = \quad O\!\sim\!(\underline{A} \cdot \underline{B})$$

The last two are deontic if-then and don't-combine forms.

Here are examples using quantifiers:

$$\text{It's obligatory that everyone do A} \quad = \quad O(x)A\underline{x}$$
$$\text{It isn't obligatory that everyone do A} \quad = \quad \sim\!O(x)A\underline{x}$$
$$\text{It's obligatory that not everyone do A} \quad = \quad O\!\sim\!(x)A\underline{x}$$
$$\text{It's obligatory that everyone refrain from doing A} \quad = \quad O(x)\!\sim\!A\underline{x}$$

These two are importantly different:

$$\text{It's obligatory that someone answer the phone} \quad = \quad O(\exists x)A\underline{x}$$
$$\text{There's someone who has the obligation to answer the phone} \quad = \quad (\exists x)OA\underline{x}$$

The first might be true while the second is false; it might be obligatory (on the group) that someone or other in the office answer the phone – while yet no

---

[1] We'll also take imperatives in an all-things-considered (not *prima facie*) sense. So we won't take "Do A" to mean "Other-things-being-equal, do A."

[2] For a discussion of these issues, see my *Ethics: A Contemporary Introduction* (London and New York: Routledge, 1998).

specific person has the obligation to answer it. To prevent the "Let the other person do it" mentality in such cases, we sometimes need to assign duties.

Compare these three:

It's obligatory that some who kill repent	=	O(∃x)(Kx • R<u>x</u>)
It's obligatory that some kill who repent	=	O(∃x)(K<u>x</u> • Rx)
It's obligatory that some both kill and repent	=	O(∃x)(K<u>x</u> • R<u>x</u>)

The three wffs are different; the underlining shows which parts are obligatory: repenting, killing, or killing-and-repenting. If we just attached "O" to indicatives, our formulas couldn't distinguish the forms; all three would translate as "O(∃x)(Kx • Rx)." Because of such examples, we need to attach "O" to imperative wffs, not to indicative ones.[1]

Wffs in deontic logic divide broadly into *descriptive*, *imperative*, and *deontic* wffs. Here are examples of each:

Descriptive	Imperative	Deontic (normative)	
You're doing A.	Do A.	You ought to do A.	It's all right for you to do A.
A	<u>A</u>	O<u>A</u>	R<u>A</u>
Au	A<u>u</u>	OA<u>u</u>	RA<u>u</u>

The type of wff can matter; for example, "O" and "R" must attach to *imperative* wffs. So we'll now give rules for distinguishing the three types of wff:

1. Any not-underlined capital letter not immediately followed by a small letter is a *descriptive* wff. Any underlined capital letter not immediately followed by a small letter is an *imperative* wff.

2. The result of writing a not-underlined capital letter and then one or more small letters, none of which are underlined, is a *descriptive* wff. The result of writing a not-underlined capital letter and then one or more small letters, one small letter of which is underlined, is an *imperative* wff.

3. The result of prefixing any wff with "~" is a wff and is *descriptive*, *imperative*, or *deontic*, depending on what the original wff was.

4. The result of joining any two wffs by "•" or "∨" or "⊃" or "≡" and enclosing the result in parentheses is a wff. The resulting wff is *descriptive* if both original wffs were descriptive; it's *imperative* if at least one was imperative; it's *deontic* if both were deontic or if one was deontic and the other descriptive.

---

[1] We can't distinguish the three as "(∃x)(Kx • ORx)," "(∃x)(OKx • Rx)," and "(∃x)O(Kx • Rx)" – since putting "(∃x)" outside the "O" changes the meaning. See the previous paragraph.

5.   The result of writing a quantifier and then a wff is a wff. The resulting wff is *descriptive, imperative,* or *deontic,* depending on what the original wff was.

6.   The result of writing a small letter and then "=" and then a small letter is a *descriptive* wff.

7.   The result of writing "◇" or "□," and then a wff, is a *descriptive* wff.

8.   The result of writing "O" or "R," and then an imperative wff, is a *deontic* wff.

9.3a   Exercise – LogiCola L (DM & DT)

Translate these English sentences into wffs; take each "you" as a singular "you."

"You ought to do A" entails "It's possible that you do A."	□(O<u>A</u> ⊃ ◇A)

Here "◇A" doesn't use underlining; "◇A" means "It's possible that you do A" – while "◇<u>A</u>" means "The imperative 'Do A' is logically consistent." Our sample sentence also could translate as "□(O<u>Au</u> ⊃ ◇Au)."

1.   If you're accelerating, then you ought not to brake.   [Use A and B.]
2.   You ought not to combine accelerating with braking.
3.   If A is wrong, then don't do A.
4.   Do A, only if A is permissible.
5.   "Do A" entails "A is permissible."
6.   Act A is morally indifferent (morally optional).
7.   If A is permissible and B is permissible, then A-and-B is permissible.
8.   It isn't your duty to do A, but it's your duty not to do A.
9.   If you believe that you ought to do A, then you ought to do A.   [Use B for "You believe that you ought to do A" and A for "You do A."]
10.   You ought not to combine believing that you ought to do A with not doing A.
11.   "Everyone does A" doesn't entail "It would be all right for you to do A."   [Use Ax and u.]
12.   If it's all right for X to do A to Y, then it's all right for Y to do A to X.   [Use Axy.]
13.   It's your duty to do A, only if it's possible for you to do A.
14.   It's obligatory that the state send only guilty persons to prison.   [Use Gx, Sxy, and s.]
15.   If it isn't possible for everyone to do A, then you ought not to do A.   [Use Ax and u.]
16.   If it's all right for someone to do A, then it's all right for everyone to do A.
17.   If it's all right for you to do A, then it's all right for anyone to do A.
18.   It isn't all right for anyone to do A.
19.   It's permissible that everyone who isn't sinful be thankful.   [Use Sx and Tx.]
20.   It's permissible that everyone who isn't thankful be sinful.

9.4 Deontic proofs

We'll now add six inference rules. The first four, following the modal and quantificational pattern, are for reversing squiggles and dropping "R" and "O."

These reverse-squiggle (RS) rules hold regardless of what pair of contradictory imperative wffs replaces "$\underline{A}$"/"$\sim\underline{A}$":

Reverse squiggle	$\sim O\underline{A} \;\rightarrow\; R\sim\underline{A}$ $\sim R\underline{A} \;\rightarrow\; O\sim\underline{A}$

These let us go from "not obligatory to do" to "permissible not to do" – and from "not permissible to do" to "obligatory not to do." Use these rules only within the same world and only when the formula begins with "$\sim$O" or "$\sim$R."

We need to expand our worlds. From now on, a **possible world** is a consistent and complete set of indicatives and imperatives. And a **deontic world** is a possible world (in this expanded sense) in which (a) the indicative statements are all true and (b) the imperatives prescribe some jointly permissible combination of actions. So then these equivalences hold:

$O\underline{A}$	=	Act A is obligatory.
	=	"Do A" is in *all* deontic worlds.

$R\underline{A}$	=	Act A is permissible.
	=	"Do A" is in *some* deontic worlds.

A *world prefix* is a string of zero or more instances of the letters "W" or "D." As before, world prefixes represent possible worlds. "D," "DD," and so on represent deontic worlds; we can use these in derived steps and assumptions, such as:

$D\therefore A$ (So A is true in deontic world D.)   DD asm: A   (Assume A is true in deontic world DD.)

We can drop deontic operators using the next two rules (which hold regardless of what imperative wff replaces "$\underline{A}$"). Here's the drop-"R" (DR) rule:

Drop "R"	$R\underline{A} \;\rightarrow\; \overset{\downarrow}{D}\therefore \underline{A},$ use a *new* string of D's

Here the line with "$R\underline{A}$" can use any world prefix – and the line with "$\therefore \underline{A}$" must use a world prefix that is the same except that it adds a *new* string (a string not occurring in earlier lines) of one or more D's at the end. If act A is permissible, then "Do A" is in some deontic world; we may give this world an

arbitrary and hence *new* name – corresponding to a new string of D's. We'll use
"D" for the first "R" we drop, "DD" for the second, and so forth. So if we drop
two R's, then we must introduce two deontic worlds:

R<u>A</u>	Act A is permissible, act B is permissible; so some
R<u>B</u>	deontic world has "Do A" and another has "Do B."
D ∴ <u>A</u>	← "D" is OK because it occurs in no earlier line.
DD ∴ <u>B</u>	← Since "D" has now occurred, we use "DD."

Permissible options need not be combinable; if it's permissible to marry Ann
and permissible to marry Beth, it needn't be permissible to marry both Ann
and Beth (bigamy). We can drop an "R" from formulas that are more complicated, so long as "R" *begins* the wff:

Right:	*Wrong:*	*Wrong:*
R(<u>A</u> · <u>B</u>)	(R<u>A</u> ⊃ B)	(R<u>A</u> · R<u>B</u>)
D ∴ (<u>A</u> · <u>B</u>)	D ∴ (<u>A</u> ⊃ B)	D ∴ (<u>A</u> · <u>B</u>)

The last two formulas doesn't *begin* with "R"; instead, they begin with a left-
hand parenthesis. Drop only an *initial* "R" – and introduce a new and different
deontic world whenever you drop an "R."

Here's the drop-"O" (DO) rule:

Drop "O"	OA → D ∴ A, ↓ use a blank or any string of D's

Here the line with "O<u>A</u>" can use any world prefix – and the line with "∴ <u>A</u>"
must use a world prefix which is either the same or else the same except that it
adds one or more D's at the end. If act A is obligatory, then "Do A" is in all
deontic worlds. So if we have "O<u>A</u>" in the actual world then we can derive "∴
<u>A</u>," "D ∴ <u>A</u>," "DD ∴ <u>A</u>," and so on; but it's good strategy to say in *old* deontic
worlds when dropping "O." As before, we can drop an "O" from formulas that
are more complicated, so long as "O" *begins* the wff:

Right:	*Wrong:*	*Wrong:*
O(A ⊃ <u>B</u>)	(O<u>A</u> ⊃ B)	(O<u>A</u> ⊃ O<u>B</u>)
D ∴ (A ⊃ <u>B</u>)	D ∴ (<u>A</u> ⊃ <u>B</u>)	D ∴ (<u>A</u> ⊃ <u>B</u>)

The last two formulas begin not with "O," but with "(." "(O<u>A</u> ⊃ B)" and
"(O<u>A</u> ⊃ O<u>B</u>)" are if-then forms and follow the if-then rules: if we have the first
part true, we can get the second true; if we have the second part false, we can
get the first false; and if we get stuck, we need to make another assumption.

Rule DO lets us go from "O<u>A</u>" in a world to "<u>A</u>" in the same world. This accords with "Hare's Law" (named after R. M. Hare):

Hare's Law	An ought judgment entails the corresponding imperative: "You ought to do A" entails "Do A."
□(O<u>A</u> ⊃ <u>A</u>)	

Hare's Law (also called "prescriptivity") equivalently claims that "You ought to do it, but don't" is inconsistent. This law fails for some weaker *prima facie* or descriptive senses of "ought"; there's no inconsistency in this: "You ought (according to company policy) to do it, but don't do it." But the law seems to hold for the all-things-considered, normative sense of "ought"; this seems inconsistent: "All things considered, you ought to do it; but don't do it." However, some philosophers reject Hare's law; those who reject it would want to specify that in applying rule DO the world prefix of the derived step can't be the same as that of the earlier step.

Here's a deontic proof using these rules:

```
         1    O~(A · B)  Valid
         2    OA
            [∴ O~B
  *      3    ┌ asm: ~O~B
  *      4    │ ∴ RB  {from 3}
         5    │ D∴ B  {from 4}
  *      6    │ D∴ ~(A · B)  {from 1}
         7    │ D∴ A  {from 2}
         8    └ D∴ ~B  {from 6 and 7}
         9    ∴ O~B  {from 3; 5 contradicts 8}
```

This is like a modal proof, except for underlining and having "O," "R," and "D" in place of "□," "◇," and "W." As in modal logic, we can star (and then ignore) a line when we use a reverse-squiggle or "R"-dropping rule on it.

Things get more complicated if we use the rules for dropping "R" and "O" on a formula in some other possible world. Consider these two cases:

R<u>A</u>	W∴ R<u>A</u>
O<u>B</u>	W∴ O<u>B</u>
D∴ <u>A</u>	WD∴ <u>A</u>
D∴ <u>B</u>	WD∴ <u>B</u>

In the case on the left, formulas "R<u>A</u>" and "O<u>B</u>" are in the actual world (using the blank world prefix); and so we put the corresponding imperatives in a deontic world "D." In the case on the right, formulas "R<u>A</u>" and "O<u>B</u>" are in world W; so here we keep the "W" and just add "D." The rules for dropping

"R" and "O" allow these moves. Here world WD is a deontic world that *depends on* possible world W; this means that (a) the indicative statements in WD are those of world W, and (b) the imperatives of WD prescribe some set of actions that are jointly permissible according to the norms of world W. The following proof uses world prefix "WD" in steps 7 to 9:

```
        [∴ □(O(A · B) ⊃ OA)        Valid
*   1   ┌ asm: ~□(O(A · B) ⊃ OA)
*   2   │  ∴ ◇~(O(A · B) ⊃ OA)   {from 1}
*   3   │  W ∴ ~(O(A · B) ⊃ OA)   {from 2}
    4   │  W ∴ O(A · B)   {from 3}
*   5   │  W ∴ ~OA   {from 3}
*   6   │  W ∴ R~A   {from 5}
    7   │  WD ∴ ~A   {from 6}
    8   │  WD ∴ (A · B)   {from 4}
    9   └  WD ∴ A   {from 8}
   10   ∴ □(O(A · B) ⊃ OA)   {from 1; 7 contradicts 9}
```

The next two chapters will often use complex world prefixes like "WD."

We have two additional inference rules. The indicative transfer rule IT lets us transfer indicatives freely between a deontic world and whatever world it depends on; we can do this because these two worlds have the same indicative (descriptive or deontic) wffs. IT holds regardless of what descriptive or deontic wff replaces "A":

$$\text{Indicative transfer} \qquad \boxed{\text{D} \therefore \text{A} \;\rightarrow\; \text{A}}$$

The world prefixes of the derived and deriving steps must be identical except that one ends in one or more additional D's. Use IT only with indicatives:

Right:	*Right:*	*Right:*	*Wrong:*
A	D ∴ A	OA	A
——	——	——	——
D ∴ A	∴ A	D ∴ OA	D ∴ A

It can be useful to move an indicative between world D and the actual world (or vice versa) when we need it elsewhere to get a contradiction or apply an I-rule.

Our final inference rule KL is named for Immanuel Kant:

$$\text{Kant's Law} \qquad \boxed{\text{OA} \;\rightarrow\; ◇\text{A}} \qquad \begin{array}{l} \text{"Ought" implies "can":} \\ \text{"You ought to do A" entails} \\ \text{"It's possible for you to do A."} \end{array}$$

This holds regardless of what imperative wff replaces "<u>A</u>" and what indicative wff replaces "A" – provided that the former is like the latter except for underlining, and every wff out of which the former is constructed is an imperative.[1] It can be useful to use Kant's Law if we have a letter that occurs underlined in a deontic wff and not-underlined in a modal wff.

Kant's Law equivalently claims that "You ought to do it, but it's impossible" is inconsistent. This law fails for some weaker *prima facie* or descriptive senses of "ought"; since company policy may require impossible things, there's no inconsistency in this: "You ought (according to company policy) to do it, but it's impossible." But the law seems to hold for the all-things-considered, normative sense of "ought"; this seems inconsistent: "All things considered, you ought to do it; but it's impossible to do it." We can't have an all-things-considered moral obligation to do the impossible.

KL is a weak form of Kant's Law. Kant thought that what we ought to do is not just *logically possible*, but also what we are *capable of doing* (physically and psychologically). Our rule KL expresses only the "logically possible" part; but, even so, it's still useful for many arguments. And it won't hurt if sometimes we interpret "◊" in terms of what we are *capable of doing* (instead of what is *logically possible*).

We've already mentioned the first two of these four "laws":[2]

Hare's Law:	An "ought" entails the corresponding imperative.
Kant's Law:	"Ought" implies "can."
Hume's Law:	You can't deduce an "ought" from an "is."
Poincaré's Law:	You can't deduce an imperative from an "is."

Now we'll briefly consider the last two.

Hume's Law (named for David Hume) claims that we can't validly deduce what we *ought* to do from premises that don't contain "ought" or similar notions.[3] Hume's Law fails for some weak senses of "ought." Given descriptions of company policy and the situation, we can sometimes validly deduce what ought (according to company policy) to be done. But Hume's Law seems to hold for the all-things-considered, normative sense of "ought."

Here's a careful wording of Hume's Law:

---

[1] The proviso outlaws "O(∃x)(Lx · ~L<u>x</u>) ∴ ◊(∃x)(Lx · ~L<u>x</u>)" ("It's obligatory that someone who is lying not lie ∴ It's possible that someone both lie and not lie"). Since "Lx" in the premise isn't an imperative wff, this (incorrect) derivation doesn't satisfy KL.

[2] The word "law," although traditional here, is really too strong, since all four are controversial.

[3] Some philosophers disagree and claim we can deduce moral conclusions using only premises about social conventions, personal feelings, God's will, or something similar. For views on both sides, see my *Ethics: A Contemporary Introduction* (London and New York: Routledge, 1998).

Hume's Law ~□(B ⊃ O<u>A</u>)	You can't deduce an "ought" from an "is": If B is a consistent non-evaluative statement and A is a simple contingent action, then B doesn't entail "Act A ought to be done."

The complex wording here sidesteps some trivial cases (see Section 9.4a) where we clearly *can* deduce an "ought" from an "is."

Poincaré's Law (named for the mathematician Jules Henri Poincaré) similarly claims that we can't validly deduce an imperative from indicative premises that don't contain "ought" or similar notions. Here's a careful wording:

Poincaré's Law ~□(B ⊃ <u>A</u>)	You can't deduce an imperative from an "is": If B is a consistent non-evaluative statement and A is a simple contingent action, then B doesn't entail the imperative "Do act A."

Again, the qualifications block trivial objections (like problems 10 and 11 of Section 9.2b). We won't build Hume's Law or Poincaré's Law into our system.

Our deontic proof strategy is much like the modal strategy. First we reverse squiggles to put "O" and "R" at the beginning of a formula. Then we drop each initial "R," putting each permissible thing into a *new* deontic world. Lastly we drop each initial "O," putting each obligatory thing into each *old* deontic world. Drop obligatory things into the actual world just if:

- the premises or conclusion have an instance of an underlined letter that isn't part of some wff beginning with "O" or "R"; or
- you've done everything else possible (including further assumptions if needed) and still have no old deontic worlds.

Use the indicative transfer rule if you need to move an indicative between the actual world and a deontic world (or vice versa). Consider using Kant's Law if you see a letter that occurs underlined in a deontic wff and not-underlined in a modal wff; some of the proofs involving Kant's Law get very tricky.

From now on, we won't do refutations for invalid arguments – since refutations get too messy when we mix various kinds of world.

9.4a   Exercise – LogiCola M (D & M)

Say whether valid (and give a proof) or invalid (no refutation necessary).

$$∴ {\sim}◇(O\underline{A} \cdot O{\sim}\underline{A})$$

```
        [ ∴ ~◇(OA · O~A)        Valid
  *  1  ┌ asm: ◇(OA · O~A)
  *  2  │  W ∴ (OA · O~A)  {from 1}
     3  │  W ∴ OA   {from 2}
     4  │  W ∴ O~A   {from 2}
     5  │  W ∴ A   {from 3}
     6  └  W ∴ ~A   {from 4}
     7  ∴ ~◇(OA · R~A)  {from 1; 5
          contradicts 6}
```

This wff says "It isn't logically possible that you ought to do A and also ought not to do A"; this formula is correct if we take "ought" in the all-things-considered, normative sense. Morality can't make impossible demands on us; if we think otherwise, our lives will likely be filled with irrational guilt for not fulfilling impossible demands. But "~◇(OA · O~A)" would be incorrect if we took "O" in it to mean something like "ought according to company policy" or "*prima facie* ought." Inconsistent company policies may require that we do A and also require that we not do A; and we can have a *prima facie* duty to do A and another to omit doing A.

1. O~A
    ∴ O~(A · B)

2. (∃x)OAx
    ∴ O(∃x)Ax

3. b=c
    ∴ (OFab ⊃ OFac)

4. ∴ O(OA ⊃ A)

5. ∴ O(A ⊃ OA)

6. ∴ O(A ⊃ RA)

7. OA
    OB
    ∴ O(A · B)

8. (x)OFx
    ∴ O(x)Fx

9. O(A ∨ B)
    ∴ (~◇A ⊃ RB)

10. (A ⊃ OB)
    ∴ O(A ⊃ B)

11. □(A ⊃ B)
    OA
    ∴ OB

12. OA
    RB
    ∴ R(A · B)

13. A
    ∴ O(B ∨ ~B)

14. (x)RAx
    ∴ R(x)Ax

15. OA
    OB
    ∴ ◇(A · B)

16. ∴ (RA ∨ R~A)

17. (OA ⊃ B)
    ∴ R(A · B)

18. ~◇A
    ∴ R~A

19. A
    ~A
    ∴ OB

20. O(x)(Fx ⊃ Gx)
    OFa
    ∴ OGa

21. O(A ⊃ B)
    ∴ (A ⊃ OB)

22. O(x)Ax
    ∴ (x)OAx

23. ∴ O(~RA ⊃ ~A)

24. A
    ∴ (A ∨ OB)

25. (A ∨ OB)
    ~A
    ∴ OB

Problems 3, 13, and 19 show how to deduce an "ought" from an "is." If "(A ∨ OB)" is an "ought," then 24 gives another example; if it's an "is," then 25 gives another example. Problem 20 of Section 9.4b gives yet another example. We formulated Hume's Law so that these examples don't refute it.

9.4b   Exercise – LogiCola M (D & M)

First appraise intuitively. Then translate into logic (using the letters given) and say whether valid (and give a proof) or invalid (no refutation necessary).

1.   It isn't all right for you to combine drinking with driving.
     You ought to drive.
     ∴ Don't drink.   [Use K for "You drink" and V for "You drive."]

2. ∴ Either it's your duty to do A or it's your duty not to do A.   [The conclusion is *rigorism* – the view that there are no morally neutral acts (acts permissible to do and also permissible not to do).]

3.   I did A.
     I ought not to have done A.
     If I did A and it was possible for me not to have done A, then I have free will.
     ∴ I have free will.   [Use A and F. Immanuel Kant thus argued that ethics requires free will.]

4. ∴ If you ought to do A, then do A.

5. ∴ If you ought to do A, then you'll in fact do A.

6.   It isn't possible for you to be perfect.
     ∴ It isn't your duty to be perfect.   [Use P.]

7.   You ought not to combine drinking with driving.
     You don't have a duty to drive.
     ∴ It's all right for you to drink.   [Use K and V.]

8. ∴ Do A, only if it would be all right for you to do A.

9.   If it's all right for you to insult Jones, then it's all right for Jones to insult you.
     ∴ If Jones ought not to insult you, then don't you insult Jones.   [Use Ixy, u, and j. The premise follows from the universalizability principle ("What is right for one person is right for anyone else in similar circumstances") plus the claim that the cases are similar. The conclusion is a distant relative of the golden rule.]

10.   It's all right for someone to do A.
      ∴ It's all right for anyone to do A.   [Can you think of an example where the premise would be true and the conclusion false?]

11.   If fatalism (the view that whatever happens couldn't have been otherwise) is true and I do A, then my doing A (taken by itself) is necessary.
      ∴ If fatalism is true and I do A, then it's all right for me to do A.   [Use F and A.]

12.   If it's all right for you to complain, then you ought to take action.
      ∴ You ought to either take action or else not complain.   [Use C and T. This is the "Put up or shut up" argument.]

13.   I ought to stay with my brother while he's sick in bed.
      It's impossible for me to combine these two things: staying with my brother while he's sick in bed and driving you to the airport.
      ∴ It's all right for me not to drive you to the airport.   [Use S and D.]

14. Jones ought to be happy in proportion to his moral virtue.
Necessarily, if Jones is happy in proportion to his moral virtue, then Jones will be rewarded either in the present life or in an afterlife.
It isn't possible for Jones to be rewarded in the present life.
If it's possible for Jones to be rewarded in an afterlife, then there is a God.
∴ There is a God. [Use H for "Jones is happy in proportion to his moral virtue," P for "Jones will be rewarded in the present life," A for "Jones will be rewarded in an afterlife," and G for "There is a God." This is Kant's moral argument for the existence of God. To make premise 3 plausible, we must take "possible" as "factually possible" (instead of "logically possible"). But does "ought to be" (premise 1 uses this – and not "ought to do") entail "is factually possible"?]

15. If killing the innocent is wrong, then one ought not to intend to kill the innocent.
If it's permissible to have a nuclear retaliation policy, then intending to kill the innocent is permissible.
∴ If killing the innocent is wrong, then it's wrong to have a nuclear retaliation policy. [Use K, I, and N.]

16. If it's all right for you to do A, then you ought to do A.
If you ought to do A, then it's obligatory that everyone do A.
∴ If it's impossible that everyone do A, then you ought not to do A. [Use Ax and u. The premises and conclusion are doubtful; the conclusion entails "If it's impossible that everyone become the first woman president, then you ought not to become the first woman president." The conclusion is a relative of Kant's formula of universal law; it's also a "formal ethical principle" – an ethical principle that we can formulate using abstract logical notions but leaving unspecified the meaning of the individual, property, relational, and statement letters.]

17. It's obligatory that Smith help someone or other whom Jones is beating up.
∴ It's obligatory that Jones beat up someone. [Use Hxy, Bxy, s, and j. This "good Samaritan paradox" is provable in most deontic systems that attach "O" to indicatives. There are similar examples where the evil deed happens after the good one. It may be obligatory that Smith warn someone or other whom Jones will try to beat up; this doesn't entail that Jones ought to try to beat up someone.]

18. If it isn't right to do A, then it isn't right to promise to do A.
∴ Promise to do A, only if it's all right to do A. [Use A and P.]

19. It's obligatory that someone answer the phone.
∴ There's someone who has the obligation to answer the phone. [Use Ax.]

20. Studying is needed to become a teacher.
"Become a teacher" entails "Do what is needed to become a teacher."
"Do what is needed to become a teacher" entails "If studying is needed to become a teacher, then study."
∴ You ought to either study or not become a teacher. [Use N for "Studying is needed to become a teacher," B for "You become a teacher," D for "You do what is needed to become a teacher," and S for "You study." This is the ought-version of problem 10 of Section 9.2b. It shows that we can deduce a complex ought judgment from purely descriptive premises.]

21.   If it's right for you to litter, then it's wrong for you to preach concern for the environment.
      ∴ It isn't right for you to combine preaching concern for the environment with littering.   [Use L and P.]

22.   If you ought to be better than everyone else, then it's obligatory that everyone be better than everyone else.
      "Everyone is better than everyone else" is self-contradictory.
      ∴ It's all right for you not to be better than everyone else.   [Use Bx (for "x is better than everyone else") and u.]

23.   You ought not to combine braking with accelerating.
      You ought to brake.
      ∴ You ought to brake and not accelerate.   [Use B and A.]

24.   "Everyone breaks promises" is impossible.
      ∴ It's all right for there to be someone who doesn't break promises.   [Use Bx. Kant thought universal promise-breaking would be impossible, since no one would make promises if everyone broke them. But he wanted to draw the stronger conclusion that it's always wrong to break promises. See problem 16.]

25.   It's all right for you to punish Judy for the accident, only if Judy ought to have stopped her car more quickly.
      Judy couldn't have stopped her car more quickly.
      ∴ You ought not to punish Judy for the accident.   [Use P and S.]

26.   You ought to pay by check or pay by Mastercard.
      If your Mastercard is expired, then you ought not to pay by Mastercard.
      ∴ If your Mastercard is expired, then pay by check.   [Use C, M, and E.]

27.   You ought to help your neighbor.
      It ought to be that, if you (in fact) help your neighbor, then you say you'll help him.
      You don't help your neighbor.
      If you don't help your neighbor, then you ought not to say you'll help him.
      ∴ You ought to say you'll help him, and you ought not to say you'll help him.
      [Use H and S. Roderick Chisholm pointed out that this clearly invalid argument was provable in many systems of deontic logic. Is it provable in our system?]

28.   If you take logic, then you'll make mistakes.
      You ought not to make mistakes.
      ∴ You ought not to take logic.   [Use T and M.]

29.   If I ought to name you acting mayor because you served ten years on the city council, then I ought to name Jennifer acting mayor because she served ten years on the city council.
      I can't name both you and Jennifer as acting mayor.
      ∴ It's not the case that I ought to name you acting mayor because you served ten years on the city council.   [Use U and J.]

CHAPTER 10
Belief Logic

B elief logic is "logic" in an extended sense. Instead of studying what follows from what, belief logic studies patterns of consistent believing and willing; it generates consistency norms that prescribe that we be consistent in various ways. We'll start with a simplified system and then add refinements.

10.1 Belief translations

We'll use ":" to construct descriptive and imperative belief formulas:

> 1. The result of writing a small letter and then ":" and then a wff is a *descriptive* wff.
> 2. The result of writing an underlined small letter and then ":" and then a wff is an *imperative* wff.

Statements about beliefs translate into *descriptive* belief formulas:

$$\begin{array}{rcl} \text{You believe that A is true} & = & \text{u:A} \\ \text{You believe that A is false} & = & \text{u:}{\sim}\text{A} \\ \text{You don't believe that A is true} & = & {\sim}\text{u:A} \end{array}$$

If you don't believe that A is true (you refrain from believing A), then you needn't believe that A is false; maybe you take no position on A (neither believing A nor believing not-A). Here are further translations:

$$\begin{array}{rcl} \text{You don't believe A and you don't believe not-A} & = & ({\sim}\text{u:A} \cdot {\sim}\text{u:}{\sim}\text{A}) \\ \\ \text{You believe that you ought to do A} & = & \text{u:OA}\underline{\text{u}} \\ \text{Everyone believes that they ought to do A} & = & \text{(x)x:OAx} \\ \\ \text{You believe that if A then not-B} & = & \text{u:(A} \supset {\sim}\text{B)} \\ \text{If you believe A, then you don't believe B} & = & \text{(u:A} \supset {\sim}\text{u:B)} \end{array}$$

Since our belief logic generates norms *prescribing* consistency, it focuses on *imperative* belief formulas – which we express by underlining the small letter:

Believe that A is true	=	u:A
Believe that A is false	=	u:~A
Don't believe that A is true	=	~u:A
Don't believe A and don't believe not-A	=	(~u:A • ~u:~A)
Believe that you ought to do A	=	u:OAu
Let everyone believe that they ought to do A	=	(x)x:OAx

As before, we distinguish between if-then and don't-combine forms:

If you in fact believe A, then don't believe B	=	(u:A ⊃ ~u:B)
Don't combine believing A with believing B	=	~(u:A • u:B)

10.1a Exercise – LogiCola N (BM & BT)

Translate these sentences into wffs (use "u" for "you" and "G" for "There is a God").

You believe that there is a God. (You're a theist.)	u:G

1.   You believe that there is no God. (You're an atheist.)
2.   You take no position on whether there is a God. (You're an agnostic.)
3.   You don't believe that there is a God. (You're a non-theist.)
4.   You believe that "There is a God" is self-contradictory.
5.   Necessarily, if you're a theist then you aren't an atheist. (Is this statement true?)
6.   Believe that there is a God.
7.   If "There is a God" is self-contradictory, then don't believe that there is a God.
8.   If you believe A, then you don't believe not-A.
9.   If you believe A, then don't believe not-A.
10.   Don't combine believing A with believing not-A.

10.2 Belief proofs

There are three approaches that we might take to belief logic. On the first approach, belief logic would study what belief formulas validly follow from what other belief formulas. We might try to prove arguments such as this one:

You believe A.	u:A
∴ You don't believe not-A.	∴ ~u:~A

But even this is invalid, since people can be confused and illogical. Students and politicians can assert A and assert not-A almost in the same breath; just given that someone believes A, we can deduce little or nothing about what else the person believes. So this first approach is doomed from the start.

A second approach would study how people would believe if they were *completely consistent believers* – where this term is defined as follows:

Person X is a **completely consistent believer** if and only if:

- X believes some things,
- the set S of things that X believes is logically consistent, and
- X believes anything that follows logically from set S.

Our previous argument would be valid if we added, as an additional premise, that you're completely consistent:

> (You're a completely consistent believer.)
> You believe A.
> ∴ You don't believe not-A.

A belief logic of this sort would take "You're a completely consistent believer" as an implicit premise of its arguments. This premise would be assumed, even though it's false, to help us explore what belief patterns a consistent believer would follow. While this approach to belief logic works,[1] I prefer a third approach, in view of what I want to do in the next chapter.

My approach is to construct a belief logic that generates consistency imperatives like this one:

> ∴ Don't combine *believing A* with *believing not-A*.   ∴ ~($\underline{u}$:A · $\underline{u}$:~A)

My belief logic tells us to avoid inconsistent combinations. The above premiseless argument isn't "valid" in the normal sense; but it becomes valid if we add the premise, "You ought to be consistent." We'll assume such an implicit premise in all our belief logic arguments. So, when we call an argument "valid in our belief logic," we'll mean that it's valid if we assume this additional premise. Here are two further consistency norms that are provable:

$(\sim\Diamond(A \cdot B) \supset \sim(\underline{u}:A \cdot \underline{u}:B))$	=	Don't combine inconsistent beliefs.
	=	If A is inconsistent with B, then don't combine *believing A* with *believing B*.
$(\Box(A \supset B) \supset \sim(\underline{u}:A \cdot \sim\underline{u}:B))$	=	Don't believe something without believing what follows from it.
	=	If A logically entails B, then don't combine *believing A* with *not believing B*.

---

[1] Jaakko Hintikka used roughly this second approach in his classic *Knowledge and Belief* (Ithaca, New York: Cornell University Press, 1962).

Belief logic forbids combinations of believing or not-believing that would remove us further from the ranks of "completely consistent believers."

Belief logic uses belief worlds and two new inference rules. Suppose that we have a set of imperatives telling person X what to believe or refrain from believing. A **belief world**, relative to these imperatives, is a possible world that contains everything that X is told to believe. We'll represent a belief world by a string of one or more one or more instances of a small letter; "x," "xx," "xxx," and so on represent belief worlds of X ("y," "yy," "yyy," and so on similarly represent belief worlds of Y). A *world prefix* is any string of zero or more instances of letters from the set <W, D, a, b, c, ...> – where <a, b, c, ...> is the set of small letters.

So X's belief worlds, again, are possible worlds that contain everything that X is told to believe (by a given set of belief imperatives). So if X is told to believe A, then *all* his belief worlds have A. Now individual belief worlds may contain further statements. For example, if X is told to be neutral about A (not to believe A and not to believe not-A), then some of his belief worlds will have A and some will have not-A. What is common to all of X's belief worlds is what X is told to believe. Accordingly, we have two inference rules:

B+	If X is told to believe A, then all of X's belief worlds have A.	"Believe A" ⟺ "All belief worlds have A"
B-	If X is told to *refrain* from believing A, then some belief world of X has not-A.	"Refrain from believing A" ⟺ "Not all belief worlds have A" ⟺ "Some belief worlds have not-A"

X is told to believe inconsistently if we can't thus construct consistent belief worlds to mirror how X is told to believe. This might happen because (1) X is told to believe incompatible things, or (2) X is told to believe certain things and also told to refrain from believing what follows from them.

Rule B+ operates on *positive* imperative belief formulas; if X is told to believe A, then all of X's belief worlds have A. Here any wff can replace "A" and any small letter can replace "x":

$$\text{B+} \quad \boxed{\begin{array}{c} \underline{x}{:}A \;\rightarrow\; x \overset{\downarrow}{\therefore} A, \\ \text{use any string of x's} \end{array}}$$

The line with "x:A" can use any world prefix not containing small letters or "W"[1] – and the line with "∴ A" must use a world prefix that is the same except that it adds a string of one or more x's at the end.

---

[1] This proviso (about small letters and "W") blocks proofs of questionable wffs that place one imperative belief operator within another, like "b:~(c:A • c:~A)," or claim logical necessity for consistency imperatives, like "□~(x:A • x:~A)."

Rule B- operates on *negative* formulas; if X is told to *refrain* from believing A, then some belief world of X has not-A. Here any pair of contradictory wffs can replace "A"/"~A" and any small letter can replace "x":

B-

$$\sim \underline{x}{:}A \quad \rightarrow \quad \overset{\downarrow}{x} \therefore \sim A,$$

use a *new* string of x's

The line with "$\sim \underline{x}{:}A$" can use any world prefix not containing small letters or "W" – and the line with "$\therefore \sim A$" must use a world prefix that is the same except that it ends a *new* string (one not occurring in earlier lines) of one or more x's at the end.

Our proof strategy goes as follows:

- First use rule B- on *negative imperative belief formulas* (formulas that say to *refrain* from believing something). Use a new belief world each time. You can star (and then ignore) a line when you use B- on it.

- Then use B+ on *positive imperative belief formulas* (formulas that say to believe something). Use *each* old belief world of the person in question each time. (Use a single new belief world if you have no old ones.) Don't star a line when you use B+ on it.

Both rules operate only on *imperative* belief formulas (like "$\sim \underline{u}{:}A$" or "$\underline{u}{:}A$") – not on *descriptive* ones (like "$\sim u{:}A$" or "$u{:}A$"). Our belief worlds are about what you are *told* to believe – not about what you *actually* believe.

Here's an example of a proof:

∴ Don't combine believing A
   with believing not-A.

```
          [ ∴ ~(u:A · u:~A)      Valid
 *   1   ┌ asm: (u:A · u:~A)
     2   │  ∴ u:A    {from 1}
     3   │  ∴ u:~A   {from 1}
     4   │  u ∴ A    {from 2}    ← using B+
     5   └  u ∴ ~A   {from 3}    ← using B+
     6    ∴ ~(u:A · u:~A)   {from 1; 4 contradicts 5}
```

We assume the opposite of the conclusion – and then show that this assumption tells you to be inconsistent. Using rules B+ and B-, we try to construct a non-empty set of possible belief worlds such that (1) whatever you're told to believe is in *all* of the worlds, and (2) the denial of whatever you're told not to believe is in *at least one* of the worlds. Since this construction is impossible (lines 4 and 5 contradict), the assumption prescribes an inconsistent combination of belief attitudes. So belief logic tells us to avoid this combination.

Our proof doesn't show that the formula is logically necessary; instead, it shows that it follows from an implicit "One ought to be consistent" premise. Using rules B+ and B- is equivalent to assuming such an implicit premise.

Here's another proof:

A logically entails B.
∴ Don't combine believing
A with not believing B.

1	□(A ⊃ B)	**Valid**		
	[∴ ~(u:A • ~u:B)			
* 2	⌐ asm: (u:A • ~u:B)			
3	│ ∴ u:A {from 2}			
* 4	│ ∴ ~u:B {from 2}			
5	│ u ∴ ~B {from 4}	←	using B-
6	│ u ∴ A {from 3}	←	using B+
* 7	│ u ∴ (A ⊃ B) {from 1}			
8	⌐ u ∴ B {from 6 and 7}			
9	∴ ~(u:A • ~u:B) {from 2; 5 contradicts 8}			

This proof goes much like before. But now we first use rule B- on the negative belief formula in step 4 (and star this step) to get 5. Then we use rule B+ on the positive belief formula in step 3 to get 6.

Our consistency norms have a don't-combine form. They tell you to make your beliefs coherent with each other; but they don't say what beliefs to add or subtract to bring this about. Let's suppose that P (*premise*) logically entails C (*conclusion*); compare these three forms:

(u:P ⊃ u:C)   If you believe *premise*, then believe *conclusion*.
(~u:C ⊃ ~u:P)   If you don't believe *conclusion*, then don't believe *premise*.
~(u:P • ~u:C)   Don't combine believing *premise* with not believing *conclusion*.

Suppose you believe *premise* but don't believe *conclusion*; then you violate all three imperatives. What should you do? The first form tells you to believe *conclusion*; but maybe *conclusion* is irrational and you should reject both *premise* and *conclusion*. The second form tells you to drop *premise*; but maybe *premise* is solidly based and you should accept both *premise* and *conclusion*. So the first two forms can tell you to do the wrong thing. The third form is better; it simply forbids the inconsistent combination of believing *premise* but not believing *conclusion* – but it doesn't tell us what to do if we get into this forbidden combination.

Here's another example. Assume that A is logically inconsistent with B; compare these three forms:

(u:A ⊃ ~u:B)   If you believe A, then don't believe B.
(u:B ⊃ ~u:A)   If you believe B, then don't believe A.
~(u:A • u:B)   Don't combine believing A with believing B.

Suppose you believe A and also believe B, even though the two are inconsistent. The first form tells you to drop B, while the second tells you to drop A; but which you should drop depends on the situation. The last form is better; it simply tells us to avoid the inconsistent combination.

Doing proofs with different kinds of operator can be confusing. This chart tells what order to use in dropping operators:

First drop these weak operators:	Then drop these strong operators:
◇ ~<u>x</u>: R (∃x)	□ <u>x</u>: O (x)
Use new worlds/constants; star the old line.	Use old worlds/constants if you have them; don't star the old line.

Within each group, the dropping order doesn't matter – except that it's wise to drop "<u>x</u>:" and "O" before dropping the very strong "□."

Section 6.2 noted that our "substitute equals" rule can fail in arguments about beliefs. Consider this argument:

> Jones believes that Lincoln is on the penny.
> Lincoln is the first Republican US president.
> ∴ Jones believes that the first Republican US president is on the penny.

> j:Pl
> l=r
> ∴ j:Pr

If Jones is unaware that Lincoln was the first Republican president, the premises could be true while the conclusion is false. So the argument is invalid. But yet we can derive the conclusion from the premises using our substitute-equals rule. So we need to qualify this rule so it doesn't apply in belief contexts. From now on, the substitute-equals rule holds only if no interchanged instance of the constants occurs within a wff immediately preceded by ":" and then a small letter (underlined or not).

10.2a   Exercise – LogiCola OB

Say whether valid (and give a proof) or invalid (no refutation necessary).

> □(A ⊃ B)
> ∴ (u:A ⊃ <u>u</u>:B)

	1	□(A ⊃ B) **Invalid**
		[∴ (u:A ⊃ <u>u</u>:B)
*	2	asm: ~(u:A ⊃ <u>u</u>:B)
	3	∴ u:A {from 2}
*	4	∴ ~<u>u</u>:B {from 2}
	5	u ∴ ~B {from 4}
*	6	u ∴ (A ⊃ B) {from 1}
	7	u ∴ ~A {from 5 and 6}

Since rules B+ and B- work only on *imperative* belief formulas, we can't go from "u:A" in line 3 to "u ∴ A." The conclusion here has the faulty if-then form. Suppose that A entails B and you believe A; it doesn't follow that you should believe B – maybe you should reject A and also reject B.

1. ~◇(A · B)
    ∴ ~(u:A · u:B)

2. ~◇(A · B)
    ∴ (u:A ⊃ ~u:B)

3. ~◇(A · B)
    ∴ (u:A ⊃ ~u:B)

4. ~◇(A · B)
    ∴ (~u:A ∨ ~u:B)

5. ~◇(A · B)
    ∴ (u:~A ∨ u:~B)

6. □(A ⊃ B)
    u:A
    ∴ u:B

7. □(A ⊃ B)
    u:A
    ∴ u:B

8. □(A ⊃ B)
    ~u:~A
    ∴ ~u:~B

9. □(A ⊃ B)
    ~u:B
    ∴ u:~A

10. ~◇(A · B)
    ∴ ~(u:A · ~u:~B)

10.2b   Exercise – LogiCola OB

First appraise intuitively. Then translate into logic and say whether valid (and give a proof) or invalid (no refutation necessary).

1. A logically entails B.
    Don't believe B.
    ∴ Don't believe A.

2. You believe A.
    ∴ You don't believe not-A.

3. You believe A.
    ∴ Don't believe not-A.

4. ∴ If A is self-contradictory, then don't believe A.

5. ∴ Either believe A or believe not-A.

6. Believe A.
    ∴ Don't believe not-A.

7. ∴ Don't combine believe that A is true with not believing that A is possible.

8. (A and B) entails C.
    ∴ Don't combine believing A and believing B and not believing C.

9. A logically entails (B and C).
    Don't believe that B is true.
    ∴ Believe that A is false.

10. ∴ If A is true, then believe A.

10.3   Believing and willing

Now we'll expand belief logic to cover willing as well as believing. We'll do this by treating "willing" as *accepting an imperative* – just as we previously treated "believing" as *accepting an indicative*:

$$u{:}A \quad \begin{array}{l} = \text{ You accept (endorse, assent to, say in your heart) ``A is true.''} \\ = \text{ You believe that A.} \end{array}$$

$$u{:}\underline{A} \quad \begin{array}{l} = \text{ You accept (endorse, assent to, say in your heart) ``Let act A be done.''} \\ = \text{ You will that act A be done.} \end{array}$$

In translating "u:$\underline{A}$," we'll often use terms more specific than "will" – terms like "act," "resolve to act," or "desire."[1] Which of these fits depends on whether the imperative is present or future, and whether it applies to oneself or to another. Here are three examples:

If A is present:	u:A$\underline{u}$	=	You accept the imperative for you to do A now.
		=	You act (in order) to do A.
If A is future:	u:A$\underline{u}$	=	You accept the imperative for you to do A in the future.
		=	You're resolved to do A.
If u≠x:	u:A$\underline{x}$	=	You accept the imperative for X to do A.
		=	You desire (or want) that X do A.

And to accept "Would that I had done that" is to wish that you had done it.

There's a subtle difference between "u:A$\underline{u}$" and "Au":

| u:A$\underline{u}$ | = | You act (in order) to do A. |
| | = | You say in your heart, "Do A" (addressed to yourself). |

| Au | = | You do A. |

The first is about what you try or intend to do, while the second is about what you actually do (perhaps accidentally).

Section 9.3 noted that we'd lose important distinctions if we just prefixed "O" to indicatives. Something similar applies here. Consider these three wffs:

u:(∃x)(Kx · R$\underline{x}$)	=	You desire that some who kill *repent*.
	=	You say in your heart "Would that some who kill *repent*."
u:(∃x)(K$\underline{x}$ · Rx)	=	You desire that some *kill* who repent.
	=	You say in your heart "Would that some *kill* who repent."
u:(∃x)(K$\underline{x}$ · R$\underline{x}$)	=	You desire that some both *kill* and *repent*.
	=	You say in your heart "Would that some *kill* and *repent*."

The three are very different. The underlining shows which parts are desired: repenting, or killing, or killing-and-repenting. If we just attached "desire" to

---

[1] "Desire" and similar terms can have a *prima facie* sense ("I have some desire to do A") or an all-things-considered sense ("All things considered, I desire to do A"). Here I intend the all-things-considered sense.

indicative formulas, all three would translate the same way, as "You desire that (∃x)(Kx • Rx)" ("You desire that there's someone who both kills and repents"). So "desire" is better symbolized in terms of accepting an imperative.

This imperative formula *tells* you to will something:

$\underline{u{:}A}$ = Accept (endorse, assent to, say in your heart) "Let act A be done."
$\underline{u{:}A}$ = Will that act A be done.

Again, our translation can use terms more specific than "will":

If A is present:	$\underline{u}{:}A\underline{u}$	=	Accept the imperative for you to do A now.
		=	Act (in order) to do A.
If A is future:	$\underline{u}{:}A\underline{u}$	=	Accept the imperative for you to do A in the future.
		=	Be resolved to do A.
If u≠x:	$\underline{u}{:}A\underline{x}$	=	Accept the imperative for X to do A.
		=	Desire (or want) that X do A.

Be careful with underlining:

- Use underlining *after* ":" if the sentence is about *willing*.
- Use underlining *before* ":" to *tell* someone what to believe or will.

Here are the basic examples:

Indicatives		
u:A	=	You believe A.
u:$\underline{A}$	=	You will A.

Imperatives		
$\underline{u}$:A	=	Believe A.
$\underline{u}$:$\underline{A}$	=	Will A.

10.3a Exercise – LogiCola N (WM & WT)

Translate these English sentences into wffs (use "u" for "you" and "j" for "Jones").

Don't act to do A without believing that A would be all right.	$\sim(\underline{u}{:}A\underline{u} \cdot \sim u{:}RA\underline{u})$

1. You want Jones to sit down. [Use Sx for "x sits down."]
2. You think that Jones ought to sit down.
3. Eat nothing. [Use Exy for "x eats y."]
4. You resolve to eat nothing.
5. You fall down, but you don't act (in order) to fall down. [Use Fx.]
6. You act to kick the goal, but you don't in fact kick the goal. [Use Kx.]
7. If you believe that you ought to do A, then do A.
8. Don't combine believing that you ought to do A with not acting to do A.

9. Don't resolve to eat nothing. [Use Exy.]
10. Don't combine resolving to eat nothing with acting to eat this. [Use Exy and t.]
11. You're resolved that if killing were needed to save your family, then you wouldn't kill. [Use N and Kx.]
12. Do A, only if you want everyone to do A. (Act only as you'd want everyone to act.) [This is crude form of Kant's formula of universal law.]
13. If X does A to you, then do A to X. (Treat others as they treat you.) [Use Axy. This principle entails "If X knocks out your eye, then knock out X's eye."]
14. If you do A to X, then X will do A to you. (People will treat you as you treat them.) [Use Axy. This is often confused with the golden rule.]
15. If you want X to do A to you, then do A to X. (Treat others as you want to be treated.) [Use Axy. This is the "literal golden rule."]

10.4   Willing proofs

Besides inconsistency in beliefs, there is inconsistency in will. I have inconsistency in will, for example, if I have inconsistent desires, violate ends–means consistency, or have my moral beliefs conflict with how I live. Belief logic also generates norms about consistent willing.

Except for having more underlining, proofs with willing formulas work like before. Here's an example:

$\therefore$ Don't combine *believing* that it's wrong for you to do A with *acting* to do A.

$$[\ \therefore \sim(\underline{u}{:}O{\sim}A\underline{u} \cdot \underline{u}{:}A\underline{u}) \qquad \text{Valid}$$

```
 *   1  ┌ asm: (u:O~Au · u:Au)
     2  │  ∴ u:O~Au   {from 1}
     3  │  ∴ u:Au    {from 1}
     4  │  u ∴ O~Au   {from 2}
     5  │  u ∴ Au    {from 3}
     6  └  u ∴ ~Au    {from 4}
     7  ∴ ~(u:O~Au · u:Au)   {from 1;
             5 contradicts 6}
```

This formula forbids combining these two:

believing that it's wrong to do A		acting (in order) to do A

The second part is expressed as "$\underline{u}{:}A\underline{u}$" (which is about what you try or intend to do) and not "$A\underline{u}$" (which is about what you actually do, perhaps accidentally). The faulty translation "$\sim(\underline{u}{:}O{\sim}A\underline{u} \cdot A\underline{u})$" forbids unintentionally doing what one thinks is wrong; there's no inconsistency in this, except maybe externally. The correct version forbids this inconsistent combination: thinking that A is wrong and at the same time acting with the intention of doing A.

10.4a   Exercise – LogiCola OW

Say whether valid (and give a proof) or invalid (no refutation necessary).

∴ (u:O~A<u>u</u> ⊃ ~<u>u</u>:A<u>u</u>)

```
       [ ∴ (u:O~Au ⊃ ~u:Au)   Invalid
*   1    asm: ~(u:O~Au ⊃ ~u:Au)
    2    ∴ u:O~Au   {from 1}
    3    ∴ u:Au   {from 1}
    4    u ∴ Au   {from 3}
```

This formula says: "If you believe that it's wrong for you to do A, then don't act to do A"; this leads to absurdities because it doesn't have the correct don't-combine form and because your belief may be mistaken. Maybe you believe that it's wrong to treat people fairly; then this formula tells you not to act to treat them fairly.

1. ∴ ~(u:A · u:~A)

2. ∴ u:(Ba ⊃ RBa)

3. ∴ (u:Ba ∨ u:~Ba)

4. ∴ ~((u:(A ⊃ B) · u:A) · ~u:B)

5.   u:(x)OAx
   ∴ u:Au

6.   ~u:Au
   ∴ ~u:OAu

7. ∴ u:(OAu ⊃ Au)

8. ∴ (u:Au ∨ ~u:OAu)

9.   u:Au
   ∴ ~u:O~Au

10.   □(A ⊃ B)
   ∴ ~(u:OA · ~u:B)

10.4b   Exercise – LogiCola OW

First appraise intuitively. Then translate into logic and say whether valid (and give a proof) or invalid (no refutation necessary).

1. ∴ If you believe that you ought to do A, then do A.   [This if-then form of the "Follow your conscience" principle is faulty: it tells people to commit mass murder if they believe that they ought to do this.]

2. ∴ Don't combine *believing* that you ought to do A with *not acting* to do A.   [This don't-combine form of "Follow your conscience" is better.]

3. ∴ Don't combine resolving to eat nothing with acting to eat this.   [Use Exy and t.]

4. ∴ Don't combine believing that everyone ought to do A with not acting/resolving to do A yourself.   [This is belief logic's version of "Practice what you preach."]

5.   "Attain this end" entails "If taking this means is needed to attain this end, then take this means."
   ∴ Don't combine (1) *wanting* to attain this end and (2) *believing* that taking this means is needed to attain this end and (3) *not acting* to take this means.   [Use E for "You attain this end," N for "Taking this means is needed to attain this end," M for "You take this means," and u. The conclusion is an ends–means consistency imperative.]

6. "Attain this end" entails "If taking this means is needed to attain this end, then take this means."
∴ If you want to attain this end and believe that taking this means is needed to attain this end, then act to take this means. [Use E, N, M, and u.]

7. ∴ Don't accept "It's wrong for anyone to kill," without being resolved that if killing were needed to save your family, then you wouldn't kill. [Use Kx and N.]

8. ∴ Don't accept "It's wrong for anyone to kill," without it being the case that if killing were needed to save your family then you wouldn't kill. [Use Kx and N. A draft board challenged a pacifist friend of mine, "If killing were needed to save your family, then would you kill?" My friend answered, "I don't know – I might lose control and kill (it's hard to predict what you'll do in a panic situation); but I now firmly hope and resolve that I wouldn't kill." Maybe my friend didn't satisfy this present formula; but he satisfied the previous one.]

9. ∴ Don't combine accepting "It's wrong for Jones to do A" with wanting Jones to do A. [Use j.]

10. ∴ Don't combine believing that the state ought to execute all murderers with not desiring that if your friend is a murderer then the state execute your friend. [Use s for "the state," Exy for "x executes y," Mx for "x is a murderer," f for "your friend," and u for "you."]

11. ∴ Don't combine acting to do A with not accepting that A is all right.

12. ∴ If you act to do A, then accept that act A is all right.

13. ∴ Don't combine acting to do A with not accepting that A is obligatory.

14. Believe that you ought to do A.
∴ Act to do A.

15. "It's all right for you to do A" entails "It's obligatory that everyone do A."
∴ Don't combine acting to do A with not willing that everyone do A. [The conclusion is a crude version of Kant's formula of universal law. To see that the premise and conclusion are questionable, substitute "become a doctor" for "do A" in both. We'll see a better version of the formula in the next chapter.]

10.5 Rationality translations

Beliefs can be "evident" or "reasonable" for a given person. As I shade my eyes from the bright sun, my belief that it's sunny is *evident*; it's very solidly grounded. As I hear the prediction of rain, my belief that it will rain is *reasonable*; my belief accords with reason but isn't solid enough to be evident. "Evident" expresses a higher certitude than does "reasonable." We'll symbolize these two notions as follows:

	=	A is evident to you.
Ou:A	=	It's obligatory (rationally required) that you believe A.
	=	Insofar as intellectual considerations are concerned (including your experiences), you ought to believe A.

	=	A is reasonable for you to believe.
Ru:A	=	It's all right (rationally permissible) that you believe A.
	=	Insofar as intellectual considerations are concerned (including your experiences), it would be all right for you to believe A.

Neither entails that you believe A; to say that a proposition A that you believe is evident/reasonable, we'll use "(u:A · Ou:A)"/"(u:A · Ru:A)." "Evident" and "reasonable" are relational; "It's raining" might be evident to one person (perhaps to someone outside) but not to another (perhaps it isn't evident to someone inside with no windows).

Here are further translations:

It would be unreasonable for you to believe A	=	~Ru:A
It's obligatory that you not believe A	=	O~u:A
It would be reasonable for you to take no position on A	=	R(~u:A · ~u:~A)
It's evident to you that if A then B	=	Ou:(A ⊃ B)
If it's evident to you that A, then it's evident to you that B	=	(Ou:A ⊃ Ou:B)
You ought not to combine believing A with believing not-A	=	O~(u:A · u:~A)

Since "O" and "R" attach only to imperatives, "Ou:A" and "Ru:A" aren't wffs. We can almost define "knowledge" in this simple way:

knowledge	=	evident true belief
You know that A	=	A is evident to you, A is true, and you believe A.
uKA	=	(Ou:A · (A · u:A))

Knowing requires more than just true belief; if you guess right, you have not knowledge, but only true belief. Knowledge must be well-grounded; it must be more than just *reasonable* (permitted by the evidence), it must be *evident* (required by the evidence). The claim that *knowledge is evident true belief* is plausible. But there are cases (like example 10 of Section 10.6b) where we have one but not the other. So this simple definition of "knowledge" is flawed; but it's still a useful approximation.

10.5a   Exercise – LogiCola N (RM & RT)

Translate these English sentences into wffs. When an example says a belief is evident or reasonable, but don't say *to whom*, assume it means evident or reasonable *to you*.

You ought to want Jones to sit down.	O̲u:S̲j

We can paraphrase the sentence as "It's obligatory that you say in your heart 'Would that Jones sit down.'"

1. You ought to believe that Jones is sitting down.
2. It's evident to you that Jones is sitting down.
3. It's reasonable for you to believe that Jones ought to sit down.
4. Belief in God is reasonable (for you).   [Use G.]
5. Belief in God is unreasonable for everyone.
6. It isn't reasonable for you to believe that belief in God is unreasonable for everyone.
7. Belief in God is reasonable only if "There is a God" is logically consistent.
8. You ought not to combine believing that there is a God with not believing that "There is a God" is logically consistent.
9. You ought not to combine believing that you ought to do A with not acting to do A.
10. You know that x=x.   [Use the flawed definition of knowledge given previously.]
11. If agnosticism is reasonable, then theism isn't evident.   [Agnosticism = not believing G and not believing not-G; theism = believing G.]
12. You have a true belief that A.   [You believe that A, and it is true that A.]
13. You mistakenly believe A.
14. It would be impossible for you mistakenly to believe A.
15. A is evident to you, if and only if it would be impossible for you mistakenly to believe A.   [This idea is attractive but quickly leads to skepticism.]
16. It's logically possible that you have a belief A that is evident to you and yet false.
17. It's evident to all that if they doubt then they exist.   [Use Dx and Ex.]
18. If A entails B, and B is unreasonable, then A is unreasonable.
19. It's permissible for you to do A, only if you want everyone to do A.
20. If you want X to do A to you, then you ought to do A to X.   [Use Axy. This one and the next are versions of the golden rule.]
21. You ought not to combine acting to do A to X with wanting X not to do A to you.
22. It's necessary that if you're in pain then it's evident to you that you're in pain. [Use Px. This claims that "I'm in pain" is a self-justifying belief. Many think that there are two kinds of self-justifying beliefs: those of experience (as in this example) and those of reason (as in the next example).]
23. It's necessary that, if you believe that x=x, then it's evident to you that x=x. [Perhaps believing "x=x" entails understanding it, and this makes it evident.]
24. If you have no reason to doubt your perceptions and it's evident to you that you believe that you see a red object, then it's evident to you that there is an actual red object.   [Use Dx for "x has reason to doubt his or her perceptions," Sx for "x sees a red object," and R for "There is an actual red object." Roderick Chisholm claimed that we need evidential principles like this (but more complex) to show how beliefs about external objects are based on beliefs about perceptions.]
25. If it's evident to you that Jenny shows pain behavior and you have no reason to doubt her sincerity, then it's evident to you that Jenny feels pain.   [Use Bx, Dx, Fx, and j. This exemplifies an evidential principle about knowing other minds.]

10.6 Rationality proofs

Deontic belief proofs, while not requiring further inference rules, often use complex world prefixes like "Du" or "Duu." Here's an example:

[∴ O~(u:O~Au · u:Au)   Valid

*	1	⌐ asm: ~O~(u:O~Au · u:Au)
*	2	∴ R(u:O~Au · u:Au) {from 1}
*	3	D ∴ (u:O~Au · u:Au) {from 2}
	4	D ∴ u:O~Au {from 3}
	5	D ∴ u:Au {from 3}
	6	Du ∴ O~Au {from 4}
	7	Du ∴ Au {from 5}
	8	└ Du ∴ ~Au {from 6}
	9	∴ O~(u:O~Au · u:Au) {from 1; 7 contradicts 8}

∴ You ought not to combine *believing* that it's wrong for you to do A with *acting* to do A.

(a conscientiousness principle)

We get to line 5 using propositional and deontic rules. Lines 6 and 7 follow using rule B+. Here we write belief world prefix "u" after the deontic world prefix "D" used in lines 4 and 5; world Du is a belief world of u that depends on what deontic world D tells u to accept. We soon get a contradiction.

"O~(u:O~Au · u:Au)" is a **formal ethical principle** – an ethical principle that can be formulated using the abstract notions of our logical systems plus variables (like "u" and "A") that stand for any person and action. The next chapter will focus on another formal ethical principle – the golden rule.

10.6a   Exercise – LogiCola O (R & M)

Say whether valid (and give a proof) or invalid (no refutation necessary).

	1	Ru:O(A · B) **Valid**
		[∴ Ru:OA
*	2	⌐ asm: ~Ru:OA
	3	∴ O~u:OA {from 2}
	4	D ∴ u:O(A · B) {from 1}
*	5	D ∴ ~u:OA {from 3}
*	6	Du ∴ ~OA {from 5}
	7	Du ∴ O(A · B) {from 4}
*	8	Du ∴ R~A {from 6}
	9	DuD ∴ ~A {from 8}
	10	DuD ∴ (A · B) {from 7}
	11	└ DuD ∴ A {from 10}
	12	∴ Ru:OA {from 2; 9 contradicts 11}

Ru:O(A · B)
∴ Ru:OA

(If you can follow this example, you needn't fear proofs involving complex world prefixes.)

1. □(A ⊃ B)
   ~Ru:B
   ∴ ~Ru:A

2. O~u:A
   ∴ Ou:~A

3. R(~u:A · ~u:~A)
   ∴ ~Ou:A

4. Ru:~A
   ∴ R~u:A

5. Oa:(C · D)
   ∴ Ob:C

6. ∴ O~(u:A · ~u:◊A)

7. ∴ (Ru:A ⊃ ◊A)

8. □(A ⊃ B)
   ∴ (R~u:B ⊃ Ru:~A)

9. Ru:OAu
   ∴ Ru:◊Au

10. Ou:(A ⊃ OBu)
    ∴ ~(u:A · ~u:Bu)

10.6b   Exercise – LogiCola O (R & M)

First appraise intuitively. Then translate into logic and say whether valid (and give a proof) or invalid (no refutation necessary). Use G for "There is a God" and u for "you." When an example says a belief is evident or reasonable, but don't say *to whom*, assume it means evident or reasonable *to you*.

1. Theism is evident.
   ∴ Atheism is unreasonable.   [Theism = believing G; atheism = believing not-G.]

2. Theism isn't evident.
   ∴ Atheism is reasonable.

3. ∴ You ought not to combine *believing* you ought to do A with *not acting* to do A.

4. ∴ If you believe you ought to do A, then you ought to do A.

5. "All men are endowed by their creator with certain unalienable rights" entails "There is a creator."
   It would be reasonable not to accept "There is a creator."
   ∴ "All men are endowed by their creator with certain unalienable rights" isn't evident.   [Use E and C. The opening lines of the US Declaration of Independence claim E to be self-evident.]

6. It would be reasonable for you to believe that A is true.
   It would be reasonable for you to believe that B is true.
   ∴ It would be reasonable for you to believe that A and B are both true.

7. "If I'm hallucinating, then physical objects aren't as they appear to me" is evident to me.
   It isn't evident to me that I'm not hallucinating.
   ∴ It isn't evident to me that physical objects are as they appear to me.   [Use H, P, and i. This argument for skepticism is essentially from Descartes.]

8. "If I'm hallucinating, then physical objects aren't as they appear to me" is evident to me.
   If I have no special reason to doubt my perceptions, then it's evident to me that physical objects are as they appear to me.
   I have no special reason to doubt my perceptions.
   ∴ It's evident to me that I'm not hallucinating.   [Use H, P, D, and i. This is John Pollock's answer to the previous argument.]

9. It's evident to you that taking this means is needed to attain this end.
    "Attain this end" entails "If taking this means is needed to attain this end, then take this means."
    ∴ You ought not to combine wanting to attain this end with not acting to take this means.   [Use N for "Taking this means is needed to attain this end," E for "You attain this end," M for "You take this means," and u.]

10. Al believes that Smith owns a Ford.
    It's evident to Al that Smith owns a Ford.
    Smith doesn't own a Ford.
    Smith owns a Chevy.
    Al believes that Smith owns a Ford or a Chevy.
    Al doesn't know that Smith owns a Ford or a Chevy.
    ∴ Al has an evident true belief that Smith owns a Ford or a Chevy; but Al doesn't know that Smith owns a Ford or a Chevy.   [Use a for "Al," F for "Smith owns a Ford," C for "Smith owns a Chevy," and K for "Al knows that Smith owns a Ford or a Chevy." This argument from Edmund Gettier attacks the definition of knowledge as evident true belief.]

11. It's evident to you that if it's all right for you to hit Jones then it's all right for Jones to hit you.
    ∴ Don't combine acting to hit Jones with believing that it would be wrong for Jones to hit you.   [Use Hxy, u, and j. The premise is normally true; but it could be false if you and Jones are in different situations (maybe Jones needs to be hit to dislodge food he's choking on). The conclusion resembles the golden rule.]

12. ∴ It's reasonable to want A to be done, only if it's reasonable to believe that A would be all right.

13. It's evident that A is true.
    ∴ A is true.

14. It's reasonable to combine believing that there is a perfect God with believing T.
    T entails that there's evil in the world.
    ∴ It's reasonable to combine believing that there is a perfect God with believing that there's evil in the world.   [Use G, T, and E. Here T (for "theodicy") is a reasonable explanation of why God permits evil. T might say: "The world has evil because God, who is perfect, wants us to make significant free choices to struggle to bring a half-completed world toward its fulfillment; moral evil comes from the abuse of human freedom and physical evil from the half-completed state of the world."]

15. It's evident to you that if there are moral obligations then there's free will.
    ∴ Don't combine accepting that there are moral obligations with not accepting that there's free will.   [Use M and F.]

16. Theism is reasonable.
    ∴ Atheism is unreasonable.

17. Theism is evident.
   ∴ Agnosticism is unreasonable.   [Agnosticism = not believing G and not believing not-G.]

18. ∴ It's reasonable for you to believe that God exists, only if "God exists" isn't self-contradictory.   [Belief logic regards a belief as "reasonable" only if *in fact* it's consistent. In a more subjective sense, someone could "reasonably" believe a proposition that's reasonably but incorrectly taken to be consistent.]

19. ∴ If A is unreasonable, then don't believe A.

20. You ought not to combine accepting A with not accepting B.
   ∴ If you accept A, then accept B.

21. ∴ You ought not to combine wanting A not to be done with believing that A would be all right.

22. It's reasonable not to believe that there is an external world.
   ∴ It's reasonable to believe that there's no external world.   [Use E.]

23. It's reasonable to believe that A ought to be done.
   ∴ It's reasonable to want A to be done.

24. ∴ Either theism is reasonable or atheism is reasonable.

25. It's evident to you that if the phone is ringing then you ought to answer it.
     It's evident to you that the phone is ringing.
   ∴ Act on the imperative "Answer the phone."   [Use P and Ax.]

26. A entails B.
     Believing A would be reasonable.
   ∴ Believing B would be reasonable.

27. Atheism isn't evident.
   ∴ Theism is reasonable.

28. Atheism is unreasonable.
     Agnosticism is unreasonable.
   ∴ Theism is evident.

29. A entails B.
     You accept A.
     It's unreasonable for you to accept B.
   ∴ Don't accept A, and don't accept B.

30. It would be reasonable for anyone to believe A.
   ∴ It would be reasonable for everyone to believe A.   [Imagine a controversial issue where everyone has the same evidence. Could it be more reasonable for the community to disagree? If so, the premises of this argument might be true but the conclusion false.]

10.7   A sophisticated system

The system of belief logic that we've developed is oversimplified in three ways. We'll now sketch a more sophisticated system.

First, our "One ought to be consistent" principle requires qualification. For the most part, we do have a duty to be consistent. But, since "ought" implies "can," this duty is nullified when we're unable to be consistent; such inability can come from emotional turmoil or our incapacity to grasp complex inferences. And the obligation to be consistent can be overridden by other factors; if Dr Evil would destroy the world unless we were inconsistent in some respect, then surely our duty to be consistent would be overridden. And the duty to be consistent applies, when it does, only to persons; yet our principles so far would entail that rocks and trees also have a duty to be consistent.

For these reasons, it would be better to qualify our "One ought to be consistent" principle, as in the following formulation:[1]

> If X is a person who is able to be consistent in certain ways, who does (or should) grasp the logical relationships involved, and whose being consistent in these ways wouldn't have disastrous consequences, then X ought to be consistent in these ways.

Let's abbreviate the qualification in the box ("X is ...") as "Px." Then we can reformulate our inference rules by adding a required "Px" premise:

$$B+ \quad \boxed{\begin{array}{l} \text{x:A, Px} \quad \rightarrow \quad \overset{\downarrow}{\text{x} \therefore \text{A,}} \\ \text{use any string of x's} \end{array}} \qquad B- \quad \boxed{\begin{array}{l} \sim\text{x:A, Px} \quad \rightarrow \quad \overset{\downarrow}{\text{x} \therefore \sim\text{A,}} \\ \text{use a } new \text{ string of x's} \end{array}}$$

So now we'd need a "Px" premise to apply either rule. Then the following argument would be provable – but it wouldn't be without premise 2:

A entails B.
You're a person who is able to be consistent ....
∴ You ought not to combine believing A with not believing B.

$\square(A \supset B)$
Pu
$\therefore O\sim(\underline{u}{:}A \cdot \sim\underline{u}{:}B)$

If we made these changes, we'd have to qualify most of our arguments with a premise like "Pu" – or else our arguments would be invalid.

A second problem is that our system can prove a questionable **conjunctivity principle:**

---

[1] Section 2.3 of my *Formal Ethics* (London and New York: Routledge, 1996) has additional qualifications.

You ought not to combine believing A and believing B and not believing (A · B). $O\sim((\underline{u}{:}A \cdot \underline{u}{:}B) \cdot \sim\underline{u}{:}(A \cdot B))$

This leads to questionable results in "the lottery paradox." Suppose that eight people have an equal chance to win a lottery. You know that someone of the eight will win; but the probability is against any given person winning. Presumably it could be reasonable for you to accept statements 1 to 8 without also accepting statement 9 (which means "None of the eight will win"):

1. Person 1 won't win.
2. Person 2 won't win.
3. Person 3 won't win.
4. Person 4 won't win.
5. Person 5 won't win.
6. Person 6 won't win.
7. Person 7 won't win.
8. Person 8 won't win.
9. Person 1 won't win, person 2 won't win, person 3 won't win, person 4 won't win, person 5 won't win, person 6 won't win, person 7 won't win, and person 8 won't win.

But multiple uses of our conjunctivity principle would entail that one ought not to accept statements 1 to 8 without also accepting their conjunction 9. So the conjunctivity principle, which is provable using our rules B+ and B-, sometimes leads to questionable results.

I'm not completely convinced that it is reasonable to accept statements 1 to 8 but not accept 9. If it *is* reasonable, then we have to reject the conjunctivity principle; this would force us to modify our ideas on what sort of consistency is desirable. Let's call the ideal of "completely consistent believer" defined in Section 10.2 *broad consistency*. Perhaps we should strive, not for broad consistency, but for *narrow consistency*. To explain this, let S be the non-empty set of indicatives and imperatives that X accepts; then:

X is *broadly consistent* just if:	X is *narrowly consistent* just if:
• set S is logically consistent, and • X accepts anything that follows from set S.	• every pair of items of set S is logically consistent, and • X accepts anything that follows from any single item of set S.

Believing eight lottery statements but not their conjunction is narrowly consistent, but it isn't broadly consistent.

To have our rules mirror the ideal of narrow consistency, we'd add an additional proviso to rule B+: "The world prefix in the derived step cannot have occurred more than once in earlier lines." With this change, only a few examples in this chapter would cease being provable. And many of these could still be salvaged by adding an additional conjunctivity premise like the following (which would be true in many cases):

You ought not to combine believing A and believing B and not believing (A · B). $O{\sim}((\underline{u}{:}A \cdot \underline{u}{:}B) \cdot {\sim}\underline{u}{:}(A \cdot B))$

Conjunctivity presumably fails only in rare lottery-type cases.

The third problem is that we've been translating these two statements in the same way, as "O$\underline{u}$:A," even though they don't mean the same thing:

"You ought to believe A."   "A is evident to you."

Suppose that you have an obligation to trust your wife and give her the benefit of every reasonable doubt. It could be that you *ought* to believe what she says, even though the evidence isn't so strong as to make this belief *evident*. So there's a difference between "ought to believe" and "evident."

So it may be better to use a different symbol (perhaps "O*") for "evident":

$O\underline{u}{:}A$ = You ought to believe A.
  = All things considered, you ought to believe A.

$O^*\underline{u}{:}A$ = A is evident to you.
  = Insofar as intellectual considerations are concerned (including your experiences), you ought to believe A.

"O" is an all-things-considered "ought," while "O*" is a *prima facie* "ought" that considers only the intellectual basis for the belief. If we added "O*" to our system, we'd need corresponding deontic inference rules for it. Since "O*$\underline{A}$" is a *prima facie* "ought," it wouldn't entail the corresponding imperative or commit one to action; so we'd have to weaken the rule for dropping "O*" so we couldn't derive "$\underline{u}$:A" from "O*$\underline{u}$:A."

These refinements would overcome problems but make our system much harder to use. We seldom need the refinements. So we'll keep the naïve belief logic of earlier sections as our "official system" and build on it in the next chapter. But we'll be conscious that this system is oversimplified in various ways. If and when the naïve system gives questionable results, we can appeal to the sophisticated system to clear things up.

CHAPTER 11
A Formalized Ethical Theory

This chapter gives a precise logical formulation of an ethical theory, one that builds on ideas from Immanuel Kant and R. M. Hare.[1] This gives an example of how to use logic to formalize larger philosophical views. As in the chapter on belief logic, we'll systematize consistency norms. But now our norms will be stronger and will feature a version of the golden rule (roughly, "Treat others as you want to be treated").

We'll first consider practical rationality in general terms, highlighting the role of consistency. Then we'll focus on one consistency principle: the golden rule. After seeing problems with the usual wording, we'll formulate a better golden rule and give an intuitive argument for it. We'll then add logical machinery (symbols and inference rules) to formalize these ideas. We'll end by giving a formal proof of the golden rule in logical symbols.

11.1   Practical rationality

While non-rational forces (like emotions and cultural influences) play a big role in our moral thinking, rational forces also can be important. Here I'll distinguish three central dimensions of practical rationality: factual understanding, imagination (role reversal), and consistency.

Factual understanding requires that we know the facts of the case: circumstances, alternatives, consequences, and so on. To the extent that we're misinformed or ignorant, our moral thinking is flawed. Of course, we can never know *all* the facts; and often we have no time to research a problem and must act quickly. But we can act out of greater or lesser knowledge. Other things being equal, a more informed judgment is a more rational one.

We also need to understand ourselves, and how our feelings and moral beliefs originated; this is important because we can to some extent neutralize

---

[1] My approach to moral rationality is presented here in a sketchy and incomplete manner. My *Formal Ethics* (London and New York: Routledge, 1996) has a fuller account; Chapters 7 to 9 of my *Ethics: A Contemporary Introduction* (London and New York: Routledge, 1998) present the same material more simply. See also Immanuel Kant's *Groundwork of the Metaphysics of Morals* (New York: Harper & Row, 1964) and R. M. Hare's *Freedom and Reason* (New York: Oxford University Press, 1963).

our biases if we understand their origin. For example, some people are hostile toward a group because they were taught this when they were young. Their attitudes might change if they understood the source of their hostility and broadened their experience; if so, then their attitudes are less rational – since they exist because of a lack of self-knowledge and experience.

Imagination (role reversal) is a vivid and accurate awareness of what it would be like to be in the place of those affected by our actions. This differs from just knowing facts. So in dealing with poor people, besides knowing facts about them, we also need to appreciate and envision what these facts mean to their lives; movies, literature, and personal experience can help us to visualize another's life. We also need to appreciate future consequences of our actions on ourselves; knowing that drugs would have harmful effects on us differs from being able to imagine these effects in a vivid and accurate way.

Consistency demands a coherence among our beliefs, between our ends and means, and between our moral judgments and how we live; it also, I'll argue, includes golden-rule consistency – that we not act toward another in a way that we're unwilling to be treated in the same situation. The rest of this chapter will focus on consistency;[1] as a logician, I have more to say about this dimension. But keep in mind that we need all the dimensions working together for our practical thinking to be fully reasonable.

Holistic rationality includes all these aspects of rationality – and others that I haven't mentioned. A more traditional term is "practical wisdom." We are "rational" (or "wise") in our ethical beliefs to the extent that we satisfy a variety of considerations. Only God (knowing everything, imagining vividly the inner life of each person, being consistent in every way, and so on) could satisfy them completely. We humans find practical rationality difficult, and we satisfy its requirements only to a lesser or greater degree.

To dramatize the problem of practical rationality, let's imagine that you were brought up in a racist society that practiced Nazism or slavery or apartheid. Suppose that racist norms were instilled in your moral intuitions; so, because of your training, it seemed "intuitively obvious" to you that it was right for whites to enslave blacks, but not vice versa. Is there any way that you could use your intelligence to criticize these racist norms? If so, how?

Let's consider parallel cases in other areas. Suppose that your society taught you that there was a highest prime number – or that the earth was flat. You could in principle use your intelligence to criticize these beliefs. There's a good argument going back to Euclid that there's no highest prime (see the end of Section 4.2b); and there are indirect signs that the earth is round – or you could build a space ship and go out and look at the earth. In practice, few people will have the independence, energy, and intelligence to pursue such ideas; but eventually someone will, and the word will spread. The morality case is similar.

---

[1] Appeals to consistency in ethics are frequently obscure and dubious. Part of my goal is to propose clear and defensible consistency norms that can be useful in ethical thinking.

To rationally criticize inherited racist norms requires the things we mentioned before: *factual accuracy* (understanding facts about race and how the victims suffer), *imagination* (role reversal – visualizing what it would be like for ourselves and our families to be treated in like manner), and *consistency* (especially the golden rule – which tells us to treat others only as we are willing to be treated ourselves in the same situation). Historically, people who criticized racist norms often appealed to the golden rule and to these other factors.

11.2   Consistency

Consistency itself has many dimensions. These include consistency among beliefs, between ends and means, and between our moral judgments and how we live. Our chapter on belief logic touched on these three consistency norms:[1]

> **Logicality**: Avoid inconsistency in beliefs.
>
> **Ends–means consistency**: Keep your means in harmony with your ends.
>
> **Conscientiousness**: Keep your actions, resolutions, and desires in harmony with your moral beliefs.

Our belief logic contains *logicality* norms forbidding inconsistent beliefs:

$$(\sim\Diamond(A \cdot B) \supset \sim(\underline{u}{:}A \cdot \underline{u}{:}B))$$

= Don't combine inconsistent beliefs.
= If A is inconsistent with B, then don't combine *believing A* with *believing B*.

$$(\Box(A \supset B) \supset \sim(\underline{u}{:}A \cdot \sim\underline{u}{:}B))$$

= Don't believe something without believing what follows from it.
= If A logically entails B, then don't combine *believing A* with *not believing B*.

We often appeal to such things when we argue about ethics. You say that such and such is wrong, and I ask why. You respond with an argument consisting in a factual premise, a moral premise, and a moral conclusion. The factual premise is challengeable on grounds of factual accuracy. The moral premise is challengeable on grounds of consistency; we look for cases where you'd reject the implications of your own principle (perhaps cases where the principle applies to how we should treat you).

---

[1] We noted at the end of the last chapter that consistency duties require qualifiers like "insofar as you are able to be consistent in these ways and no disaster would result from so doing ...." This also applies to the golden rule. We'll regard such a qualifier as implicit throughout.

Here's a concrete example. When I was ten years old, I heard a racist argue something like this: "Blacks ought to be treated poorly, because they're inferior." How can we respond? Should we dispute the racist's factual premise and say "All races are genetically equal"? Or should we counter with our own moral principle and say "People of all races ought to be treated equally"? Either strategy will likely lead to a stalemate, where the racist has his premises and we have ours, and neither side can convince the other.

I suggest instead that we formulate the racist's argument clearly and then watch it explode in his face. First we need to clarify what the racist means by "inferior." Is "being inferior" a matter of IQ, education, wealth, physical strength, or what? Let's suppose that he defines "inferior" as "having an IQ of less than 80." Since the racist's conclusion is about how *all* blacks ought to be treated, his premises also have to use "all." So his argument goes:

> All blacks have an IQ of less than 80.
> All who have an IQ of less than 80 ought to be treated poorly.
> ∴ All blacks ought to be treated poorly.

While this is valid, we can easily appeal to factual accuracy against premise 1 and to consistency against premise 2. Regarding consistency, we could ask the racist whether he accepts what his premise 2 logically entails about whites:

> All who have an IQ of less than 80 ought to be treated poorly. .
> ∴ All *whites* who have an IQ of less than 80 ought to be treated poorly.

The racist won't accept this conclusion. But then he inconsistently believes a premise but refuses to believe what follows from it. To restore consistency, he must either give up his principle or else accept its implications about whites. It would be very difficult for the racist to reformulate his argument to avoid such objections; he needs some criterion that crisply divides the races (as IQ doesn't) and that he applies consistently (including to people of his own race).

Appealing to consistency in beliefs is often useful in moral disputes. The appeal is powerful, since it doesn't presume material moral premises (which the other party may reject) but just points out problems in one's belief system. But at times, of course, consistency won't do the job by itself and we need other ways to carry the argument further.

Our belief logic can prove this *ends–means consistency* argument (example 5 of Section 10.4b):

$\Box(\underline{E} \supset (N \supset \underline{M}))$	"Attain this end" entails "If taking this means is needed to attain this end, then take this means."
$\therefore \sim((\underline{u}{:}\underline{E} \cdot \underline{u}{:}N) \cdot \sim\underline{u}{:}\underline{M})$	$\therefore$ Don't combine (1) *wanting* to attain this end and (2) *believing* that taking this means is needed to attain this end and (3) *not acting* to take this means.

It's easy to violate the conclusion. Many want to lose weight and believe that eating less is needed to do this; yet they don't take steps to eat less. Insofar as we violate ends–means consistency, we're flawed in our rationality. People of all cultures implicitly recognize this – or else they wouldn't survive.

We could incorporate ends–means consistency more fully into our approach if we added the symbol "⊡" for "It's causally necessary that."[1] Then we could translate "Taking this means is needed to attain this end" as "⊡(~M ⊃ ~E)" ("It's causally necessary that if you don't take this means then you won't attain this end"); our premise above would then be "□(E ⊃ (⊡(~M ⊃ ~E) ⊃ M))." If we added rules of inference to prove this premise, then this form of the conclusion would be provable by itself:

$$\sim((\underline{u}{:}\underline{E} \cdot \underline{u}{:}⊡(\sim M \supset \sim E)) \cdot \sim\underline{u}{:}\underline{M})$$

> Don't combine (1) *wanting* to attain this end and (2) *believing* that taking this means is needed to attain this end and (3) *not acting* to take this means.

While all this would be easy to do, we won't do it here.

Our belief logic also can prove *conscientiousness* principles that prescribe a harmony between our moral beliefs and how we live. Here's one example:

$$\sim(\underline{u}{:}O{\sim}A\underline{u} \cdot \underline{u}{:}A\underline{u}))$$

> Don't combine *believing* that it's wrong for you to do A with *acting* to do A.

This is a **formal ethical principle** – an ethical principle that can be formulated using the abstract notions of our logical systems plus variables (like "u" and "A") that stand for any person and action. All our consistency requirements are *formal* in this sense.

Here are three further formal consistency requirements:

> **Impartiality**: Make similar evaluations about similar actions, regardless of the individuals involved.
>
> **Golden rule**: Treat others only as you consent to being treated in the same situation.
>
> **Formula of universal law**: Act only as you're willing for anyone to act in the same situation – regardless of imagined variations of time or person.

We'll add logical machinery for all three, but mostly focus on the golden rule.

---

[1] For more about "⊡" and the logic of causal necessity, see pages 337–478 of Arthur Burks's *Chance, Cause, Reason* (Chicago: University of Chicago Press, 1977).

11.3 The golden rule

The golden rule (GR) says "Treat others as you want to be treated." All the major religions and many non-religious thinkers teach this rule. For example, Jesus gave the rule as the summary of the Law and the Prophets (Mt 7:12), the Rabbi Hillel used it to summarize the Jewish law, and Confucius used it to sum up his teachings. And GR is important in our own culture.

The golden rule seems clear and simple; but this clarity and simplicity disappear when we try to explain what the rule means. We can't take the usual wording of the rule literally. GR seems to say this:

> **Literal golden rule (LR):**
>
> If you want X to do A to you,
> then do A to X.
>
> $(u:A\underline{x}u \supset A\underline{u}x)$

LR often works well. Suppose that you want Suzy to be kind to you; then LR tells you to be kind to her. Or suppose that you want Tom not to hurt you (or rob you, or be selfish to you); then you are not to do these things to him. These applications seem sensible. But LR can lead to absurdities in two ways. First, there are cases where you are in *different circumstances* from X:

- To a patient: If you want the doctor to remove your appendix, then remove the doctor's appendix.
- To a violent little boy who loves to fight: If you want your sister to fight with you, then fight with her.
- To a parent: If you want your child not to punish you, then don't punish him.

Second, there are cases where you have *defective desires* about how you are to be treated:

- To one who desires hatred: If you want others to hate you, then hate them.

LR leads to absurdities because its wording is defective.[1]

I suggest that the following wording will avoid the objections:

---

[1] Some suggest that we apply GR only to "general" actions (such as treating someone with kindness) and not to "specific" ones (such as removing someone's appendix). But our last example used a general action; so this restriction wouldn't solve the problem.

Golden rule:	GR forbids this combination:
Treat others only as you consent to being treated in the same situation.	• I do something to another. • I'm unwilling that this be done to me in the same situation.

Our formulation has a don't-combine form (forbidding a combination) and has you imagine an exactly reversed situation where you are on the receiving end of the action. These features avoid the objections to the "literal golden rule."

GR's same-situation clause avoids the first kind of objection. Consider this case. I speak loudly to my father (who is hard of hearing); but I don't want him to speak loudly to me (since my hearing is normal). While this is sensible, it violates the literal LR. LR says that if I want my father to speak normally (not loudly) to me, then this is how I am to speak to him. LR ignores differences in circumstances. LR says: "If you want others to treat you in a given way in your present situation, then this is how you are to treat them – even if their situation is very different."

With GR, I'd ask how I desire that I'd be treated if I were in the *same situation* as my father (and thus hard of hearing). I desire that if I were in his same situation then people would speak loudly to me. So I'd speak loudly to him.

We can take "same" situation here as "exactly similar" or "relevantly similar." In the first case, I'd imagine myself in my father's *exact place* (with all his properties). In the second, I'd imagine myself having those of his properties (such as being hard of hearing) that I think are or might be *relevant* to deciding how loudly one should speak to him. Either approach works fine.

The same-situation clause also is important for the appendix case. Recall that LR told the patient to remove the doctor's appendix. The same-situation clause would block this, since the patient clearly doesn't desire that if he were in the place of his doctor (with a healthy appendix), then his appendix be removed by a sick patient ignorant of medicine. In applying GR, we need to ask, "Am I willing that the same thing be done to me *in the same situation?*"

In the fighting case, LR told the violent little boy to fight with his sister. The same-situation clause would block this. The little boy should imagine himself in the place of his sister (who is terrorized by fighting) and ask "Am I willing that I be fought with in this way if I were in her place?" Since the answer is "no," he wouldn't fight with his sister.

We need to be careful about something else. GR is about *our present reaction to a hypothetical case.* It isn't about how we would react if we were in the hypothetical case. We have to ask the right question:

Ask this	➡	Am I willing that this be done to me in the same situation?
Not this	➡	If I were in the same situation, would I then be willing that this be done to me?

The difference here is important, but subtle. Let me try to clarify it.

Suppose that I have a two-year-old son, little Will, who keeps putting his fingers into electrical outlets. I try to discourage him from doing this, but nothing works. Finally, I decide that I need to spank him when he does it. I want to see if I can spank him without violating GR. In determining this, I should ask the first question – not the second:

Good form: Am I now willing that if I were in Will's place then I be spanked?	This has "willing that if." It's about my present adult desire toward a hypothetical case.

Bad form: If I were in Will's place, would I then be willing to be spanked?	This has "if" before "willing." It's about the desires I'd have as a small child.

With the *good form*, I imagine the case in the following box:

I'm a two-year-old child. I put my fingers into electrical outlets, and the only way to discourage me from doing this is through a spanking. Of course, I know nothing about electricity and I desire not to be spanked.

As an adult, I say "I *now* desire that if I were in this situation then I be spanked." I might add, "I'm thankful that my parents spanked me in such cases – even though I wasn't pleased then." Thus I can spank my child without breaking GR, since I'm willing that I would have been treated the same way in the same situation.

On the other hand, if I were in Will's place, and thus judged things from a two-year-old mentality, then I'd desire not to be spanked. That's what the *bad form* is about. If we formulated GR using this, then I'd break GR if I spanked Will. But this is absurd. We need to formulate GR using the *good form*, in terms of my present reaction to a hypothetical case. I can satisfy GR because I'm now (as an adult) willing that I would have been spanked in this situation.

This point is subtle, but of central importance. If you don't get the idea, I suggest you reread the last few paragraphs a few times until it comes through.

This distinction is crucial when we deal with someone who isn't very rational – such as a person who is in a coma, or who is senile or confused. We need to ask the right question:

Ask this	➜	Am I now willing that if I were in a coma then this be done to me?
Not this	➜	If I were in a coma, would I then be willing that this be done to me?

GR is about our *present* attitude toward a hypothetical case. To use GR correctly, say "I AM WILLING THAT IF"; don't say "I WOULD BE WILLING."

Let me sum up where we are. Recall that the literal golden rule LR can lead to absurdities in two ways. First, there are cases where you are in *different circumstances* from the other person. We can get around these by including a same-situation clause and being careful to ask the right question. Second, there are cases where you have *defective desires* about how you are to be treated. LR can tell a person with defective desires to do evil things. For example, it can tell someone who desires hatred to hate others. Here we'll consider a simpler case that shows why we need to take GR not as a direct guide to action, but rather as prescribing consistency between our actions (toward another) and our desires (about a reversed-situation action).

Imagine this case. We own a very profitable coal mine but act wrongly in paying our workers only a miserly $1 a day. People ask if we're willing to be paid $1 a day in their place. We answer "yes" and thus are consistent. But we answer "yes" only because we think (incorrectly) that our workers can live tolerably on this amount. If we knew the truth, we wouldn't answer "yes." So here we're consistent and follow GR, but only because we're ignorant.

GR gives a useful tool for attacking certain inconsistencies. But here we need something else. We need to correct our view of the facts; only then can GR show us our error in how we pay our workers.

So here we satisfy GR-consistency but act wrongly. This shows that we shouldn't take GR to be an infallible guide on what is right or wrong. Properly understood, GR doesn't tell us what specific action to take; instead, it forbids inconsistent combinations. Formally, we need to express GR as a don't-combine consistency principle – not as an if-then:

The *good form* forbids a combination:	Don't combine acting to do A to X with …
• I do something to another. • I'm unwilling that this be done to me in the same situation.	$\sim(\underline{u}{:}A\underline{u}x \cdot \sim\underline{u}{:}\ldots)$

This **bad form** is defective, since your desires can be defective: "If you desire that you be treated in a given way in similar circumstances, then treat others this way."	If you desire ..., then do A to X. (u:... ⊃ A<u>u</u>x)

We've seen that other consistency principles require this *don't-combine* form, and that the *if-then* form can lead to absurdities when we have defective beliefs or desires. So our GR formulation has three key features:

- a same-situation clause,
- a present attitude toward a hypothetical situation, and
- a don't-combine form.

We need these features to avoid absurd implications.

Suppose that I'm about to do something to another, and I want to see if I can treat the other this way without violating GR. I'd imagine myself in the other person's place on the receiving end of the action; and I'd ask "Am I willing that if I were in this person's exact place then this be done to me?" If I do something to another, and yet am unwilling that this be done to me in the same situation, then I'm inconsistent and I violate the rule.

As I stressed before, consistency principles like the golden rule aren't sufficient in themselves. To apply GR most rationally, we need to know how our actions would influence the lives of others, and we need to develop and exercise the ability to imagine ourselves in the place of another. When combined with these and other elements, GR can be a powerful tool of ethical thinking.

But we shouldn't make excessive claims for the golden rule. It doesn't give all the answers to ethical problems. It doesn't separate concrete actions into "right actions" and "wrong actions." It only prescribes consistency – that we not have our actions (toward another) be out of harmony with our desires (about a reversed-situation action). Despite its limitations, GR is very useful. The golden rule expresses a formal rational condition that we often violate.

11.4 Starting the GR proof

GR follows from requirements to be conscientious and impartial. Suppose that you want to steal Detra's bicycle. And suppose that you're *conscientious* (keep your actions and desires in harmony with your moral beliefs) and *impartial* (make similar evaluations about similar actions). Then you won't steal her bicycle unless you're also willing that your bicycle be stolen in the same situation. This chart shows the steps in the derivation:

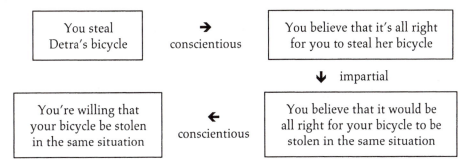

Here's a less graphical argument. If we're conscientious and impartial, then:

> We won't *act* to do something to another unless we *believe* that this act is all right.
> We won't *believe* that this act is all right unless we *believe* that it would be all right for this to be done to us in the same situation.
> We won't *believe* that it would be all right for this to be done to us in the same situation unless we're *willing* that this be done to us in the same situation.
> ∴ We won't *act* to do something to another unless we're *willing* that this be done to us in the same situation.

So if we're conscientious and impartial, then we'll follow GR: we won't do something to another unless we're willing that it be done to us in the same situation.

So GR follows from the requirements to be conscientious and impartial. But why be conscientious and impartial? Why care about consistency at all?

Different views could answer differently. Maybe we ought to be consistent because this is inherently right; our minds grasp the duty to be consistent as the first duty of a rational being. Or maybe we accept the consistency norms because they are commanded by God, are useful to social life, or accord with how we want to live (perhaps because inconsistency brings painful "cognitive dissonance" and social sanctions). And perhaps demands to be conscientious and impartial are built into our moral language (so violating them involves a strict logical inconsistency), or perhaps not. I'll abstract from these issues here and assume only that there's *some* reason to be consistent (in a broad sense that includes being conscientious and impartial). I won't worry about the details. I'm trying to develop consistency norms that appeal to a wide range of views – even though these views may explain and justify the norms differently.

To incorporate GR into our logical framework, then, we need to add requirements to be *conscientious* and *impartial*. Our belief logic already has a good part of the conscientiousness requirement. We already can prove the imperative analogue of the first step of our GR argument:

Don't *act* to do A to
X without *believing*
that it's all right for
you to do A to X.[1]

$$
\begin{array}{ll}
 & [\ \therefore \sim(\underline{u}{:}A\underline{u}x \cdot \sim\underline{u}{:}RA\underline{u}x) \\
* \quad 1 & \quad \text{asm: } (\underline{u}{:}A\underline{u}x \cdot \sim\underline{u}{:}RA\underline{u}x) \\
\quad 2 & \quad \therefore \underline{u}{:}A\underline{u}x \quad \{\text{from } 1\} \\
* \quad 3 & \quad \therefore \sim\underline{u}{:}RA\underline{u}x \quad \{\text{from } 1\} \\
* \quad 4 & \quad u\therefore \sim RA\underline{u}x \quad \{\text{from } 3\} \\
\quad 5 & \quad u\therefore O\sim A\underline{u}x \quad \{\text{from } 4\} \\
\quad 6 & \quad u\therefore A\underline{u}x \quad \{\text{from } 2\} \\
\quad 7 & \quad u\therefore \sim A\underline{u}x \quad \{\text{from } 5\} \\
\quad 8 & \quad \therefore \sim(\underline{u}{:}A\underline{u}x \cdot \sim\underline{u}{:}RA\underline{u}x) \\
 & \qquad \{\text{from } 1; \ 6 \text{ contradicts } 7\}
\end{array}
$$

However, we can't yet prove the imperative analogue of our GR argument's third step – which also deals with conscientiousness:

> Don't *believe* that it would be all right for X to do A to you in the same situation without *being willing* that X do A to you in the same situation.

The hard part here is to symbolize "in the same situation." If we ignore this for the moment, then what we need is this:

> Don't *believe* that it would be all right for X to do A to you without *being willing* that X do A to you.

We'll interpret "being willing that A be done" as "accepting 'A *may* be done.'" Here the permissive "A *may* be done" isn't another way to say "A is all right." Instead, it's a member of the imperative family, but weaker than "Do A," expressing only one's consent to the action. We'll symbolize "A *may* be done" as "M$\underline{A}$." Then we can symbolize the imperative mentioned above as follows:

$\sim(\underline{u}{:}RA\underline{u}x \cdot \sim\underline{u}{:}MA\underline{u}x)$

= Don't *believe* that it would be all right for X to do A to you without *being willing* that X do A to you.

= Don't combine (1) *believing* "It would be all right for X to do A to me" with (2) *not accepting* "X may do A to me."

To prove this, we need a principle like "$\Box(R\underline{A} \supset M\underline{A})$" – which says that a permissibility judgment entails the corresponding permissive. This is like the prescriptivity principle ("Hare's Law") discussed in Section 9.4, which says that an ought judgment entails the corresponding imperative: "$\Box(O\underline{A} \supset \underline{A})$."[2]

---

[1] For some discussion on this principle, see my "Acting commits one to ethical beliefs," *Analysis* 42 (1983), pages 40–3.

[2] For some discussion on this "$\Box(R\underline{A} \supset M\underline{A})$" principle, see my "How incomplete is prescriptivism?" *Mind* 93 (1984), pages 103–7. My "$\Box(R\underline{A} \supset M\underline{A})$" and "$\Box(O\underline{A} \supset \underline{A})$" assume that

Our biggest task is to give logical machinery to symbolize and prove the impartiality requirement – and the imperative analogue of our GR argument's second step:

> Don't combine (1) *believing* that it's all right for you to do A to X with (2) *not believing* that it would be all right for X to do A to you in the same situation.

$\sim(\underline{u}{:}RA\underline{u}x \cdot \sim\underline{u}{:}...)$

To symbolize this, we need to replace "..." with a formula that means "it would be all right for X to do A to you in *the same situation*." And to prove this, we need an inference rule to reflect universalizability – which is one of the few principles on whose truth almost all moral philosophers agree.

The **universalizability principle** (U) says that whatever is right (wrong, good, bad, etc.) in one case would also be right (wrong, good, bad, etc.) in any exactly or relevantly similar case, regardless of the individuals involved. Here are three equivalent formulations of U for "all right" (similar formulations work for "ought"):

Universalizability

If it's all right for X to do A, then it would be all right for anyone else to do A in the same situation.

If act A is permissible, then there is some universal property (or conjunction of such properties) F, such that: (1) act A is F, and (2) in any actual or hypothetical case every act that is F is permissible.

$$(R\underline{A} \supset (\exists F)(F\underline{A} \cdot \blacksquare(\underline{X})(F\underline{X} \supset R\underline{X})))$$

The second phrasing, which is more technically precise, uses the notion of a "universal property." A **universal property** is any non-evaluative property describable without proper names (like "Gensler" or "Cleveland") or pointer terms (like "I" or "this"). Let me give examples. Suppose that I am tempted to steal my neighbor Patrick's new computer. This possible act has several properties or characteristics; for example, it is:

- *wrong* (evaluative term),
- an act of stealing *Pat's* computer (proper name), and
- something *I* would be doing (pointer word).

---

violations of conscientiousness involve a strict logical inconsistency. One who didn't accept this, but who still thought that violations of conscientiousness were in some way objectionable, could endorse the weaker principles "$(R\underline{A} \supset M\underline{A})$" and "$(O\underline{A} \supset \underline{A})$" – and weaker versions of the corresponding inference rules; the golden rule proof at the end of this chapter would still work.

These aren't universal, since they use evaluative terms, proper names, or pointer words. But the act also has universal properties; for example, it is:

- an act of stealing a new computer from one's neighbor,
- an act whose agent has blue eyes, and
- an act that would greatly distress the owner of the computer.

U says that the morality of an act depends on its universal properties – like those of the second group – properties expressible without evaluative terms, proper names, or pointer words. Two acts with the same universal properties must have the same moral status, regardless of the individuals involved.

Here's an important corollary of universalizability:

U* If it's all right for you to do A to X, then it would be all right for X to do A to you in the same situation.

= If it's all right for you to do A to X, then, for some universal property F, F is the complete description of your-doing-A-to-X in universal terms, and, in any actual or hypothetical case, if X's-doing-A-to-you is F, then it would be all right for X to do A to you.

$$(RA\underline{u}x \supset (\exists F)(F^*A\underline{u}x \cdot \blacksquare(FA\underline{x}u \supset RA\underline{x}u)))$$

U* relates closely to the second step in our argument for GR.

11.5 GR logical machinery

Now we'll add logical machinery to formulate and prove our version of the golden rule. This involves adding:

- letters for universal properties and for actions,
- "M" ("may") for permissives,
- "$\blacksquare$" ("in every actual or hypothetical case") for hypothetical cases, and
- "*" for the complete description of an act in universal terms.

We also need to add inference rules. This section will get complicated; you may need to read it a couple of times to follow what's happening.

First, we'll use letters of two new sorts (both can be used in quantifiers):

- "F," "G," "H," and these with primes stand for universal properties of actions (including conjunctions of such properties).
- "X," "Y," "Z," and these with primes stand for actions.

These examples use letters for universal properties:

$$\begin{array}{rcl} F\underline{A} & = & \text{Act A has universal property F.} \\ & = & \text{Act A is F (e.g., act A is an act of stealing).} \end{array}$$

$$\begin{array}{rcl} (F\underline{A} \supset {\sim}R\underline{A}) & = & \text{If act A is an act of stealing, then act A is wrong.} \end{array}$$

$$\begin{array}{rcl} G\underline{A} & = & \text{Act A is an act of a blue-eyed philosophy teacher} \\ & & \text{stealing a bicycle from an impoverished student.} \end{array}$$

We translate "F$\underline{A}$" as "Act A is F" – not as "Imperative 'Do A' is F." This next example uses a universal-property quantifier:

$$\begin{array}{rcl} (F)(F\underline{A} \equiv F\underline{B}) & = & \text{Acts A and B have all the same universal properties.} \\ & = & \text{For every universal property F, act A has property F} \\ & & \text{if and only if act B has property F.} \end{array}$$

These examples use action quantifiers:

$$\begin{array}{rcl} (\exists\underline{X})F\underline{X} & = & \text{Some act has universal property F.} \\ & = & \text{For some act X, X has universal property F.} \end{array}$$

$$\begin{array}{rcl} (\underline{X})(F\underline{X} \supset O\underline{X}) & = & \text{Every act that is F ought to be done.} \\ & = & \text{For every act X, if act X is F, then act X ought to be done.} \end{array}$$

$$\begin{array}{rcl} (\underline{X})(\exists F)F\underline{X} & = & \text{Every act has some universal property.} \\ & = & \text{For every act X there's some universal property F, such} \\ & & \text{that act X is F.} \end{array}$$

Our two new kinds of letter require two new formation rules:

> 1. The result of writing "F," "G," "H," or one of these with primes, and then an imperative wff is itself a descriptive wff.
> 2. The result of writing "(" or "($\exists$," and then "F," "G," "H," "$\underline{X}$," "$\underline{Y}$," "$\underline{Z}$," or one of these with primes, and then ")" is a quantifier.

Assume expanded versions of our quantifier rules for the new quantifiers. We have to substitute the right sort of thing for the quantified letter:

> For *individual variables*: x, y, z, x′, …, substitute individual constants: a, b, c, d, …
>
> For *universal-property variables*: F, G, H, F′, …, substitute universal-property letters not bound to quantifiers: F, G, H, F′, …
>
> For *action variables*: $\underline{X}$, $\underline{Y}$, $\underline{Z}$, $\underline{X}$′, …, substitute imperative wffs: A$\underline{a}$, $\underline{B}$, A$\underline{xy}$, …[1]

---

[1] The last case requires two technical provisos. Suppose that we drop a quantifier containing an action variable and substitute an imperative wff for the variable. Then we must be sure that

When "M" is prefixed to an imperative wff, we'll translate it as "may":[1]

> 3. The result of prefixing an imperative wff with "M" is a wff.

$$\text{M}\underline{\text{A}} \quad = \quad \text{Act A may be done.}$$

$$\text{MA}\underline{\text{xu}} \quad = \quad \text{X may do A to you.}$$

$$
\text{u:MA}\underline{\text{xu}} \quad
\begin{aligned}
&= \quad \text{You accept "X may do A to me."}\\
&= \quad \text{You consent to X's doing A to you.}\\
&= \quad \text{You're willing that X do A to you.}
\end{aligned}
$$

Permissives like "M$\underline{\text{A}}$" are weaker members of the imperative family. They express our consent to the act, but not necessarily our positive desire that the act take place. We can consistently consent both to the act and to its omission – saying "You may do A and you may omit A." Here are further wffs:

$$\sim\!\text{M}\!\sim\!\underline{\text{A}} \quad = \quad \text{Act A may not be omitted.}$$

$$
\text{u:}\!\sim\!\text{M}\!\sim\!\text{A}\underline{\text{xu}} \quad
\begin{aligned}
&= \quad \text{You accept "X may not omit doing A to me."}\\
&= \quad \text{You demand that X do A to you.}
\end{aligned}
$$

"M$\underline{\text{A}}$" is weaker and "$\sim\!\text{M}\!\sim\!\underline{\text{A}}$" is stronger than "$\underline{\text{A}}$."[2]

Inference rule G1 is the principle that "A is all right" entails "A may be done." G1 holds regardless of what imperative wff replaces "$\underline{\text{A}}$":[3]

> G1 $\quad$ R$\underline{\text{A}}$ $\;\to\;$ M$\underline{\text{A}}$

Given this and the rules for "M," "O," and "R," we also can prove the reverse entailment from "M$\underline{\text{A}}$" to "R$\underline{\text{A}}$." Then either of the two logically entails the

---

(1) this imperative wff contains no variable that also occurs in a quantifier in the derived wff, and (2) if we dropped an existential quantifier, this substituted imperative wff must be an underlined capital letter that isn't an action variable and that hasn't occurred before in the proof.

[1] Capital letters have various uses, depending on context. In "((M · Ma) ⊃ (Mbc · M$\underline{\text{A}}$))," for example, "M" is used first for a statement, then for a property of an individual, then for a relation between individuals, and finally for "may." It's usually clearer to use different letters.

[2] The relationship between permissives and standard imperatives is tricky. See my *Formal Ethics* (London and New York: Routledge, 1996), pages 185–6, and my "How incomplete is prescriptivism?" *Mind* 93 (1984), pages 103–7.

[3] Thinking that an act is *all right* commits one to *consenting* to the idea of it being done (or, equivalently, *being willing* that it be done). We also could use words like "approve," "accept," "condone," or "tolerate" – in one sense of these terms. The sense of "consent" that I have in mind refers to an inner attitude incompatible with inwardly objecting to (condemning, disapproving, forbidding, protesting, objecting to) the act. Consenting here is a minimal attitude and needn't involve favoring or advocating or welcoming the act. It's consistent to both consent to the idea of A being done and also consent to the idea of A not being done.

other; so accepting one commits a person to accepting the other. But the distinction between the two doesn't vanish. "R<u>A</u>" is true or false; to accept "R<u>A</u>" is to believe that something is true. But "M<u>A</u>" isn't true or false; to accept "M<u>A</u>" isn't to believe something but to will something – to consent to the idea of something being done.

Some of our inference rules for "M" and "■" involve new kinds of world. A *world prefix* is now any string of zero-or-more instances of letters from the set <W, D, H, P, a, b, c, ...> – where <a, b, c, ...> is the set of small letters. Here "P," "PP," "PPP," and so on are "permission worlds," much like deontic worlds. A permission world that depends on a given world W1 is a possible world that contains the indicative judgments of W1 and some set of imperatives prescribing actions jointly permitted by the permissives of W1.

Inference rules G2 to G4 (which won't be used in our GR proof) govern permissions and are much like the deontic rules. G2 and G3 hold regardless of what pair of contradictory imperative wffs replaces "<u>A</u>" / "~<u>A</u>":

$$\text{G2} \quad \boxed{\begin{array}{c} \sim\text{M}\underline{\text{A}} \;\rightarrow\; \overset{\downarrow}{\text{P}} \therefore \sim\underline{\text{A}}, \\ \text{use a blank or any string of P's} \end{array}}$$

In G2, the world prefix of the derived step must be either the same as that of the earlier step or else the same except that it adds one or more P's at the end.

$$\text{G3} \quad \boxed{\begin{array}{c} \text{M}\underline{\text{A}} \;\rightarrow\; \overset{\downarrow}{\text{P}} \therefore \underline{\text{A}}, \\ \text{use a \textit{new} string of P's} \end{array}}$$

In G3, the world prefix of the derived step must be the same as that of the earlier step except that it adds a *new* string (a string not occurring in earlier lines) of one or more P's at the end. G4 mirrors the deontic indicative transfer rule; it holds regardless of what descriptive or deontic wff replaces "A":

$$\text{G4} \quad \boxed{\text{P} \therefore \text{A} \;\rightarrow\; \text{A}}$$

In G4, the world prefixes in the derived and deriving steps must be identical except that one ends in one or more additional P's.

"■" is a modal operator somewhat like "□":

$$\boxed{\text{4.} \quad \text{The result of prefixing any wff with "■" is a wff.}}$$

"■" translates as "in every actual or hypothetical case" or "in every possible world having the same basic moral principles as those true in the actual world." Here's a wff using "■":

$$\blacksquare(F\underline{A} \supset O\underline{A}) \quad \begin{aligned} &= && \text{If act A is or were F, then act A ought to be done.} \\ &= && \text{In every actual or hypothetical case, if act A is F,} \\ & && \text{then act A ought to be done.} \end{aligned}$$

Suppose that, while act A may or may not have property F (e.g., it may or may not maximize pleasure), still, if it did, then it would be what ought to be done. We'll use "$\blacksquare(F\underline{A} \supset O\underline{A})$" for this idea. "$(F\underline{A} \supset O\underline{A})$" is too weak to express this (since this wff is trivially true if "$F\underline{A}$" is false); "$\square(F\underline{A} \supset O\underline{A})$" is too strong (since there's no such entailment). So we'll use "$\blacksquare$" to formulate claims about what would be right or wrong in hypothetical situations (such as imagined exactly reversed situations).

We can now symbolize the universalizability principle:

U If act A is permissible, then there is some universal property (or conjunction of such properties) F, such that: (1) act A is F, and (2) in any actual or hypothetical case every act that is F is permissible.

$$(R\underline{A} \supset (\exists F)(F\underline{A} \cdot \blacksquare(\underline{X})(F\underline{X} \supset R\underline{X})))$$

G5 and G6 are the "all right" and "ought" forms of the corresponding inference rules. These hold regardless of what imperative wff replaces "$\underline{A}$," what universal-property variable replaces "F," and what action variable replaces "$\underline{X}$":

G5	$R\underline{A}$	$\rightarrow$	$(\exists F)(F\underline{A} \supset \blacksquare(\underline{X})(F\underline{X} \supset R\underline{X}))$
G6	$O\underline{A}$	$\rightarrow$	$(\exists F)(F\underline{A} \supset \blacksquare(\underline{X})(F\underline{X} \supset O\underline{X}))$

In G5 and G6, the world prefix of the derived and deriving steps must be identical and must contain no "W." The proviso prevents us from being able to prove that violations of universalizability are logically self-contradictory (I don't think they are).

The rules for "$\blacksquare$" resemble those for "$\square$." Recall that our expanded world prefixes can use "H," "HH," and "HHH"; these represent *hypothetical situation worlds* – which are possible worlds having the same basic moral principles as those of the actual world (or whatever world the H-world depends on). G7 and G8 hold regardless of what pair of contradictory wffs replaces "A" / "~A":

G7	$\blacksquare A \quad \rightarrow \quad \overset{\downarrow}{H} \therefore A,$ use a blank or any string of H's

In G7, the world prefixes in the derived and deriving steps must either be the same or the same except that one adds one or more H's at the end.

$$\text{G8} \quad \boxed{\begin{array}{c} \sim\blacksquare A \;\;\rightarrow\;\; \overset{\downarrow}{H} \therefore \sim A, \\ \text{use a } \textit{new} \text{ string of H's} \end{array}}$$

In G8, the derived step's world prefix must be the same as that of the earlier step except that it adds a *new* string (a string not occurring in earlier lines) of one or more H's at the end. Rule G9 (which won't be used in our proof of the golden rule) says that "□" and "■" are equivalent when prefixed to descriptive wffs; this holds regardless of what *descriptive* wff replaces "A":

$$\text{G9} \quad \boxed{\; \blacksquare A \;\;\leftrightarrow\;\; \square A \;}$$

Our final symbol is "*"; this is used with universal-property letters to represent the complete description of an action in universal terms. Here's the rule for constructing wffs with "*," with an example:

> 5. The result of writing "F," "G," "H," or these with primes, then "*,"and then an imperative wff is itself a descriptive wff.

$$F^*\underline{A} \quad \begin{array}{l} = \quad \text{F is the complete description of act A in universal terms.} \\ = \quad \text{F is the description of act A in universal terms which includes} \\ \quad\;\;\; \text{all the universal properties of act A.} \end{array}$$

"F*$\underline{A}$" means the same as this longer wff:

$$(F\underline{A} \cdot (G)(G\underline{A} \supset \square(\underline{X})(F\underline{X} \supset G\underline{X})))$$
= Act A is F, and every universal property G that A has is included as part of F.
= Act A is F, and, for every universal property G that A has, it's logically necessary that every act that's F also is G.

We adopt the corresponding inference rule G10, which lets us go back and forth between "F*$\underline{A}$" and this longer wff. G10 holds regardless of what distinct universal-property letters replace "F" and "G," what imperative wff replaces "$\underline{A}$," and what action variable replaces "$\underline{X}$":

$$\text{G10} \quad \boxed{\; F^*\underline{A} \;\;\leftrightarrow\;\; (F\underline{A} \cdot (G)(G\underline{A} \supset \square(\underline{X})(F\underline{X} \supset G\underline{X}))) \;}$$

Rule G11, our final inference rule, says that every act has a complete description in universal terms (even though it may be too long to write down). G11 is an axiom; it lets us put wff "$(\underline{X})(\exists F)F^*\underline{X}$" on any line of a proof:

$$\text{G11} \quad \boxed{\quad \rightarrow \quad (\underline{X})(\exists F)F^*\underline{X} \quad}$$

We'll use "*" in symbolizing "exactly similar situation." Let's take an example. Let "Amx" represent the act of my attacking X. Suppose that this act has complete description F:

> F*A$\underline{m}$x = My-attacking-X has *complete universal description* F.

Let's flesh this out. Let "G," "G'," ... represent my universal properties; these include properties like being a logician. Let "H," "H'," ... represent X's universal properties; these might include being an impoverished student. Let "R," "R'," ... represent the relationships between X and me; these might include X's being my student. Now property F would look like this, which describes the *actual situation*:

> FA$\underline{m}$x = My-attacking-X is an act of someone who
> is G, G', ... attacking someone who is H,
> H', ... and related to me in ways R, R', ...

Now we imagine an *exactly similar situation* if we imagine the situation where X's-attacking-me has this same description F:

> FA$\underline{x}$m = X's-attacking-me is an act of someone who
> is G, G', ... attacking someone who is H,
> H', ... and related to X in ways R, R', ...

In this imagined exactly similar situation, X is in my exact place – and I am in X's exact place. All our universal properties and relationships are switched.

We can now symbolize the reversed-situation corollary of universalizability:

> U* If it's all right for you to do A to X, then it would be all right for X to do A to you in the same situation.
>
> = If it's all right for you to do A to X, then, for some universal property F, F is the complete description of your-doing-A-to-X in universal terms, and, in any actual or hypothetical case, if X's-doing-A-to-you is F, then it would be all right for X to do A to you.
>
> $(RA\underline{u}x \supset (\exists F)(F^*A\underline{u}x \cdot \blacksquare(FA\underline{x}u \supset RA\underline{x}u)))$

Also, and most importantly, we can symbolize the golden rule:

GR Treat others only as you consent to being treated in the same situation.

= Don't combine *acting* to do A to X with *being unwilling* that A be done to you in the same situation.

= Don't combine (1) accepting "Do A to X" with (2) not accepting "For some universal property F, F is the complete description in universal terms of my-doing-A-to-X, and, in any actual or hypothetical situation, if X's-doing-A-to-me is F, then X may do A to me."

$$\sim(\underline{u}{:}A\underline{u}x \cdot \sim\underline{u}{:}(\exists F)(F^*A\underline{u}x \cdot \blacksquare(FA\underline{x}u \supset MA\underline{x}u)))$$

While we're at it, here are the symbolizations of two other consistency principles that we mentioned in Section 11.2:

Impartiality: Make similar evaluations about similar actions, regardless of the individuals involved.

= Don't accept "Act A is permissible" without accepting "Any act exactly or relevantly similar to act A is permissible."

= Don't accept "Act A is permissible" without accepting "For some universal property F, act A is F and, in any actual or hypothetical situation, any act that is F is permissible."

$$\sim(\underline{u}{:}R\underline{A} \cdot \sim\underline{u}{:}(\exists F)(F\underline{A} \cdot \blacksquare(X)(F\underline{X} \supset R\underline{X})))$$

Formula of universal law: Act only as you're willing for anyone to act in the same situation – regardless of imagined variations of time or person.[1]

= Don't combine *acting* to do A with *not being willing* that any similar action be done in the same situation.

= Don't combine (1) accepting "Do A" with (2) not accepting "For some universal property F, F is the complete description in universal terms of my doing A, and, in any actual or hypothetical situation, any act that is F may be done."

$$\sim(\underline{u}{:}A\underline{u} \cdot \sim\underline{u}{:}(\exists F)(F^*A\underline{u} \cdot \blacksquare(X)(F\underline{X} \supset M\underline{X})))$$

Since "same situation" covers imagined cases where I am in the place of *anyone* affected by my action, this "formula of universal law" is a generalized GR that

---

[1] My "formula of universal law" resembles Immanuel Kant's principle. His wording went, "Act only on that maxim through which you can at the same time will that it should be a universal law." Depending on how this is interpreted, it could be quite different from my principle.

applies equally to situations involving more than two people. It also can apply to situations involving only one person (for example, cases where my present action can harm my future self).

11.6   The symbolic GR proof

Before we do our proof of the golden rule, let's review the larger picture.

We began this chapter by sketching various dimensions of ethical rationality. Then we narrowed our focus, first to rationality as consistency, and then to a single consistency principle – the golden rule. We had to formulate GR carefully to avoid absurd implications. We arrived at this wording:

Golden rule:	GR forbids this combination:
Treat others only as you consent to being treated in the same situation.	• I do something to another. • I'm unwilling that this be done to me in the same situation.

After sketching an intuitive proof of the golden rule, we noted that incorporating GR and its proof into our logical framework requires adding impartiality and strengthening conscientiousness. So we added logical machinery to do this. And so now we are ready to give a formal proof of the golden rule.

Our proof goes as follows ("#" marks steps that use our new inference rules):

$$[\therefore \sim(\underline{u}{:}A\underline{u}x \cdot \sim\underline{u}{:}(\exists F)(F^*A\underline{u}x \cdot \blacksquare(FA\underline{x}u \supset MA\underline{x}u)))$$

1	┌ asm: $(\underline{u}{:}A\underline{u}x \cdot \sim\underline{u}{:}(\exists F)(F^*A\underline{u}x \cdot \blacksquare(FA\underline{x}u \supset MA\underline{x}u)))$	
2	│ $\therefore \underline{u}{:}A\underline{u}x$ {from 1}	
3	│ $\therefore \sim\underline{u}{:}(\exists F)(F^*A\underline{u}x \cdot \blacksquare(FA\underline{x}u \supset MA\underline{x}u))$ {from 1}	
4	│ $u \therefore \sim(\exists F)(F^*A\underline{u}x \cdot \blacksquare(FA\underline{x}u \supset MA\underline{x}u))$ {from 3}	
5	│ $u \therefore A\underline{u}x$ {from 2}	
6	│ ┌ u asm: $\sim RA\underline{u}x$ {we need to derive "RA$\underline{u}$x"}	
7	│ │ $u \therefore O\sim A\underline{u}x$ {from 6}	
8	│ └ $u \therefore \sim A\underline{u}x$ {from 7}	
9	│ $u \therefore RA\underline{u}x$ {from 6; 5 contradicts 8}	
# 10	│ $u \therefore (\exists F)(FA\underline{u}x \cdot \blacksquare(\underline{X})(F\underline{X} \supset R\underline{X}))$ {from 9 by G5}	
11	│ $u \therefore (GA\underline{u}x \cdot \blacksquare(\underline{X})(G\underline{X} \supset R\underline{X}))$ {from 10}	
12	│ $u \therefore GA\underline{u}x$ {from 11}	
13	│ $u \therefore \blacksquare(\underline{X})(G\underline{X} \supset R\underline{X})$ {from 11}	
# 14	│ $u \therefore (\underline{X})(\exists F)F^*\underline{X}$ {by rule G11}	
15	│ $u \therefore (\exists F)F^*A\underline{u}x$ {from 14}	
16	│ $u \therefore H^*A\underline{u}x$ {from 15}	
# 17	│ $u \therefore (HA\underline{u}x \cdot (F)(FA\underline{u}x \supset \Box(\underline{X})(H\underline{X} \supset F\underline{X})))$ {from 16 by G10}	
18	│ $u \therefore HA\underline{u}x$ {from 17}	
19	│ $u \therefore (F)(FA\underline{u}x \supset \Box(\underline{X})(H\underline{X} \supset F\underline{X}))$ {from 17}	

	20	u ∴ (GA<u>u</u>x ⊃ □(<u>X</u>)(H<u>X</u> ⊃ G<u>X</u>)) {from 19}
	21	u ∴ □(<u>X</u>)(H<u>X</u> ⊃ G<u>X</u>) {from 12 and 20}
	22	u ∴ (F)~(F*A<u>u</u>x · ■(FA<u>x</u>u ⊃ MA<u>x</u>u)) {from 4}
	23	u ∴ ~(H*A<u>u</u>x · ■(HA<u>x</u>u ⊃ MA<u>x</u>u)) {from 22}
	24	u ∴ ~■(HA<u>x</u>u ⊃ MA<u>x</u>u) {from 16 and 23}
#	25	uH ∴ ~(HA<u>x</u>u ⊃ MA<u>x</u>u) {from 24 by G8}
	26	uH ∴ HA<u>x</u>u {from 25}
	27	uH ∴ ~MA<u>x</u>u {from 25} ◀······┐
	28	uH ∴ (<u>X</u>)(H<u>X</u> ⊃ G<u>X</u>) {from 21} ┊
	29	uH ∴ (HA<u>x</u>u ⊃ GA<u>x</u>u) {from 28} ┊
	30	uH ∴ GA<u>x</u>u {from 26 and 29} ┊
#	31	uH ∴ (<u>X</u>)(G<u>X</u> ⊃ R<u>X</u>) {from 13 by G7} ┊
	32	uH ∴ (GA<u>x</u>u ⊃ RA<u>x</u>u) {from 31} ┊
	33	uH ∴ RA<u>x</u>u {from 30 and 32} ┊
#	34	⌐ uH ∴ MA<u>x</u>u {from 33 by G1} ◀·····┘
	35	∴ ~(<u>u</u>:A<u>u</u>x · ~<u>u</u>:(∃F)(F*A<u>u</u>x · ■(FA<u>x</u>u ⊃ MA<u>x</u>u))) {from 1; 27 contradicts 34}

While this is a difficult proof, you should be able to follow the individual steps and see that everything follows correctly.

Our proof begins as usual; we assume the opposite of what we want to prove and then try to derive a contradiction. Soon we get these in lines 4 and 5 (where 5 is addressed to yourself):

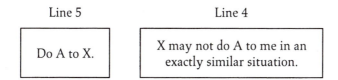

Line 5

Line 4

Do A to X.

X may not do A to me in an exactly similar situation.

Using line 4, we get these key steps:

16 Let H be the complete description of my doing A to X.
26 In an imagined situation, X's-doing-A-to-me is H.
27 In our imagined situation, X may not do A to me.

We use line 5 to get "It's all right for me to do A to X":

6 ⌐ Assume that it's *not* all right for me to do A to X.
7 │ ∴ I ought not to do A to X.
8 └ ∴ Don't do A to X.   (This is addressed to yourself.)
9 ∴ It's all right for me to do to X.   {8 contradicts 5}

Then we use universalizability on "It's all right for me to do A to X" to get "Any act relevantly or exactly similar to my-doing-A-to-X would be all right." We specify that G is the morally relevant complex of properties here; so:

12   My-doing-A-to-X has property G.
13   Any act that has property G would be all right.

We get a contradiction in a few more steps:

16   H is the complete description of my doing A to X.   {above}
12   My-doing-A to-X has property G.   {above}
21   So G is part of H – and every act that is H is G.
26   In our imagined situation, X's-doing-A-to-me is H.   {above}
30   So in our imagined situation, X's-doing-A-to-me is G.
13   Any act that has property G would be all right.   {above}
33   So in our imagined situation, X's-doing-A-to-me is all right.
34   So in our imagined situation, X may do A to me.

Since 34 contradicts 27, we derive our conclusion. This ends our proof of the golden rule:[1]

Always treat others as you want to be treated; that is
the summary of the Law and the Prophets. (Mt 7:12)

---

[1] If you want a challenging exercise, prove the impartiality and universal law formulas – as given at the end of the previous section.

CHAPTER 12
Metalogic

M etalogic studies logical systems. It focuses not on how to use these systems to test arguments, but rather on the systems themselves. This chapter provides an introduction to metalogic.

12.1 Metalogical questions

Metalogic is the study of logical systems; when we do metalogic, we try to prove things about these systems. Here's an example. Recall our first two rules for forming propositional wffs:

> 1. Any capital letter is a wff.
> 2. The result of prefixing any wff with "~" is a wff.

It follows from these that there's no longest wff – since, if there were a longest wff, then we could make a longer one by adding another "~." This simple proof is about a logical system, so it's part of *metalogic*.

Consider our system of propositional logic; metalogic would ask questions like: Do we need all five symbols ("~," "•," "∨," "⊃," and "≡")? Could we define some symbols in terms of others? Did we set up our proof system right? Are any of the inference rules defective? Can we prove invalid arguments or self-contradictions? Do we have enough inference rules to prove all valid propositional arguments? Could other approaches systematize propositional logic?

These are typical metalogical questions. This book focuses on logic, not metalogic (which can get highly technical). But this chapter will do a little metalogic, to give you an idea of what this is like.

12.2 Symbols

We don't need all five propositional symbols ("~," "•," "∨," "⊃," and "≡"). We could symbolize and test the same arguments if we had just "~" and "•"; then, instead of writing "(P ∨ Q)," we could write "~(~P • ~Q)":

$$(P \lor Q) \quad = \quad {\sim}({\sim}P \cdot {\sim}Q)$$

At least one is true $\quad = \quad$ Not both are false.

The two forms are equivalent, in that both are true or false under the same conditions; we could show this using a truth table. Similarly, we could express "⊃" and "≡" using "~" and "·":

$$(P \supset Q) \quad = \quad {\sim}(P \cdot {\sim}Q)$$
If P then Q $\quad = \quad$ We don't have P true and Q false.

$$(P \equiv Q) \quad = \quad ({\sim}(P \cdot {\sim}Q) \cdot {\sim}(Q \cdot {\sim}P))$$
P if and only if Q $\quad = \quad$ We don't have P true and Q false, and
we don't have Q true and P false.

Or we might translate the other symbols into "~" and "∨":

$$(P \cdot Q) \quad = \quad {\sim}({\sim}P \lor {\sim}Q)$$
$$(P \supset Q) \quad = \quad ({\sim}P \lor Q)$$
$$(P \equiv Q) \quad = \quad ({\sim}(P \lor Q) \lor {\sim}({\sim}P \lor {\sim}Q))$$

Or we might use just "~" and "⊃" – in light of these equivalences:

$$(P \cdot Q) \quad = \quad {\sim}(P \supset {\sim}Q)$$
$$(P \lor Q) \quad = \quad ({\sim}P \supset Q)$$
$$(P \equiv Q) \quad = \quad {\sim}((P \supset Q) \supset {\sim}(Q \supset P))$$

Systems with only two symbols are more elegantly simple but harder to use. However, logicians are sometimes more interested in proving results about a system than in using it to test arguments; and it may be easier to prove these results if we use fewer symbols.

Another approach is to use all five symbols but divide them into undefined (primitive) symbols and defined ones. We could take "~" and either "·" or "∨" or "⊃" as undefined, and then define the others using these. We'd then view the defined symbols as abbreviations; whenever we liked, we could eliminate them and use only the undefined symbols.

There are further options about notation. While we use capital letters for statements, some logicians use small letters (often just "p," "q," "r," and "s") or Greek letters. Some use "-" or "¬" for negation, "&" or "∧" for conjunction, "→" for conditional, or "↔" for equivalence. Various conventions are used for dropping parentheses. It's easy to adapt to these differences.

Polish notation avoids parentheses and has shorter formulas. "K," "A," "C," and "E" go in place of the left-hand parentheses for "·," "∨," "⊃," and "≡"; and "N" is used for "~." Here are four examples:

$$
\begin{array}{llll}
{\sim}(P \cdot Q) \;=\; NKpq & \qquad & ((P \cdot Q) \supset R) \;=\; CKpqr \\
({\sim}P \cdot Q) \;=\; KNpq & & (P \cdot (Q \supset R)) \;=\; KpCqr
\end{array}
$$

Advocates of Polish notation say they can actually understand the formulas.

12.3 Soundness

The most important questions of metalogic are about whether a system is **sound** (won't prove bad things – so every argument provable in the system is valid) and **complete** (can prove every good thing – so every valid argument expressible in the system is provable in the system).

Could the following case happen?

> A student named Logicus found a flaw in our proof system. Logicus produced a formal proof of a propositional argument; and he then showed by a truth table that this argument is invalid. So some arguments provable on our proof system are invalid.

People have found such flaws in logical systems. How do we know that our propositional system is free from such flaws? How can we prove soundness?

> *Soundness:* Any propositional argument for which we can give a formal proof is valid (on the truth-table test).

We first must show that all the propositional inference rules are *truth preserving* (which means that, when applied to true wffs, they yield only further true wffs). We have 13 inference rules: 6 S-rules, 6 I-rules, and RAA. It's easy (but tedious) to use the truth-table method of Section 3.6 to show that the S- and I-rules are truth preserving. All these rules pass the test (as you could check for yourself); when applied to true wffs, they yield only true wffs.

RAA is more difficult to check. We first show that the *first* use of RAA in a proof is truth preserving. Suppose that all previous not-blocked-off lines in a proof are true, and we use RAA to derive a further line; we have to show that this further line is true:

1	... = 1	⇐	Suppose that all these are true.
2	... = 1	⇐	
	asm: ~A	←	We assume that A is false.
	...		
	∴ B	⇐	We derive a contradiction.
	∴ ~B	⇐	
	∴ A	←	Does A then have to be true?

From previous true lines plus assumption "~A," we derive contradictory wffs "B" and "~B" using the S- and I-rules. We just saw that the S- and I-rules are truth preserving. So if the lines used to derive "B" and "~B" were all true, then both "B" and "~B" would have to be true – which is impossible. Hence the lines used to derive them can't all be true. Since the lines before the assumption are presumed to be true, assumption "~A" has to be false. So its opposite ("A") has to be true. So the first use of RAA in a proof is truth preserving.

We can similarly show that if the first use of RAA is truth preserving, then the second also must be. And we can show that if the first n uses of RAA are truth preserving, then the n+1 use also must be. Then we can apply the principle of mathematical induction:

Mathematical Induction

Suppose that something holds in the first case, and if it holds in the first n cases, then it holds in the n+1 case. Then it holds in all cases.

Using this principle, it follows that *all* uses of RAA are truth preserving.

Now suppose that an argument is provable in our propositional system. Then there's some proof that derives the conclusion from the premises using truth-preserving rules. So if the premises are true, then the conclusion also must be true – and so the argument is valid. So if an argument is provable in our propositional system, then it's valid. This establishes soundness.

Isn't this reasoning circular? Aren't we just assuming principles of propositional inference as we defend our propositional system? Of course we are. Nothing can be proved without assuming logical rules. We aren't attempting the impossible task of proving things about a logical system without assuming any logical rules. Instead, we are doing something more modest. We are trying to show, relying on ordinary reasoning, that we didn't make certain errors in setting up our system.

12.4 Completeness

Our soundness proof shows that our propositional system won't prove invalid arguments. You probably didn't doubt this anyway. But you may have doubted whether our system is strong enough to prove all valid propositional arguments. After all, the single-assumption method of doing proofs wasn't strong enough; Section 4.4 uncovered valid arguments that required further assumptions. How do we know that our expanded method is enough? Maybe Logicus will find a further propositional argument that's valid but not provable; then we'd have to strengthen our system still further. To calm these doubts, we'll show that our propositional system is complete:

> *Completeness:* Any propositional argument that is valid (on the truth-table test) can be proved using a formal proof.

By our definitions, a capital letter or its negation is a *simple* wff; all other wffs are *complex*. Any complex wff has one of these nine basic forms (where α and β represent any wffs):

$$\sim\sim\alpha \qquad \begin{array}{llll} (\alpha \cdot \beta) & (\alpha \vee \beta) & (\alpha \supset \beta) & (\alpha \equiv \beta) \\ \sim(\alpha \cdot \beta) & \sim(\alpha \vee \beta) & \sim(\alpha \supset \beta) & \sim(\alpha \equiv \beta) \end{array}$$

If we follow our full proof strategy (Section 4.5) but don't get a proof, then each complex not-blocked-off wff will be either *starred* (and we'll have further not-blocked-off lines that are or can be derived from it using an S- or I-rule) or *already broken up* (we have one side or its negation – but not what we need to apply an I-rule). Let's say that the complex wff then "breaks down" into the smaller wffs just mentioned. The nine basic forms will break down as follows:

This form:	breaks down into these:
$\sim\sim\alpha$	α [S-rule]
$(\alpha \cdot \beta)$	α and β [S-rule]
$\sim(\alpha \cdot \beta)$	~α or ~β [I-rule or already broken up]
$(\alpha \vee \beta)$	α or β [I-rule or already broken up]
$\sim(\alpha \vee \beta)$	~α and ~β [S-rule]
$(\alpha \supset \beta)$	~α or β [I-rule or already broken up]
$\sim(\alpha \supset \beta)$	α and ~β [S-rule]
$(\alpha \equiv \beta)$	(α ⊃ β) and (β ⊃ α) [S-rule]
$\sim(\alpha \equiv \beta)$	(α ∨ β) and ~(α · β) [S-rule]

Forms that break down using an S-rule always break down the same way. Other forms can break down in two ways. Take "~(A · B)." If this wff is starred, then we've derived "~A" or "~B" using an I-rule (or perhaps have one of these from some other source); if this wff is already broken up, then we have one side or its negation, but not what we need to apply an I-rule (or else we would have done this and the wff would be starred), so again we have "~A" or "~B." So, after applying our directions, every not-blocked-off complex wff is broken down into further not-blocked-off wffs.

Each wff is true if the wffs it breaks down into are true. We can check this by going through the nine cases given in the box. For example, ~~α breaks down into α – and is true if α is true. (α · β) breaks down into α and β – and is true if both of these are true. Similarly, ~(α · β) breaks down into ~α or ~β – and is true if either of these is true.

Suppose that we correctly apply our proof strategy to a *valid* propositional argument but don't get a proof. We can easily show that this is impossible. Let sets R and T be as follows:

- Set R (for "refutation") is the set of all the simple not-blocked-off wffs.
- Set T (for "total") is the set of all the not-blocked-off wffs. (Set T contains, among other things, the premises and the first assumption.)

Set R is consistent (or else we'd have applied RAA); so its members could all be true together. The truth of set R would ensure the truth of all the members of set T (since the complex members of T broke down into the members of R) – and set T contains the premises and denial of the conclusion. So set R gives truth conditions making the premises true and conclusion false. So the argument is *invalid*. This contradicts our supposition that we correctly applied our proof strategy to a *valid* argument and yet didn't get a proof.

This reasoning establishes the premise of the following valid argument:

> If we correctly apply our proof strategy to a propositional argument but don't get a proof, then the argument is invalid.
> ∴ If we correctly apply our proof strategy to a propositional argument and the argument is valid, then we'll get a proof.

$$((C \cdot {\sim}P) \supset {\sim}V)$$
$$\therefore ((C \cdot V) \supset P)$$

Now it's always possible to apply our proof strategy correctly to a propositional argument (since our strategy is consistent and will finish after a finite number of steps). So it's always possible to generate a proof for a valid propositional argument. This establishes the completeness of our propositional system.

So we've proved both soundness and completeness:

> *Soundness:* Every provable propositional argument is valid.
> *Completeness:* Every valid propositional argument is provable.

From both together, we conclude that a propositional argument is provable if and only if it's valid.

12.5 Corollaries

We'll now prove two more things about our propositional system. Let's say that a wff is a **theorem** if it's derivable from zero premises; "(P ∨ ~P)" is an example of a theorem. We can prove that a wff is a theorem if and only if it's a truth-table tautology. In this proof, "α" represents any wff:

1. α is a theorem if and only if "∴ α" is provable.
2. "∴ α" is provable if and only if "∴ α" is valid.
3. "∴ α" is valid if and only if α has an all-1 truth table.
4. α has an all-1 truth table if and only if α is a truth-table tautology.
   ∴ α is a theorem if and only if α is a truth-table tautology.

Premise 1 is true by the definition of "theorem." Premise 2 follows from our soundness and completeness proofs. Premise 3 is true because an argument without premises is valid if and only if its conclusion is true in all possible cases. Premise 4 is true by the definition of "truth-table tautology."

We also can prove that our propositional system is *consistent* – in the sense that no pair of contradictory wffs are both theorems. Our proof goes as follows:

1. All theorems are truth-table tautologies.
2. No pair of contradictory wffs are both truth-table tautologies.
∴ No pair of contradictory wffs are both theorems.

We just proved premise 1. Premise 2 is true; if it were false, then some wff α and its contradictory $\sim\alpha$ would both have all-1 truth tables – which is impossible. The conclusion follows. So our propositional system is consistent.

12.6   An axiomatic system

Our propositional system is an *inferential system,* since it uses mostly **inference rules** (rules that let us derive formulas from earlier formulas). It's also possible to systematize propositional logic as an *axiomatic system,* which uses mostly **axioms** (formulas that can be put on any line, regardless of earlier lines). Both approaches can be set up to be equally powerful – so that anything provable with one is provable with the other. Axiomatic systems tend to have a simpler structure, while inferential systems tend to be easier to use. The pioneers of symbolic logic used axiomatic systems.

I'll now sketch a version of an axiomatic system from *Principia Mathematica.*[1] We'll use the definitions of "wff," "premise," and "derived step" from our propositional system – and this definition of "proof":

> A *proof* is a vertical sequence of zero or more premises followed by one or more derived steps, where each derived step is an axiom or follows from earlier lines by the inference rule or the substitution of definitional equivalents.

There are four axioms; these axioms, and the inference rule and definitions, hold regardless of what wffs uniformly replace "A," "B," and "C":

Axiom 1. $((A \lor A) \supset A)$
Axiom 2. $(A \supset (A \lor B))$
Axiom 3. $((A \lor B) \supset (B \lor A))$
Axiom 4. $((A \supset B) \supset ((C \lor A) \supset (C \lor B)))$

---

[1] Bertrand Russell and Alfred North Whitehead (Cambridge: Cambridge University Press, 1910).

The system has one inference rule (*modus ponens*):

$$\text{Inference rule:} \quad (A \supset B), \ A \ \rightarrow \ B$$

It takes "∨" and "~" as undefined; it defines "⊃," "•," and "≡" as follows:

Definition 1. $(A \supset B) = (\sim A \lor B)$
Definition 2. $(A \cdot B) = \sim(\sim A \lor \sim B)$
Definition 3. $(A \equiv B) = ((A \supset B) \cdot (B \supset A))$

Let's prove "$(P \lor \sim P)$" two ways: first using our inferential system and then using the axiomatic system. Our inferential proof is trivially simple:

```
        [ ∴ (P ∨ ~P)          Valid
  *   1   ┌ asm: ~(P ∨ ~P)
      2   │ ∴ ~P  {from 1}
      3   └ ∴ P  {from 1}
      4   ∴ (P ∨ ~P)   {from 1; 2 contradicts 3}
```

The axiomatic proof is rather difficult:

1   ∴ $(((P \lor P) \supset P) \supset ((\sim P \lor (P \lor P)) \supset (\sim P \lor P)))$ {from axiom 4, substituting "$(P \lor P)$" for "A," "P" for "B," and "$\sim P$" for "C"}
2   ∴ $((P \lor P) \supset P)$ {from axiom 1, substituting "P" for "A"}
3   ∴ $((\sim P \lor (P \lor P)) \supset (\sim P \lor P))$ {from 1 and 2}
4   ∴ $(P \supset (P \lor P))$ {from axiom 2, substituting "P" for "A" and "P" for "B"}
5   ∴ $(\sim P \lor (P \lor P))$ {from 4, substituting things equivalent by definition 1}
6   ∴ $(\sim P \lor P)$ {from 3 and 5}
7   ∴ $((\sim P \lor P) \supset (P \lor \sim P))$ {from axiom 3, substituting "$\sim P$" for "A" and "P" for "B"}
8   ∴ $(P \lor \sim P)$ {from 6 and 7}

Since there's no automatic strategy, creating such proofs requires guesswork and intuition. And we might work for hours trying to prove an argument that's actually invalid. Axiomatic systems tend not to be user-friendly.

12.7   Gödel's theorem

Now we'll consider metalogic's most surprising discovery: Gödel's theorem.

Let's define a **formal system** (or **calculus**) to be an artificial language with notational grammar rules and notational rules for determining validity. Formal systems typically are either inferential (our usual approach) or axiomatic.

It's fairly easy to put propositional logic into a sound and complete formal system. Our inferential system does the job – as does the axiomatic system of Russell and Whitehead. In either system, a propositional argument is valid if and only if it's provable.

You might think that arithmetic could similarly be put into a sound and complete system. If we succeeded, we'd have an inferential or axiomatic system that could prove any truth of arithmetic but no falsehood. Then a statement of arithmetic would be true if and only if it's provable in the system.

But this is impossible. **Gödel's theorem** showed that we can't systematize arithmetic in this way. For any attempted formalization, one of two bad things will happen: some true statements of arithmetic won't be provable (making the system incomplete), or some false statements of arithmetic will be provable (making the system unsound). Gödel's theorem shows that any formal system attempting to encompass arithmetic will be incomplete or unsound.

You may find Gödel's theorem hard to believe. Arithmetic seems to be an area where everything can be proved one way or the other. But Kurt Gödel in 1931 showed the world that this was wrong. The reasoning behind his theorem is difficult; here I'll just try to give a glimpse of what it's about.[1]

What exactly is this "arithmetic" that we can't systematize? "Arithmetic" here is roughly like high-school algebra, but limited to positive whole numbers. It includes truths like these three:

$$2+2=4$$
$$\text{If } x+y=z, \text{ then } y+x=z.$$
$$\text{If } xy=18 \text{ and } x=2y, \text{ then } x=6 \text{ and } y=3.$$

More precisely, **arithmetic** is the set of truths and falsehoods that can be expressed using symbols for the vocabulary items in these boxes:

Mathematical vocabulary	*Logical vocabulary*
positive numbers: 1, 2, 3, ...	not, and, or, if-then
plus, times	variables: x, y, z, ...
to the power of	every, some
parentheses, equals	parentheses, equals

Gödel's theorem claims that no formal system with symbols for all the items in these two boxes can be both sound and complete.

The notions in our mathematical box can be reduced to a sound and complete formal system: one that we'll call the "number calculus." And the notions in our logical box can be reduced to a sound and complete formal system: our

---

[1] My little book, *Gödel's Theorem Simplified* (Langham, Maryland: University Press of America, 1984), tried to explain the theorem. Refer to this book for further information.

quantificational system. But combining these two systems produces a monster that can't be put into a sound and complete formal system.

We'll now construct a number calculus (NC) that uses seven symbols:

$$/ \quad + \quad \cdot \quad ^\wedge \quad (\quad) \quad =$$

"/" means "one" ("1"). We'll write 2 as "//" ("one one"), 3 as "///" ("one one one"), and so on. "+" is for "plus," "·" for "times," and "^" for "to the power of." Our seven symbols cover all the notions in our mathematical box.

Meaningful sequences of NC symbols are *numerals*, *terms*, and *wffs*:

---

1. Any string consisting of one or more instances of "/" is a *numeral*.
2. Every numeral is a *term*.
3. The result of joining any two terms by "+," "·," or "^" and enclosing the result in parentheses is a *term*.
4. The result of joining any two terms by "=" is a *wff*.

Here are examples (with the more usual equivalents below):

Numerals:	//	///////	
	2	7	
Terms:	///////	(// · //)	((/ + /) ^ //)
	7	2 · 2	(1+1)²
Wffs:	/// = ///	(// + //) = ////	
	3=3	2+2=4	

Our NC will be able to prove just the true wffs. NC uses one axiom and six inference rules; here's our axiom (in which any numeral can replace "a"):

$$\text{Axiom:} \quad a = a$$

Any instance of this (any self-identity using the same numeral on both sides) is an axiom: "/=/" ["1=1"], "//=//" ["2=2"], "///=///" ["3=3"], and so on.

Our inference rules let us substitute one string of symbols for another. We'll use "↔" to say that we can substitute the symbols on either side for those on the other side. We have two rules for "plus" (where "a" and "b" in our inference rules stand for any numerals):

$$\text{R1.} \quad (a+/) \leftrightarrow a/$$
$$\text{R2.} \quad (a+/b) \leftrightarrow (a/+b)$$

For example, R1 lets us interchange "(///+/)" ["3+1"] and "/////" ["4"]. R2 lets us interchange "(//+//)" ["2+2"] and "(///+/)" ["3+1"] – moving the "+" one "/" to the right. We'll see R3 to R6 in a moment.

An *NC proof* is a vertical sequence of wffs, each of which is either an axiom or else follows from earlier members by one of the inference rules R1 to R6. A *theorem* is any wff of a proof.

Using our axiom and inference rules R1 and R2, we can prove any true wff of NC that doesn't use "•" or "^." Here's a proof of "(//+//)=////" ["2+2=4"]:

1. ////=////   {from the axiom}
2. (///+/)=////   {from 1 using R1}
3. (//+//)=////   {from 2 using R2}

We start with a self-identity. We get line 2 by substituting "(///+/)" for "/////" (as permitted by rule R1). We get line 3 by further substituting "(//+//)" for "(///+/)" (as permitted by rule R2). So "(//+//)=////" is a theorem.

Here are our rules for "times" and "to the power of":

R3. $(a \cdot /) \leftrightarrow a$
R4. $(a \cdot /b) \leftrightarrow ((a \cdot b) + a)$
R5. $(a \wedge /) \leftrightarrow a$
R6. $(a \wedge /b) \leftrightarrow ((a \wedge b) \cdot a)$

Our NC is sound and complete; any wff of NC is true if and only if it's provable in NC. This is easy to show, but we won't do the proof here.

Suppose that we take our number calculus, add the symbols and inference rules of our quantificational logic, add a few more axioms and inference rules, and call the result the "arithmetic calculus" (AC). We could then symbolize any statement of arithmetic in AC. So we could symbolize these:

If x+y=z, then y+x=z.
= $((x+y)=z \supset (y+x)=z)$

If xy=8 and x=2y, then x=4 and y=2.
= $(((x \cdot y)=//////// \cdot x=(//\cdot y)) \supset (x=//// \cdot y=//))$

x is even.
=   For some number y, x = 2 times y.
= $(\exists y)x=(// \cdot y)$

x is prime.
=   For every number y and z, if x = y times z, then y=1 or z=1.
= $(y)(z)(x=(y \cdot z) \supset (y=/ \vee z=/))$

We could even symbolize Goldbach's conjecture (which no one has yet been able to prove or disprove):

Every even number is the sum of two primes.
= $(x)((\exists y)x=(2 \cdot y) \supset (\exists x')(\exists x'')(x=(x'+x'') \cdot ((y)(z)(x'=(y \cdot z)$
    $\supset (y=/ \vee z=/)) \cdot (y)(z)(x''=(y \cdot z) \supset (y=/ \vee z=/)))))$

Gödel's theorem shows that any such arithmetic calculus has a fatal flaw: either it *can't* prove some arithmetic truths, or it *can* prove some arithmetic falsehoods. This flaw comes not from an accidental defect in our choice of axioms and inference rules, but from the fact that any such system can encode messages about itself.

To show how this works, it's helpful to use a version of AC with minimal vocabulary. The version that we've sketched so far uses these symbols:

$$/ \quad + \quad \cdot \quad \wedge \quad (\quad) \quad = \quad \sim \quad \vee \quad \supset \quad \exists \quad \text{x, y, z, x}', \ldots$$

We'll now economize. Instead of writing "∧" ("to the power of"), we'll write "⋅⋅." We'll drop "∨" and "⊃," and express the same ideas using "∼" and "⋅" (see Section 12.2). We'll use "n," "nn," "nnn," "nnnn," … for our variables (instead of "x," "y," "z," "x'," …). We'll drop "∃," and write "∼(n)∼" instead of "(∃n)." Our minimal-vocabulary version of AC uses only eight symbols:

$$/ \quad + \quad \cdot \quad (\quad) \quad = \quad \sim \quad \text{n}$$

Any statement of arithmetic can be symbolized by combining these symbols.

Our strategy for proving Gödel's theorem goes as follows. First we give ID numbers to AC formulas. Then we see how AC formulas can encode messages about other AC formulas. Then we construct a special formula, called the Gödel formula G, that encodes this message about itself: "G isn't provable." G asserts its own unprovability; this is the key to Gödel's theorem.

It's easy to give ID numbers to AC formulas. Let's assign to each of the eight symbols a digit from 1 to 8:

Symbol:	/	+	⋅	(	)	=	∼	n
ID Number:	1	2	3	4	5	6	7	8

Thus "/" has ID # 1 and "+" has ID # 2. To get the ID number for a formula, we replace each symbol by its one-digit ID number. So we replace "/" by "1," "+" by "2," and so on. Here are two examples:

The ID # for: "/=/"	The ID # for: "(//+//)"
is: 161	is: 4112115

The ID numbers follow patterns. For example, each numeral has an ID number consisting of all 1's:

Numeral:	/	//	///	////
ID Number:	1	11	111	1111

So we can say:

| Formula # n is a numeral | if and only if | n consists of all 1's. |

We can express the right-hand box as the equation "(nine-times-n plus one) equals some power of ten," or "($\exists$x)9n+1=10^x," which can be symbolized in an AC formula.[1] This AC formula is true of any number n if and only if formula # n is a numeral. This is how system AC encodes messages about itself.

An AC theorem is any formula provable in AC. The ID numbers for theorems follow definite but complex patterns. It's possible to find an equation that's true of any number n if and only if formula # n is a theorem. If we let "n is ..." represent this equation, we can say:

| Formula # n is a theorem | if and only if | n is .... |

The equation in the right-hand box would be very complicated.

To make things more intuitive, let's pretend that all and only theorems have *odd* ID numbers. Then "n is odd" encodes "Formula # n is a theorem":

| Formula # n is a theorem | if and only if | n is odd. |

For example, "161 is odd" encodes the message that formula # 161 (which is "/=/") is a theorem:

| Formula # 161 is a theorem | if and only if | 161 is odd. |

Then "n is even" would encode the message that formula # n is a non-theorem:

| Formula # n is a non-theorem | if and only if | n is even. |

Imagine that "485..." is some specific very large number. Let the following box represent the AC formula that says that 485... is even:

| 485... is even. |

This formula would encode the following message:

---

[1] The AC formula for this equation is "~(nn)~(((\\\\\\\\\ • n) + \) = (\\\\\\\\\ •• nn))." This formula has ID # 7488574441111111113852156411111111111338855. It's important that the statements in our right-hand boxes can be symbolized in AC formulas with definite ID numbers. It isn't important that we write out the formulas or their ID numbers.

> Formula # 485... is a non-theorem.

So the AC formula is true if and only if formula # 485... is a non-theorem. Now let us suppose that this formula itself happens to have ID number 485.... Then the formula would be talking about itself, declaring that it itself is a non-theorem. This is what the Gödel formula G does. G, which itself has a certain ID number, encodes the message that the formula with this ID number is a non-theorem. G in effect says this:

G | G is not a theorem.

So G encodes the message "G is not a theorem." But this means that G is true if and only if it isn't a theorem.

So G is true if and only if it isn't provable. Now G, as a formula of arithmetic, is either true or false. Is G true? Then it isn't provable – and our system contains unprovable truths. Or maybe G is false? Then it's provable – and our system contains provable falsehoods. In either case, system AC is flawed.

We can't remove the flaw by adding further axioms or inference rules. No matter what we add to the arithmetic calculus, we can use Gödel's technique to find a formula of the system that's true-but-unprovable or false-but-provable. Hence arithmetic can't be reduced to any sound and complete formal system.

This completes our sketch of the reasoning behind Gödel's proof. To fill in the details would require answering two further questions:

- Consider the equation that's true of any number n if and only if formula # n is a theorem. This equation would have to be much more complicated than "n is odd." How can we produce this equation?
- If we have the equation, how do we then produce a formula with a given number that says that the formula with that number is a non-theorem?

The answers to these questions are too complicated to go into here. The important thing is that the details can be worked out; we won't worry about how to work them out.[1]

Most people find the last two chapters surprising. We tend to think that *everything* can be proved in math, and that *nothing* can be proved in ethics. But Gödel's theorem shows that not everything can be proved in math. And our golden-rule formalization shows that some important ideas (like the golden rule) can be proved in ethics. Logic can surprise us.

---

[1] For the technical details, see my *Gödel's Theorem Simplified* (Langham, Maryland: University Press of America, 1984).

CHAPTER 13
Inductive Reasoning

Much of our everyday reasoning deals with probabilities. We observe patterns and conclude that, based on these, such and such a belief is *probably* true. This is inductive reasoning.

13.1 The statistical syllogism

The Appalachian Trail (AT), a 2,160-mile footpath from Georgia to Maine in the eastern US, has a series of lean-to shelters. Suppose we backpack on the AT and plan to spend the night at Rocky Gap Shelter. We'd like to know before-hand whether there's water (a spring or stream) close by. If we knew that *all* AT shelters have water, or that *none* do, we could reason *deductively*:

All AT shelters have water.　　　　No AT shelters have water.
Rocky Gap is an AT shelter.　　　Rocky Gap is an AT shelter.
∴ Rocky Gap has water.　　　　∴ Rocky Gap doesn't have water.

Both are deductively valid. Both have a tight connection between premises and conclusion; if the premises are true, the conclusion *has* to be true. Deductive validity is an all-or-nothing affair. Deductive arguments can't be "half-valid," nor can one be "more valid" than another.

Actually, most of the shelters have water, but a few don't. In my experience, roughly 90 percent have water. (This varies somewhat by season and rainfall.) If we knew that 90 percent of them have water, we could reason *inductively*:

90 percent of the AT shelters have water.
Rocky Gap is an AT shelter.
This is all we know about the matter.
∴ Probably Rocky Gap has water.

This is a strong inductive argument. Relative to the premises, the conclusion is a good bet. But it's partially a guess; it could turn out false, even though the premises are all true.

The "This is all we know about the matter" premise means "We have no further information that influences the probability of the conclusion." Suppose that we just met a thirsty backpacker complaining that the water at Rocky Gap had dried up; that would change the probability of the conclusion. The premise claims that we have no such further information.

Two features set inductive arguments apart from deductive ones. (1) Inductive arguments vary in how strongly the premises support the conclusion. The premise "99 percent of the AT shelters have water" supports the conclusion more strongly than does "60 percent of the AT shelters have water." We have shades of gray here – not the black and white of deductive validity/invalidity. (2) Even a strong inductive argument has only a loose connection between premises and conclusion. The premises make the conclusion at most only highly probable; the premises might be true while the conclusion is false. Inductive reasoning is a form of guessing based on recognizing and extending known patterns and resemblances.

Let me sum up. A **deductive argument** claims that it's *logically necessary* that if the premises are all true then so is the conclusion. An **inductive argument** claims that it's *likely* (but not logically necessary) that if the premises are all true then so is the conclusion. While this book is mostly about deductive arguments, this chapter focuses on inductive ones.

We can refine our AT conclusion by specifying a probability:

> 90 percent of the AT shelters have water.
> Rocky Gap is an AT shelter.
> This is all we know about the matter.
> ∴ *It's 90 percent probable that* Rocky Gap has water.

The general principle is this:

Statistical Syllogism

N percent of A's are B's.
X is an A.
This is all we know about the matter.
∴ It's N percent probable that X is a B.

Here's another example:

> 50 percent of coin tosses are heads.
> This is a coin toss.
> This is all we know about the matter.
> ∴ It's 50 percent probable that this is heads.

Suppose that all we know affecting the probability of the toss being heads is that 50 percent of coin tosses are heads and that this is a coin toss. Then it's 50 percent probable to us that the toss is heads. This holds if we didn't yet toss the coin, or if we tossed it but didn't yet know how it landed. The matter is different if we know how it landed. Then it's no longer just 50 percent probable to us that it's heads; rather, we *know* that it's heads or that it's tails.

Statistical syllogisms apply most cleanly if we know little about the subject. Suppose we know these two things about Michigan's football team:

1. It's first down – and Michigan runs 70 percent of the time on first down.
2. Michigan is behind – and passes 70 percent of the time when it's behind.

Relative to 1, Michigan probably will run. Relative to 2, Michigan probably will pass. But it's unclear what Michigan probably will do relative to 1 and 2. It gets worse if we add facts about the score, the time left, and the offensive formation. Each fact by itself may lead to a clear conclusion about what Michigan probably will do; but the combination muddies the issue. Too much information can confuse us when we apply statistical syllogisms.

Chapter 1 distinguished between *valid* and *sound* deductive arguments. *Valid* asserts a correct relation between premises and conclusion, but says nothing about the truth of the premises; *sound* includes both "valid" and "has true premises." It's convenient to have similar terms for inductive arguments. Let's say that an argument is **strong** inductively if the conclusion is probable relative to the premises. And let's say that an argument is **reliable** inductively if it's strong and has true premises. Here's a chart:

	Deductively	Inductively
Correct premise/conclusion link ➜	*valid*	*strong*
This plus true premises ➜	*sound*	*reliable*

Here's a very strong inductive argument that isn't reliable:

> Michigan loses 99 percent of the time it plays.
> Michigan is playing today.
> This is all we know about the matter.
> ∴ Probably Michigan will lose today.

This is very strong, because in relation to the premises the conclusion is very probable. But the argument isn't reliable, since premise 1 is false.

We'll see that inductive logic (unlike deductive logic) is highly controversial and difficult to reduce to neat and tidy principles.

13.2 Probability calculations

Sometimes we can calculate probabilities rather precisely. Experience shows that coins tend to land heads half the time and tails the other half; each coin has a 50 percent chance of landing heads and a 50 percent chance of landing tails. Suppose we toss two coins. There are four possible combinations of heads (**H**) and tails (**T**) for the two coins:

HH HT TH TT

Each combination is equally probable. So our chance of getting two heads is 25 percent (.25 or ¼), since it happens in 1 out of 4 cases. Here's the rule (where "prob" is short for "the probability" and the "favorable cases" are those in which A is true):

This rule holds if every case is equally likely:

$$\text{Prob of A} = \frac{\text{the number of favorable cases}}{\text{the total number of cases}}$$

Our chance of getting at least one head is 75 percent (.75 or ¾), since it happens in 3 out of 4 cases. So here probability is based on a ratio between the number of favorable cases and the total number of cases.

With odds, the ratio concerns favorable and unfavorable cases (where the "unfavorable cases" are those in which A is false). The odds are in your favor if the number of favorable cases is greater (then your probability is greater than 50 percent):

$$\text{The odds \textit{in favor of} A} = \frac{\text{the number of favorable cases}}{\text{the number of unfavorable cases}}$$

So the odds are 3 to 1 in favor of getting at least one head – since it happens in 3 cases and fails in only 1 case. The odds are against you if the number of unfavorable cases is greater (so your probability is less than 50 percent):

$$\text{The odds \textit{against} A} = \frac{\text{the number of unfavorable cases}}{\text{the number of favorable cases}}$$

Odds are usually given in whole numbers, with the larger number first. We wouldn't say "The odds are 1 to 3 *in favor of* getting two heads"; rather, we'd put the larger number first and say "The odds are 3 to 1 *against* getting two heads." Here are examples of how to convert between odds and probability:

- The odds are even (1 to 1) that we'll win = The probability of our winning is 50 percent.

- The odds are 7 to 5 in favor of our winning = The probability of our winning is 7/12 (7 favorable cases out of 12 total cases, or 58.3 percent).
- The odds are 7 to 5 against our winning = The probability of our winning is 5/12 (5 favorable cases out of 12 total cases, 41.7 percent).
- The probability of our winning is 70 percent = The odds are 7 to 3 in favor of our winning (70 percent favorable to 30 percent unfavorable).
- The probability of our winning is 30 percent = The odds are 7 to 3 against our winning (70 percent unfavorable to 30 percent favorable).

We'll now learn some rules for calculating probabilities. The first two rules are about necessary truths and self-contradictions:

If A is a necessary truth:	If A is a self-contradiction:
Prob of A = 100 percent.	Prob of A = 0 percent.

Our chance of a specific coin being *either heads or not heads* is 100 percent. And our chance of it being *both heads and not heads* (at one time) is 0 percent.

This next rule relates the probability of a given event happening to the probability of that event not happening:

$$\text{Prob of not-A} = 100 \text{ percent - prob of A.}$$

So if our chance of getting two heads is 25 percent, then our chance of *not* getting two heads is 75 percent (100 percent - 25 percent).

The next rule concerns events that are **independent** of each other, in that the occurrence of one doesn't make the occurrence of the other any more or any less likely (the first coin being heads, for example, doesn't make it any more or any less likely that the second coin will be heads):

$$\text{If A and B are independent:}$$
$$\text{Prob of (A and B)} = \text{prob of A} \cdot \text{prob of B.}$$

Probabilities multiply with AND. So our chance of throwing two heads (25 percent) *and then* throwing two heads again (25 percent) is 6.25 percent (25 percent · 25 percent).

This next rule holds for events that are **mutually exclusive**, in that they can't both happen together:

$$\text{If A and B are mutually exclusive:}$$
$$\text{Prob of (A or B)} = \text{prob of A} + \text{prob of B.}$$

Probabilities add with OR. It can't happen that we throw two heads and also (on the same toss of two coins) throw two tails. The probability of either event is 25 percent. So the probability of one *or* the other happening (getting two heads *or* two tails) is 50 percent (25 percent + 25 percent). When the two events aren't mutually exclusive, we have to follow this more complex rule:

> This holds even if A and B aren't mutually exclusive:
>
> Prob of (A or B) = Prob of A + prob of B - prob of (A and B).

Suppose we calculate the probability of getting at least one head when we flip two coins. Coin 1 being heads and coin 2 being heads aren't mutually exclusive events, since they might both happen together; so we have to apply the more complex rule. The chance of coin 1 being heads *or* coin 2 being heads = the chance of coin 1 being heads (50 percent) + the chance of coin 2 being heads (50 percent) - the chance of coin 1 and coin 2 both being heads (25 percent). So our chance of getting at least one head is 75 percent (50 percent + 50 percent - 25 percent). If A and B are mutually exclusive then the probability of (A and B) = 0; then the simpler rule gives the same result as the more complex rule.

Suppose we throw two dice. There are six equally probable possibilities for each die. Here are the possible combinations and resulting totals:

	1	2	3	4	5	6	← second die
1	2	3	4	5	6	7	
2	3	4	5	6	7	8	
first 3	4	5	6	7	8	9	← TOTALS
die 4	5	6	7	8	9	10	
5	6	7	8	9	10	11	
6	7	8	9	10	11	12	

There are 36 possible combinations; each has an equal 1/36 probability. The chance of getting a 12 is 1/36, since we get a 12 in only 1 out of 36 cases. The chance of getting an 11 is 1/18 (2/36) – since we get an 11 in 2 out of 36 cases. Similarly, we have a 1/6 (6/36) chance of getting a 10 or higher, and a 5/6 (30/36) chance of getting a 9 or lower.

Cards provide another example. What's our chance of getting 2 aces when dealt 2 cards from a standard 52-card deck? We might think that, since 1/13 of the cards are aces, our chance of getting two aces is 1/169 (1/13 · 1/13). But that's wrong. Our chance of getting an ace on the first draw is 1/13, since there are 4 aces out of the 52 cards, and 4/52 = 1/13. But if we get an ace on the first draw, then there are only 3 aces left out of 51 cards. So our chance of getting a second ace is 1/17 (3/51). Thus, our chance of getting 2 aces when dealt 2 cards from a standard 52-card deck is 1/221 (1/13 · 1/17), or about 0.45 percent.

Here the events aren't independent. Getting an ace on the first card reduces the number of aces left and lowers our chance of drawing an ace for the second card. This is unlike coins, where getting heads on one toss doesn't affect our chance of getting heads on the next toss. If events A and B aren't independent, we need this rule for determining the probability of the conjunction (A and B):

> This holds even if A and B aren't independent:
>
> Prob of (A and B)   =   Prob of A · (prob of B after A occurs).

This reflects the reasoning we used to calculate our chance of getting 2 aces from a 52-card deck. What's our chance if we use a double 104-card deck? Our chance of getting a first ace is again 1/13 (since there are 8 aces out of the 104 cards, and 8/104 = 1/13). After we get a first ace, there are 7 aces left in the 103 cards. Our chance of getting a second ace is 7/103. So the probability of getting a first ace and then a second ace = 1/13 (the probability of the first ace) · 7/103 (the probability of the second ace). This works out to 7/1339 (1/13 · 7/103), or about 0.52 percent. So our chance of getting 2 aces when dealt 2 cards from a double 104-card deck is about 0.52 percent. We have a better chance with the double deck (0.52 percent instead of 0.45 percent).

Mathematically fair betting odds are in reverse proportion to probability. Suppose we bet on whether, in drawing 2 cards from a standard 52-card deck, we'll draw 2 aces. There's a 1/221 chance of getting 2 aces, so the odds are 220 to 1 against us. If we bet $1, we should get $220 if we win. If we play for a long time under such betting odds, our gains and losses probably will roughly equalize. In practice, of course, the casino takes its cut; then we get less than mathematically fair earnings if we win. If we play for a long time under such odds, probably we'll lose and the casino will win. That's why Las Vegas casinos look like the palaces of emperors.

13.2a   Exercise – LogiCola P (P, O, & C)

Work out the following problems. A calculator is useful for some of them.

You're playing blackjack and your first card is an ace. What's your chance of getting a card worth 10 (a 10, jack, queen, or king) for your next card? You're using a standard 52-card deck.	There are 16 such cards (one 10, J, Q, and K for each suit) from 51 remaining cards. So your chance is 16/51 (about 31.4 percent).

1. What would the answer to the sample problem be with a double 104-card deck?
2. Suppose that the Cubs and Mets play baseball today. There's a 60 percent chance of rain, which would cancel the game. If the teams play, the Cubs have a 20 percent chance of winning. What chance do the Cubs have of winning today?

3. You're tossing coins. You tossed 5 heads in a row using a fair coin. What's the probability now that the next coin will be heads?

4. You're about to toss 6 coins. What's the probability that all 6 will be heads?

5. Suppose that there's an 80 percent chance that the winner of the Michigan versus Ohio State game will go to the Rose Bowl, a 60 percent chance that Michigan will beat Ohio State, and a 30 percent chance that Michigan will win the Rose Bowl if it goes. Then what's the probability that Michigan will win the Rose Bowl?

6. Suppose you bet $10 that Michigan will win the Rose Bowl. Assuming the probabilities of the last example and mathematically fair betting odds, how much money should you win if Michigan wins the Rose Bowl?

7. You're playing blackjack and get an ace for the first card. You know that the cards used on the only previous hand were a 5, a 6, two 7s, and two 9s, and that all these are in the discard pile. What's your chance of getting a card worth 10 (that is, a 10, jack, queen, or king) for the next card? Presume that you're using a standard 52-card deck.

8. What would the answer to the last problem be with a double 104-card deck?

9. You're throwing a pair of dice. Your sister bets you even money that you'll throw an even number (adding both together). Is she playing you for a sucker?

10. Your sister is throwing a pair of dice. She says, "I bet I'll throw a number divisible by three." What are the mathematically fair betting odds?

11. You're dealt five cards: two 3s, a 4, a 6, and a 7. If you get another card, what's the probability that it will be a 5? What's the probability that it will be a 3?

12. You're at a casino in Las Vegas and walk by a $1 slot machine that says "Win $2,000!" Assume that this is the only way you can win and that it gives mathematically fair odds or worse. What's your chance of winning if you deposit $1?

13. What's the antecedent probability that both your parents have their birthday on the same day of the year? (Ignore leap-year complications.)

14. Our football team, Michigan, is 2 points behind with a few seconds left. We have the ball, fourth and two, on the Ohio State 38. We could have the kicker try a long field goal, which would win the game. The probability of his kicking this goal is 30 percent. Or we could try to make a first down and then kick from a shorter distance. There's a 70 percent probability of making a first down and a 50 percent probability of making the shorter field goal if we make the first down. Which alternative gives us a better chance to make the field goal?

15. Our team, Michigan, is 2 points ahead with a minute left. Ohio State is going for it on fourth down. It's 60 percent probable that they'll pass, and 40 percent probable that they'll run. We can defense the pass or defense the run. If we defense the pass, then we're 70 percent likely to stop a pass but only 40 percent likely to stop a run. If we defense the run, then we're 80 percent likely to stop a run but only 50 percent likely to stop a pass. What should we do?

13.3 Philosophical questions

We'll now consider four philosophical questions on probability. Philosophers disagree on how to answer these questions.

1. Are the ultimate scientific laws governing the universe *deterministic* or *probabilistic* in nature?

Some philosophers contend that all ultimate scientific laws are *deterministic*. They think we speak of probability only because we lack knowledge. Suppose that we knew all the laws of nature and all the concrete facts about the world at a given time, and could apply this knowledge. Then we could infallibly predict whether the coin will come up heads, whether it will rain three years from today, and who will win the World Cup 30 years from now. This is the thesis of determinism.

Other philosophers say that some or all of the ultimate laws governing our world are *probabilistic*. Such laws say not that under given conditions a result necessarily obtains, but rather that under these conditions the result *probably* obtains. They see the probabilistic laws of quantum physics as evidence that the world is a big dice game.

Since the empirical evidence is inconclusive, it's hard to be sure which side is correct. Physics today embraces probabilistic laws, but could some day return to deterministic laws. The issue is complicated by the controversy over whether determinism is an empirical or an *a priori* issue (see Section 14.8); some think reason (and not experience) gives us certainty that the world is deterministic. The debate goes on.

2. What does "probable" mean? And can every statement be assigned a numerical probability relative to given evidence?

Philosophers distinguish various senses of "probable." "The *probability* of heads is 50 percent" could be taken in at least four different ways:

- *Ratio of observed frequencies*: We've observed that coins land heads about half of the time.
- *Ratio of abstract possibilities*: Heads is one of the two equally likely abstract possibilities.
- *Measure of actual confidence*: We have the same degree of confidence in the toss being heads as we have in it not being heads.
- *Measure of rational confidence*: It's rational to have the same degree of confidence in the toss being heads as in it not being heads.

We used a *ratio of observed frequencies* to calculate the probability of finding water at Rocky Gap Shelter. And we used a *ratio of abstract possibilities* to calculate the probability of being dealt two aces. So sometimes these ratio approaches can give numerical probabilities. But sometimes they can't. Neither ratio approach gives a numerical probability to "Michigan will run" relative to information about ancient Greek philosophy – or relative to this combination:

1. It's first down – and Michigan runs 70 percent of the time on first down.
2. Michigan is behind – and passes 70 percent of the time when it's behind.

Only in special cases do the ratio approaches give numerical probabilities.

The *measure of actual confidence* sometimes yields numerical probabilities. Consider these statements:

> "There is life on other galaxies."
> "Michigan will beat Ohio State this year."
> "There is a God."

If you regard 1-to-1 betting odds on one of these as fair, then your actual confidence in the statement is 50 percent. But you may be unwilling to commit yourself on fair betting odds. Maybe you can't even say if your confidence in the statement is less or greater than your confidence that a coin toss will be heads. Then we likely can't assign numbers to your actual confidence.

The *rational confidence* approach would seem able to assign numerical probabilities only if these can be based on one of the other approaches. But some suggest a possible-world (see Section 7.1) analysis of rational confidence, which assigns numerical probabilities to *any* statement. This approach defines "Statement A has a probability of N percent relative to data B" to mean "In N percent of the possible worlds where B is true, A also is true." This approach shows promise, but it isn't yet clear whether it can work in real cases.

Some doubt whether probability as rational confidence satisfies the standard probability rules of the last section. These rules say that all necessary statements have a probability of 100 percent relative to any data. But consider a complicated propositional logic formula A that is a necessary truth, even though your evidence suggests that it isn't; perhaps your normally reliable logic teacher tells you that A isn't a necessary truth – or perhaps in error you get a truth-table line where A is false. Relative to your data, it seems rational not to put 100 percent confidence in formula A (even though A in fact is a necessary truth). So is probability theory wrong?

Probability theory is idealized rather than wrong. It describes the confidence an ideal reasoner would have, based on an ideal analysis of the data; an ideal reasoner would always recognize necessary truths and put 100 percent confidence in them. So we have to be careful in applying probability theory to the beliefs of non-ideal human beings; we must be like physicists who give simple equations for "frictionless bodies" and then make allowances for the idealization when applying the equations to real cases.

Probability as *actual confidence* definitely can violate the probability rules. Many would calculate the probability of drawing 2 aces from a 52 or 104 card deck as 1/169 (1/13 · 1/13); so they'd regard 168-to-1 betting odds as fair. But the probability rules say this is wrong (see Section 13.2).

3. How does probability relate to how ideally rational persons *believe*?

On one view, an ideally rational person would believe all and only those statements that are more than 50 percent probable relative to the person's data. But this view has strange implications. Suppose that each of these statements has an equal 33 1/3 percent probability:

> "Austria will win the World Cup."
> "Brazil will win the World Cup."
> "China will win the World Cup."

Then each of these three has a 66 2/3 percent probability:

> "Austria won't win it, but Brazil or China will."
> "Brazil won't win it, but Austria or China will."
> "China won't win it, but Austria or Brazil will."

On the view just described, an ideally rational person would believe all three statements. But this is silly; only a very confused person could do this.

The view has other problems. Why pick a 50 percent figure? Why wouldn't an ideally rational person believe all and only those statements that are at least 60 percent (or 75 percent or 90 percent) probable? There are further problems if sometimes (or usually?) there is no way to work out numerical probabilities.

The view gives an ideal of selecting all beliefs in a way that's free of subjective factors (like feelings and practical interests). Some find this ideal attractive. Pragmatists find it repulsive. They believe in following subjective factors on issues that our intellects can't decide. They think numerical probability doesn't apply to life's deeper issues (like free will, God, or basic moral principles).

4. How does probability relate to how ideally rational persons *act*?

On one view, an ideally rational person always acts to maximize **expected gain**. In working out what to do, such a person would list the possible alternative actions (A, B, C, ...) and then consider the possible outcomes (A1, A2, A3, ...) of each action. The gain or loss of each outcome would be multiplied by the probability of that outcome occurring; adding these together gives the action's expected gain. So an action's expected gain is the sum of probability-times-gain of its various possible outcomes. An ideally rational person, on this view, would always do whatever had the highest expected gain; this entails going for the lowest expected loss when every alternative loses.

What is "gain" here? Is it pleasure or satisfaction of desires – for oneself or for one's group or for all affected by the action? Or is it financial gain – for oneself or for one's company? To keep things concrete, let's focus on an economic version of the theory. Let's consider the view that ideally rational gamblers would always act to maximize their expected financial gain.

Imagine that you're such an "ideally rational gambler." You find a game of dice that pays $3,536 on a $100 bet if you throw a 12. You'd work out the expected gain of playing or not playing (alternatives P and N) in this way:

P. PLAYING. There are two possible outcomes: P1 (I win) and P2 (I lose). P1 is 1/36 likely and gains $3,536; P1 is worth (1/36 · $3,536) or $98.22. P2 is 35/36 likely and loses $100; P2 is worth (35/36 · -$100), or -$97.22. The expected gain of alternative P is ($98.22 - 97.22), or $1.

N. NOT PLAYING. On this alternative, I won't win or lose anything. The expected gain of alternative N is (100 percent · $0), or $0.

So then you'd play – unless you found another game with a greater expected gain. If you played this dice game only once, you'd be 97 percent likely to lose money. But the occasional payoff is great; you'd likely gain about a million dollars if you played a million times.

An "ideally rational gambler" would gamble if the odds were favorable, but not otherwise. Since Las Vegas casinos take their cut, the odds there are against the individual gambler; so an ideally rational gambler wouldn't gamble at these places. But people have interests other than money; for many, gambling is great fun – and they're willing to pay for the fun.

Some whose only concern is money refuse to gamble even when the odds are in their favor. Their concern may be to have *enough* money. They may better satisfy this by being cautious; they don't want to risk losing what they have for the sake of gaining more. Few people would endanger their total savings for the 1-in-900 chance of gaining a fortune 1000 times as great.

Another problem with "maximize expected gain" is that it's difficult or impossible to give objective numerical probabilities except in cases involving things like dice or cards. How can we multiply probability by gain unless we can express both probability and gain by numbers?

This imperative to "maximize expected gain" thus faces grave difficulties if taken as an overall guide to life. But it can sometimes be useful as a rough guide. At times it's helpful to work out the expected gain of the various alternatives, perhaps guessing at the probabilities and gains involved.

Here's an actual example involving the flight for a hiking trip. My travel agent gave me two alternatives:

Ticket A costs $250 and allows me to change my return date.	Ticket B costs $200 but has a $125 charge if I change my return date.

Which ticket is a better deal for me? Intuitively, A is better if a change is very likely, while B is better if a change is very unlikely. But we can be more precise than that. Let x represent the probability of my changing the return. Then:

Expected cost of A = $250.   Expected cost of B = $200 + ($125 · x).

Some algebra shows the expected costs to be identical if x is 40 percent. Thus A is better if a change is more than 40 percent likely, while B is better if a change is less likely than that. The actual probability of my having to change the return was clearly less than 40 percent; judging from my past, it was more like 10 percent. Thus, ticket B minimized my expected cost. So I bought ticket B.

In some cases, however, it might be more rational to pick A. Maybe I have $250 but I don't have the $325 that option B might cost me – so I'd be in great trouble if I had to change the return date. It might then be more rational to follow the "better safe than sorry" principle and pick A.

13.3a   Exercise – LogiCola P (G, D, & V)

Suppose that you decide to believe all and only statements that are more probable than not. You're tossing three coins; which of the next six statements would you believe?

Either the first coin will be heads, or all three will be tails.	You'd believe this, since it happens in 5 out of 8 cases:	**HHH** THH **HHT** THT **HTH** TTH **HTT** **TTT**

1. I'll get three heads.
2. I'll get at least one tail.
3. I'll get two heads and one tail.
4. I'll get either two heads and one tail, or else two tails and one head.
5. The first coin will be heads.

For problems 6 through 10, suppose that you decide to do in all cases whatever would maximize your expected financial gain.

6. You're deciding whether to keep your life savings in a bank (which pays a dependable 10 percent) or invest in Mushy Software. If you invest in Mushy, you have a 99 percent chance of losing everything and a 1 percent chance of making 120 times your investment this year. What should you do?

7. You're deciding whether to get hospitalization insurance. There's a 1 percent chance per year that you'll have a $10,000 hospital visit (ignore other hospitalizations); the insurance would cover it all. What's the most you'd agree to pay per year for this insurance?

8. You're running a company that offers hospitalization insurance. There's a 1 percent chance per year that a customer will have a $10,000 hospital visit (ignore other hospitalizations); the insurance would cover it all. What's the least you could charge per year for this insurance to break even?

9. You're deciding whether to invest in Mushy Software or in Enormity Incorporated. Mushy stock has a 30 percent probability of gaining 80 percent, and a 70 percent probability of losing 20 percent. Enormity stock has a 100 percent probability of gaining 11 percent. Which should you invest in?

10.   You're deciding whether to buy a Cut-Rate computer or one from Enormity Incorporated. Both models perform identically. There's a 60 percent probability that either machine will need repair over the period you'll keep it. The Cut-Rate model is $600 but will be a total loss (requiring the purchase of another computer for $600) if it ever needs repair. The Enormity Incorporated model is $900 but offers free repairs. Which should you buy?

13.4   Reasoning from a sample

Recall our statistical-syllogism example about the Appalachian Trail:

> 90 percent of the AT shelters have water.
> Rocky Gap is an AT shelter.
> This is all we know about the matter.
> ∴ Probably Rocky Gap has water.

Premise 1 says 90 percent of the shelters have water. I might base this on an examination of all the shelters; if I checked each for water, then I could argue:

> There are 300 AT shelters.
> 270 AT shelters have water.
> If there are 300 AT shelters and 270 AT shelters have water,
>   then 90 percent (270/300) of the AT shelters have water.
> ∴ 90 percent of the AT shelters have water.

This is deductively valid. If the premises are true, the conclusion *must* be true; there's no guessing.

In fact, I base my claim on inductive reasoning. On my AT hikes, I've observed a large and varied group of shelters; about 90 percent of these have had water. I conclude that probably roughly 90 percent of *all* the shelters (including those not observed) have water. I argue as follows:

> 90 percent of examined AT shelters have water.
> A large and varied group of AT shelters has been examined.
> ∴ Probably roughly 90 percent of all AT shelters have water.

This presumes that a large and varied sample probably gives us a good idea of the whole. Here's the general principle:

Sample-Projection Syllogism

N percent of examined A's are B's.
A large and varied group of A's has been examined.
∴ Probably roughly N percent of all A's are B's.

Three factors determine the strength of a sample-projection argument: (1) *size* of sample, (2) *variety* of sample, and (3) *cautiousness* of conclusion.

1. Other things being equal, a *larger sample* gives a stronger argument. A projection based on a small sample (ten shelters, for example) would be weak. My sample included about 150 shelters.

2. Other things being equal, a *more varied sample* gives a stronger argument. A sample is *varied* to the extent that it proportionally represents the diversity of the whole. AT shelters differ. Some are on high ridges, while others are in valleys. Some are on the main trail, while others are on blue-blazed side trails. Some are in wilderness areas of New England and the South, while others are in rural areas of the middle states. A sample of shelters is varied to the extent that it reflects this diversity.

We'd have a weak argument if we examined only the dozen or so shelters in Georgia. This sample is small, has little variety, and covers only one part of the trail; but the poor sample might be all that we have to go on. Background information can help us to criticize a sample. Suppose that we checked only AT shelters located on mountain tops or ridges. If we knew that water is more scarce in such places, we'd also judge this sample to be biased.

3. Other things being equal, we get a stronger argument if we have a *more cautious conclusion* (one that gives a wider range of percentages):

Less cautious: Between 89 and 91 percent of the shelters have water.
More cautious: Between 80 and 95 percent of the shelters have water.

Our original argument says "roughly 90 percent." This is vague; whether it's too vague depends on our purposes.

Suppose that our sample-projection argument is strong and has true premises. Then it's likely that roughly 90 percent of the shelters have water. But the conclusion is only a rational guess; it could be far off. It's even could happen that every shelter we didn't check is bone dry.

Here's another sample-projection argument:

52 percent of the voters we checked favor the Democrat.
A large and varied group of voters has been checked.
∴ Probably roughly 52 percent of all voters favor the Democrat.

Again, our argument is stronger if we have a larger and more varied sample and a more cautious conclusion. A sample of 500 to 1000 people supposedly yields a margin of likely error of less than 5 percent; we should then construe our conclusion as "Probably between 57 percent and 47 percent of all voters favor the Democrat." To get a varied sample, we might select people using a random process that gives everyone an equal chance of being included. We also might try to have our sample proportionally represent groups (like farmers and the elderly) that tend to vote in a similar way. We should word our survey fairly and clearly and not intimidate people into giving a certain answer. And we should be clear whether we're checking registered voters or probable voters.

A sample-projection argument ends the way a statistical syllogism begins – with "N percent of all A's are B's." It's natural to connect the two:

> 90 percent of examined AT shelters have water.
> A large and varied group of AT shelters has been examined.
> ∴ Probably roughly 90 percent of all AT shelters have water.
> Rocky Gap is an AT shelter.
> This is all we know about the matter.
> ∴ It's roughly 90 percent probable that Rocky Gap has water.

Other variations are possible. We might use "all" instead of a percentage:

> All examined cats purr.
> A large and varied group of cats has been examined.
> ∴ Probably all cats purr.

This conclusion makes a strong claim, since a single non-purring cat would make it false; this makes the argument riskier and weaker. We could expand the argument further to draw a conclusion about a specific cat:

> All examined cats purr.
> A large and varied group of cats has been examined.
> ∴ Probably all cats purr.
> Socracat is a cat.
> ∴ Probably Socracat purrs.

Thus sample-projection syllogisms can have various forms.

13.4a Exercise

Evaluate the following inductive arguments.

After contacting 2 million voters using telephone lists, we conclude that Landon will beat Roosevelt in 1936 by a landslide for the US presidency. (This was an actual prediction.)	The sample was biased. Those who could afford telephones during the Depression tended to be richer and more Republican. Roosevelt won easily.

1. I randomly examined 200 Loyola University of Chicago students at the law school and found that 15 percent were born in Chicago. So probably 15 percent of all Loyola students were born in Illinois.
2. I examined every Loyola student whose Social Security number ended in 3 and I found that exactly 78.4 percent of them were born in Chicago. So probably 78.4 percent of all Loyola students were born in Chicago.

3. Italians are generally fat and lazy. How do I know? Well, when I visited Rome for a weekend last year, all the hotel employees were fat and lazy – all six of them.
4. I meet many people in my daily activities; the great majority of them intend to vote for the Democrat. So the Democrat probably will win.
5. The sun has risen every day as long as humans can remember. So the sun will likely rise tomorrow. (How can we put this argument into standard form?)

Consider this inductive argument: "Lucy got an A on the first four logic quizzes, so probably she'll also get an A on the fifth logic quiz." Would each of the statements 6 through 10 strengthen or weaken this argument?

6. Lucy has been sick for the last few weeks and has missed most of her classes.
7. The first four quizzes were on formal logic, while the fifth is on informal logic.
8. Lucy has never received less than an A in her life.
9. A student in this course gets to drop the lowest of the five quizzes.
10. Lucy just took her Law School Admissions Test.

We saw a deductive version of the classic argument from design for the existence of God in Section 4.2b (problem 4). The following inductive version of the argument has a sample-projection form and is very controversial. Evaluate the truth of the premises and the general inductive strength of the argument.

11. The universe is orderly (like a watch that follows complex laws).
    Most orderly things we've examined have intelligent designers.
    We've examined a large and varied group of orderly things.
    This is all we know about the matter.
    ∴ The universe probably has an intelligent designer.

13.5   Analogical reasoning

Suppose that you're exploring your first Las Vegas casino. The casino is huge and filled with people. There are slot machines for nickels, dimes, quarters, and dollars. There are tables for blackjack and poker. There's a big roulette wheel. There's a bar and an inexpensive all-you-can-eat buffet.

You then go into your second Las Vegas casino and notice many of the same things: the size of the casino, the crowd, the slot machines, the blackjack and poker tables, the roulette wheel, and the bar. You're hungry. Recalling what you saw in your first casino, you conclude, "I bet this place has an inexpensive all-you-can-eat buffet, just like the first casino."

This is an argument by analogy. The first and second casinos are alike in many ways, so they're probably alike in some further way:

> Most things true of casino 1 also are true of casino 2.
> Casino 1 has an all-you-can-eat buffet.
> This is all we know about the matter.
> ∴ Probably casino 2 also has an all-you-can-eat buffet.

Here's a more wholesome example (about Appalachian Trail shelters):

> Most things true of the first AT shelter are true of this second one.
> The first AT shelter had a logbook for visitors.
> This is all we know about the matter.
> ∴ Probably this second shelter also has a logbook.

We argue that things similar in many ways are likely similar in a further way. Statistical and analogical arguments are closely related:

Statistical	*Analogical*
Most large casinos have buffets.	Most things true of casino 1 are true of casino 2.
Circus Circus is a large casino.	
This is all we know.	Casino 1 has a buffet.
∴ Probably Circus Circus has a buffet.	This is all we know.
	∴ Probably casino 2 has a buffet.

The first rests on our experience of *many casinos*, while the second rests on our experience of *many features* that two casinos have in common.

Here's the general form of the analogy syllogism:

> **Analogy Syllogism**
>
> Most things true of X also are true of Y.
> X is A.
> This is all we know about the matter.
> ∴ Probably Y is A.

Premise 1 is rough. In practice, we don't just count similarities; rather we look for how relevant the similarities are to the conclusion. While the two casinos were alike in many ways, they also differed in some ways:

- Casino 1 has a name whose first letter is "S," while casino 2 doesn't.
- Casino 1 has a name whose second letter is "A," while casino 2 doesn't.
- Casino 1 has quarter slot machines by the front entrance, while casino 2 has dollar slots there.

These factors aren't relevant and so don't weaken our argument that casino 2 has a buffet. But the following differences would weaken the argument:

- Casino 1 is huge, while casino 2 is small.
- Casino 1 has a bar, while casino 2 doesn't.
- Casino 1 has a big sign advertising a buffet, while casino 2 has no such sign.

These factors would make a buffet in casino 2 less likely.

So we don't just count similarities when we argue by analogy; many similarities are trivial and unimportant. Rather, we look to *relevant* similarities. But how do we decide which similarities are relevant? We somehow appeal to our background information about what kinds of things are likely to go together. It's difficult to give rules here – even vague ones.

Our "Analogy Syllogism" formulation is a rough sketch of a subtle form of reasoning. Analogical reasoning is elusive and difficult to put into strict rules.

13.5a   Exercise – LogiCola P (I)

Suppose you're familiar with this Gensler logic book but with no others. Your friend Sarah is taking logic and uses another book. You think to yourself, "My book discusses analogical reasoning, and so Sarah's book likely does too." Which of these bits of information would strengthen or weaken this argument – and why?

Sarah's course is a specialized graduate course on quantified modal logic.	This weakens the argument; such a course probably wouldn't discuss analogical reasoning. (This answer presumes background information.)

1. Sarah's book has a different color.
2. Sarah's book also has chapters on syllogisms, propositional logic, quantificational logic, and meaning and definitions.
3. Sarah's course is taught by a member of the mathematics department.
4. Sarah's chapter on syllogisms doesn't use the star test.
5. Sarah's book is abstract and has few real-life examples.
6. Sarah's book isn't published by Routledge Press.
7. Sarah's book is entirely on informal logic.
8. Sarah's book has cartoons.
9. Sarah's book has 100 pages on inductive reasoning.
10. Sarah's book has 10 pages on inductive reasoning.

Suppose your friend Tony at another school took an ethics course that discussed utilitarianism. You're taking an ethics course next semester. You think to yourself, "Tony's course discussed utilitarianism, and so my course likely will too." Which of these bits of information would strengthen or weaken this argument – and why?

11. Tony's teacher transferred to your school and will teach your course as well.
12. Tony's course was in medical ethics, while yours is in general ethical theory.
13. Both courses use the same textbook.
14. Tony's teacher has a good reputation, while yours doesn't.
15. Your teacher is a Marxist, while Tony's isn't.

13.6   Analogy and other minds

We'll now study a classic philosophical example of analogical reasoning. This will help us to appreciate the elusive nature of such arguments.

Consider these two hypotheses:

There are other conscious beings besides me, other beings with inner thoughts and feelings.	I'm the only conscious being. Other humans are like cleverly constructed robots; they have outer behavior but no inner thoughts and feelings.

We all accept the first hypothesis and reject the second. How can we justify this intellectually? Consider that I can directly feel my own pain, but not the pain of others. When I experience the *pain behavior* of others, how do I know that this behavior manifests an inner experience of pain?

One approach appeals to an argument from analogy:

> Most things true of me also are true of Jones. (We are both alike in general behavior, nervous system, and so on.)
> I generally feel pain when I show outward pain behavior.
> This is all I know about the matter.
> ∴ Probably Jones also feels pain when showing outward pain behavior.

By this argument, Jones and I are alike in most ways. So probably we're alike in a further respect – that we both feel pain when we show pain behavior. But then there would be other conscious beings besides me.

Here are four ways to criticize this argument:

1. Jones and I also *differ* in many ways. These differences, if relevant, would weaken the argument.

2. Since I can't directly feel Jones's pain, I can't have direct access to the truth of the conclusion. This makes the argument peculiar and may weaken it.

3. I have a sample-projection argument *against* the claim that there are other conscious beings besides me:

    > All the conscious experiences that I've experienced are mine.
    > I've examined a large and varied group of conscious experiences.
    > ∴ Probably *all* conscious experiences are mine.

    The conclusion is another way to say that I'm the only conscious being. Is this a strong argument? Can we disqualify my sample as "not varied" without already presuming that other conscious beings exist (which would beg the question)? Any strength that this argument has detracts from the strength of the analogical argument for other minds.

4.   Since the analogical argument is weakened by such considerations, it at most makes it only *somewhat probable* that there are other conscious beings. But normally we take this belief to be *solidly based.*

Suppose we reject the analogical argument. Then *why* should we believe in other minds? Perhaps because it's is a commonsense belief that hasn't been disproved and that's in our practical and emotional interests to accept. Or perhaps because of a special rule of evidence, not based on analogy, that experiencing another's behavior justifies beliefs about the other's mental states. Or perhaps because talk about mental states is really just talk about behavior (so "being in pain" means "showing pain behavior"). Or maybe there's no answer – and I don't really *know* if there are other conscious beings besides me.

The analogical argument for other minds highlights some problems with induction. Philosophers seldom dispute whether *deductive* arguments have a correct connection between premises and conclusion; instead, they dispute the truth of the premises. But *inductive* arguments are different. Here, it's often hotly disputed whether and to what extent the premises, if true, provide good reason for accepting the conclusion. Those who like things neat and tidy prefer deductive to inductive reasoning.

13.7   Mill's methods

John Stuart Mill, a nineteenth-century British philosopher, formulated five methods for arriving at and justifying beliefs about causes. We'll study three of his methods. His basic idea is that factors that regularly occur together are likely to be causally related.

Imagine that Alice, Bob, Carol, and David were at a party. Alice and David got sick, and food poisoning is suspected. Hamburgers, pie, and ice cream were served. This chart shows who ate what and who got sick:

	Hamburger	Pie	Ice Cream	Sick
Alice	yes	yes	no	yes
Bob	no	no	yes	no
Carol	yes	no	no	no
David	no	yes	yes	yes

To find what caused the sickness, we'd search for a factor that correlates with the "yes" answers in the "sick" column. This suggests that the pie did it. Pie is the only thing eaten by all and only those who got sick. This reasoning reflects Mill's method of agreement:

Agreement

A occurred more than once.
B is the only additional factor that occurred if and only if A occurred.
∴ Probably B caused A, or A caused B.

Sickness occurred more than once.
Eating pie is the only additional factor that occurred if and only if sickness occurred.
∴ Probably eating pie caused sickness, or sickness caused the eating of pie.

The second alternative, that sickness caused the eating of pie (perhaps by bringing about a special craving?), is interesting but implausible. So we'd conclude that the people probably got sick because of eating pie.

The "probably" is important. Eating the pie and getting sick might just happen to have occurred together; maybe there's no causal connection between the two. Some factor not on our chart might have caused the sickness; maybe Alice and David got sick from backpacking in the rain. Or maybe Alice's sickness and David's had different causes.

We took for granted a simplifying assumption. We assumed that the two cases of sickness had the same cause which was a single factor on our list and always caused sickness. Our investigation may force us to give up this assumption and consider more complex solutions. But it's good to try simple solutions first and avoid complex ones as long as we can.

We also can conclude that eating the hamburgers doesn't necessarily make a person sick, since Carol ate them but didn't get sick. Similarly, eating the ice cream doesn't necessarily make a person sick, since Bob ate it but didn't get sick. Let's call this sort of reasoning the "method of disagreement":

Disagreement

A occurred in some case.
B didn't occur in the same case.
∴ A doesn't necessarily cause B.

Eating the ice cream occurred in Bob's case.
Sickness didn't occur in Bob's case.
∴ Eating the ice cream doesn't necessarily cause sickness.

Mill used this form of reasoning but didn't include it in his five methods.

Suppose that *two* factors – eating pie and eating hamburgers – occurred in just those cases where someone got sick. Then the method of agreement wouldn't lead to any definite conclusion about which caused the sickness. To make sure it was the pie, we might do an experiment. We take two people, Eduardo and Frank, who are as alike as possible in health and diet. We give them all the same things to eat, except that we feed pie to Eduardo but not to Frank. (This is unethical, but it makes a good example.) Then we see what happens. Suppose Eduardo gets sick but Frank doesn't:

	Pie	Sick
Eduardo	yes	yes
Frank	no	no

Then we can conclude that the pie probably caused the sickness. This follows Mill's method of difference:

<table>
<tr>
<td>
Difference

A occurred in the first case but not the second.
The cases are otherwise identical, except that B also occurred in the first case but not in the second.
∴ Probably B is (or is part of) the cause of A, or A is (or is part of) the cause of B.
</td>
<td>
Sickness occurred in Eduardo's case but not Frank's.
The cases are otherwise identical, except that eating pie occurred in Eduardo's case but not Frank's.
∴ Probably eating pie is (or is part of) the cause of the sickness, or the sickness is (or is part of) the cause of eating pie.
</td>
</tr>
</table>

Since we caused Eduardo to eat the pie, we reject the second pair of alternatives. So probably eating pie is (or is part of) the cause of the sickness. The cause might simply be the eating of the pie (which contained a virus). Or the cause might be this combined with one's poor physical condition.

Another unethical experiment illustrates Mill's method of variation. This time we find four victims (George, Henry, Isabel, and Jodi) and feed them varying amounts of pie. They get sick in varying degrees:

	Pie	Sick
George	tiny slice	slightly
Henry	small slice	somewhat
Isabel	normal slice	very
Jodi	two slices	wants to die

We conclude that the pie probably caused the sickness. This follows Mill's method of variation:

<table>
<tr>
<td>
Variation

A changes in a certain way if and only if B also changes in a certain way.
∴ Probably B caused A, or A caused B, or some C caused both A and B.
</td>
<td>
The person's sickness was greater if and only if the person ate more pie.
∴ Probably eating pie caused the sickness, or the sickness caused the eating of pie, or something else caused both the eating and the sickness.
</td>
</tr>
</table>

The last two alternatives are implausible. So we conclude that eating pie probably caused the sickness.

Mill's methods often give us a conclusion with several alternatives. Sometimes we can eliminate an alternative because of temporal sequence; the cause can't happen after the effect. Suppose we conclude this:

> Either laziness during previous months caused the F on the final exam,
> or the F on the final exam caused laziness during the previous months.

Here we'd reject the second alternative.

In applying Mill's methods, we should be aware of some ambiguities of the word "cause." For one thing, "cause" can mean either "total cause" or "partial cause." Suppose that Jones got shot and then died. Misapplying the method of disagreement, we might conclude that being shot didn't cause the death, since some who are shot don't die. But the proper conclusion is rather that being shot doesn't necessarily cause death. We also can conclude that just being shot wasn't the *total* cause of Jones's death (even though it might be a partial cause). What caused Jones's death wasn't just that he was shot. What caused the death was that he was shot in a certain way (for example, through the head) in certain circumstances (for example, with no medical help available). This is the total cause; anyone shot in that way in those circumstances would have died. The method of disagreement deals with total causes, not partial causes.

The ambiguities of the word "cause" run deep. "Factor A causes factor B" could mean any combination of these:

> The presence of factor A will always (or probably) by itself (or in combination with some factor C) directly (or through a further causal chain) bring about the presence of factor B; or the absence of factor A will … bring about the absence of factor B; or both.

The probabilistic sense is controversial. Suppose that the incidence of lung cancer varies closely with heavy smoking, so heavy smokers are much more likely to get lung cancer. Could this probabilistic connection be enough for us to say that heavy smoking is a (partial) cause of lung cancer? Or is it wrong to use "cause" unless we come up with some factor C such that heavy smoking when combined with factor C *always* results in lung cancer? At least part of the debate over whether a "causal connection" exists between heavy smoking and lung cancer is semantic. Does it make sense to use "cause" with probabilistic connections? If we can speak of Russian roulette *causing* death, then we can speak of heavy smoking *causing* lung cancer.

13.7a Exercise – LogiCola P (M & B)

Draw whatever conclusions you can using Mill's methods; supplement Mill's methods by common sense when appropriate. Say which method you're using, what alternatives you conclude from the method itself, and how you narrow the conclusion down to a single alternative. Also say when Mill's methods lead to no definite conclusion.

Kristen's computer gave error messages when she booted up. We changed things one at a time to see what would stop the error messages. What worked was updating the video driver.	By the difference method, probably updating the driver caused (or partially caused) the error messages to stop, or stopping the messages caused (or partially caused) us to update the driver. The latter can't be, since the cause can't happen after the effect. So probably updating the driver caused (or partially caused) the error messages to stop.

1. Experiments show that a person's reaction time is much longer after a few drinks but is relatively uninfluenced by a series of other factors.
2. A study showed that people with no bacteria in their mouth get no cavities – and that people with no food particles in their mouth get no cavities. However, people with both bacteria and food particles in their mouth get cavities.
3. Whenever Michelle drinks scotch and *soda*, she has a hangover the next day. Whenever she drinks gin and *soda*, she gets a hangover. Likewise, whenever she drinks rum and *soda*, she gets a hangover.
4. The morning disc jockey on a Cleveland radio station remarked in early December that the coldest temperature of the day seemed to occur later and later in the morning. The weather person pointed out that the sunrise had been getting later and later. In a few weeks both processes would reverse themselves, with the sunrise and the coldest temperature of the day both occurring earlier every day.
5. Our research team at the medical center just discovered a new blood factor called "factor K." Factor K occurs in everyone who has cancer but in no one else.
6. When I sat eating on the rock slab in Grand Gulch, armies of little ants invaded the slab. Later I sat on the slab in the same way except that I didn't eat anything. In the second case the ants didn't invade the slab.
7. We just did an interesting study comparing the vacation periods of employees and the disappearance of food items. We found that when Megan is working the items disappear, and when she's away they don't disappear.
8. People in several parts of the country have lower rates of tooth decay. Investigations show that the only thing different about these places is that their water supply contains fluoride.
9. We did an experiment where we selected two more or less identical groups and put fluoride in the first group's water but not in the second group's. The first group had a lower rate of tooth decay.
10. Many backpackers think eating raw garlic gives you an odor that causes mosquitoes not to bite you. When hiking a mosquito-infested part of the Bruce Trail, I ate much raw garlic. The mosquitoes bit me in their usual bloodthirsty manner.
11. Little Will throws food on the floor and receives signs of disapproval from Mommy and Daddy. Such things happen regularly. When he eats his food without throwing it on the floor, he doesn't get any disapproval.
12. Everyone in our study who became a heroin addict had first tried marijuana.

13. If you rub two surfaces together, the surfaces get warm. They'll get warmer and warmer as you rub the surfaces together harder and faster.

14. When we plot how many hours Alex studies against the grades he gets for his various exams, we see a close correlation.

15. Matches that aren't either heated or struck don't light. Matches that are wet don't light. Matches that aren't in the presence of oxygen don't light. Matches that are heated or struck, dry, and in the presence of oxygen do light.

16. Little Will made a discovery. He keeps moving the lever on the radio up and down. He notices that the music gets louder and softer when he does this.

17. We made a careful study of the heart rate of athletes and how it correlates with various factors. The only significant correlation we found is that those who do aerobic exercise (and those alone) have lower heart rates.

18. We investigated many objects with a crystalline structure. The only thing they have in common is that all solidified from a liquid state. (Mill used this example.)

19. After long investigation, we've found a close correlation between night and day. If you have night, then there invariably, in a few hours, follows day. If you have day, then invariably, in a few hours, there follows night.

20. Young Will has been experimenting with his electrical meter. He found that if he increases the electrical voltage, then he also increases the current.

21. Whenever Kurt wears his headband, he makes all his field goals. Whenever he doesn't wear his headband, he misses all his field goals. This has been going on for many years.

22. The fish in my father's tank all died. We suspected either the fish food or the water temperature. We bought more fish and did everything the same except for changing the fish food. All the fish died. We then bought more fish and did everything the same except for changing the water temperature. The fish lived.

23. Bacteria introduced by visitors from the planet Krypton is causing an epidemic. We've found that everyone exposed to the bacteria gets sick and dies – except those who have a higher-than-normal heart rate.

24. When we chart the inflation rate next to the growth in the national debt over several years, we find a close correlation.

25. On my first backpack trip, I hiked long distances but wore only a single pair of socks. I got bad blisters on my feet. On my second trip, I did everything the same except that I wore two pairs of socks. I got only minor blisters.

13.8 Scientific laws

Ohm's Law is an important principle with many electrical applications. "Law" here suggests great scientific dignity and backing. Ohm's Law is more than a mere *hypothesis* (preliminary conjecture) or even a *theory* (with more backing than a hypothesis but less than a law).

Ohm's Law is a formula relating electric current, voltage, and resistance:

Ohm's Law:

I = E/R

where:
I = current (in amps)
E = voltage (in volts)
R = resistance (in ohms)

An electric current of 1 amp (ampere) is a flow of 6,250,000,000,000,000,000 electrons per second; a 100-watt bulb draws almost an amp, and the fuse blows if you draw over 15 amps. To push the electrons, you need a voltage; your outlet may have 117 volts, and your flashlight battery 1.5 volts. The voltage encounters an electrical resistance, which influences how many electrons flow per second. A short thick wire has low resistance (less than an ohm) while an inch of air has high resistance (billions of ohms). Small carbon resistors go from less than an ohm to millions of ohms. Ohm's Law says that the current increases if you raise the voltage or lower the resistance.

Electric current is like the flow of water through a garden hose. Voltage is like water pressure. Electrical resistance is like the resistance to the water flow provided by your hose; a long, thin hose has greater resistance than a short, thick one. The current or flow of water is measured in gallons per minute; it increases if you raise the water pressure or use a hose with less resistance.

Ohm's Law is a mathematical formula that lets us calculate various results. Suppose we put a 10-ohm resistor across your 117-volt electrical outlet; we'd get a current of 11.7 amps (not quite enough to blow your fuse):

$$I = E/R = 117 \text{ volts}/10 \text{ ohms} = 11.7 \text{ amps}.$$

Ohm's Law deals with unobservable properties (current, voltage, resistance) and entities (electrons). Science allows unobservables if they have testable consequences or can somehow be measured. The term "unobservable" is vague. Actually we can feel certain voltages. The 1.5 volts from your flashlight battery can't normally be felt, slightly higher voltages give a slight tingle, and the 117 volts from your outlet can give a dangerous jolt.

Philosophers dispute the status of unobservable entities. Here are four views:

- Electrons, atoms, and other unobservables are the only real entities; chairs and other commonsense objects have no ultimate reality.
- Chairs and other commonsense objects are real; electrons and other unobservables are just fictions to help us visualize scientific equations.
- Both electrons and chairs are real; real entities are of various sorts.
- Neither electrons nor chairs have any ultimate reality; both are just fictions to help us talk about our sensations.

Metaphysics and philosophy of science deal with such issues.

We can ask how scientific laws are *discovered*, or we can ask how they're *verified*. History can tell us how Georg Simon Ohm discovered his law in 1827; philosophy is more concerned with how such laws are verified (or shown to be true), regardless of their origins. Basically, scientific laws are verified by a combination of observation and argument; but the details get complicated.

Suppose that we want to verify Ohm's Law. We are given batteries and resistors. We also are given a meter for measuring current, voltage, and resistance; the meter simplifies our task; we don't have to worry about defining the fundamental units (ampere, volt, and ohm) and inventing ways to measure them. Wouldn't the meter make our task too easy? Couldn't we just do a few experiments and then base Ohm's Law on the results, using standard deductive and inductive reasoning? Unfortunately, it isn't that simple.

Suppose we hook up batteries of different voltages to a resistor:

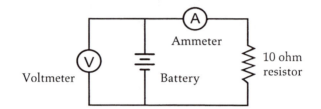

The voltmeter measures the voltage, and the ammeter measures the current. We start with a 10-ohm resistor. We try voltages of 1 volt and 2 volts and find that we get currents of .1 amp and .2 amp. Here's a chart with the results:

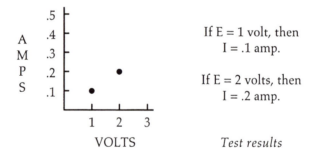

If E = 1 volt, then
    I = .1 amp.

If E = 2 volts, then
    I = .2 amp.

Test results

This accords with Ohm, since:

If E = 1 volt, then I = .1 amp.   If E = 2 volts, then I = .2 amp.
  (I = E/R = 1/10 = .1)   (I = E/R = 2/10 = .2)

On this basis, we argue inductively as follows:

      All examined voltage–resistance–current cases follow Ohm.
      A large and varied group of such cases has been examined.
  ∴ Probably all such cases follow Ohm.

Premise 2 is weak, since we tried only two cases. But we can easily perform more experiments; after we do so, Ohm would seem to be securely based.

The problem is that we can give an equally strong inductive argument for a second and incompatible hypothesis:

$$I = (E^2 - 2E + 2)/R$$

Let's call this *Mho's Law* (although it isn't a "law"). Surprisingly, our test results also accord with Mho:

If E = 1 volt, then I = .1 amp.

$$\begin{aligned} I &= (E^2 - 2E + 2)/R \\ &= (1^2 - 2 \cdot 1 + 2)/10 \\ &= (1 - 2 + 2)/10 = 1/10 = .1 \end{aligned}$$

If E = 2 volts, then I = .2 amp.

$$\begin{aligned} I &= (E^2 - 2E + 2)/R \\ &= (2^2 - 2 \cdot 2 + 2)/10 \\ &= (4 - 4 + 2)/10 = 2/10 = .2 \end{aligned}$$

So each examined case follows Mho. We can argue inductively as follows:

> All examined voltage–resistance–current cases follow Mho.
> A large and varied group of such cases has been examined.
> ∴ Probably all such cases follow Mho.

This inductive argument for Mho seems as strong as the one we gave for Ohm. Judging just from these arguments and test results, there seems to be no reason for preferring Ohm over Mho, or Mho over Ohm.

The two laws, while agreeing on both test cases so far, give conflicting predictions for further cases. Ohm says we'll get 0 amps with 0 volts, and .3 amp with 3 volts; Mho says we'll get .2 amp with 0 volts, and .5 amp with 3 volts:

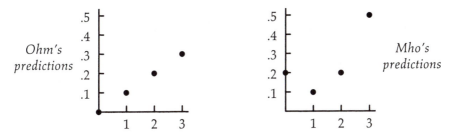

The two laws are genuinely different, even though they give the same results for a voltage of 1 or 2 volts.

We have to try a crucial experiment to decide between the theories. What happens with 3 volts? Ohm says we'll get .3 amp, but Mho says we'll get .5 amp. If we do the experiment and get .3 amp, this would falsify Mho:

If Mho is correct and we apply 3 volts to this   **Valid**
    10-ohm resistor, then we get .5 amp current.
We apply 3 volts to this 10-ohm resistor.   If M and A, then G
We don't get .5 amp current.   A
∴ Mho isn't correct.   Not-G
    ∴ Not-M

Premise 1 links a scientific hypothesis (Mho) to antecedent conditions (that 3 volts have been applied to the 10-ohm resistor) to give a testable prediction (that we'll get .5 amp current). Premise 2 says the antecedent conditions have been fulfilled. Premise 3 says the results conflict with what was predicted. The argument has true premises and is deductively valid. So our experiment shows Mho to be wrong.

Does our experiment similarly show that Ohm is correct? Unfortunately not. Consider this argument:

If Ohm is correct and we apply 3 volts to this   **Invalid**
    10-ohm resistor, then we get .3 amp current.
We apply 3 volts to this 10-ohm resistor.   If O and A, then G
We get .3 amp current.   A
∴ Ohm is correct.   G
    ∴ O

This is invalid, as we could check using propositional logic (Chapter 3). So the premises don't prove that Ohm is correct; and Ohm might fail for further cases. But the experiment strengthens our inductive argument for Ohm, since it gives a larger and more varied sample. So we can have greater trust that the pattern observed to hold so far will continue to hold.

Three aspects of scientific method should be stressed:

1. *Scientists often set up crucial experiments to decide between conflicting theories.* Scientists like to dream up alternative theories and look for ways to decide between them.
2. *We can sometimes deductively refute a theory through a crucial experiment.* Experimental results, when combined with other suitable premises, can logically entail the falsity of a theory.
3. *We can't deductively prove a theory using experiments.* Experiments can inductively support a theory and deductively refute opposing theories. But they can't eliminate the possibility of the theory's failing for further cases.

Recall how the Mho problem arose. We had two test cases that agreed with Ohm. These test cases also agreed with another formula, one we called "Mho"; and the inductive argument for Mho seemed as strong as the one for Ohm. But Ohm and Mho gave conflicting predictions for further test cases. So we did a crucial experiment to decide between the two. Ohm won.

But there's always another Mho behind the bush – so our problems aren't over. However many experiments we do, there are always alternative theories that agree with all test cases so far but disagree on some further predictions. In fact, there's always an *infinity* of theories that do this. No matter how many dots we put on the chart (representing test results), we could draw an unlimited number of lines that go through all these dots but otherwise diverge.

Suppose that we conduct 1000 experiments in which Ohm works. There are alternative theories Pho, Qho, Rho, and so on that agree on these 1000 test cases but give conflicting predictions about further cases. And each theory seems to be equally supported by the same kind of inductive argument:

> All examined voltage-resistance-current cases follow this theory.
> A large and varied group of such cases has been examined.
> ∴ Probably all such cases follow this theory.

Even after 1000 experiments, Ohm is just one of infinitely many formulas that seem equally probable on the basis of the test results and inductive logic.

In practice, we prefer Ohm on the basis of *simplicity*. Ohm is the simplest formula that agrees with all our test results. So we prefer Ohm to the alternative theories and regard Ohm as firmly based.

What is simplicity and how can we decide which of two scientific theories is simpler? We don't have a neat and tidy answer to these questions. In practice, though, we can tell that Ohm is simpler than Mho; we judge that Ohm's formula is simpler and that its straight line is simpler than Mho's curved line. We don't have a clear and satisfying definition of "simplicity"; yet we can apply this notion in a rough way in many cases.

We can express the simplicity criterion this way:

> **Simplicity criterion:** Other things being equal, we ought to prefer a simpler theory to a more complex one.

The "other things being equal" qualification is important. Experiments may force us to accept very complex theories; but we shouldn't take such theories seriously until we're forced into it.

It's unclear how to justify the simplicity criterion. Since inductive reasoning stumbles unless we presuppose the criterion, an inductive justification would be circular. Perhaps the criterion is a self-evident truth not in need of justification. Or perhaps the criterion is pragmatically justified:

> If the simplicity criterion isn't correct, then no scientific laws are justified.
> Some scientific laws are justified.
> ∴ The simplicity criterion is correct.

Does premise 2 beg the question against the skeptic? Can this premise be defended without appealing to the criterion? The simplicity criterion is vague and raises complex problems, but we can't do without it.

Coherence is another factor that's important for choosing between theories:

> **Coherence criterion**: Other things being equal, we ought to prefer a theory that harmonizes with existing well-established beliefs.

Mho has trouble here, since it predicts that 0 volts across a 10-ohm resistor produces a current of .2 amp. But then it follows, given an existing well-grounded belief that current through a resistor produces heat, that a 10-ohm resistor with no voltage applied produces heat. This, while nice for portable handwarmers, would be difficult to harmonize with the principle of conservation of mass and energy. So the coherence criterion leads us to doubt Mho.

Do further tests continue to confirm Ohm? The answer is complicated. Some resistors give, not a straight-line chart, but something of a curve; this happens if we use a regular light bulb for the resistor. Instead of rejecting Ohm, scientists say that heating the resistor changes the resistance. This seems satisfactory, since the curve becomes straighter if the resistor is kept cooler. And we can measure changes in resistance when the resistor is heated externally.

Another problem is that resistors will burn up or explode if enough voltage is applied. This brings an irregularity into the straight-line chart. But again, scientists regard this as changing the resistance – and as not falsifying Ohm.

A more serious problem is that some devices don't even roughly approximate the pattern predicted by Ohm. A Zener diode, for example, draws almost no current until a critical voltage is reached; then it draws a high current:

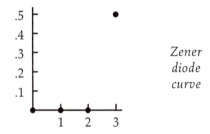

Do such devices refute Ohm? Not necessarily. Scientists implicitly qualify Ohm so it applies just to "pure resistances" and not to things like Zener diodes. This seems circular. Suppose that a "pure resistor" is any device that satisfies Ohm. Then isn't it circular to say that Ohm holds for "pure resistors"? Doesn't this just mean that Ohm works for any device for which it works?

In practice, people working in electronics learn quickly which devices satisfy Ohm and which don't. The little tubular "resistors" follow Ohm closely (neglecting slight changes caused by heating and major changes when we burn up the resistor). Zener diodes, transistors, and other semiconductors generally don't follow Ohm. So Ohm can be a useful principle, even though it's difficult to specify in any precise and non-circular manner the cases where it applies.

13.8a Exercise

Sketch in a rough way how we might verify or falsify these hypotheses. Point out any special difficulties likely to arise.

<table>
<tr>
<td>

Women have less innate logical ability than men.

</td>
<td>

We'd give a logic test to large and varied groups of either sex, and see how results differ. If women tested lower [they don't – judging from a test I designed for a friend in psychology], this wouldn't itself prove lower innate ability, since the lower scores might come from different social expectations or upbringing. It would be difficult to avoid this problem completely; but we might try testing groups in cultures with less difference in social expectations and upbringing.

</td>
</tr>
</table>

1. Neglecting air resistance, objects of any weight fall at the same speed.
2. Germs cause colds.
3. A huge Ice-Age glacier covered most of Wisconsin about 10,000 years ago.
4. Regular moderate use of marijuana is no more harmful than regular moderate use of alcohol.
5. When couples have several children, the child born first tends to have greater innate intelligence than the one born last.
6. Career-oriented women tend to have marriages that are more successful than those of home-oriented women.
7. Factor K causes cancer.
8. Water is made up of molecules consisting of two atoms of hydrogen and one atom of oxygen.
9. Organisms of a given biological species randomly develop slightly different traits; organisms with survival-promoting traits tend to survive and pass on these traits to their offspring. New biological species result when this process continues over millions of years. This is how complex species developed from simple organisms, and how humans developed from lower species.
10. Earth was created 5,000 years ago, complete with all current biological species.

13.9 Problems with induction

We've seen in previous sections that inductive logic isn't as neat and tidy as deductive logic. Now we'll consider two further perplexing problems: how to *formulate* principles of inductive logic and how to *justify* these principles.

We've formulated inductive principles in a rough way that can lead to absurdities if taken literally. Consider this statistical syllogism:

> 60 percent of all Cleveland voters are Democrats.
> This non-Democrat is a Cleveland voter.
> This is all we know about the matter.
> ∴ It's 60 percent probable that this non-Democrat is a Democrat.

Actually, "This non-Democrat is a Democrat" is 0 percent probable, since it's a self-contradiction. So our statistical syllogism principle isn't entirely correct.

We noted that the analogy syllogism is over-simplified in its formulation. We need to rely on *relevant similarities* instead of just counting resemblances. But "relevant similarities" is hard to pin down.

The sample-projection syllogism suffers from a problem raised by Nelson Goodman. Consider this argument:

> All examined diamonds are hard.
> A large and varied group of diamonds has been examined.
> ∴ Probably all diamonds are hard.

Let's suppose that the premises are true; then the argument would seem to be a good one. But consider this second argument, which has the same form except that we substitute a more complex phrase for "hard":

> All examined diamonds are such that they are hard-if-
> and-only-if-they-were-examined-before-2200.
> A large and varied group of diamonds has been examined.
> ∴ Probably all diamonds are such that they are hard-if-and-
> only-if-they-were-examined-before-2200.

Premise 1 is tricky to understand. It isn't yet 2200. So if all examined diamonds are hard, then they are such that they are hard-if-and-only-if-they-were-examined-before-2200. So premise 1 is true. Premise 2 also is true. Then this second argument also would seem to be a good one.

Consider a *diamond X* that will be first examined after 2200. By our first argument, diamond X probably *is* hard; by the second, it probably *isn't* hard. So our sample projection argument leads to conflicting conclusions.

Philosophers have discussed this problem for decades. Some suggest that we qualify the sample-projection syllogism form to outlaw the second argument; but it's not clear how to eliminate the bad apples without also eliminating the good ones. As yet, there's no agreement on how to solve the problem.

Goodman's problem is somewhat like one we saw in the last section. Here we had similar inductive arguments for two incompatible laws – Ohm and Mho:

All examined electrical cases follow Ohm's Law.	All examined electrical cases follow Mho's Law.
A large and varied group of cases has been examined.	A large and varied group of cases has been examined.
∴ Probably all electrical cases follow Ohm's Law.	∴ Probably all electrical cases follow Mho's Law.

Even after 1000 experiments, there are an *infinity* of theories that give the same test results in these 1000 cases but conflicting results in further cases. And we could "prove," using an inductive argument, that each of these incompatible theories probably is true. But this is absurd. We can't have each of an infinity of conflicting theories be probably true. Our sample-projection syllogism thus leads to absurdities.

We got around this problem in the scientific-theory case by appealing to simplicity: "Other things being equal, we ought to prefer a *simpler* theory to a more complex one." While "simpler" here is vague and difficult to explain, we seem to need some such simplicity criterion to justify any scientific theory.

Simplicity is important in our diamond case, since 1 is simpler than 2:

1. All diamonds are hard.
2. All diamonds are such that they are hard-if-and-only-if-they-were-examined-before-2200.

By our simplicity criterion, we ought to prefer 1 to 2, even if both have equally strong inductive backing. So the sample-projection syllogism needs a simplicity qualification; but it's not clear how to formulate it.

So it's difficult to formulate clear inductive-logic principles that don't lead to absurdities. Inductive logic is less neat and tidy than deductive logic.

Our second problem is how to justify inductive principles. For now, let's ignore the problem we just talked about; let's pretend that we have clear inductive principles that roughly accord with our practice and don't lead to absurdities. Why follow these principles?

Consider this inductive argument (which says roughly that the sun will probably come up tomorrow, since it has come up every day in the past):

> All examined days are days on which the sun comes up.
> A large and varied group of days has been examined.
> Tomorrow is a day.
> ∴ Probably tomorrow is a day on which the sun comes up.

But even though the sun has come up every day in the past, it still might not come up tomorrow. Why think that the premise gives good reason for accepting the conclusion? Why accept this or any inductive argument?

David Hume several centuries ago raised this problem about the justification of induction. We'll discuss five responses.

1. Some suggest that, to justify induction, we need to presume that nature is uniform. If nature works in regular patterns, then the cases we haven't examined will likely follow the same patterns as the ones we have examined.

There are two problems with this suggestion. First, what does it mean to say "Nature is uniform"? Let's be concrete. What would this principle imply about the regularity (or lack thereof) of Cleveland weather patterns? "Nature is uniform" seems either obviously false or else hopelessly vague.

Second, what's the backing for the principle? Justifying "Nature is uniform" by experience would require inductive reasoning. But then we're arguing in a circle – using the uniformity idea to justify induction, and then using induction to justify the uniformity idea. This presumes what's being doubted: that it's reasonable to follow inductive reasoning in the first place. Or is the uniformity idea perhaps a self-evident truth not in need of justification? But it's implausible to claim self-evidence for a claim about what the world is like.

2. Some suggest that we justify induction by its success. Inductive methods work. Using inductive reasoning, we know what to do for a toothache and how to fix cars. We use such reasoning continuously and successfully in our lives. What better justification for inductive reasoning could we have than this?

This seems like a powerful justification. But there's a problem. Let's assume that inductive reasoning has worked in the past; how can we then conclude that it probably will work in the future? The argument is inductive, much like our sunrise argument:

Induction has worked in the past.	The sun has come up every day in the past.
∴ Induction probably will work in the future.	∴ The sun probably will come up tomorrow.

So justifying inductive reasoning by its past successes is circular; it uses inductive reasoning and thus presupposes that such reasoning is legitimate.

3. Some suggest that it's part of the meaning of "reasonable" that beliefs based on inductive reasoning are *reasonable*. "Reasonable belief" just means "belief based on experience and inductive reasoning." So it's true by definition that beliefs based on experience and inductive reasoning are reasonable.

There are two problems with this. First, the definition is wrong. It really isn't true by definition that all and only things based on experience and inductive reasoning are reasonable. There's no contradiction in disagreeing with this standard of reasonableness – as there would be if this definition were correct. Mystics see their higher methods as reasonable, and skeptics see the ordinary methods as unreasonable. Both groups might be wrong; but they aren't simply contradicting themselves.

Second, even the correctness of the definition wouldn't solve the problem. Suppose that standards of inductive reasoning are built into the conventional meaning of our word "reasonable." Suppose that "reasonable belief" simply means "belief based on experience and inductive reasoning." Then why follow what's "reasonable" in this sense? Why not instead follow the skeptic's advice and avoid believing such things? So this approach doesn't answer the main question – why follow inductive reasoning at all?

4. Karl Popper suggests that we avoid inductive reasoning. But we seem to need such reasoning in our lives; without inductive reasoning, we have no basis for believing that bread nourishes and arsenic kills. And suggested substitutes for inductive reasoning don't seem adequate.

5. Some suggest that we approach justification in inductive logic in the same way we approach it in deductive logic. How can we justify the validity of a deductive principle like *modus ponens* ("If A then B, A ∴ B")? Can we prove such a principle? Perhaps we could prove *modus ponens* by doing a truth table (see Section 3.6) and then arguing this way:

> If the truth table for *modus ponens* never gives true premises
> and a false conclusion, then *modus ponens* is valid.
> The truth table for *modus ponens* never gives true premises
> and a false conclusion.
> ∴ *Modus ponens* is valid.

Premise 1 is a necessary truth and premise 2 is easy to check. The conclusion follows. Therefore, *modus ponens* is valid. But the problem is that the argument itself uses *modus ponens*. So this attempted justification is circular, since it presumes from the start that *modus ponens* is valid.

Aristotle long ago showed that every proof must eventually rest on something unproved; otherwise, we'd need either an infinite chain of proofs or circular arguments – and neither is acceptable. So why not just accept the validity of *modus ponens* as a self-evident truth – a truth that's evident but can't be based on anything more evident? If we have to accept some things as evident without proof, why not accept *modus ponens* as evident without proof?

I have some sympathy with this approach. But, if we accept it, we shouldn't think that picking logical principles is purely a matter of following "logical intuitions." Logical intuitions vary enormously among people. The pretest that I give my class shows that beginning logic students generally have poor intuition about the validity of simple arguments.

Even though untrained logical intuitions differ, still we can reach agreement on basic principles of logic. Early on, we introduced the notion of logical form. And we distinguished between valid and invalid forms – such as these two:

Modus ponens:	*Affirming the consequent:*
If A then B **Valid**	If A then B **Invalid**
A	B
∴ B	∴ A

Students at first are poor at distinguishing valid from invalid forms. They need concrete examples like these:

If you're a dog, then **Valid**	If you're a dog, then **Invalid**
you're an animal.	you're an animal.
You're a dog.	You're an animal.
∴ You're an animal.	∴ You're a dog.

After enough well-chosen examples, the validity of *modus ponens* and the invalidity of affirming the consequent become clear.

So, despite the initial clash of intuitions, we eventually reach clear logical principles of universal rational appeal. We do this by searching for clear formal principles that lead to intuitively correct results in concrete cases without leading to any clear absurdities.

We might think that this procedure proves *modus ponens*:

If *modus ponens* leads to intuitively correct results in concrete cases
    without leading to any clear absurdities, then *modus ponens* is valid.
Modus ponens leads to intuitively correct results in concrete cases
    without leading to any clear absurdities.
∴ *Modus ponens* is valid.

But this reasoning itself uses *modus ponens*; the justification is circular, since it presumes from the start that *modus ponens* is valid. So this procedure of testing *modus ponens* by checking its implications doesn't prove *modus ponens*. But I think it gives a "justification" for it, in some sense of "justification." This is vague, but I don't know how to make it more precise.

I suggested that we justify inductive principles in the same way we justify deductive ones. Realizing that we can't prove everything, we wouldn't demand a proof. Rather, we'd search for clear formal inductive principles that lead to intuitively correct results in concrete cases without leading to any clear absurdities. Once we reached such inductive principles, we'd rest content with them and not look for any further justification.

This is the approach that I'd use in justifying inductive principles. But the key problem is the one discussed earlier. As yet we seem unable to find clear formal inductive principles that lead to intuitively correct results in concrete cases without leading to any clear absurdities. We just don't know how to formulate inductive principles very rigorously. This is what makes the current state of inductive logic intellectually unsatisfying.

Inductive reasoning has been very useful. Inductively, we assume that it will continue to be useful. In our lives, we can't do without it. But the intellectual basis for inductive reasoning is shaky.

CHAPTER 14
Meaning and Definitions

Logic is the analysis and appraisal of arguments. So far, we've focused on the link between premises and conclusion – whether this link be deductive or inductive. But there are other things we need to consider when we appraise arguments; one of these is language.

14.1   Logic and meaning

To determine whether an argument is sound, we need to appraise the truth of the premises; this requires some understanding of what the premises mean. Meaning is often crucial. Imagine that someone proposes this argument:

>   If there's a cosmic force, then there's a God.   .
>   There's a cosmic force.
> ∴ There's a God.

While this is deductively valid, the premises are obscure. What is a "cosmic force"? Or, better yet, what (if anything) does the person proposing the argument mean by this phrase? We can't intelligently either agree or disagree with the premises if we don't understand what they mean. One of my favorite slogans is: "Understand before you criticize."

In this chapter, after first exploring some general uses of language, we'll examine definitions and other ways to make our meaning clear. Then we'll learn more about making distinctions and detecting unclarities. Finally, we'll consider the distinction between analytic and synthetic statements, and the related distinction between knowledge based on reason and knowledge based on experience. The goal of this investigation into language is to enhance our ability to analyze and appraise arguments.

14.2   Uses of language

Grammarians distinguish four sentence types, which broadly reflect four important uses of language:

Declarative:	"Michigan beat Ohio State."	*make assertions*
Interrogatory:	"Did Michigan win?"	*ask questions*
Imperative:	"Beat Ohio State."	*tell what to do*
Exclamatory:	"Hurrah for Michigan!"	*express feelings*

Sentences can do various jobs at the same time. These next examples, while making assertions, also can ask questions, tell what to do, or express feelings:

- "I wonder whether Michigan won." (This can ask a question.)
- "I want you to throw the ball." (This can tell what to do.)
- "Michigan won!" (This can express feelings of joy or sadness.)

Arguments too can exemplify different uses of language. Suppose that someone argues this way about the Cleveland river that used to catch on fire: "You can see that the Cuyahoga River is polluted from the fact that it even catches on fire!" We could make this into an explicit argument:

> No pure water is burnable.
> Some Cuyahoga River water is burnable.
> ∴ Some Cuyahoga River water is not pure water.

One who argues about water purity also can (perhaps implicitly) be raising a question, directing people to do something, or expressing feelings:

- What can we do to clean up this polluted river?
- Let's all resolve to take action on this problem.
- How disgusting is this polluted river!

Arguments have a wider human context and purpose. We should remember this when we study detached specimens of argumentation.

When we do logic, our focus narrows and we concentrate on assertions and reasoning. For this purpose, detached specimens of argumentation are better. Expressing an argument in a clear, direct, emotionless way can make it easier to appraise the truth of the premises and the validity of the inference.

It's important to avoid emotional language when we reason. Of course, there's nothing wrong with feelings or emotional language. Reason and feeling are both important parts of life; we needn't choose between the two. But we often need to focus on one or the other for a given purpose. At times, expressing our feelings is the important thing and argumentation only gets in the way. At other times, we need to reason things out in a cool-headed manner.

Emotional language can discourage clear reasoning. When reasoning about abortion, for example, it's wise to avoid slanted phrases like "the atrocious, murderous crime of abortion" or "Neanderthals who oppose the rights of women." Bertrand Russell gave this example of how we slant language:

I am *firm*; you are *obstinate*; he is *pig-headed*.

Slanted phrases can mislead us into thinking we've defended our view by an argument (premises and conclusion), when in fact we've only expressed our feelings. Careful thinkers try to avoid highly emotional terms when constructing their arguments.

In the rest of this chapter, we'll explore aspects of the "making assertions" side of language that relate closely to analyzing and appraising arguments.

14.2a Exercise

For each word or phrase, say whether it has a positive or negative or neutral emotional tone. Then find another word or phrase with more or less the same assertive meaning but a different emotional tone.

old maid	This has a negative tone. A more neutral phrase is "elderly woman who has never married."

(The term "old maid" suggests that a woman's goal in life is to get married and that an older woman who has never married is unfortunate. I can't think of a corresponding negative term for an older man who never married. A single word or phrase sometimes suggests a whole attitude toward life – and often an unexamined attitude.)

1.	a cop	11.	a hair-splitter	21.	brazen
2.	filthy rich	12.	an egghead	22.	an old broad
3.	heroic	13.	a bizarre idea	23.	old moneybags
4.	an extremist	14.	a kid	24.	a busybody
5.	an elderly gentleman	15.	booze	25.	a bribe
6.	a bastard	16.	a gay	26.	old fashioned
7.	baloney	17.	abnormal	27.	brave
8.	a backward country	18.	bureaucracy	28.	garbage
9.	authoritarian	19.	abandoning me	29.	a cagey person
10.	a do-gooder	20.	babbling	30.	a whore

14.3 Lexical definitions

We noted earlier that the phrase "cosmic force" in this example is obscure:

> If there's a cosmic force, then there's a God.
> There's a cosmic force.
> ∴ There's a God.

Unless the speaker tells us what is meant by "cosmic force," we won't be able to understand what's said or tell whether it's true. But how can the speaker explain what he or she means by "cosmic force"? Or, more generally, how can we explain the meaning of a word or phrase?

Definitions are an important way to explain meaning – but not the only way. We'll consider definitions now and other ways to explain meaning later.

A **definition** is a rule of paraphrase intended to explain meaning. More precisely, a definition of a word or phrase is a rule saying how to eliminate this word or phrase in any sentence using it and produce a second sentence that means the same thing – the purpose of this being to explain or clarify the meaning of the word or phrase.

Suppose the person with the cosmic-force argument gives us this definition:

> "Cosmic force" means "force, in the sense used in physics, whose influence covers the entire universe."

This tells us that we can interchange "cosmic force" and a second phrase ("force, in the sense used in physics, whose influence covers the entire universe") in any sentence without changing the sentence's meaning. We can use this definition to paraphrase out the words "cosmic force" in the original argument. We'd get this equivalent argument:

> If there's a force, in the sense used in physics, whose influence covers the entire universe, then there's a God.
> There's a force, in the sense used in physics, whose influence covers the entire universe.
> ∴ There's a God.

This helps us understand what the speaker is getting at – and to see that premise 1 is doubtful. Suppose that there is a force, such as gravity, whose influence covers the entire universe. Why should we think that if there is such a force then there's a God? This is unclear.

So a definition is a rule of paraphrase intended to explain meaning. Definitions may be **lexical** (explaining current usage) or **stipulative** (specifying your own usage). Here's a correct lexical definition:

> "Bachelor" means "unmarried man."

This says we can interchange "bachelor" and "unmarried man" in any sentence; the resulting sentence will mean the same as the original, according to current usage. This leads to the interchange test for lexical definitions:

> **Interchange test:** To test a lexical definition claiming that A means B, try switching A and B in a variety of sentences. If some resulting pair of sentences don't mean the same thing, then the definition is incorrect.

According to our definition of "bachelor" as "unmarried man," for example, these two sentences would mean the same thing:

"Al is a *bachelor*."   "Al is an *unmarried man*."

These two *do* seem to mean the same thing. To refute the definition, we'd have to find a pair of sentences that are alike, except that "bachelor" and "unmarried man" are interchanged, and that don't mean the same thing.

Here's an incorrect lexical definition:

"Bachelor" means "happy man."

This leads to incorrect paraphrases. If the definition were correct, then these two sentences would mean the same thing:

"Al is a *bachelor*."   "Al is a *happy man*."

But they don't mean the same thing, since we could have one true but not the other. So the definition is wrong.

The interchange test is subject to at least two restrictions. First, definitions are often intended to cover just one sense of a word that has various meanings; we should then use the interchange test only on sentences using the intended sense. Thus it wouldn't be a good objection to our definition of "bachelor" as "unmarried man" to claim that these two sentences don't mean the same:

"I have a *bachelor* of arts degree."   "I have an *unmarried man* of arts degree."

The first sentence uses "bachelor" in a sense the definition doesn't try to cover.

Second, we shouldn't use the test on sentences where the word appears in quotes. Consider this pair of sentences:

"'*Bachelor*' has eight letters."   "'*Unmarried man*' has eight letters."

The two don't mean the same thing, since the first is true and the second false. But this doesn't show that our definition is wrong.

Lexical definitions are important in philosophy. Many philosophers, from Socrates to the present, have sought correct lexical definitions for some of the central concepts of human existence. They've tried to define concepts such as knowledge, truth, virtue, goodness, and justice. Such definitions are important for understanding and applying the concepts. Defining "good" as "what society approves of" would lead us to base our ethical beliefs on what is socially approved. We'd reject this method if we defined "good" as "what I like" or "what God desires," or if we regarded "good" as indefinable.

We can evaluate philosophical lexical definitions using the interchange test; Socrates was adept at this. Consider cultural relativism's definition of "good":

"X is good" means "X is approved by my society."

To evaluate this, we'd try switching "good" and "approved by my society" in a sentence to get a second sentence. Here's such a pair of sentences:

"Slavery is *good*."   "Slavery is *approved by my society*."

Then we'd see if the two sentences mean the same thing. Here they clearly don't, since it's consistent to affirm one but deny the other. Those who disagree with the norms of their society often say things like "Slavery is approved by my society, but it isn't good." Given this, we can argue against cultural relativism's definition of "good" as follows:

> If cultural relativism's definition is correct, then these
> two sentences mean the same thing.
> They don't mean the same thing.
> ∴ Cultural relativism's definition isn't correct.

To counter this, the cultural relativist would have to claim that the sentences *do* mean the same thing. But this claim is implausible.

Here are five rules for good lexical definitions:

1.   A good lexical definition is neither too broad nor too narrow.

Defining "bachelor" as "man" is too broad, since there are men who aren't bachelors. And defining "bachelor" as "unmarried male astronaut" is too narrow, since there are bachelors who aren't astronauts.

2.   A good lexical definition avoids circularity and poorly understood terms.

Defining "true" as "known to be true" is circular, since it defines "true" using "true." And defining "good" as "having positive aretaic value" uses poorly understood terms, since "aretaic" is less clear than "good."

3.   A good lexical definition matches in vagueness the term defined.

Defining "bachelor" as "unmarried male over 18 years old" is overly precise. The ordinary sense of "bachelor" is vague, since it's unclear on semantic grounds exactly at what age the term begins to apply. So "over 18" is too precise to be used to define "bachelor." "Man" or "adult" are better choices, since these match "bachelor" fairly well in vagueness.

4.   A good lexical definition matches, as far as possible, the emotional tone (positive or negative or neutral) of the term defined.

It won't do to define "bachelor" as *"fortunate* man who never married" or *"unfortunate* man who never married." These have positive and negative emotional slants; the original term "bachelor" is fairly neutral.

>   5.   A good lexical definition includes only properties essential to the term.

Suppose that all bachelors live on the planet earth. Even so, living on planet earth isn't a property *essential* to the term "bachelor" – since we could imagine a bachelor who lives on the moon. So it's wrong to include "living on planet earth" in the definition of "bachelor."

14.3a   Exercise – LogiCola Q

Give objections to these proposed lexical definitions.

"Game" means "anything that involves competition between two parties, and winning and losing."	By this definition, solitaire isn't a game, but a military battle is a game. This goes against the normal usage of the word "game."

1. "Lie" means "false statement."
2. "Adolescent" means "person between 9 and 19 years old."
3. "God" means "object of ultimate concern."
4. "Metaphysics" means "any sleep-inducing subject."
5. "Good" means "of positive value."
6. "Human being" means "featherless biped."
7. "I know that P" means "I believe that P."
8. "I know that P" means "I believe that P, and P is true."
9. "Chair" means "what you sit on."
10. "True" means "believed."
11. "True" means "proved to be true."
12. "Valid argument" means "argument that persuades."
13. "Murder" means "killing."
14. "Morally wrong" means "against the law."
15. "Philosopher" means "someone who has a degree in philosophy" and "philosophy" means "study of the great philosophers."

14.3b   Exercise

Cultural relativism claims that "good" (in its ordinary usage) is equivalent to "socially approved" or "approved by the majority (of the society in question)." What does this definition entail about the statements below? If this definition were correct, then would each of the following be true (1), false (0), or undecided by such considerations (?)?

If torturing for religious beliefs is *socially approved* in country X, then it's *good* in country X.	1 (for "true"). On cultural relativism, the statement would mean this (and thus be true): "If torturing for religious beliefs is *socially approved* in country X, then it's *socially approved* in country X."

1. Conclusions about what is good are deducible from sociological data (based, for example, on opinion surveys) describing one's society and what it approves.
2. If I say "Infanticide isn't good" but an ancient Roman says "Infanticide is good," then one or the other of us must be mistaken.
3. The norms set up by my society about what is good couldn't be mistaken.
4. Judgments about what is good aren't true or false.
5. It's good to respect the values of other societies.
6. If our society were to favor intolerance, then intolerance would be good.
7. Representational democracy will work anywhere.
8. From an analysis of how people use the word "good," it can be proved that whatever is socially accepted must be good.
9. Different cultures accept different moral beliefs.
10. "The majority favors this" logically entails "This is good."
11. If the majority favors war (sexual stereotypes, conservative politics, abortion, and so on), then this has to be good.
12. "Do good" means "Do what the majority favors."
13. Doing something because it's good isn't the same as doing it because the majority favors it.
14. People who said "Racism is favored by the majority but it isn't good" were contradicting themselves.
15. Something that's bad might nevertheless be socially approved (because society may be misinformed or irrational in its evaluations).
16. The majority knows what it favors.
17. If Nazism became widespread and genocide came to be what most people favored, then genocide would have to be good.
18. It isn't necessarily good for me to do what society favors.
19. Suppose that a survey showed that 90 percent of the population disapprove of people always following social approval. Then it follows that it's bad to always follow social approval – in other words, it's bad to always follow what is good.
20. Suppose that your fellow Americans as a group and your fellow Anglicans as a group disapprove of racism, whereas your fellow workers and your social group (friends and relatives) approve of racism. Then racism is bad.

14.4 Stipulative definitions

A **stipulative definition** specifies how you're going to use a term. Since your use may differ from conventional usage, it would be unfair to criticize a stipulative definition for clashing with the latter. Stipulative definitions should be judged, not as correct or incorrect, but rather as useful or useless.

This book has many stipulative definitions. I continually define terms like "logic," "argument," "valid," "wff," and so forth. These definitions specify the meaning I'm going to use for the terms (which sometimes is close to their standard meaning). The definitions create a technical vocabulary.

A **clarifying definition** is one that stipulates a clearer meaning for a vague term. For example, a scientist might stipulate a technical sense of "pure water" in terms of bacteria level; this technical sense, while related to the normal one, is more scientifically precise. Likewise, courts might stipulate a more precise definition of "death" to resolve certain legal disputes; the definition might be chosen on moral and legal grounds to clarify the law.

Philosophers often use stipulative definitions. Here's an example:

> In this discussion, I use "rational" to mean "always adopting the means believed necessary to achieve one's goals."

This definition signals that the author will use "rational" to abbreviate a certain longer phrase; there's no claim that this exactly reflects the ordinary meaning of the term. Other philosophers may use "rational" in quite different senses, such as "logically consistent," "emotionless," or "always forming beliefs solely by the methods of science." These philosophers needn't be disagreeing; they may just be specifying their technical vocabulary differently. We could use subscripts for different senses; "rational$_1$" might mean "logically consistent," and "rational$_2$" might mean "emotionless." Don't be misled into thinking that, because being *rational* in one sense is desirable, therefore being *rational* in some other sense must also be desirable.

Stipulative definitions, while they needn't accord with current usage, should:

- use clear terms that the parties involved will understand,
- avoid circularity,
- allow us to paraphrase out the defined term,
- accord with how the person giving it is going to use the term, and
- help our understanding and discussion of the subject matter.

Let me elaborate on the last norm. A stipulative definition is a device for abbreviating language. Chapter 1 of this book starts with a stipulative definition: "Logic is the analysis and appraisal of arguments." This definition lets us use the one word "logic" in place of the six words "the analysis and appraisal of arguments." Without the definition, our explanations would be wordier and harder to grasp; so the definition is useful.

Stipulative definitions should promote understanding. It's seldom useful to stipulate that a well established term will be used in a radical new sense (for example, that "biology" will be used to mean "the study of earthquakes"); this

would create confusion. And it's seldom useful to multiply stipulative definitions for terms that we'll seldom use. But at times we find ourselves repeating a
cumbersome phrase over and over; then a stipulative definition can be helpful.
Suppose your essay keeps repeating the phrase "action that satisfies criteria 1,
2, and 3 of the previous section"; your essay may be easier to follow if some
short term were stipulated to mean the same as this longer phrase.

Some of our definitions seem to violate the "avoid circularity" norm. Section
3.1 defined "wffs" as sequences that we can construct using these rules:

> 1. Any capital letter is a wff.
> 2. The result of prefixing any wff with "~" is a wff.
> 3. The result of joining any two wffs by "·" or "∨" or "⊃"
>   or "≡" and enclosing the result in parentheses is a wff.

Clauses 2 and 3 define "wff" in terms of "wff." And the definition doesn't seem
to let us paraphrase out the term "wff"; we don't seem able to take a sentence
using "wff" and say the same thing without "wff."

Actually, our definition is perfectly fine. We can rephrase it in the following
way to avoid circularity and show how to paraphrase out the term "wff":

> "Wff" means "member of every set S of strings that satis-
> fies these conditions: (1) Every capital letter is a member of
> set S; (2) the result of prefixing any member of set S with
> '~' is a member of set S; and (3) the result of joining any
> two members of set S by '·' or '∨' or '⊃' or '≡' and enclosing
> the result in parentheses is a member of set S."

Our definition of "wff" is a **recursive definition** – one that first specifies some
things that the term applies to and then specifies that if the term applies to
certain things then it also applies to certain other things. Here's a recursive
definition of "ancestor of mine":

> 1. My father and mother are ancestors of mine.
> 2. Any father or mother of an ancestor of mine
>   is an ancestor of mine.

Here's an equivalent non-recursive definition:

> "Ancestor of mine" means "member of every set
> S that satisfies these conditions: (1) my father and
> mother are members of S; and (2) every father or
> mother of a member of S is a member of S."

14.5   Explaining meaning

If we avoid circular sets of definitions, we can't define all our terms; instead, we must leave some terms undefined. But how can we explain the *undefined* terms? One way is by examples.

To teach "red" to someone who understands no language that we speak, we could point to red objects and say "Red!" We'd want to point to different sorts of red objects; if we pointed only to red shirts, the person might think that "red" meant "shirt." If the person understands "not," we also could point to non-red objects and say "Not red!" The person, unless color blind, soon will catch our meaning and be able to point to red objects and say "Red!" This is a basic, primitive way to teach language. It explains a word, not by using other words, but by relating a word to concrete experiences.

We sometimes point to examples through words. We might explain "plaid" to a child by saying "It's a color pattern like that of your brother's shirt." We might explain "love" by mentioning examples: "Love is getting up to cook a sick person's breakfast instead of staying in bed, encouraging someone instead of complaining, listening to other people instead of telling them how great you are, and similar things." It's often helpful to combine a definition with examples, so the two can reinforce each other; so Chapter 1 defined "argument" and then gave examples.

In abstract discussions, people sometimes use words so differently that they fail to communicate. People almost seem to speak different languages. Asking for definitions may then lead to the frustration of hearing one term you don't understand being defined using other terms you don't understand. In such cases, it might be more helpful to ask for examples instead of definitions. We might say, "Give me examples of an *analytic statement* (or of a *deconstruction*)." The request for examples can bring an bewilderingly abstract discussion back down to earth and mutual understanding.

Logical positivists and pragmatists suggested other ways to clarify statements. The positivists proposed that we explain the meaning of a statement by specifying which experiences would show the statement to be true, and which would show it to be false. Operational definitions such as these connect meaning to an experimental test:

- To say that rock A is "harder than" rock B means that A would scratch B but B wouldn't scratch A.
- To say that this string is "1 meter long" means that, if you stretch it over the standard meter stick, then the ends of both will coincide.
- To say that the person "has an IQ of 100" means that the person would get an average score on a standard IQ test.

Such definitions are important in science.

Logical positivists like A. J. Ayer appealed to a verifiability criterion of meaning as the cornerstone of their philosophy. We can formulate their principle (to be applied only to synthetic statements – see Section 14.7) as follows:

Logical Positivism (LP)

This question can help us find a statement's meaning: "How could the truth or falsity of the statement in principle be discovered by conceivable observable tests?"

If there's no way to test a statement, then it has no meaning (it makes no assertion that could be true or false). If tests are given, they specify the meaning.

There are problems with taking LP to be literally true. LP says *any untestable statement is without meaning*. But LP itself is untestable. Hence LP is without meaning on its own terms – it's self-refuting. For this reason and others, few hold this view anymore, even though it was popular decades ago.

Still, the LP way to clarify statements can sometimes be useful. Consider this claim of Thales, the ancient Greek alleged to be the first philosopher:

"Water is the primal stuff of reality."

The meaning of this claim is unclear. We might ask Thales for a definition of "primal stuff"; this would clarify the claim. Or we might follow LP and ask, "How could we test whether your claim is correct?" Suppose that Thales says the following, thus giving an operational definition of his claim:

Try giving living things no water. If they die, then this proves my claim. If they live, then this refutes my claim.

We'd then understand Thales to be claiming that water is needed for life. Or suppose that Thales replies this way:

Let scientists work on the task of transforming each kind of matter (gold, rock, air, and so on) into water, and water back into each kind of matter. If they eventually succeed, then that proves my claim.

Again, this would help us understand the claim. But suppose Thales says this:

No conceivable experimental test could show my claim to be true or show it to be false.

The positivists would then conclude that Thales's claim is meaningless – that it makes no factual assertion that could be true or false. Those of us who aren't positivists needn't draw this conclusion so quickly; but we might remain suspicious of Thales's claim and wonder what he's getting at.

LP demands that a statement *in principle* be able to be tested. The "in principle" qualification is important. Consider this example: "There are mountains on the other side of the moon." When the positivists wrote, rocket technology was less advanced and we couldn't actually test this statement. But that didn't matter to its meaningfulness, since we could describe what a test would be like. That this claim was *testable in principle* was enough to make it meaningful.

LP's question hides an ambiguity:

> How could the truth or falsity of the statement in principle
> be discovered by conceivable observable tests?

Observable by whom? Is it enough that one person can make the observation? Or does it have to be publicly observable? Is a statement about my present feelings meaningful if I alone can observe whether it's true?

Historically, most of the positivists demanded that a statement be *publicly verifiable*. But the weaker version of the theory that allows *verification by one person* seems more plausible. After all, a statement about my present feelings does make sense – and only I can verify it.

William James suggested a related way to clarify statements. His "Pragmatism" essay suggests that we determine the meaning, or "cash value," of a statement by relating it to practical consequences. James's view is broader and more tolerant than that of the positivists. We can formulate his pragmatism principle as follows (again, it's to be applied only to synthetic statements):

Pragmatism (PR)

This question can help us find a statement's meaning: "What conceivable practical differences to someone could the truth or falsity of the statement make?" Here "practical differences to someone" covers what *experiences* one would have or what *choices* one ought to make.

If the truth or falsity of a statement could make no practical difference to anyone, then it has no meaning; it makes no assertion that could be true or false. If practical differences are given, they specify the meaning.

I'm inclined to think that something close to PR is literally true. But here I'll just stress that PR can be useful in clarifying meaning.

In many cases, PR applies in much the same way as LP. At least, PR applies like the weaker version of LP that allows verification by one person. LP focuses on what we could experience if the statement were true or false; and PR includes such experiences under practical differences.

But PR also includes under "practical differences" what choices one ought to make. This makes PR broader than LP, since what makes a difference to choices need not be testable by observation. Consider the view called "hedonism":

"Only pleasure is worth striving for."

LP asks, "How could the truth or falsity of hedonism in principle be discovered by conceivable observable tests?" The answer may be "It can't"; then LP would see hedonism as meaningless. But PR asks, "What conceivable practical differences to someone could the truth or falsity of hedonism make?" Here, "practical differences" include what *choices* one ought to make. The truth of hedonism could make many specifiable differences about such choices; if hedonism is true, for example, then we should pursue knowledge, not for its own sake, but only insofar as it promotes pleasure. Ethical claims like hedonism are meaningless on LP but meaningful on the more tolerant PR.

In addition, PR isn't self-refuting. LP says "Any untestable statement is without meaning." But LP itself is untestable – and so is meaningless on its own terms. But PR says "Any statement whose truth or falsity could make no conceivable practical difference is without meaning." PR makes a practical difference to our choices about beliefs; presumably we shouldn't believe statements that fail the PR test. And so PR can be meaningful on its own terms.

So we can explain words by definitions, examples, verification conditions, and practical differences. Another way to convey the meaning of words is by contextual use: we use a word in such a way that its meaning can be gathered from surrounding "clues." Suppose a person getting in a car says "I'm getting in my C"; we can surmise that C means "car." We all learned most of our first language by picking up the meaning of words from their contextual use.

Some thinkers want us to pick up their technical terms in this same way. We are given no definitions of key terms, no examples to clarify their use, and no explanations in terms of verification conditions or practical differences. We are just told to dive in and catch the lingo by getting used to it. We should be suspicious of this. We may catch the lingo, but it may turn out to be empty and without meaning. That's why the positivists and pragmatists emphasized finding the "cash value" of ideas in terms of verification conditions or practical differences. We must be on guard against empty jargon.

14.5a Exercise

Would each claim be meaningful or meaningless on LP? (Take LP to require that a statement be publicly testable.) Would each be meaningful or meaningless on PR?

Unless we have strong reasons to the contrary, we *ought* to believe what sense experience seems to reveal.	This is meaningless on LP, since claims about what one ought to do aren't publicly testable. It's meaningful on PR, since its truth could make a difference about what choices we ought to make about beliefs.

1. It's cold outside.
2. That clock is fast.
3. There are five-foot-long blue ants in my bedroom.
4. Nothing is real.
5. Form is metaphysically prior to matter.
6. At noon all objects, distances, and velocities in the universe will double.
7. I'm wearing an invisible hat that can't be felt or perceived in any way.
8. Regina has a pain in her little toe but shows no signs of this and will deny it if you ask her.
9. Other humans have no thoughts or feelings but only act as if they do.
10. Manuel will continue to have conscious experiences after his physical death.
11. Angels exist (that is, there are thinking creatures who have never had spatial dimensions or weights).
12. God exists (that is, there's a very intelligent, powerful, and good personal creator of the universe).
13. One ought to be logically consistent.
14. Any statement whose truth or falsity could make no conceivable practical difference is meaningless. (PR)
15. Any statement that isn't observationally testable is meaningless. (LP)

14.6 Making distinctions

Philosophers faced with difficult questions often begin by making distinctions:

> "If your question means ... [and then the question is rephrased simply and clearly], then my answer is .... But if you're really asking ..., then my answer is ...."

The ability to formulate various possible meanings of a question is a valuable skill. Many of the questions that confront us are vague or confused; we often have to clarify a question before we can answer it intelligently. Getting clear on a question can be half the battle.

Consider this question:

> "Are some beliefs <u>indubitable</u>?"

I underlined the tricky word "indubitable." What does it mean? Does it mean *not actually doubted*? Or *not able (psychologically) to be doubted*? Or *irra-*

tional to doubt? And what is it to doubt? Is it to *refrain from believing?* Or is it to *have some suspicion* toward the belief (although we might still believe it)? And indubitable by whom? By *everyone* (even crazy people)? By *all rational persons?* By at least *some* individuals? By *me?* Our little question hides a sea of ambiguities. It's unwise to try to answer such a question without first spelling out what we take it to mean.

Here are three of the many things that our little question could be asking:

- Are there some beliefs that no one at all has ever refused to believe? (To answer this, we'd need to know whether people in insane asylums sometimes refuse to believe that they exist or that "2=2.")
- Are there some beliefs that no rational person has suspicions about? (To answer this, we'd first have to decide what we mean by "rational.")
- Are there some beliefs that some specific individuals are psychologically unable to regard with any suspicion? (Perhaps many are unable to doubt beliefs about what their name is or where they live.)

Our little question could have many different meanings.

Unnoticed ambiguities can block communication. Often people are unclear about what they're asking, or take the question of another in an unintended sense. This is more likely if the discussion goes abstractly, without examples.

14.6a Exercise

Each of the following questions is obscure or ambiguous as it stands. You are to distinguish at least three interesting senses of each question. Formulate each sense simply, clearly, and briefly – and without using the underlined words.

> Can one <u>prove</u> that there are external objects?

> - Can we deduce, from premises expressing immediate experience (like "I seem to see a blue shape"), that there are external objects?
> - Can anyone give an argument that will convince (all or most) skeptics that there are external objects?
> - Can anyone give a good deductive or inductive argument, from premises expressing their immediate experience in addition to true principles of evidence, to conclude that it's reasonable to believe that there are external objects? (These "principles of evidence" might include things like "Unless we have strong reasons to the contrary, it's reasonable to believe what sense experience seems to reveal.")

1. Is ethics a <u>science</u>?
2. Is this monkey a <u>rational</u> animal?
3. Is this belief part of <u>common sense</u>?
4. Are material objects <u>objective</u>?

5. Are values <u>relative</u> (or <u>absolute</u>)?
6. Are scientific generalizations ever <u>certain</u>?
7. Was the action of that monkey a <u>free</u> act?
8. Is <u>truth</u> <u>changeless</u>?
9. How are moral beliefs <u>explainable</u>?
10. Is that judgment based on <u>reason</u>?
11. Is a fetus a <u>human being</u> (or <u>human person</u>)?
12. Are values <u>objective</u>?
13. What is the <u>nature</u> of <u>man</u>?
14. Can I ever <u>know</u> what someone else feels?
15. Do you have a <u>soul</u>?
16. Is the world <u>illogical</u>?

14.7 Analytic and synthetic

Immanuel Kant long ago introduced two related distinctions. He divided statements, on the basis of their meaning, into *analytic* and *synthetic* statements. He divided knowledge, on the basis of how it's known, into *a priori* and *a posteriori* knowledge. We'll consider these distinctions, which many philosophers find useful, in this section and the next.

First let's try to understand what an *analytic statement* is. One problem is that Kant gave two definitions:

1. An *analytic statement* is one whose subject contains its predicate.
2. An *analytic statement* is one that's self-contradictory to deny.

Consider these examples (and take "bachelor" to mean "unmarried man"):

(a) "All bachelors are unmarried."
(b) "If it's raining, then it's raining."

Both examples are analytic by definition 2, since both are self-contradictory to deny. But only (a) is analytic by definition 1. In (a), the subject "bachelor" (= "unmarried man") contains the predicate "unmarried"; but in (b), the subject "it" doesn't contain the predicate.

We'll adopt definition 2; so we define an **analytic statement** as one that's self-contradictory to deny. *Logically necessary truth* is another term for the same idea; such truths are based on logic, the meaning of concepts, or necessary connections between properties. Here are some further examples of analytic statements:

"2=2"   "If everything is green, this is green."
"1>0"   "If there's rain, there's precipitation."
"All frogs are frogs."   "If this is green, this is colored."

By contrast, a **synthetic statement** is one that's neither analytic nor self-contradictory; *contingent* is another term for the same idea. Statements divide into analytic, synthetic, and self-contradictory; here's an example of each:[1]

> *Analytic:* "All bachelors are unmarried."
> *Synthetic:* "Daniel is a bachelor."
> *Self-contradictory:* "Daniel is a married bachelor."

While there are three kinds of statement, there are only two kinds of truth: analytic and synthetic. Self-contradictory statements are necessarily false.

14.7a Exercise

Say whether each of these statements is analytic or synthetic. Take the various terms in their most natural senses. Some examples are controversial.

All triangles are triangles.	This is analytic. It would be self-contradictory to deny it and say "Some triangles aren't triangles."

1. All triangles have three angles.
2. $2 + 2 = 4$.
3. Combining two drops of mercury with two other drops results in one big drop.
4. There are ants that have established a system of slavery.
5. Either some ants are parasitic or else none are.
6. No three-year-old is an adult.
7. No three-year-old understands symbolic logic.
8. Water boils at 90°C on that 10,000-foot mountain.
9. Water boils at 100°C at sea level.
10. No uncle who has never married is an only child.
11. All swans are white.
12. Every material body is spatially located and has spatial dimensions.
13. Every material body has weight.
14. The sum of the angles of a Euclidian triangle equals 180°.
15. If all Parisians are French and all French are European, then all Parisians are European.
16. Every event has a cause.
17. Every effect has a cause.
18. We ought to treat a person not simply as a means but always as an end in itself.
19. One ought to be logically consistent.
20. God exists.
21. Given that we have observed that the sun rose every day in the past, it's reasonable for us to believe that the sun will rise tomorrow.

---

[1] Modal logic (see Chapter 7) symbolizes "A is analytic (necessary)" as "□A," "A is synthetic (contingent)" as "(◇A · ◇~A)," and "A is self-contradictory" as "~◇A."

22. Unless we have strong reasons to the contrary, we ought to believe what sense experience seems to reveal.
23. Everything red is colored.
24. Nothing red is blue (at the same time and in the same part and respect).
25. Every synthetic statement that's known to be true is known on the basis of sense experience. (There's no synthetic *a priori* knowledge.)

14.8 *A priori* and *a posteriori*

Philosophers traditionally distinguish two kinds of knowledge. *A posteriori* (**empirical**) **knowledge** is knowledge based on sense experience. *A priori* (**rational**) **knowledge** is knowledge not based on sense experience. Here is an example of each kind of knowledge:

> *A posteriori:* "Some bachelors are happy."
> *A priori:* "All bachelors are unmarried."

While we know both to be true, *how* we know differs in the two cases. We know the first statement from our experience of bachelors; we've met many bachelors and recall that some of them have been happy. In contrast, we know the second statement by grasping what it means and seeing that it must be true; we don't have to appeal to our experience of bachelors.

Most of our knowledge is *a posteriori* – based on sense experience. "Sense experience" here covers the five "outer senses" (sight, hearing, smell, taste, and touch). It also covers "inner sense" (the awareness of our own thoughts and feelings) and any other experiential access to the truth that we might have (perhaps mystical experience or extrasensory perception).

Logical and mathematical knowledge is generally *a priori*. To test the validity of an argument, we don't go out and do experiments. Instead, we just think and reason; sometimes we write things out to help our thinking. The validity tests in this book use rational (*a priori*) methods. "Reason" in a narrow sense (in which it contrasts with "experience") deals with what we can know *a priori*.

A priori knowledge requires some experience. We can't know that all bachelors are unmarried unless we've learned the concepts involved; this requires experience of language and of (married and unmarried) humans. And knowing that all bachelors are unmarried requires the experience of thinking. So *a priori* knowledge depends somewhat on experience. But it still makes sense to call such knowledge *a priori*. Suppose that we've gained the concepts using experience. Then to know that all bachelors are unmarried, we don't have to appeal to any further experience, other than thinking. In particular, we don't have to investigate bachelors to see whether they're all unmarried.

Here are some further examples of statements known *a priori*:

"2=2"	"If everything is green, this is green."
"1>0"	"If there's rain, there's precipitation."
"All frogs are frogs."	"If this is green, this is colored."

We also gave these as examples of analytic statements.

So far, we've used only analytic statements as examples of *a priori* knowledge, and only synthetic statements as examples of *a posteriori* knowledge. Some philosophers think both distinctions coincide; they think there's only one distinction, although it's drawn in two ways. They suggest that:

$$a \text{ } priori \text{ knowledge } = \text{ analytic knowledge}$$
$$a \text{ } posteriori \text{ knowledge } = \text{ synthetic knowledge}$$

Is this view true? If it's true at all, it isn't true just because of how we defined the terms. By our definitions, the basis for the analytic / synthetic distinction differs from the basis for the *a priori* / *a posteriori* distinction. A statement is analytic or synthetic depending on whether its denial is self-contradictory. Knowledge is *a posteriori* or *a priori* depending on whether it rests on sense experience. Our definitions leave it open whether the two distinctions coincide.

These two combinations are very common:

analytic *a priori* knowledge   synthetic *a posteriori* knowledge

Most of our knowledge in math and logic is analytic and *a priori*. Most of our scientific knowledge and everyday knowledge about the world is synthetic and *a posteriori*. These next two combinations are more controversial:

analytic *a posteriori* knowledge   synthetic *a priori* knowledge

Can we know any analytic statements *a posteriori*? It seems that we can. "π is a little over 3" is presumably an analytic truth that can be known either by *a priori* calculations (the more precise way to compute π) – or by measuring circles empirically (as the ancient Egyptians did). And "It's raining or not raining" is an analytic truth that can be known either *a priori* (and justified by truth tables) – or by deducing it from the empirical statement "It's raining."

But perhaps any analytic statement that is known *a posteriori* also could be known *a priori*. This claim seems very plausible. Saul Kripke has questioned it, but his arguments are too complex to consider here.

The biggest controversy has raged over this question:

Do we have any synthetic *a priori* knowledge?

Equivalently, is there any statement A such that:

- A is synthetic (neither self-contradictory to affirm nor self-contradictory to deny),
- we know A to be true, and
- our knowledge of A is based on reason (not on sense experience)?

In one sense of the term, an **empiricist** is one who rejects such knowledge – and who thus limits what we can know by reason alone to analytic statements. By contrast, a **rationalist** is one who accepts such knowledge – and who thus gives a greater scope to what we can know by reason alone.[1] Our view on this issue has an important impact on the rest of our philosophy.

Empiricists deny the possibility of synthetic *a priori* knowledge for two main reasons. First, it's difficult to understand how there could be such knowledge. Analytic *a priori* knowledge is fairly easy to grasp. Suppose a statement is true simply because of the meaning and logical relations of the concepts involved; then we can know it in an *a priori* fashion, by reflecting on these concepts and logical relations. But suppose a statement could logically be either true or false. How could we then possibly know by pure thinking which it is?

Second, those who claim to know synthetic *a priori* truths don't agree much on what these truths are. They just seem to follow their prejudices and call them "deliverances of reason."

Rationalists affirm the existence of synthetic *a priori* knowledge for two main reasons. First, the opposite view (at least if it's claimed to be known) is self-refuting. Consider empiricists who claim to know this to be true:

"There's no synthetic *a priori* knowledge."

This statement itself would have to represent synthetic *a priori* knowledge. For the statement is synthetic (it isn't true by virtue of how we defined the terms "synthetic" and "*a priori*" – and it isn't self-contradictory to deny). And it would have to be known *a priori* (since surely we can't know it on the basis of sense experience). So the empiricist's claim would be synthetic *a priori* knowledge – the very thing it rejects.

Second, we seem to have synthetic *a priori* knowledge of various truths – such as the following:

If you believe that you see an object to be red and you have no special reason for doubting your perception, then it's reasonable for you to believe that you see an actual red object.

This claim is synthetic; it isn't true because of how we've defined terms – and skeptics can deny it without self-contradiction. It's known to be true; if we

---

[1] More broadly, *empiricists* are those who emphasize *a posteriori* knowledge, while *rationalists* are those who emphasize *a priori* knowledge.

don't know truths like this one, then we can't justify any empirical beliefs. And it's known *a priori*; it can't be based on sense experience – instead, knowledge from sense experience is based on truths like this one. So we have synthetic *a priori* knowledge of this claim. So there is synthetic *a priori* knowledge.

The dispute over synthetic *a priori* knowledge deeply influences how we do philosophy. The dispute concerns the power of pure thinking. Is pure *a priori* knowledge limited to analytic truths? Consider this question about basic ethical principles (which are generally conceded to be synthetic):

> Are basic ethical principles known *a priori*?

Empiricists answer no and thus deny that we know basic ethical principles *a priori*; so empiricists think knowledge of basic ethical principles is either empirical or non-existent. But rationalists can (and often do) think that we know basic ethical truths *a priori*, from reason alone (either through intuition or through some rational consistency test).

14.8a   Exercise

Suppose that we knew each of these statements to be true. Would our knowledge likely be *a priori* or *a posteriori*? Take the various terms in their most natural senses. Some examples are controversial.

All triangles are triangles.	This would be known *a priori*.

Use the examples from Section 14.7a.

CHAPTER 15
Fallacies and Argumentation

This final chapter has five related topics. These deal with characteristics of a good argument, recognizing common fallacies, avoiding inconsistency, developing your own arguments, and analyzing arguments that you read.

15.1 Good arguments

A **good argument**, to be logically correct and to fulfill the purposes for which we use arguments, should:

1. be deductively valid (or inductively strong) and have all true premises;
2. have its validity and truth-of-premises be as evident as possible to the parties involved;
3. be clearly stated (using understandable language and making clear what the premises and conclusion are);
4. avoid circularity, ambiguity, and emotional language; and
5. be relevant to the issue at hand.

First and most obviously, a good argument should be deductively valid (or inductively strong) and have all true premises. Correspondingly, we often criticize an argument by trying to show that the conclusion doesn't follow from the premises or that one or more of the premises are false.

Second, a good argument should have its validity and truth-of-premises be as evident as possible to the parties involved. Arguments are less effective if they involve ideas that others see as false or controversial. Ideally, we'd like to use only premises that everyone will accept as immediately obvious; in practice, this is too high an ideal. We sometimes appeal to premises that only some will accept – perhaps those of similar philosophical, religious, or political commitments. And sometimes we appeal to personal hunches (like "I can get to the gun before the thief does"); while far from ideal, this may be the best we can do at a given moment.

Third, a good argument should be clearly stated; it should use understandable language and make clear what the premises and conclusion are. Obscure or overly complex language makes reasoning harder to grasp.

When we develop an argument, a good strategy is to put it down on paper in a preliminary way and then go through it several times trying to make improvements. Try to express the ideas more clearly and simply – and bear in mind how others may object to or misconstrue what is said. Ideas often come to us in a confused form; clarity typically comes later, after much hard work. While mushy thinking is often unavoidable in the early development of an idea, it isn't acceptable in the final product.

People often argue without making clear what their premises and conclusions are; sometimes we get stream-of-consciousness ramblings sprinkled with an occasional "therefore." While this is unacceptable, a good argument needn't spell everything out; it's often fine to omit premises that are obvious to the parties involved. If I'm hiking on the Appalachian Trail, I might say this to my hiking partner: "We can't still be on the right trail, since we don't see white blazes on the trees." This is fine if my partner knows that we'd see white blazes if we were on the right trail; then the full argument would be pedantic:

> If we were still on the right trail, then
> we'd see white blazes on the trees.
> We don't see white blazes on the trees.
> ∴ We aren't still on the right trail.

In philosophy, it's wise to spell out *all* our premises, since implicit ideas are often crucial but unexamined. Suppose someone argues: "We can't be free, since all our actions are determined." This assumes the italicized premise:

> All human actions are determined.
> *No determined action is free.*
> ∴ No human actions are free.

We should be aware that we're assuming this controversial premise.

So a good argument should be valid (or strong) and have all true premises, this truth and validity should be evident, and the argument should be clearly stated. We gave two further conditions; a good argument should:

    4. avoid circularity, ambiguity, and emotional language; and
    5. be relevant to the issue at hand.

I'll now introduce five common fallacies that correspond to these conditions.
  Our first fallacy is *circularity*:

An argument is **circular** (**question begging**) if it presumes the truth of what is to be proved.	A series of arguments is **circular** if it uses a given premise to prove a conclusion – and then uses that conclusion to prove the premise.

A simple example is "The soul is immortal because it can't die"; the premise here just repeats the conclusion in different words – so the argument takes for granted what it's supposed to prove. A circular *series* of arguments might have this form: "A is true because B is true, and B is true because A is true."

Here's a second fallacy – and a crude argument that exemplifies the fallacy:

An argument is **ambiguous** if it changes the meaning of a term or phrase within the argument.	Love is an emotion. God is love. ∴ God is an emotion.

Premise 1 requires that we take "love" to mean "the feeling of love" – which makes premise 2 false or doubtful. Premise 2 requires that we take "love" to mean "a supremely loving person" or "the source of love" – which makes premise 1 false or doubtful. So we can have both premises clearly true only by shifting the meaning of "love."

It's important to avoid emotionally slanted terms when we reason:

> To **appeal to emotion** is to stir up feelings instead of arguing in a logical manner.

Students, when asked on an exam to argue (reason) against a theory, often just describe the theory in derogatory language; but such verbal abuse doesn't give any reason for thinking a view wrong. Often the best way to argue against a theory is to try to find some false implication and then reason as follows:

> If the theory is true, then this other thing also would be true.
> This other thing isn't true.
> ∴ The theory isn't true.

Recall that an argument consists of premises and a conclusion.

Our last condition says that a good argument must be relevant to the issue at hand. A clearly stated argument might prove something and yet still be defective – since it may be beside the point in the current context:

> An argument is **beside the point** if it argues for a conclusion irrelevant to the issue at hand.

Hitler, when facing a group opposed to the forceful imposition of dictatorships, sidetracked their attention by attacking pacifism; his arguments, even if sound, were beside the point. Such arguments are called "red herrings," after a practice used in training hunting dogs: a red herring fish would be dragged across the trail to distract the dog from tracking an animal. In arguing, we must keep the point at issue clearly in mind and not be misled by smelly fish.

Students sometimes use this "beside the point" label too broadly, to apply to almost any fallacy. Keep in mind that this fallacy isn't about the *premises being irrelevant* to the conclusion. Instead, it's about the *conclusion* (regardless of whether it's proved) *being irrelevant to the issue at hand.*

One common form of this fallacy has its own name:

> A **straw man** argument misrepresents an opponent's views.

This is common in politics. Candidate A for mayor suggests cutting a few seldom-used stations on the rapid transit system. Then candidate B portrays A as wanting to eliminate the whole system; B devotes speeches to showing how the rapid transit system is needed. But B is then attacking, not what A actually holds, but only a "straw man" – a scarecrow of his own invention.

Let's get back to our discussion of good arguments. Briefly, a good argument is deductively valid (or inductively strong) and has all true premises; has this validity and truth be as evident as possible to the parties involved; is clearly stated; avoids circularity, ambiguity, and emotional language; and is relevant to the issue at hand.

A good argument normally convinces others, but it need not. Some people aren't open to rational argument on certain issues. Some believe that the earth is flat – despite good arguments to the contrary. On the other hand, bad arguments sometimes convince people. Hitler's use of the "beside the point" fallacy and the candidate's use of the "straw man" fallacy can mislead and convince. Studying logic can help to protect us from bad reasoning.

"Proof" is roughly like "good argument." But we can *prove* something even if our argument is unclear, contains emotional language, or is irrelevant to the issue at hand. And a proof must be *very* strong in its premises and in how it connects the premises to the conclusion; for the latter reason, it seems wrong to call inductive arguments "proofs." Here's a definition:

> A **proof** is a non-circular, non-ambiguous, deductively valid argument with clearly true premises.

A **refutation** of A is a proof of the denial of A.

"Proof" can have other meanings. Previous chapters used "proof" in the technical sense of "formal proof," to cover logical derivations that follow certain specified rules. And exercise 14.6a explained that "prove" could have various meanings in the question, "Can we prove that there are external objects?" The word "proof" has a cluster of related meanings.

Students often misuse the words "prove" and "refute." These words properly apply only to successful arguments. If you *prove* something, it's true – and you've shown that it's true. If you *refute* something, it's false – and you've shown that it's false. Compare these two:

> *Wrong:*   "Hume proved this, but Kant refuted him."
> *Right:*   "Hume argued for this, but Kant criticized his reasoning."

The first is self-contradictory, since it implies that Hume's claim is both true and false – and that Hume showed it was true and Kant showed it was false.

15.2   Informal fallacies

A **fallacy** is a deceptive error of thinking; an **informal fallacy** is a fallacy that isn't covered by some system of deductive or inductive logic. In working out the conditions for a good argument, we've already introduced five fallacies:

Circular   Ambiguous   Appeal to emotion   Beside the point   Straw man

We'll now add thirteen more, loosely divided into three groups. Our full list includes eighteen of the more common fallacies. We'll now list six fallacies that are conveniently expressed in a premise–conclusion format.

Appeal to the crowd	Most people believe A. ∴ A is true.

Most people think Wheaties is very nutritious.
∴ Wheaties is very nutritious.

Despite popular opinion (perhaps influenced by health-oriented advertising), Wheaties cereal could have little nutritional value. Discovering its nutritional value requires checking its nutrient content; group opinion proves nothing. When we think about it, we all recognize the fallacy here; yet group opinion still may sway us. Reasoning that we know to be flawed may continue to influence us. We humans are only partially rational.

Opposition	Our opponents believe A. ∴ A is false.

Those blasted liberals say we should raise taxes.
∴ We shouldn't raise taxes.

The problem here is that our opponents are often right.

Genetic fallacy	We can explain why you believe A. ∴ A is false.

Any psychologist would see that you believe A because of such and such.
∴ A is false.

One who has superficially studied a little psychology might dismiss another's views in this way. An appropriate (but nasty) reply is, "And what is the psychological explanation for why you confuse psychological explanations with logical disproofs?" To show a belief to be false, we must argue against the *content* of the belief; it isn't enough to explain how the belief came to be.

Appeal to ignorance	No one has proved A. ∴ A is false.	No one has disproved A. ∴ A is true.

No one has proved that there is a God. ∴ There is no God.	No one has proved that there is no God. ∴ There is a God.

Neither is correct. Something that isn't proved might still be true, just as something that isn't refuted might still be false. An "appeal to ignorance" must have one of these forms; it isn't just any case in which someone speaks out of ignorance.

Post hoc ergo propter hoc	A happened after B. ∴ A was caused by B.

Paul had a beer and then got 104% on his logic test.
∴ He got 104% because he had beer.

The premise was true (there were bonus points). Some creative students added their own conclusions: "So if I have a beer before the next test, I'll get 104%" and "If I have a six-pack, I'll get 624%." The Latin name for this fallacy means "after this therefore because of this." To prove causal connections requires more than just the premise that one factor occurred after another; the two factors might just *happen* to have occurred together. It isn't even enough that two factors *always* occur together; day always follows night, and night follows day, but neither causes the other. Proving causal connections is difficult (see Mill's methods in Section 13.7).

Division-composition	This is F. ∴ Every part of this is F.	Every part of this is F. ∴ This is F.

My essay is well done. ∴ Every sentence of my essay is well done.	Every sentence of my essay is well done. ∴ My essay is well done.

The first argument is wrong because an essay might be good despite having some poor sentences. The second is wrong because each sentence of the essay might be well done without the essay as a whole being good; the well-written individual sentences might not make sense together. So something might be true of the whole without being true of the parts; and something might be true of the parts without being true of the whole.

In unusual cases, these six forms might be abbreviated forms of good reasoning. Suppose you know that people in your society almost never have false beliefs; then this "appeal to the crowd" could be correct reasoning:

> Almost always, what most people in my society believe is true.
> Most people in my society believe A.
> This is all we know about the matter.
> ∴ Probably A is true.

Or suppose you know that your opponent Jones is always wrong. This opposition argument would then be correct reasoning:

> Everything Jones says is false.
> Jones says A.
> ∴ A is false.

Correct forms of these six fallacies are unusual in real life. But our next three fallacies have common correct forms; so we'll consider their correct and incorrect forms together.

Appeal to authority – correct form:

X holds that A is true.
X is an authority on the subject.
The consensus of authorities agrees with X.
∴ There's a presumption that A is true.

Incorrect forms omit premise 2 or 3, or conclude that A *must* be true.

> Your doctor tells you A.
> She's an authority on the subject.
> The other authorities agree with her.
> ∴ There's a presumption that A is true.

This example about your doctor is good reasoning; the conclusion means that you ought to believe A unless you have special evidence to the contrary. If your doctor is a great authority and the consensus of authorities is large, then the argument becomes stronger; but it's never 100 percent conclusive. All the authorities in the world *might* agree on something that they later discover to be wrong; so we shouldn't think that something *must* be so because the authorities say it is. It's also wrong to appeal to a person who isn't an authority in the field (a sports hero endorsing coffee makers, for example). And finally, it's weak to appeal to one authority (regarding the safety of an atomic power plant, for example) when the authorities disagree widely. The appeal to authority can go wrong in many ways. Yet many of our trusted beliefs (that Washington was the first US president, for example, or that there's such a country as Japan) rest quite properly on the say so of others.

An "authority" might be a calculator or computer instead of a human. My calculator has proved itself reliable, and it gives the same result as other reliable calculators. So I believe it when it tells me that 679 · 177 = 120,183.

Ad hominem – correct form:

X holds that A is true.
In holding this, X violates legitimate rational standards (for example, X is inconsistent, biased, or not correctly informed).
∴ X isn't fully reasonable in holding A.

Incorrect forms use factors not about rational competence (for example, X is a member of a hated minority group or beats his wife) or conclude that A is false.

Rick holds that people of such and such a race ought to be treated poorly.
In holding this, Rick is inconsistent (because he doesn't think that he ought to be treated that way if he were in their exact place) and so violates legitimate rational standards.
∴ Rick isn't fully reasonable in his views.

Ad hominem (Latin for "against the person") is opposed to *ad rem* ("on the issue"). A "personal attack" argument can be either legitimate or fallacious. It's legitimate in our example; here we conclude that Rick, because he violates rational standards, isn't fully reasonable in his beliefs. It would be fallacious to draw the stronger conclusion that his beliefs must be wrong; to show his beliefs to be wrong, we must argue against the beliefs, not against the person. A more extreme case of the *ad hominem* fallacy was exemplified by those Nazis who argued that Einstein's theories must be wrong since he was Jewish; being Jewish was irrelevant to Einstein's competence as a scientist.

Pro-con – correct form:

The reasons in favor of act A are ....
The reasons against act A are ....
The former reasons outweigh the latter.
∴ Act A ought to be done.

Incorrect form:

The reasons in favor of act A are ....
∴ Act A ought to be done.

The reasons in favor of getting an internal-frame backpack are ....
The reasons against getting an internal frame backpack are ....
The former reasons outweigh the latter.
∴ I ought to get an internal-frame backpack.

This can be good reasoning. People sometimes make decisions by folding a piece of paper in half, and listing reasons in favor on one side and reasons against on the other; then they decide intuitively which side has stronger (not necessarily more) reasons. This method forces us to look at both sides of an issue before we decide. In the incorrect form, we just look at half the picture; this is called "stacking the deck."

We can expand our three "correct forms" into standard inductive and deductive arguments. A correct appeal to authority becomes a strong inductive argument if we add this inductively confirmed premise: "The consensus of authorities on a subject is usually right." Correct *ad hominem* arguments become deductively valid if we add: "Anyone who, in believing A, violates legitimate rational standards is thereby not fully reasonable in believing A." And correct pro-con arguments become deductively valid if we add: "If the reasons in favor of A outweigh the reasons against A, then A ought to be done."

Our final four fallacies go together. None of them necessarily involves reasoning from premises to a conclusion.

> **Black-and-white** thinking oversimplifies by assuming that one or another of two extreme cases must be true.

One commits this fallacy in thinking that people must be *logical* or *emotional*, but can't be both. My thesaurus incorrectly lists these two terms as having *opposite* meanings; but if they really had opposite meanings, then no one could be both at once – which indeed is possible. In fact, all four combinations are common:

logical and emotional	illogical and emotional
logical and unemotional	illogical and unemotional

People who think in a black-and-white manner prefer simple dichotomies, like logical-emotional, Capitalist-Communist, or intellectual-jock. Such people have a hard time seeing that the world is more complicated than that.

> To use a **false stereotype** is to assume that members of a certain group are more alike than they actually are.

People commit this fallacy in thinking that all Italians exist only on spaghetti, that all New Yorkers are uncaring, or that all who read Karl Marx want to overthrow the government.

> To **appeal to force** is to use threats or intimidation to get a conclusion accepted.

A parent might say, "Just agree and shut up!" Parents and teachers hold inherently intimidating positions and are often tempted to appeal to force.

> A **complex question** is a question that assumes
> the truth of something false or doubtful.

The standard example is: "Are you still beating your wife?" A "yes" implies that you still beat your wife, while a "no" implies that you used to beat her. The question combines a statement with a question: "You have a wife and used to beat her; do you still beat her?" The proper response is: "Your question presumes something that's false – namely that I have a wife and used to beat her." Sometimes it's misleading to give a "yes" or "no" answer.

15.2a   Exercise – LogiCola R

Identify the fallacies in the following examples. Not all are clear-cut; some examples are controversial and some commit more than one fallacy. All the examples here are fallacious. Use these labels to identify the fallacies:

AA = appeal to authority	AM = ambiguous	FS = false stereotype
AC = appeal to the crowd	BP = beside the point	GF = genetic fallacy
AE = appeal to emotion	BW = black and white	OP = opposition
AF = appeal to force	CI = circular	PC = pro-con
AH = *ad hominem*	CQ = complex question	PH = *post hoc*
AI = appeal to ignorance	DC = division-composition	SM = straw man

> This sports hero advertises a popcorn popper on TV. He says it's the best popcorn popper, so this must be true.

> This is an incorrect appeal to authority. There's no reason to think the sports hero is an authority on popcorn poppers.

1. Are you still wasting time with all that book-learning at the university?
2. The Bible tells the truth because it's God's word. We know the Bible is God's word because the Bible says so and it tells the truth.
3. You should vote for this candidate because she's intelligent and has much experience in politics.
4. The Equal Rights Amendment was foolish because its feminist sponsors were nothing but bra-less bubbleheads.
5. No one accepts this theory any more, so it must be wrong.
6. Either you favor a massive arms buildup, or you aren't a patriotic American.
7. The president's veto was the right move. In these troubled times we need decisive leadership, even in the face of opposition. We should all thank the president for his courageous move.
8. Each member of this team is unbeatable, so this team must be unbeatable.
9. My doctor told me to lose weight and give up smoking. But she's an overweight smoker herself, so I can safely ignore her advice.
10. Belief in God is explained in terms of one's need for a father figure; so it is false.

11. There are scientific laws. Where there are laws there must be a lawgiver. Hence someone must have set up the scientific laws to govern our universe, and this someone could only be God.

12. The defense claims that there's doubt that Smith committed the crime. But, I ask, are you going to let this horrible crime go unpunished because of this? Look at the crime; see how horrible it was! So you see clearly that the crime was horrible and that Smith should be convicted.

13. Free speech is for the common good, since unrestrained expression of opinion is in people's interest.

14. This is a shocking and stupid proposal. Its author must be either a dishonest bum or a complete idiot.

15. Aristotle said that heavy objects fall faster than light ones, so it must be true.

16. Each of these dozen cookies (or drinks) by itself isn't harmful; one little one won't hurt! Hence having these dozen cookies (or drinks) isn't harmful.

17. We've had war with almost every Democratic president of the last hundred years. So if you don't want a president who causes war, don't vote Democratic.

18. Only men are rational animals. No woman is a man. Therefore no woman is a rational animal.

19. I'm right, because you flunk if you disagree with me!

20. The discriminating backpacker prefers South Glacier tents.

21. Those who opposed the war were obviously wrong; they were just a bunch of cowardly homosexual Communists.

22. We should legalize gambling in our state, because it would bring in new tax revenue, encourage tourists to come and spend money here, and cost nothing (just the passing of a new law).

23. Do you want to be a good little boy and go to bed?

24. This man is probably a Communist. After all, nothing in the files disproves his Communist connections.

25. People who read *Fortune* magazine make a lot of money. So if I subscribe to *Fortune*, then I too will make a lot of money.

26. Feminists deny all difference between male and female. But this is absurd, as anyone with eyes can see.

27. Each part of life (eyes, feet, and so on) has a purpose. Hence life itself must have a purpose.

28. So you're a business major? You must be one of those people who care only about the almighty dollar and aren't concerned about ideas.

29. My opponent hasn't proved that I obtained these campaign funds illegally. So we must conclude that I'm innocent.

30. Those dirty Communists said we should withdraw from the Panama Canal, so obviously we should have stayed there.

31. Karl Marx was a personal failure who couldn't even support his family, so his political theory must be wrong.

32. Religion originated from myth (which consists of superstitious errors). So religion must be false.

33. Suzy brushed with Ultra Brilliant and then attracted boys like a magnet! Wow – I'm going to get some Ultra Brilliant. Then I'll attract boys too!

34. Did you kill the butler because you hated him or because you were greedy?

35. My parents will be mad at me if I get a D, and I'll feel so stupid. Please? You know how I loved your course. I surely deserve at least a C.
36. Miracles are impossible because they simply can't happen.
37. I figure that a person must be a Communist if he doesn't think the American free-enterprise system is flawless and the greatest system in the world.
38. Everyone thinks this beer is simply the best. So it must be the best.
39. We ought to oppose this, since it's un-American.
40. Practically every heroin addict first tried marijuana. Therefore, marijuana causes heroin addiction.
41. Most college students are mainly concerned with sports, liquor, and sex. So this is normal. But Duane is mainly concerned with poetry. So he must be abnormal and thus unhealthy.
42. Each of the things in my backpack is light, so my loaded backpack must be light.
43. You're wrong in disagreeing with me, because what I said is true.
44. Everyone thinks the Democrat is the better candidate, so it must be true.
45. We should reject Mendel's genetic theories, since he was a monk and thus couldn't have known anything about science.
46. Every time I backpack it seems to rain. I'm going backpacking next week. So this will cause it to rain.
47. It hasn't been proved that cigarettes are dangerous, so it's only reasonable to conclude that they aren't dangerous.
48. In a commercial filled with pleasant scenery, sexy girls, and soft music: "Buy a Ford Mustang – it's a super car!"
49. Atheism is absurd. Atheists deny God because they can't see him. But who has seen electrons either?
50. Look at all the bad things that happened to our country while my opponent was in office! If you don't want to elect an official who'll bring about such bad things, then you should vote against my opponent.

15.3 Inconsistency

Inconsistency is probably the most important fallacy – the most important of the deceptive errors of thinking. Students writing on philosophical issues for the first time often express inconsistent views; this example is typical:

> Since morality is relative to culture, no duties bind universally. What's right in one culture is wrong in another. Universal duties are a myth. Relativism should make us tolerant toward others; we can't say that we're right and they're wrong. So everyone ought to respect the values of others.

Here the first statement is incompatible with the last:

1. No duties bind universally.
2. Everyone ought to respect the values of others.

If *everyone* ought to respect the values of others, then some duties bind universally. And if *no* duties bind universally, then neither does the duty to respect others. This inconsistency isn't trivial; it cuts deeply. The unexamined views that we use to guide our lives are often radically incoherent; putting these views into words often brings out their incoherence. The ancient Greek philosopher Socrates was adept at showing people how difficult it was to have consistent beliefs on the deeper issues of life.

Inconsistency is common in other areas too. Someone running for political office might talk to environmentalists one day and to industrialists the next. Each group might be told exactly what it wants to hear. The first group is told "I'll support stronger emission standards"; the second is told "I'll try to lower emission standards." We can be sure that the politician, if elected, will violate some of the promises. One can't fulfill incompatible promises.

We often aren't aware of our inconsistency. For example, one might believe all three of these:

1. God is good.
2. Predestination is true. (God immediately causes everything that happens.)
3. God damns sinners to eternal punishment.

These three beliefs aren't inconsistent in themselves. But the believer might have these other beliefs that add to these three to make an inconsistent set:

4. If predestination is true, then God causes us to sin.
5. If God causes us to sin and yet damns sinners to eternal punishment, then God isn't good.

This set of five beliefs is inconsistent. Beliefs 2 and 4 entail "God causes us to sin." This, with 3 and 5, entails "God isn't good" – which contradicts 1. So the five beliefs can't all be true together. Someone who believes all five might not be aware of the inconsistency; the beliefs might not have come together in the person's consciousness at the same time.

Inconsistency is a sign that our belief system is flawed and that we need to change something. Logic can tell us that our belief system is inconsistent. But it can't tell us how to rearrange our beliefs to regain consistency; that's up to us.

Controversies often arise when we have a set of individually plausible statements that can't consistently be combined. Consider this group of statements:

$$F \ = \ \text{Some human actions are free.}$$
$$D \ = \ \text{All human actions are determined.}$$
$$I \ = \ \text{No determined actions are free.}$$

Even though each claim by itself is plausible, the set is inconsistent. If we take any two of the statements as premises, we can infer the denial of the third.

Hard determinists take D (determinism) and I (that determinism is incompatible with free will) as premises. They conclude not-F (that we have no free will):

All human actions are determined.	D
No determined actions are free.	I
∴ No human actions are free.	∴ Not-F

Indeterminists take F (free will) and I (that determinism is incompatible with free will) as premises. They conclude not-D (the falsity of determinism):

Some human actions are free.	F
No determined actions are free.	I
∴ Some human actions aren't determined.	∴ Not-D

Soft determinists take F (free will) and D (determinism) as premises. They conclude not-I (that determinism isn't incompatible with free will):

Some human actions are free.	F
All human actions are determined.	D
∴ Some determined actions are free.	∴ Not-I

Each of the three arguments has plausible premises. All three arguments are valid, but at most only one of them can have true premises.

The three arguments relate to each other in an interesting way. Each argument is a "turnaround" of the other two. An argument is a **turnaround** of another if each results from the other by switching the denial of a premise with the denial of the conclusion. Here is an example:

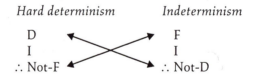

Hard determinism   *Indeterminism*

As you'll see from the exercises, several classical philosophical disputes involve turnaround arguments. In each dispute, we have a set of individually plausible statements that can't consistently be combined.

A single statement may be inconsistent with itself. The most interesting case is that of a **self-refuting statement** – a statement that makes such a sweeping claim that it ends up denying itself. Suppose I tell you this:

Everything that I tell you is false.

Could this be true? Not if I tell it to you; then it has to be false. The statement refutes itself. Here's another example:

> I know that there's no human knowledge.

This couldn't be true. If it were true, then there would be some human knowledge – thus refuting the claim. A self-refuting claim often starts as a seemingly big, bold insight. The bubble bursts when we see that it destroys itself.

Consistency relates ethical beliefs to actions in a special way. Suppose that I believe that this man is bleeding. That belief doesn't commit me, under pain of inconsistency, to any specific act; how I live can't be inconsistent with this belief (taken by itself). But suppose that I believe that I *ought* to call the doctor. This ethical belief does commit me, under pain of inconsistency, to action. If I don't act to call the doctor, then the way I live is inconsistent with my belief. Consistency requires that we work out a harmony between our ethical beliefs and the way we live.

Many consistency arguments in ethics depend on the universalizability principle, which is one of the few principles on which almost all philosophers agree. Here's one formulation of the principle:

> **Universalizability:** Whatever is right (wrong, good, bad, etc.) in one case also would be right (wrong, good, bad, etc.) in any exactly or relevantly similar case, regardless of the individuals involved.

Here's an example adapted from the Good Samaritan parable (Luke 10:30–5). Suppose that, while I'm jogging, I see a man who's been beaten, robbed, and left to die. Should I help him, perhaps by running back to make a phone call? I think of excuses why I shouldn't. I'm busy, don't want to get involved, and so on. I say to myself, "It would be all right for me not to help him." But then I consider an exactly reversed situation. I imagine myself in his place; I'm the one who's been beaten, robbed, and left to die. And I imagine him being in my place; he's jogging and sees me in my sad state. I ask myself, "Would it be all right for this man not to help me in this situation? Surely not!" But then I'm inconsistent. What is all right for me to do to another has to be all right for the other to do to me in an imagined exactly reversed situation.[1]

15.3a   Exercise

Construct a turnaround argument based on the three incompatible statements in the box below. Include statement C as a premise of your argument.

---

[1] For more on the use of consistency in ethics, see Chapters 10 and 11 (especially Section 11.2) of this present book – and Chapters 7 to 9 of my *Ethics: A Contemporary Introduction* (London and New York: Routledge, 1998).

<table>
<tr><td>

A. There are no universal duties.
B. Everyone ought to respect the dignity of others.
C. If everyone ought to respect the dignity of others, then there are universal duties.

</td><td>

Everyone ought to respect the dignity of others.
If everyone ought to respect the dignity of others, then there are universal duties.
∴ There are universal duties.

</td></tr>
</table>

1. Construct a different turnaround argument based on the three statements in this first box. Again, include statement C as a premise of your argument.
2. Construct a turnaround argument based on the four incompatible statements in this second box. Include statement A as a premise of your argument.

> A. If we have ethical knowledge, then either ethical truths are provable or there are self-evident ethical truths.
> B. We have ethical knowledge.
> C. Ethical truths aren't provable.
> D. There are no self-evident ethical truths.

3. Following the directions in 2, construct a second such turnaround argument.
4. Following the directions in 2, construct a third such turnaround argument.
5. Construct a turnaround argument based on the three incompatible statements in this third box.

> A. All human concepts come from sense experience.
> B. The concept of logical validity is a human concept.
> C. The concept of logical validity doesn't come from sense experience.

6. Following the directions in 5, construct a second such turnaround argument.
7. Following the directions in 5, construct a third such turnaround argument.
8. If an argument is valid, then is its turnaround necessarily also valid? Argue for the correctness of your answer.

The next seven examples are self-refuting statements. Explain how each self-refutes.

9. No statement is true.
10. Every rule has an exception.
11. One ought not to accept statements that haven't been proved.
12. Any statement whose truth or falsity we can't decide through scientific experiments is meaningless.
13. There's no such thing as something being "true." There are only opinions, each being "true for" the person holding it, none being just "true."
14. We can know only what's been proved using experimental science. I know this.
15. It's impossible to express truth in human concepts.

15.4 Constructing arguments

This book presents many logical tools; these can help turn mushy thinking into clear reasoning. You should use these logical tools where appropriate in your own reading and writing.

Imagine that your teacher in business ethics gives you this assignment:

> Suppose that you work for a small, struggling company called Mushy Software. You can get a lucrative contract for your company, but only by bribing an official of Enormity Incorporated. Would it be right for you to offer the bribe? Write a paper taking a position on this. Give a clear argument explaining the reasoning behind your answer.

Many of your fellow students probably don't even know what an argument is. But you've studied logic; you know that an argument is a set of statements divided into premises and a conclusion. The assignment tells you to construct an argument with these features:

- The conclusion is either "Offering the bribe *is* right" or "Offering the bribe *isn't* right."
- The conclusion follows logically from the premises.
- The premises are plausible ones that you believe in – or at least are willing to support for purposes of the assignment.

You now have to try various arguments until you find one that does the job. Your argument should look like this:

> [Insert plausible premise.]
> [Insert plausible premise.]
> ∴ Offering the bribe is/isn't right.

Phrase your argument as clearly and simply as possible, and make sure that it's valid in some acceptable logical system. After sketching various arguments, you might arrive at this (which is valid in syllogistic and quantificational logic):

> No dishonest act is right.
> Offering the bribe is a dishonest act.
> ∴ Offering the bribe isn't right.

When you propose an argument, it's wise to ask how an opponent could object to it. While the form here is clearly valid, there might be some difficulty with the premises. How could an opponent attack the premises?

One simple way to attack a universal claim is to find a counterexample:

Counterexample

To refute "all A is B," find something that's A but not B.
To refute "no A is B," find something that's A and also B.

Premise 1 says "No dishonest act is right." You could refute this by finding an action that's dishonest and also right. Can you think of any such action? Imagine a case in which the only way to provide food for your starving family is by stealing. Presumably, stealing here is dishonest but also right:

> This act of stealing is a dishonest act.
> This act of stealing is right.
> ∴ Some dishonest acts are right.

This is valid in syllogistic and quantificational logic. So if the premises here are true, then premise 1 of your original argument is false.

Modus tollens gives another simple way to attack a claim:

Modus tollens

To refute claim A, find a clearly	If A then B.
false claim B that A implies. Then	Not-B.
argue as on the right:	∴ Not-A.

Here you'd try to find some clearly false claim that one of the premises implies. This argument seems to work:

> If no dishonest act is right, then it wouldn't be right to
>   steal food for your starving family when this is needed
>   to keep them from starving.
> It would be right to steal food for your starving family
>   when this is needed to keep them from starving.
> ∴ Some dishonest acts are right.

This is valid in propositional logic. If the premises are true, then premise 1 of your original argument is false. This *modus tollens* objection is similar in content to the counterexample objection, but phrased differently.

How can you respond to the objection? You have three options:

- *Counterattack*: Attack the arguments against your premise.
- *Reformulate*: Reword your original premises so they avoid the objection but still lead to your conclusion.
- *Change strategy*: Trash your original argument and try another approach.

On the *counterattack* option, you'd maintain that the arguments against your premise either are invalid or else have false premises. Here you might claim that stealing is wrong in this hypothetical case. This would be **biting the bullet** – taking a stand that seems to go against common sense in order to defend your theory. Here you'd claim that it's wrong to steal to keep your family from starving; this is a difficult bullet to bite.

On the *reformulate* option, you'd rephrase premise 1 to avoid the objection but still lead to your conclusion. You might add the italicized qualification:

No dishonest act *that isn't needed to avoid disaster* is right.

You'd have to explain what "avoid disaster" here means and you'd have to add another premise that says "Offering the bribe isn't needed to avoid disaster." Then you'd look for further objections to the revised argument.

On the *change strategy* option, you'd trash your original argument and try another approach. You might, for example, argue that offering the bribe is right (or wrong) because it's legal (or illegal), or accords with (or violates) the self-interest of the agent, or maximizes (or doesn't) the long-term interests of everyone affected by the action. Then, again, you'd have to ask whether there are objections to your new argument.

As you refine your reasoning, it's helpful to imagine a little debate going on. First present your argument to yourself. Then pretend to be your opponent and try to attack the argument. You might even enlist your friends to come up with objections; that's what professional philosophers do. Then imagine yourself trying to reply to your opponent. Then pretend to be your opponent and try to attack your reply. Repeat the process until you're content with the position you're defending and the argumentation behind it.

15.4a Exercise

Give a valid argument with plausible premises for or against these statements. For this exercise, you needn't believe these premises, but you have to regard them as plausible. Don't forget what you learned in Chapter 14 ("Meaning and Definitions") about the need to understand what a statement means before you defend or attack it.

Any act is right if and only if it's in the agent's self-interest.
(This is called *ethical egoism*.)

If ethical egoism is true, then it would be right for Jones to torture and kill you if this were in Jones's self-interest.
It wouldn't be right for Jones to torture and kill you if this were in Jones's self-interest.
∴ Ethical egoism isn't true.

1. Offering the bribe is in the agent's self-interest.
2. Every act is right if and only if it's legal.
3. All acts that maximize good consequences are right.

4. Offering the bribe maximizes the long-term interests of everyone concerned.
5. Offering the bribe is a dishonest act.
6. Some wrong actions are errors made in good faith.
7. No error made in good faith is blameworthy.
8. All socially useful acts are right.
9. No acts of punishing the innocent are right.
10. The belief that there is a God is unnecessary to explain our experience.
11. All beliefs unnecessary to explain our experience ought to be rejected.
12. All beliefs that give practical life benefits are pragmatically justifiable.
13. The idea of a perfect circle is a human concept.
14. The idea of a perfect circle doesn't derive from sense experience.
15. All ideas gained in our earthly existence derive from sense experience.

[I took many examples from Section 2.3a. The exercises with English arguments are a rich source of further problems for this exercise.]

15.5 Analyzing arguments

I'll now sketch four steps that are helpful in analyzing arguments in things you read. These steps are especially useful when you write an essay on an author's reasoning; but you also can use them to critique your own writing. These steps assume that the passage contains reasoning (and not just description).

1. *Formulate the argument in English.* Identify and write out the premises and conclusion. Try to arrive at a valid argument expressed as clearly and directly as possible. Use the "principle of charity": interpret unclear reasoning in the way that gives the best argument. Supply implicit premises where needed, avoid emotional terms, and phrase similar ideas in similar words. This step can be difficult if the author's argument is unclear.

2. *Translate into some logical system and test for validity.* If the argument is invalid, you might return to step 1 and try a different formulation. If you can't get a valid argument, you can skip the next two steps.

3. *Identify difficulties.* Star controversial premises. Underline obscure or ambiguous terms; explain what you think the author meant by these.

4. *Appraise the premises.* Try to decide if the premises are true. Look for informal fallacies, especially circularity and ambiguity. Give further arguments (your own or the author's) for or against the premises.

Let's try this on a famous passage from David Hume:

> Since morals, therefore, have an influence on the actions and affections, it follows, that they cannot be deriv'd from reason; and that because reason alone, as we have already prov'd, can never have any such influence. Morals excite passions, and produce or

prevent actions. Reason of itself is utterly impotent in this particular. The rules of morality, therefore, are not conclusions of our reason. No one, I believe, will deny the justness of this inference; nor is there any other means of evading it, than by denying that principle, on which it is founded. As long as it is allow'd, that reason has no influence on our passions and actions, 'tis in vain to pretend, that morality is discover'd only by a deduction of reason. An active principle can never be founded on an inactive ....[1]

First read the passage several times. Focus on the reasoning and try to put it into words; it usually takes several tries to get a clear argument. Here our argument might look like this:

> All moral judgments influence our actions and feelings.
> Nothing from reason influences our actions and feelings.
> ∴ No moral judgments are from reason.

Next translate into some logical system and test for validity. Here we could use either syllogistic or quantificational logic:

> all M is I $\qquad$ $(x)(Mx \supset Ix)$
> no R is I $\qquad$ $\sim(\exists x)(Rx \cdot Ix)$
> ∴ no M is R $\qquad$ ∴ $\sim(\exists x)(Mx \cdot Rx)$

The argument tests out valid in either case.

Next identify difficulties. Star controversial premises and underline obscure or ambiguous terms:

> * All moral judgments <u>influence</u> our actions and feelings.
> * Nothing from <u>reason</u> <u>influences</u> our actions and feelings.
> ∴ No moral judgments are from <u>reason</u>.

Try to figure out what Hume meant by these underlined words. By "reason," Hume seems to mean "the discovery of truth or falsehood." Thus we can rephrase his argument as follows:

> * All moral judgments <u>influence</u> our actions and feelings.
> * No discovery of truth or falsehood <u>influences</u> our actions
> and feelings.
> ∴ No moral judgments are a discovery of truth or falsehood.

"Influences" also is tricky. "X influences Y" could have either of two meanings:

---

[1] David Hume, *A Treatise of Human Nature* (Oxford: Clarendon Press, 1888), page 457 (Book III, Part I, Section I).

> "X *independently of*   "X *when combined with*
> *our desires* influences Y."   *our desires* influences Y."

Finally, appraise the premises. Since "influences" has two senses, we have to appraise the premises using each sense. Taking "influences" in the first sense, premise 1 means:

> All moral judgments, *independently of our*
> *desires*, influence our actions and feelings.

This seems false, since there are people who accept moral judgments but have no desire or motivation to follow them; the actions and feelings of such a person thus wouldn't be influenced by these moral judgments. Taking "influences" in the second sense, premise 2 means:

> No discovery of truth or falsehood, *when combined*
> *with our desires*, influences our actions and feelings.

This also seems false. The discovery of the truth that this flame would burn our finger, combined with our desire not to get burned, surely influences our actions and desires.

Hume's argument is plausible because "influences" is ambiguous. Depending on how we take this term, one premise or the other becomes false or doubtful. So Hume's argument is flawed.

Here we've combined formal techniques (logical systems) with informal ones (common-sense judgments, definitions, the fallacy of ambiguity, and so on). We've used these to formulate and criticize a classic argument on the foundations of ethics. Our criticisms, of course, might not be final. A defender of Hume might attack our arguments against Hume's premises, suggest another reading of the argument, or rephrase the premises to avoid our criticisms. But our criticisms, if clearly and logically expressed, will help the discussion go forward. At its best, philosophical discussion involves reasoning together in a clear-headed, logical manner.

It's important to be fair when we criticize the reasoning of others. Such criticism can be part of a common search for truth; we shouldn't let it descend into a vain attempt to score points. In appraising the reasoning of others, we should follow the same standards of fairness that we want others to follow in their appraisal of *our* reasoning. Distortions and other fallacies are beneath the dignity of beings, such as ourselves, who are capable of reasoning.

Appendix
LogiCola Software

LogiCola (LC) is a computer program to help students learn logic. LC generates homework problems, gives feedback on answers, and records progress. Most of the exercises in this book have corresponding LogiCola computer exercises. There are LC versions for Windows, DOS, and Macintosh.

Section A tells how to get LogiCola (and the accompanying score processor and various teaching aids) from the Internet Web. If you already have LogiCola on a floppy disk, go directly to Section B, which tells how to use the program.

A.   Getting the software

You can download LogiCola (and the score processor and teaching aids) without cost from the Web. First start your Web browser (usually Internet Explorer or Netscape). Then go to either of these addresses:

> http://www.routledge.com/textbooks/gensler_logic
> http://www.jcu.edu/philosophy/gensler/logicola.htm

The first address gives the Routledge site for this book; the second gives my own site. Both should have the program.

My Web page starts like this:

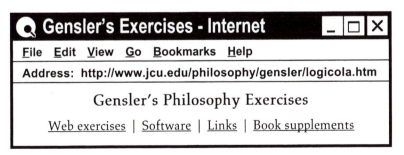

Click "Software" with your mouse. Then look for the line that says:

> LogiCola software for *Introduction to Logic*:
> in Windows and DOS format – or in Macintosh format.

Click the desired format with the right mouse button (if you're using Windows), and pick "Save Target As" (or "Save Link As"); then you'll have to specify what folder to put the file in. A big compressed file will be copied to your hard disk. You'll have to uncompress this file; ask someone how to do this if you don't know how. Then you'll need to copy the resulting files[1] (minus the original compressed file, which you can erase) to floppy disks – which can be used to run LogiCola on a personal computer.

Teachers also may want to download (and then uncompress) the accompanying score processing program, which is available in Windows and Macintosh formats; the Windows version has a convenient option for copying LogiCola files to student disks. Teachers also can download various teaching aids from the "Book supplements" part of the same Web page.

B. Starting LogiCola

This section assumes that you have a LogiCola disk, either from the Web or from your teacher:

A PC disk will have LogiCola in both Windows and DOS formats; a Mac disk will just have Macintosh LogiCola. How you start the program depends on which format you are using.

To start *Windows LogiCola*, first start Windows; you normally do this by just turning on the computer and waiting for the screen to settle down. Then put the PC LogiCola disk into the floppy disk drive. Bring up the Run Box in one of these ways:

1. If you see a Start Button, point to it with your mouse and click the left mouse button. Then point to the word "<u>R</u>un" and click again.
2. If you see a Program Manager window, point to the word "<u>F</u>ile" in its menubar with your mouse and click the left mouse button. Then point to the word "<u>R</u>un" and click again.

---

[1] Before copying files, teachers may want to customize the LC.TXT file to give special information (about things like assignments and office hours) which will be accessible from within the LogiCola program. File README.TXT tells how to customize the LC.TXT file.

3. If you see neither of the above, then hold down these two keys simultaneously: CTRL + ESC (CTRL ESC). You'll then see the Start Button, or a task manager that leads to the Program Manager.

In the Run Box, type **A:RUN** (using a colon but no spaces) and click "OK" (or hit the ENTER key ENTER). The program should start in a few seconds.

DOS LogiCola is for old computers that don't run Windows. First start DOS; with an older computer, you normally do this by just turning on the computer and waiting for the screen to settle down. If you see a DOS prompt on the screen that looks like "C:\> _" on the left below (with "_" flashing on and off), then put the PC LogiCola disk into the floppy disk drive. Type **A:DOS** (using a colon but no spaces) and then hit the ENTER key ENTER:

The program should start in a few seconds.

Starting *Macintosh LogiCola* requires an Apple Macintosh computer and the Mac LogiCola disk. First turn on your Macintosh computer. After the screen settles down, insert the Mac LogiCola disk. You'll see a LogiCola disk icon (⌹) on the screen; point to it with your mouse and double-click the mouse button. Then double-click the cola-can icon (⌷). LC will start. When you're done, eject the disk by dragging it to the trash can.

Most students like having the program on a floppy disk, since they can carry the disk with them and do LogiCola on any computer. But if you have your own computer, you may prefer to put the program into some folder on your hard disk; you'll then need to copy the SCORE.LC score file from your hard disk to a floppy when your teacher wants to record scores.

If you have difficulty starting the program – using any of the formats – ask someone for help and show them these directions. If you continue to have problems, your disk may be bad and you may need to get another one.

LogiCola starts with a welcome screen:

If someone used the disk before, LC will ask if you are this last user. If you answer "YES," you'll return to where you were before. If you answer "NO," you'll be asked for your name and other information.

When you're asked for your name, give it correctly. Since scores record under your name, you may not get credit for your work if you call yourself "Mickey Mouse"; and if you change your name from "Sue" to "Susan," the scoring program will list your scores under two different names. You'll also be asked about sound effects (keep them OFF if others may be disturbed) and scoring level (I suggest you pick 9).

Soon you'll see a menu bar with the words "File," "Options," "Tools," and "Help" near the top of the screen. Picking one of these pulls down a menu with further choices. "File" gives you these choices:

So the "File" menu lets you load a new exercise set, change exercise settings, print the current problem, or quit the program.

To pick a menu (like "File"), point to its key word with your mouse (↖) and then click the *left* mouse button. Or hold down the ALT key and press the item's first letter; so ALT+F gives you "File." When a menu pops up, click on the item you want with your mouse, or hit the number or letter, or highlight the item (using the arrow keys) and then hit the ENTER key. In Windows, clicking the *right* mouse button brings up a shortcut menu of useful commands; this can be more convenient than the main menu bar.

To learn more about the program, play around with the various options and explore the on-screen help (under the "Help" menu).

C. Doing an exercise

Let's say you want to do exercise A (EM) – which is set A (with settings E and M). From the "File" menu, pick "Load new exercise set." Then you'll pick a set:

Click the "A translations" button, or type "A." When set A loads, the bottom of the screen will say "Set A (EM): Syllogism Translations (Easier, Multiple choice)." Use the "File" menu if you want to switch between "easier" and "harder" problems, or between "multiple choice" and "type the answer" formats. The top of the screen will tell you the current exercise, like "A (EM)."

A problem looks like this:

Instead of giving the right answer, you might first play around a little. Give some wrong answers and see how the program responds; or use the "Tools" menu to have LogiCola simulate a student doing the exercise.

When you feel comfortable with the exercise, start doing it seriously. You begin with 0 points. You gain points as you get answers right; you lose points as you get them wrong (or have the program give you the answer). How much you lose for wrong answers depends on your scoring level. At a scoring level of "1," you lose very few points for wrong answers; at a level of "9," you lose lots of points – so it become much more difficult to reach the goal of 100 points. When you reach 100 points, LogiCola congratulates you. You'll see a graphics display and perhaps hear music. And your score records to the disk; use the "Tools" menu to view your scores.

After this, you return to 0 points. You can do the exercise again if you need more practice; you can do an exercise as many times as you like. Or you might want to use the "File" menu to switch the exercise set or settings – or to quit the program.

With the translation exercises, I suggest you start with multiple-choice problems. When you master these, shift to type-the-answer; these are harder, since you can't get the right answer by eliminating alternatives.

If you get stuck (or just want to play around), you can have LogiCola give you the answer. To do this, use the "Tools" menu and pick "Get answer" – or hit ALT+G – or click your mouse at the bottom of the screen where the pointer becomes a little man (😀).

D.   Some tricky areas

This book assigns exercises by set and setting. So exercise "G (EV)" is set G (propositional proofs) with settings E & V (Easier & Valid). Use the "File" menu to load a new exercise set or change exercise settings.

To get credit for your work, you must have scoring set to some scoring level between "1" and "9"; use the "Options" menu to set scoring level. It's good to write down the highest level at which you do each exercise. If you complete an exercise at various levels, the highest one counts.

LC randomly generates problems using an electronic dice throw. Some sets have a huge number of problems; set G, for example, has 20 billion problems. So don't expect to get the same problems each time you do an exercise.

When you exit properly (for example, by using the "Exit" command on the "File" menu), LC records your name, current exercise, point total, and so on. The next time, you can continue where you left off – and you won't have to tell the program your name. The current information won't update properly if you just turn off the machine instead of exiting properly.

Take care of your floppy disk. Keep it away from magnets and coffee – and don't bend it. Be careful of the metal shutter; it dents easily and then may jam when you put it into the computer. If your disk acts up, get another one.

E.   Proof exercises

A proof begins like this:

```
L🔘  LogiCola Set G (EV)        _ □ ✕
File  Options  Tools  Info  Help

    1     (S ⊃ ~C)
    2     (S ∨ ~A)
    [  ∴ ~(A · C)

What's next, Harry? _

Type a derived step ("A"), assumption ("ASM: A"),
or "REFUTE" (to finish an invalid argument). "Info"
reviews the rules. Click a wff (or use the PgUp-
PgDn keys) to copy it to the answer space.
```

You type formulas until the proof is completed. First assume the opposite of the conclusion by typing "ASM: (A · C)." LC will accept this answer, add it to the proof, and ask for the next step.

LC rejects steps that violate the inference rules or are poor strategy. Then you get the "Sorry, I don't like your answer" message and have to try again. On your first error, you get a hint about what to do next; on your second, you're told what answer to give. For some typing errors, like misspelling "ASM" or not balancing parentheses, you're given a hint but don't lose points.

You could complete the proof this way:

```
L🔘  LogiCola Set G (EV)        _ □ ✕
File  Options  Tools  Info  Help

  * 1     (S ⊃ ~C)              VALID
  * 2     (S ∨ ~A)
    [  ∴ ~(A · C)
  * 3   ┌ ASM: (A · C)
    4   │ ∴ A   {from 3}
    5   │ ∴ C   {from 3}
    6   │ ∴ ~S  {from 1 and 5}
    7   └ ∴ ~A  {from 2 and 6}
    8  ∴ ~(A · C)  {from 3; 4 contradicts 7}
```

Here you'd type "ASM: (A · C)," "A," "C," "~S," "~A," and "~(A · C)." Don't type line numbers, justifications, the three dots for "therefore," or stars;

LC types these for you. To derive a formula from previous steps, just type the formula and hit ENTER.

You could do the sample proof in various other ways; for example, you could derive "S" in steps 6 or 7. LogiCola accepts any way of doing the proof that accords with our normal strategy.

With invalid arguments, do the proof as far as you can and then type "REFUTE." LC uses the steps you've derived to construct a refutation – truth conditions making the premises all true and conclusion false.

Normally use the "program stars" setting. To make sure you understand how to star, you might occasionally use "you star"; you don't lose points for mistakes about starring.

If you get really confused on what to do, you can hit ALT+G ("Get answer") to have LC give you the next step. You normally lose points for this; but if LC just rejected your answer, you won't lose further points.

F. Sets for each chapter

This chart shows which LogiCola exercise sets (from A to R) go with which book chapters:

Chapter 2: A & B	Chapter 9: L & M
Chapter 3: C, D, E, & F	Chapter 10: N & O
Chapter 4: F & G	Chapter 13: P
Chapters 5 & 6: H & I	Chapter 14: Q
Chapters 7 & 8: J & K	Chapter 15: R

The Web (at http://www.jcu.edu/philosophy/gensler/logic.htm) has an interactive logic pretest that goes along with Chapter 1 of the book. This is a good thing to do at the very beginning of your study of logic.

Answers to Selected Problems

For each exercise set in the book, answers are given for problems 1, 3, 5, 10, 15, 20, 25, and so on.

2.1a

1. This isn't a wff; both letters after "no" have to be capitals.
3. This isn't a wff; a wff that begins with a letter must begin with a small letter.
5. This isn't a wff; both letters after "some" have to be capitals.

2.1b

1. t is S
3. no L is B
5. all D is H
10. a is s
15. m is A

2.2a

1. This isn't a syllogism, because "D" and "E" occur only once.
3. This isn't a syllogism, because "Y" occurs three times and "G" occurs only once.
5. This isn't a syllogism, because "Z is N" isn't a wff.

2.2b

1. w is not s̲
3. no R̲ is S̲
5. all P̲ is B

2.2c

1. no P* is B*   Invalid
   some C is not B*
   ∴ some C* is P*
3. no H* is B*   Invalid
   no H* is D*
   ∴ some B* is not D
5. g is not s*   Valid

∴ s* is not g
10. all D* is A   Invalid
    ∴ all A is D*

2.3a

1. all S* is D   Valid
   all D* is U
   ∴ all S is U*
3. all T* is C   Valid
   no C* is R*
   ∴ no T is R
5. all M* is R   Valid
   some P is M
   ∴ some P* is R*
10. all S* is Y   Invalid
    m is Y
    ∴ m* is S*
15. all N* is L   Valid
    m is N
    ∴ m* is L*
20. b is W   Invalid
    u is W
    ∴ u* is b*
25. some S is W   Valid
    all S* is L
    all L* is H
    ∴ some W* is H*

2.3b

1. We can't prove either "Bob stole money" or "Bob didn't steal money." 2+7 or 3+8 yield no valid argument with either conclusion.
3. 5+10+11 prove David stole money: "d is W, all W is H, all H is S ∴ d is S."
5. This would show that our data was inconsistent and hence contains false information.

2.4a

1. all J is F
3. all S is R
5. some H is L
10. no S is H
15. all M is B
20. some H is not G

2.5a

1. "No human acts are free" or "No free acts are human acts."
3. "Some free acts are determined" or "Some determined acts are free."
5. No conclusion validly follows.
10. "No culturally taught racial hatreds are rational" or "No rational thing is a culturally taught racial hatred."
15. "Some who like raw steaks like champagne" or "Some who like champagne like raw steaks."
20. "No basic moral norms are based on human nature" or "No principles based on human nature are basic moral norms."
25. "No moral judgments are objective truths" or "No objective truths are moral judgments."

2.6a

1. Invalid

   all A is B
   some C is B
   ∴ some C is A

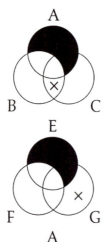

3. Valid

   all E is F
   some G is not F
   ∴ some G is not E

5. Valid

   all A is B
   all B is C
   ∴ all A is C

10. Invalid

    some V is W
    some W is Z
    ∴ some V is Z

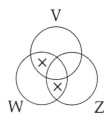

2.7a

1. all R* is G   Valid
   all G* is T
   all T* is V
   all V* is U
   ∴ all R is U*

3. g is A   Valid
   all A* is R
   no R* is C*
   ∴ g* is not C

5. no S* is A*   Valid
   all W* is A
   ∴ no S is W

Premise 2 (implicit but false) is "All garments that should be worn next to the skin while skiing are garments that absorb moisture."

10. all P* is O   Valid
    all O* is E
    no M* is E*
    ∴ no M is P

15. e is C   Invalid
    all S* is C
    ∴ e* is S*

20. all N* is C   Valid
    g is not C*
    ∴ g* is not N

25. all D* is F   Valid
    some P is not F*
    ∴ some P* is not D

3.1a

1. ~(A · B)
3. ((A · B) ∨ C)
5. ((A ⊃ B) ∨ C)
10. (A ⊃ ~(~B · ~C))
15. (~(E ∨ P) ⊃ ~R)
20. E ("(M ∨ F)" is wrong, since the English sentence doesn't mean "Everyone is male or everyone is female.")

3.2a

1.	1	5.	0	15.	0
3.	1	10.	1		

3.3a

1. $\sim(1 \cdot 0) = \sim0 = 1$
3. $\sim(\sim1 \cdot \sim0) = \sim(0 \cdot 1) = \sim0 = 1$
5. $(\sim0 \equiv 0) = (1 \equiv 0) = 0$
10. $(\sim1 \vee \sim(0 \supset 0)) = (0 \vee \sim1) = (0 \vee 0) = 0$
15. $\sim((1 \supset 1) \supset (1 \supset 0)) = \sim(1 \supset 0) = \sim0 = 1$

3.4a

1. $(? \cdot 0) = 0$
3. $(? \vee \sim0) = (? \vee 1) = 1$
5. $(0 \supset ?) = 1$
10. $(? \supset \sim0) = (? \supset 1) = 1$

3.5a

1.

P Q	$(P \equiv \sim Q)$
0 0	0
0 1	1
1 0	1
1 1	0

3.

P Q R	$(P \vee (Q \cdot \sim R))$
0 0 0	0
0 0 1	0
0 1 0	1
0 1 1	0
1 0 0	1
1 0 1	1
1 1 0	1
1 1 1	1

5.

P Q	$((P \equiv Q) \supset Q)$
0 0	0
0 1	1
1 0	1
1 1	1

3.6a

1. Invalid: second row has 110.

C D	$(C \supset D)$,	D	$\therefore$	C
0 0	1	0		0
0 1	1	1		0
1 0	0	0		1
1 1	1	1		1

3. Valid: no row has 110.

T B	$(T \supset B)$,	$(T \supset \sim B)$	$\therefore$	$\sim T$
0 0	1	1		1
0 1	1	1		1
1 0	0	1		0
1 1	1	0		0

5. Invalid: row 4 has 1110. (I once got a group together but couldn't get Grand Canyon backcountry reservations. So we instead explored canyons near Escalante, Utah. This made R=0, T=1, and E=1.)

R T E	$((R \cdot T) \supset E)$,	T	$\sim R$	$\therefore$	$\sim E$
0 0 0	1	0	1		1
0 0 1	1	0	1		0
0 1 0	1	1	1		1
0 1 1	1	1	1		0
1 0 0	1	0	0		1
1 0 1	1	0	0		0
1 1 0	0	1	0		1
1 1 1	1	1	0		0

10. Invalid: row 1 has 110.

S E R	$(S \supset (E \cdot \sim R))$,	$\sim E$	$\therefore$	R
0 0 0	1	1		0
0 0 1	1	1		1
0 1 0	1	0		0
0 1 1	1	0		1
1 0 0	0	1		0
1 0 1	0	1		1
1 1 0	1	0		0
1 1 1	0	0		1

3.7a

1. $\sim(N^1 \equiv H^1) \neq 1$ Valid
   $N^1 = 1$
   $\therefore \sim H^1 = 0$

3. $((T \vee M^1) \supset Q^0) \neq 1$ Valid
   $M^1 = 1$
   $\therefore Q^0 = 0$

5. $((L^0 \cdot F^1) \supset S^1) = 1$ Invalid
   $S^1 = 1$
   $F^1 = 1$
   $\therefore L^0 = 0$

10. $(\sim T^0 \supset (P^1 \supset J^0)) \neq 1$ Valid
    $P^1 = 1$
    $\sim J^0 = 1$
    $\therefore T^0 = 0$

15. $A^1 = 1$ Valid
    $\sim A^1 \neq 1$
    $\therefore B^0 = 0$

(An argument with inconsistent premises is always valid: if the premises can't all be true, we can't have premises all true and conclusion false. But such an argument can't be sound, since the premises can't all be true.)

3.7b

1.   C   Valid
     A
     ((C · A) ⊃ (F ∨ I))
     ~I
     ∴ F

3.   ((U · ~R) ⊃ C)   Valid
     ~C
     U
     ∴ R

5.   ((S · ~M) ⊃ D)   Valid
     ~D
     S
     ∴ M

10. (I ⊃ (U ∨ ~P))   Invalid
     ~U
     ~P
     ∴ I

15. ((M · S) ⊃ G)   Valid
     S
     ~G
     ∴ ~M

20. ((I · ~D) ⊃ R)   Valid
     ~D
     I
     ∴ R

3.8a

1.   (S ⊃ (Y · I))
3.   (Q ∨ R)
5.   (~T ⊃ ~P)
10. (A ⊃ E) *or, equivalently,* (~E ⊃ ~A)
15. (S ⊃ W)

3.9a

1.   (S ⊃ ~K)   Valid
     K
     ∴ ~S

The implicit premise 2 is "We can know something that we aren't presently sensing."

3.   ((B · ~Q) ⊃ O)   Invalid
     ~B
     ∴ ~O

5.   (S ⊃ A)   Valid
     ~A
     ∴ ~S

The implicit premise 2 is "The basic principles of ethics aren't largely agreed upon by intelligent people who have studied ethics."

10. (K ⊃ (P ∨ S))   Valid
     ~P
     ~S
     ∴ ~K

15. (O ⊃ (H ∨ C))   Valid
     ~C
     O
     ∴ H

20. G   Valid
     ~S
     ((M · G) ⊃ S)
     ∴ ~M

3.10a

1.	~I, V	10.	F, ~M
3.	no conclusion	15.	~D, ~Z
5.	no conclusion	20.	no conclusion

3.11a

1.	~T	10.	~B
3.	~L	15.	no conclusion
5.	no conclusion	20.	Y

3.12a

1.	no conclusion	10.	~A
3.	B, ~C	15.	no conclusion
5.	no conclusion		

3.13a

| 1. | (A · B), C | 5. | no conclusion |
| 3. | no conclusion | | |

4.2a

1.   Valid
*   1   (A ⊃ B)
       [∴ (~B ⊃ ~A)
*   2   ⌈ asm: ~(~B ⊃ ~A)
   3 | ∴ ~B   {from 2}
   4 | ∴ A   {from 2}
   5   ⌊ ∴ ~A   {from 1 and 3}
   6   ∴ (~B ⊃ ~A)   {from 2; 4 contradicts 5}

3.   Valid
*   1   (A ⊃ B)
*   2   (~A ⊃ B)
       [∴ B

3 ⌐ asm: ~B
4 │ ∴ ~A {from 1 and 3}
5 └ ∴ A {from 2 and 3}
6 ∴ B {from 3; 4 contradicts 5}

5. Valid
* 1 (A ∨ B)
* 2 (A ⊃ C)
* 3 (B ⊃ D)
  [∴ (C ∨ D)
* 4 ⌐ asm: ~(C ∨ D)
5 │ ∴ ~C {from 4}
6 │ ∴ ~D {from 4}
7 │ ∴ ~A {from 2 and 5}
8 │ ∴ B {from 1 and 7}
9 └ ∴ ~B {from 3 and 6}
10 ∴ (C ∨ D) {from 4; 8 contradicts 9}

10. Valid
* 1 (A ⊃ (B ⊃ C))
  [∴ ((A · B) ⊃ C)
* 2 ⌐ asm: ~((A · B) ⊃ C)
* 3 │ ∴ (A · B) {from 2}
4 │ ∴ ~C {from 2}
5 │ ∴ A {from 3}
6 │ ∴ B {from 3}
* 7 │ ∴ (B ⊃ C) {from 1 and 5}
8 └ ∴ ~B {from 4 and 7}
9 ∴ ((A · B) ⊃ C) {from 2; 6 contradicts 8}

4.2b

1. Valid
* 1 ((H · T) ⊃ B)
2 H
  [∴ (T ⊃ B)
* 3 ⌐ asm: ~(T ⊃ B)
4 │ ∴ T {from 3}
5 │ ∴ ~B {from 3}
* 6 │ ∴ ~(H · T) {from 1 and 5}
7 └ ∴ ~T {from 2 and 6}
8 ∴ (T ⊃ B) {from 3; 4 contradicts 7}

3. Valid
* 1 (W ⊃ (F ∨ M))
2 ~F
* 3 (M ⊃ A)
  [∴ (W ⊃ A)
* 4 ⌐ asm: ~(W ⊃ A)
5 │ ∴ W {from 4}
6 │ ∴ ~A {from 4}
* 7 │ ∴ (F ∨ M) {from 1 and 5}
8 │ ∴ ~M {from 3 and 6}
9 └ ∴ M {from 2 and 7}
10 ∴ (W ⊃ A) {from 4; 8 contradicts 9}

5. Valid
* 1 (~W ⊃ ~G)
* 2 (~A ⊃ ~P)
* 3 (~W ∨ ~A)
  [∴ (~P ∨ ~G)
* 4 ⌐ asm: ~(~P ∨ ~G)
5 │ ∴ P {from 4}
6 │ ∴ G {from 4}
7 │ ∴ W {from 1 and 6}
8 │ ∴ A {from 2 and 5}
9 └ ∴ ~A {from 3 and 7}
10 ∴ (~P ∨ ~G) {from 4; 8 contradicts 9}

10. Valid
* 1 (I ⊃ ~R)
* 2 (~R ⊃ ~T)
3 T
* 4 (~I ⊃ F)
  [∴ F
5 ⌐ asm: ~F
6 │ ∴ R {from 2 and 3}
7 │ ∴ ~I {from 1 and 6}
8 └ ∴ I {from 4 and 5}
9 ∴ F {from 5; 7 contradicts 8}

4.3a

1. Invalid
* 1 (A ∨ B)
  [∴ A
2 asm: ~A
3 ∴ B {from 1 and 2}

⬚ ~A, B

3. Invalid
1 ~(A · ~B)
  [∴ ~(B · ~A)
* 2 asm: (B · ~A)
3 ∴ B {from 2}
4 ∴ ~A {from 2}

⬚ B, ~A

5. Invalid
1 ((A ⊃ B) ⊃ (C ⊃ D))
* 2 (B ⊃ D)
* 3 (A ⊃ C)
  [∴ (A ⊃ D)
* 4 asm: ~(A ⊃ D)
5 ∴ A {from 4}
6 ∴ ~D {from 4}
7 ∴ ~B {from 2 and 6}
8 ∴ C {from 3 and 5}

⬚ A, ~D, ~B, C

10. Invalid
* 1 ~(~A · ~B)
2 ~C
* 3 (D ∨ ~A)
* 4 ((C · ~E) ⊃ ~B)

⬚ ~C, ~D, E ~A, B

    5   ~D
       [∴ ~E
    6   asm: E
    7   ∴ ~A {from 3 and 5}
    8   ∴ B {from 1 and 7}
    9   ∴ ~(C · ~E) {from 4 and 8}

4.3b

1.   Invalid

    1   (S ⊃ K)
*   2   (M ⊃ K)
    3   M
       [∴ S
    4   asm: ~S
    5   ∴ K {from 2 and 3}

M, ~S, K

3.   Valid

    1   E
*   2   (E ⊃ ~R)
*   3   ((I · ~A) ⊃ R)
    4   I
       [∴ A
    5   ┌ asm: ~A
    6   │ ∴ ~R {from 1 and 2}
*   7   │ ∴ ~(I · ~A) {from 3 and 6}
    8   └ ∴ A {from 4 and 7}
    9   ∴ A {from 5; 5 contradicts 8}

5.   Valid

*   1   (E ⊃ W)
*   2   (W ⊃ (~R · I))
       [∴ (R ⊃ ~E)
*   3   ┌ asm: ~(R ⊃ ~E)
    4   │ ∴ R {from 3}
    5   │ ∴ E {from 3}
    6   │ ∴ W {from 1 and 5}
    7   │ ∴ (~R · I) {from 2 and 6}
    8   └ ∴ ~R {from 7}
    9   ∴ (R ⊃ ~E) {from 3; 4 contradicts 8}

10. Valid

*   1   (G ∨ H)
*   2   ((G · K) ⊃ F)
*   3   (H ⊃ C)
*   4   ((C · K) ⊃ U)
       [∴ (K ⊃ (U ∨ F))
*   5   ┌ asm: ~(K ⊃ (U ∨ F))
    6   │ ∴ K {from 5}
*   7   │ ∴ ~(U ∨ F) {from 5}
    8   │ ∴ ~U {from 7}
    9   │ ∴ ~F {from 7}
*   10   │ ∴ ~(G · K) {from 2 and 9}
*   11   │ ∴ ~(C · K) {from 4 and 8}
    12   │ ∴ ~G {from 6 and 10}
    13   │ ∴ H {from 1 and 12}

    14   │ ∴ C {from 3 and 13}
    15   └ ∴ ~C {from 6 and 11}
    16   ∴ (K ⊃ (U ∨ F)) {from 5; 14 contradicts 15}

15. Invalid

*   1   (A ⊃ B)
*   2   (B ⊃ (F ⊃ M))
*   3   (M ⊃ ~H)
    4   H
       [∴ ~A
    5   asm: A
    6   ∴ B {from 1 and 5}
*   7   ∴ (F ⊃ M) {from 2 and 6}
    8   ∴ ~M {from 3 and 4}
    9   ∴ ~F {from 7 and 8}

H, A, B,
~M, ~F

An "F" premise would make it valid.

20. Valid

*   1   (~A ⊃ (F · C))
*   2   (~G ⊃ ~F)
       [∴ (~A ⊃ G)
*   3   ┌ asm: ~(~A ⊃ G)
    4   │ ∴ ~A {from 3}
    5   │ ∴ ~G {from 3}
*   6   │ ∴ (F · C) {from 1 and 4}
    7   │ ∴ F {from 6}
    8   │ ∴ C {from 6}
    9   └ ∴ ~F {from 2 and 5}
    10   ∴ (~A ⊃ G) {from 3; 7 contradicts 9}

25. Valid

*   1   (F ⊃ (F′ · S))
*   2   (F′ ⊃ T)
*   3   (T ⊃ T′)
*   4   (T′ ⊃ X)
*   5   ((X · T′) ⊃ Y)
*   6   ((X · Y) ⊃ ~S)
       [∴ ~F
    7   ┌ asm: F
*   8   │ ∴ (F′ · S) {from 1 and 7}
    9   │ ∴ F′ {from 8}
    10   │ ∴ S {from 8}
    11   │ ∴ T {from 2 and 9}
    12   │ ∴ T′ {from 3 and 11}
    13   │ ∴ X {from 4 and 12}
*   14   │ ∴ ~(X · Y) {from 6 and 10}
    15   │ ∴ ~Y {from 13 and 14}
*   16   │ ∴ ~(X · T′) {from 5 and 15}
    17   └ ∴ ~X {from 12 and 16}
    18   ∴ ~F {from 7; 13 contradicts 17}

4.5a

1.   Valid

*   1   (A ⊃ B)

2   (A ∨ (A · C))
   [∴ (A · B)
* 3 ┌ asm: ~(A · B)
4   ┌ asm: ~A {break up 1}
5   │ ∴ (A · C) {from 2 and 4}
6   └ ∴ A {from 5}
7   ∴ A {from 4; 4 contradicts 6}
8   ∴ B {from 1 and 7}
9   └ ∴ ~B {from 3 and 7}
10 ∴ (A · B) {from 3; 8 contradicts 9}

3.   Valid

* 1   (B ⊃ A)
* 2   ~(A · C)
3   (B ∨ C)
   [∴ (A ≡ B)
* 4 ┌ asm: ~(A ≡ B)
5   │ ∴ (A ∨ B) {from 4}
* 6 │ ∴ ~(A · B) {from 4}
7   │ ┌ asm: ~B {break up 1}
8   │ │ ∴ C {from 3 and 7}
9   │ │ ∴ ~A {from 2 and 8}
10 │ └ ∴ A {from 5 and 7}
11 │ ∴ B {from 7; 9 contradicts 10}
12 │ ∴ A {from 1 and 11}
13 │ ∴ ~C {from 2 and 12}
14 └ ∴ ~A {from 6 and 11}
15 ∴ (A ≡ B) {from 4; 12 contradicts 14}

5.   Valid

* 1   ((A ⊃ B) ⊃ C)
* 2   (C ⊃ (D · E))
   [∴ (B ⊃ D)
* 3 ┌ asm: ~(B ⊃ D)
4   │ ∴ B {from 3}
5   │ ∴ ~D {from 3}
6   │ ┌ asm: ~(A ⊃ B) {break up 1}
7   │ │ ∴ A {from 6}
8   │ └ ∴ ~B {from 6}
9   │ ∴ (A ⊃ B) {from 6; 4 contradicts 8}
10 │ ∴ C {from 1 and 9}
11 │ ∴ (D · E) {from 2 and 10}
12 └ ∴ D {from 11}
13 ∴ (B ⊃ D) {from 3; 5 contradicts 12}

4.5b

1.   Valid

* 1   ((P · T) ⊃ (K · G))
2   P
3   T
   [∴ G
4 ┌ asm: ~G
5   │ ┌ asm: ~(P · T) {break up 1}
6   │ └ ∴ ~T {from 2 and 5}
7   │ ∴ (P · T) {from 5; 3 contradicts 6}

* 8 │ ∴ (K · G) {from 1 and 7}
9   │ ∴ K {from 8}
10 └ ∴ G {from 8}
11 ∴ G {from 4; 4 contradicts 10}

3.   Valid

* 1   (A ≡ (H ∨ B))
2   ~H
   [∴ (A ≡ B)
* 3 ┌ asm: ~(A ≡ B)
* 4 │ ∴ (A ⊃ (H ∨ B)) {from 1}
5   │ ∴ ((H ∨ B) ⊃ A) {from 1}
6   │ ∴ (A ∨ B) {from 3}
* 7 │ ∴ ~(A · B) {from 3}
8   │ ┌ asm: ~A {break up 4}
9   │ │ ∴ ~(H ∨ B) {from 5 and 8}
10 │ │ ∴ ~B {from 9}
11 │ └ ∴ B {from 6 and 8}
12 │ ∴ A {from 8; 10 contradicts 11}
* 13 │ ∴ (H ∨ B) {from 4 and 12}
14 │ ∴ ~B {from 7 and 12}
15 └ ∴ B {from 2 and 13}
16 ∴ (A ≡ B) {from 3; 14 contradicts 15}

5.   Valid

1   C
2   ~D
* 3   (C ⊃ (~D ⊃ B))
4   P
5   ~E
* 6   ((P · ~E) ⊃ (B ⊃ S))
   [∴ S
7 ┌ asm: ~S
* 8 │ ∴ (~D ⊃ B) {from 1 and 3}
9   │ ∴ B {from 2 and 8}
10 │ ┌ asm: ~(P · ~E) {break up 6}
11 │ └ ∴ E {from 4 and 10}
12 │ ∴ (P · ~E) {from 10; 5 contradicts 11}
* 13 │ ∴ (B ⊃ S) {from 6 and 12}
14 └ ∴ ~B {from 7 and 13}
15 ∴ S {from 7; 9 contradicts 14}

10. Valid

* 1   ((D · L) ⊃ (F · A))
2   ((D · ~L) ⊃ (G · A))
   [∴ (D ⊃ A)
* 3 ┌ asm: ~(D ⊃ A)
4   │ ∴ D {from 3}
5   │ ∴ ~A {from 3}
6   │ ┌ asm: ~(D · L) {break up 1}
7   │ │ ∴ ~L {from 4 and 6}
8   │ │ ┌ asm: ~(D · ~L) {break up 2}
9   │ │ └ ∴ L {from 4 and 8}
10 │ ∴ (D · ~L) {from 8; 7 contradicts 9}
11 │ ∴ (G · A) {from 2 and 10}
12 │ ∴ G {from 11}
13 │ └ ∴ A {from 11}

```
 * 14  │ ∴ (D · L)   {from 6; 5 contradicts 13}
   15  │ ∴ L   {from 14}
 * 16  │ ∴ (F · A)   {from 1 and 14}
   17  │ ∴ F   {from 16}
   18  └ ∴ A   {from 16}
   19   ∴ (D ⊃ A)   {from 3; 5 contradicts 18}
```

4.6a

```
1.    Invalid
  1     ~(A · B)                          ~A, B
      [ ∴ (~A · ~B)
** 2     asm: ~(~A · ~B)
   3       asm: ~A   {break up 1}
   4       ∴ B   {from 2 and 3}

3.    Invalid
  1     ((A · B) ⊃ ~(C · D))              C, E, B, ~A
  2     C
 * 3     (E ⊃ B)
      [ ∴ ~E
   4     asm: E
   5     ∴ B   {from 3 and 4}
** 6       asm: ~(A · B)   {break up 1}
   7       ∴ ~A   {from 5 and 6}

5.    Invalid
  1     (A ⊃ B)                           ~D, ~F, ~A, ~C
  2     (C ⊃ (~D · E))
      [ ∴ (D ∨ F)
 * 3     asm: ~(D ∨ F)
   4     ∴ ~D   {from 3}
   5     ∴ ~F   {from 3}
   6       asm: ~A   {break up 1}
   7       asm: ~C   {break up 2}
```

4.6b

```
1.    Invalid
  1     (M ⊃ ~B)                          ~M, ~G, ~B
  2     ~M
  3     (B ⊃ (P · G))
      [ ∴ G
   4     asm: ~G
   5       asm: ~B   {break up 3}

3.    Invalid
  1     (~R ⊃ (O · ~S))                   R, ~C
      [ ∴ (R ⊃ (C · S))
 * 2     asm: ~(R ⊃ (C · S))
   3     ∴ R   {from 2}
   4     ∴ ~(C · S)   {from 2}
   5       asm: ~C   {break up 4}
```

```
5.    Invalid
  1     ((A · L) ⊃ (D · M))               ~C, A,
  2     (M ⊃ ~C)                          ~S, ~L
  3     (S ⊃ L)
      [ ∴ ((A · ~S) ⊃ C)
 * 4     asm: ~((A · ~S) ⊃ C)
 * 5     ∴ (A · ~S)   {from 4}
   6     ∴ ~C   {from 4}
   7     ∴ A   {from 5}
   8     ∴ ~S   {from 5}
** 9       asm: ~(A · L)   {break up 1}
   10      ∴ ~L   {from 7 and 9}

10.   Invalid
  1     H                                 H, P, H′, M
  2     P
  3     H′
 * 4     (M ⊃ ((H · P) ⊃ H′))
  5     (~M ⊃ S)
      [ ∴ (~M · S)
   6     asm: ~(~M · S)
   7       asm: ~M   {break up 4}
   8       ∴ S   {from 5 and 7}
   9       ∴ ~S   {from 6 and 7}
   10    ∴ M   {from 7; 8 contradicts 9}
   11    ∴ ((H · P) ⊃ H′)   {from 4 and 10}

15.   Invalid
  1     ((E · F) ⊃ W)                     N, F, ~E, ~W
  2     ((W · M) ⊃ (B · ~N))
      [ ∴ (N ⊃ ~F)
 * 3     asm: ~(N ⊃ ~F)
   4     ∴ N   {from 3}
   5     ∴ F   {from 3}
** 6       asm: ~(E · F)   {break up 1}
   7       ∴ ~E   {from 5 and 6}
   8         asm: ~(W · M)   {break up 2}
   9         asm: ~W   {break up 8}
```

5.1a

```
 1.   ~Ex
 3.   (∃x)Ex
 5.   (x)Ex
10.   ~(∃x)(Lx · Ex)
15.   (∃x)(Cx · ~(Ex · Lx))
20.   (x)(~Lx ⊃ Ex)
25.   ~(∃x)(~(Ex · Lx) · Cx)
```

5.2a

```
1.    Valid
  1     (x)Fx
      [ ∴ (x)(Gx ∨ Fx)
```

* 2   asm: ~(x)(Gx ∨ Fx)
* 3   ∴ (∃x)~(Gx ∨ Fx)   {from 2}
* 4   ∴ ~(Ga ∨ Fa)   {from 3}
  5   ∴ ~Ga   {from 4}
  6   ∴ ~Fa   {from 4}
  7   ∴ Fa   {from 1}
  8   ∴ (x)(Gx ∨ Fx)   {from 2; 6 contradicts 7}

  3.   Valid

* 1   ~(∃x)(Fx · Gx)
* 2   (∃x)Fx
     [∴ (∃x)~Gx
* 3   asm: ~(∃x)~Gx
  4   ∴ (x)~(Fx · Gx)   {from 1}
  5   ∴ Fa   {from 2}
  6   ∴ (x)Gx   {from 3}
* 7   ∴ ~(Fa · Ga)   {from 4}
  8   ∴ ~Ga   {from 5 and 7}
  9   ∴ Ga   {from 6}
  10   ∴ (∃x)~Gx   {from 3; 8 contradicts 9}

  5.   Valid

  1   (x)(Fx ⊃ Gx)
* 2   (∃x)Fx
     [∴ (∃x)(Fx · Gx)
* 3   asm: ~(∃x)(Fx · Gx)
  4   ∴ Fa   {from 2}
  5   ∴ (x)~(Fx · Gx)   {from 3}
* 6   ∴ (Fa ⊃ Ga)   {from 1}
  7   ∴ Ga   {from 4 and 6}
* 8   ∴ ~(Fa · Ga)   {from 5}
  9   ∴ ~Ga   {from 4 and 8}
  10   ∴ (∃x)(Fx · Gx)   {from 3; 7 contradicts 9}

  10.   Valid

  1   (x)(Fx ≡ Gx)
* 2   (∃x)~Gx
     [∴ (∃x)~Fx
* 3   asm: ~(∃x)~Fx
  4   ∴ ~Ga   {from 2}
  5   ∴ (x)Fx   {from 3}
* 6   ∴ (Fa ≡ Ga)   {from 1}
* 7   ∴ (Fa ⊃ Ga)   {from 6}
  8   ∴ (Ga ⊃ Fa)   {from 6}
  9   ∴ ~Fa   {from 4 and 7}
  10   ∴ Fa   {from 5}
  11   ∴ (∃x)~Fx   {from 3; 9 contradicts 10}

5.2b

  1.   Valid

  1   (x)(Dx ⊃ Bx)
  2   (x)Dx
     [∴ (x)Bx

* 3   asm: ~(x)Bx
* 4   ∴ (∃x)~Bx   {from 3}
  5   ∴ ~Ba   {from 4}
* 6   ∴ (Da ⊃ Ba)   {from 1}
  7   ∴ ~Da   {from 5 and 6}
  8   ∴ Da   {from 2}
  9   ∴ (x)Bx   {from 3; 7 contradicts 8}

  3.   Valid

* 1   ~(∃x)(Fx · Ox)
  2   (x)(Cx ⊃ Ox)
     [∴ ~(∃x)(Fx · Cx)
* 3   asm: (∃x)(Fx · Cx)
  4   ∴ (x)~(Fx · Ox)   {from 1}
* 5   ∴ (Fa · Ca)   {from 3}
  6   ∴ Fa   {from 5}
  7   ∴ Ca   {from 5}
* 8   ∴ (Ca ⊃ Oa)   {from 2}
  9   ∴ Oa   {from 7 and 8}
* 10   ∴ ~(Fa · Oa)   {from 4}
  11   ∴ ~Oa   {from 6 and 10}
  12   ∴ ~(∃x)(Fx · Cx)   {from 3; 9 contradicts 11}

  5.   Valid

  1   (x)(Kx ⊃ Ex)
* 2   ~(∃x)(Ex · Kx)
     [∴ ~(∃x)Kx
* 3   asm: (∃x)Kx
  4   ∴ (x)~(Ex · Kx)   {from 2}
  5   ∴ Ka   {from 3}
* 6   ∴ (Ka ⊃ Ea)   {from 1}
  7   ∴ Ea   {from 5 and 6}
* 8   ∴ ~(Ea · Ka)   {from 4}
  9   ∴ ~Ea   {from 5 and 8}
  10   ∴ ~(∃x)Kx   {from 3; 7 contradicts 9}

  10.   Valid

* 1   ~(∃x)(Bx · Cx)
* 2   (∃x)(Lx · Cx)
  3   (x)(Cx ⊃ Rx)
     [∴ (∃x)(Rx · (Cx · ~Bx))
* 4   asm: ~(∃x)(Rx · (Cx · ~Bx))
  5   ∴ (x)~(Bx · Cx)   {from 1}
* 6   ∴ (La · Ca)   {from 2}
  7   ∴ (x)~(Rx · (Cx · ~Bx))   {from 4}
  8   ∴ La   {from 6}
  9   ∴ Ca   {from 6}
* 10   ∴ (Ca ⊃ Ra)   {from 3}
  11   ∴ Ra   {from 9 and 10}
* 12   ∴ ~(Ba · Ca)   {from 5}
  13   ∴ ~Ba   {from 9 and 12}
* 14   ∴ ~(Ra · (Ca · ~Ba))   {from 7}
* 15   ∴ ~(Ca · ~Ba)   {from 11 and 14}
  16   ∴ Ba   {from 9 and 15}
  17   ∴ (∃x)(Rx · (Cx · ~Bx))   {from 4; 13 contradicts 16}

5.3a

1. Invalid   a, b

* 1   (∃x)Fx   ┌──────────┐
  [∴ (x)Fx]   │ Fa, ~Fb │
* 2   asm: ~(x)Fx   └──────────┘
  3   ∴ Fa {from 1}
* 4   ∴ (∃x)~Fx {from 2}
  5   ∴ ~Fb {from 4}

3. Invalid   a, b

* 1   (∃x)(Fx ∨ Gx)   ┌──────────┐
* 2   ~(x)Fx   │ Fa, ~Ga │
  [∴ (∃x)Gx]   │ ~Fb, ~Gb │
* 3   asm: ~(∃x)Gx   └──────────┘
* 4   ∴ (Fa ∨ Ga) {from 1}
* 5   ∴ (∃x)~Fx {from 2}
  6   ∴ (x)~Gx {from 3}
  7   ∴ ~Fb {from 5}
  8   ∴ ~Ga {from 6}
  9   ∴ Fa {from 4 and 8}
  10   ∴ ~Gb {from 6}

5. Invalid   a

* 1   ~(∃x)(Fx · Gx)   ┌──────────┐
  2   (x)~Fx   │ ~Ga, ~Fa │
  [∴ (x)Gx]   └──────────┘
* 3   asm: ~(x)Gx
  4   ∴ (x)~(Fx · Gx) {from 1}
* 5   ∴ (∃x)~Gx {from 3}
  6   ∴ ~Ga {from 5}
  7   ∴ ~Fa {from 2}
  8   ∴ ~(Fa · Ga) {from 4}

10. Invalid   a,b

* 1   (∃x)~Fx   ┌──────────┐
* 2   (∃x)~Gx   │ Ga, ~Fa │
  [∴ (∃x)(Fx ≡ Gx)]   │ Fb, ~Gb │
* 3   asm: ~(∃x)(Fx ≡ Gx)   └──────────┘
  4   ∴ ~Fa {from 1}
  5   ∴ ~Gb {from 2}
  6   ∴ (x)~(Fx ≡ Gx) {from 3}
* 7   ∴ ~(Fa ≡ Ga) {from 6}
* 8   ∴ (Fa ∨ Ga) {from 7}
  9   ∴ ~(Fa · Ga) {from 7}
  10   ∴ Ga {from 4 and 8}
* 11   ∴ ~(Fb ≡ Gb) {from 6}
* 12   ∴ (Fb ∨ Gb) {from 11}
  13   ∴ ~(Fb · Gb) {from 11}
  14   ∴ Fb {from 5 and 12}

5.3b

1. Invalid   a

* 1   ~(∃x)(Px · Bx)   ┌──────────────┐
* 2   (∃x)(Cx · ~Bx)   │ Ca, ~Ba, ~Pa │
                                                                   └──────────────┘
  [∴ (∃x)(Cx · Px)]
* 3   asm: ~(∃x)(Cx · Px)
  4   ∴ (x)~(Px · Bx) {from 1}
* 5   ∴ (Ca · ~Ba) {from 2}
  6   ∴ (x)~(Cx · Px) {from 3}
  7   ∴ Ca {from 5}
  8   ∴ ~Ba {from 5}
  9   ∴ ~(Pa · Ba) {from 4}
* 10   ∴ ~(Ca · Pa) {from 6}
  11   ∴ ~Pa {from 7 and 10}

3. Invalid   a, b

* 1   (∃x)Sx   ┌──────────┐
* 2   ~(x)Cx   │ Sa, Ca │
  [∴ (∃x)(Sx · ~Cx)]   │ ~Sb, ~Cb │
* 3   asm: ~(∃x)(Sx · ~Cx)   └──────────┘
  4   ∴ Sa {from 1}
* 5   ∴ (∃x)~Cx {from 2}
  6   ∴ (x)~(Sx · ~Cx) {from 3}
  7   ∴ ~Cb {from 5}
* 8   ∴ ~(Sa · ~Ca) {from 6}
  9   ∴ Ca {from 4 and 8}
* 10   ∴ ~(Sb · ~Cb) {from 6}
  11   ∴ ~Sb {from 7 and 10}

5. Valid

  1   (x)((Vx · Cx) ⊃ Px)
  2   (x)(Dx ⊃ (Cx · ~Px))
  [∴ ~(∃x)(Dx · Vx)]
* 3   ┌ asm: (∃x)(Dx · Vx)
* 4   │ ∴ (Da · Va) {from 3}
  5   │ ∴ Da {from 4}
  6   │ ∴ Va {from 4}
* 7   │ ∴ ((Va · Ca) ⊃ Pa) {from 1}
* 8   │ ∴ (Da ⊃ (Ca · ~Pa)) {from 2}
* 9   │ ∴ (Ca · ~Pa) {from 5 and 8}
  10   │ ∴ Ca {from 9}
  11   │ ∴ ~Pa {from 9}
* 12   │ ∴ ~(Va · Ca) {from 7 and 11}
  13   └ ∴ ~Ca {from 6 and 12}
  14   ∴ ~(∃x)(Dx · Vx) {from 3; 10 contradicts 13}

10. Valid

  1   (x)(Sx ⊃ Vx)
  [∴ (x)(~Vx ⊃ ~Sx)]
* 2   ┌ asm: ~(x)(~Vx ⊃ ~Sx)
* 3   │ ∴ (∃x)~(~Vx ⊃ ~Sx) {from 2}
* 4   │ ∴ ~(~Va ⊃ ~Sa) {from 3}
  5   │ ∴ ~Va {from 4}
  6   │ ∴ Sa {from 4}
* 7   │ ∴ (Sa ⊃ Va) {from 1}
  8   └ ∴ ~Sa {from 5 and 7}
  9   ∴ (x)(~Vx ⊃ ~Sx) {from 2; 6 contradicts 8}

5.4a

1. $(Cg \vee Eg)$
3. $((x)Lx \supset (x)Ex)$
5. $((\exists x)Ex \supset R)$
10. $((x)Ex \supset (x)(Lx \supset Ex))$
15. $\sim(\exists x)Ex$ or, equivalently, $(x)\sim Ex$
20. $\sim(\exists x)(Lx \cdot Ex)$ or, equivalently,
    $(x)\sim(Lx \cdot Ex)$

5.5a

1. Valid

   1    $(x)(Fx \vee Gx)$
   2    $\sim Fa$
       $[\therefore (\exists x)Gx$
   * 3   asm: $\sim(\exists x)Gx$
   4     $\therefore (x)\sim Gx$ {from 3}
   * 5 $\therefore (Fa \vee Ga)$ {from 1}
   6     $\therefore Ga$ {from 2 and 5}
   7     $\therefore \sim Ga$ {from 4}
   8   $\therefore (\exists x)Gx$ {from 3; 6 contradicts 7}

3. Invalid   a, b

   * 1 $((x)Ex \supset R)$ ┌─────┐
       $[\therefore (x)(Ex \supset R)$ │ Ea │
   * 2   asm: $\sim(x)(Ex \supset R)$ │ $\sim Eb$ │
   * 3 $\therefore (\exists x)\sim(Ex \supset R)$ {from 2} │ $\sim R$ │
   * 4 $\therefore \sim(Ea \supset R)$ {from 3} └─────┘
   5     $\therefore Ea$ {from 4}
   6     $\therefore \sim R$ {from 4}
   * 7 $\therefore \sim(x)Ex$ {from 1 and 6}
   * 8 $\therefore (\exists x)\sim Ex$ {from 7}
   9     $\therefore \sim Eb$ {from 8}

5. Invalid   a, b

   * 1 $((\exists x)Fx \supset (\exists x)Gx)$ ┌─────┐
       $[\therefore (x)(Fx \supset Gx)$ │ Fa │
   * 2   asm: $\sim(x)(Fx \supset Gx)$ │ $\sim Ga$ │
   * 3 $\therefore (\exists x)\sim(Fx \supset Gx)$ {from 2} │ Gb │
   * 4 $\therefore \sim(Fa \supset Ga)$ {from 3} └─────┘
   5     $\therefore Fa$ {from 4}
   6     $\therefore \sim Ga$ {from 4}
   7   asm: $\sim(\exists x)Fx$ {break up 1}
   8     $\therefore (x)\sim Fx$ {from 7}
   9     $\therefore \sim Fa$ {from 8}
   10    $\therefore (\exists x)Fx$ {from 7; 5 contradicts 9}
   * 11 $\therefore (\exists x)Gx$ {from 1 and 10}
   12    $\therefore Gb$ {from 11}

10. Invalid   d

   * 1 $\sim(\exists x)(Fx \cdot Gx)$ ┌──────┐
   2     $\sim Fd$ │ $\sim Fd, \sim Gd$ │
       $[\therefore Gd$ └──────┘
   3   asm: $\sim Gd$
   4     $\therefore (x)\sim(Fx \cdot Gx)$ {from 1}

---

5    $\therefore \sim(Fd \cdot Gd)$ {from 4}

15. Valid

   * 1 $((\exists x)Ex \supset R)$
       $[\therefore (x)(Ex \supset R)$
   * 2   asm: $\sim(x)(Ex \supset R)$
   * 3 $\therefore (\exists x)\sim(Ex \supset R)$ {from 2}
   * 4 $\therefore \sim(Ea \supset R)$ {from 3}
   5     $\therefore Ea$ {from 4}
   6     $\therefore \sim R$ {from 4}
   * 7 $\therefore \sim(\exists x)Ex$ {from 1 and 6}
   8     $\therefore (x)\sim Ex$ {from 7}
   9     $\therefore \sim Ea$ {from 8}
   10   $\therefore (x)(Ex \supset R)$ {from 2; 5 contradicts 9}

5.5b

1. Valid

   1    $(x)Cx$
   * 2 $(Cw \supset G)$
       $[\therefore G$
   3   asm: $\sim G$
   4     $\therefore \sim Cw$ {from 2 and 3}
   5     $\therefore Cw$ {from 1}
   6   $\therefore G$ {from 3; 4 contradicts 5}

3. Valid

   1    $(x)(Bx \supset Cx)$
   2   Bw
   * 3 $(Cw \supset G)$
       $[\therefore G$
   4   asm: $\sim G$
   5     $\therefore \sim Cw$ {from 3 and 4}
   * 6 $\therefore (Bw \supset Cw)$ {from 1}
   7     $\therefore Cw$ {from 2 and 6}
   8   $\therefore G$ {from 4; 5 contradicts 7}

5. Valid

   1    $(x)(Ex \supset (Ix \vee Fx))$
       $[\therefore (\sim(\exists x)Ix \supset (x)(\sim Fx \supset \sim Ex))$
   * 2   asm: $\sim(\sim(\exists x)Ix \supset (x)(\sim Fx \supset \sim Ex))$
   * 3 $\therefore \sim(\exists x)Ix$ {from 2}
   * 4 $\therefore \sim(x)(\sim Fx \supset \sim Ex)$ {from 2}
   5     $\therefore (x)\sim Ix$ {from 3}
   * 6 $\therefore (\exists x)\sim(\sim Fx \supset \sim Ex)$ {from 4}
   * 7 $\therefore \sim(\sim Fa \supset \sim Ea)$ {from 6}
   8     $\therefore \sim Fa$ {from 7}
   9     $\therefore Ea$ {from 7}
   * 10 $\therefore (Ea \supset (Ia \vee Fa))$ {from 1}
   * 11 $\therefore (Ia \vee Fa)$ {from 9 and 10}
   12    $\therefore Ia$ {from 8 and 11}
   13    $\therefore \sim Ia$ {from 5}
   14   $\therefore (\sim(\exists x)Ix \supset (x)(\sim Fx \supset \sim Ex))$ {from 2;
           12 contradicts 13}

10. Valid

   1    $(x)(Ax \supset Px)$

* 2   (Ae · Ad)
     [∴ (Pe · Pd)
* 3 ┌ asm: ~(Pe · Pd)
 4 │ ∴ Ae {from 2}
 5 │ ∴ Ad {from 2}
* 6 │ ∴ (Ad ⊃ Pd) {from 1}
 7 │ ∴ Pd {from 5 and 6}
 8 │ ∴ ~Pe {from 3 and 7}
* 9 │ ∴ (Ae ⊃ Pe) {from 1}
10 └ ∴ Pe {from 4 and 9}
11 ∴ (Pe · Pd) {from 3; 8 contradicts 10}

15. Valid

* 1   (T ⊃ (H · (x)(Mx ⊃ Ex)))
 2   (x)(Ex ⊃ Ix)
 3   Mt
 4   ~It
     [∴ ~T
 5 ┌ asm: T
* 6 │ ∴ (H · (x)(Mx ⊃ Ex)) {from 1 and 5}
 7 │ ∴ H {from 6}
 8 │ ∴ (x)(Mx ⊃ Ex) {from 6}
* 9 │ ∴ (Et ⊃ It) {from 2}
10 │ ∴ ~Et {from 4 and 9}
* 11 │ ∴ (Mt ⊃ Et) {from 8}
12 └ ∴ Et {from 3 and 11}
13 ∴ ~T {from 5; 10 contradicts 12}

20. Valid

* 1   ~(∃x)(~Cx · Ix)
 2   (x)(Ex ⊃ Ix)
     [∴ (x)(Ex ⊃ Cx)
* 3 ┌ asm: ~(x)(Ex ⊃ Cx)
 4 │ ∴ (x)~(~Cx · Ix) {from 1}
* 5 │ ∴ (∃x)~(Ex ⊃ Cx) {from 3}
* 6 │ ∴ ~(Ea ⊃ Ca) {from 5}
 7 │ ∴ Ea {from 6}
 8 │ ∴ ~Ca {from 6}
* 9 │ ∴ (Ea ⊃ Ia) {from 2}
10 │ ∴ Ia {from 7 and 9}
* 11 │ ∴ ~(~Ca · Ia) {from 4}
12 └ ∴ ~Ia {from 8 and 11}
13 ∴ (x)(Ex ⊃ Cx) {from 3; 10 contradicts 12}

6.1a

 1.   La
 3.   ~a=p
 5.   (∃x)(∃y)(~x=y · (Lx · Ly))
10.   (∃x)(Lx · ~(∃y)(~y=x · Ly))
15.   (Ra · ~a=f)

6.2a

 1. Invalid

                   a, b
 1   Fa
     [∴ ~(∃x)(Fx · ~x=a)   ┌────┐
* 2 asm: (∃x)(Fx · ~x=a)   │ Fa │
* 3 ∴ (Fb · ~b=a) {from 2}   │ ~Fb │
 4 ∴ Fb {from 3}   │ ~b=a │
 5 ∴ ~b=a {from 3}   └────┘

 3. Valid

 1   a=b
 2   b=c
     [∴ a=c
 3 ┌ asm: ~a=c
 4 └ ∴ ~b=c {from 1 and 3}
 5 ∴ a=c {from 3; 2 contradicts 4}

 5. Invalid

                  a, b, c
 1   ~a=b   ┌─────────┐
 2   ~c=b   │ ~a=b, ~a=c │
     [∴ a=c   │ ~c=b │
 3   asm: ~a=c   └─────────┘

10. Invalid

                      a
     [∴ (∃x)(∃y)~y=x   ┌───┐
* 1 asm: ~(∃x)(∃y)~y=x │ a=a │
 2 ∴ (x)~(∃y)~y=x {from 1} └───┘
* 3 ∴ ~(∃y)~y=a {from 2}
 4 ∴ (y)y=a {from 3}
 5 ∴ a=a {from 4}

6.2b

 1. Valid

 1   k=n
 2   Bn
 3   Tk
     [∴ (∃x)(Tx · Bx)
* 4 ┌ asm: ~(∃x)(Tx · Bx)
 5 │ ∴ Bk {from 1 and 2}
 6 │ ∴ (x)~(Tx · Bx) {from 4}
* 7 │ ∴ ~(Tk · Bk) {from 6}
 8 └ ∴ ~Bk {from 3 and 7}
 9 ∴ (∃x)(Tx · Bx) {from 4; 5 contradicts 8}

 3. Valid

 1   Oc
 2   ~Op
     [∴ ~p=c
 3 ┌ asm: p=c
 4 └ ∴ ~Oc {from 2 and 3}
 5 ∴ ~p=c {from 3; 1 contradicts 4}

5. Invalid

    1   ~Bm   m, u
    2   ~Bu   ┌──────────────┐
      [∴ u=m   │ ~Bm, ~Bu   │
    3   asm: ~u=m   │   ~u=m   │
                                      └──────────────┘

10. Valid

*   1   (Ku ∨ Kt)
    2   ~Ku
      [∴ ~u=t
    3 ┌ asm: u=t
    4 │ ∴ Kt   {from 1 and 2}
    5 └ ∴ ~Kt   {from 2 and 3}
    6 ∴ ~u=t   {from 3; 4 contradicts 5}

15. Valid

*   1   (∃x)(Lx · ~(∃y)(~y=x · Ly))
    2   Lp
    3   Fp
      [∴ (x)(Lx ⊃ Fx)
*   4 ┌ asm: ~(x)(Lx ⊃ Fx)
*   5 │ ∴ (∃x)~(Lx ⊃ Fx)   {from 4}
*   6 │ ∴ ~(La ⊃ Fa)   {from 5}
    7 │ ∴ La   {from 6}
    8 │ ∴ ~Fa   {from 6}
*   9 │ ∴ (Lb · ~(∃y)(~y=b · Ly))   {from 1}
    10 │ ∴ Lb   {from 9}
*   11 │ ∴ ~(∃y)(~y=b · Ly)   {from 9}
    12 │ ∴ (y)~(~y=b · Ly)   {from 11}
*   13 │ ∴ ~(~a=b · La)   {from 12}
    14 │ ∴ a=b   {from 7 and 13}
*   15 │ ∴ ~(~p=b · Lp)   {from 12}
    16 │ ∴ p=b   {from 2 and 15}
    17 │ ∴ ~Fb   {from 8 and 14}
    18 └ ∴ ~Fp   {from 16 and 17}
    19 ∴ (x)(Lx ⊃ Fx)   {from 4; 3 contradicts 18}

6.3a

1.   Cgw
3.   ~(∃x)Gxx
5.   (∃x)(Ex · Gax)
10. (∃x)~(∃y)Gyx
15. (x)(∃y)Cyx
20. (∃x)((∃y)Cxy · ~(∃y)Cyx)

6.4a

1.   Invalid

                                            a, b
    1   (x)Lxa   ┌──────────────┐
      [∴ (x)Lax   │ Lab, Laa   │
*   2   asm: ~(x)Lax   │ ~Lab   │
*   3   ∴ (∃x)~Lax   {from 2}   └──────────────┘
    4   ∴ ~Lab   {from 3}
    5   ∴ Laa   {from 1}
    6   ∴ Lba   {from 1}

3.   Invalid

                                            a
    1   (x)(y)(Lxy ⊃ x=y)   ┌────────┐
      [∴ (x)Lxx   │ ~Laa   │
*   2   asm: ~(x)Lxx   └────────┘
*   3   ∴ (∃x)~Lxx   {from 2}
    4   ∴ ~Laa   {from 3}
    5   ∴ (y)(Lay ⊃ a=y)   {from 1}
    6   ∴ (Laa ⊃ a=a)   {from 5}

5.   Valid

    1   (x)(y)Lxy
      [∴ (x)(y)((Fx · Gy) ⊃ Lxy)
*   2 ┌ asm: ~(x)(y)((Fx · Gy) ⊃ Lxy)
*   3 │ ∴ (∃x)~(y)((Fx · Gy) ⊃ Lxy)   {from 2}
*   4 │ ∴ ~(y)((Fa · Gy) ⊃ Lay)   {from 3}
*   5 │ ∴ (∃y)~((Fa · Gy) ⊃ Lay)   {from 4}
*   6 │ ∴ ~((Fa · Gb) ⊃ Lab)   {from 5}
*   7 │ ∴ (Fa · Gb)   {from 6}
    8 │ ∴ ~Lab   {from 6}
    9 │ ∴ Fa   {from 7}
    10 │ ∴ Gb   {from 7}
    11 │ ∴ (y)Lay   {from 1}
    12 │ ∴ (y)Lby   {from 1}
    13 │ ∴ Laa   {from 11}
    14 └ ∴ Lab   {from 11}
    15 ∴ (x)(y)((Fx · Gy) ⊃ Lxy)   {from 2; 8
          contradicts 14}

10. Valid

    1   Lab
    2   Lbc
      [∴ (∃x)(Lax · Lxc)
*   3 ┌ asm: ~(∃x)(Lax · Lxc)
    4 │ ∴ (x)~(Lax · Lxc)   {from 3}
    5 │ ∴ ~(Laa · Lac)   {from 4}
*   6 │ ∴ ~(Lab · Lbc)   {from 4}
    7 └ ∴ ~Lbc   {from 1 and 6}
    8 ∴ (∃x)(Lax · Lxc)   {from 3; 2 contradicts
          7}

15. Valid

    1   (x)(y)(Lxy ⊃ (Fx · ~Fy))
      [∴ (x)(y)(Lxy ⊃ ~Lyx)
*   2 ┌ asm: ~(x)(y)(Lxy ⊃ ~Lyx)
*   3 │ ∴ (∃x)~(y)(Lxy ⊃ ~Lyx)   {from 2}
*   4 │ ∴ ~(y)(Lay ⊃ ~Lya)   {from 3}
*   5 │ ∴ (∃y)~(Lay ⊃ ~Lya)   {from 4}
*   6 │ ∴ ~(Lab ⊃ ~Lba)   {from 5}
    7 │ ∴ Lab   {from 6}
    8 │ ∴ Lba   {from 6}
    9 │ ∴ (y)(Lay ⊃ (Fa · ~Fy))   {from 1}
    10 │ ∴ (y)(Lby ⊃ (Fb · ~Fy))   {from 1}
*   11 │ ∴ (Lab ⊃ (Fa · ~Fb))   {from 9}
*   12 │ ∴ (Fa · ~Fb)   {from 7 and 11}
    13 │ ∴ Fa   {from 12}
    14 │ ∴ ~Fb   {from 12}
*   15 │ ∴ (Lba ⊃ (Fb · ~Fa))   {from 10}

16 ∴ (Fb · ~Fa) {from 8 and 15}
17 ∴ Fb {from 16}
18 ∴ (x)(y)(Lxy ⊃ ~Lyx) {from 2; 14 contradicts 17}

6.4b

1. Valid

1 (x)Ljx
 [∴ (∃x)Lxu
* 2 ┌ asm: ~(∃x)Lxu
3 │ ∴ (x)~Lxu {from 2}
4 │ ∴ Ljj {from 1}
5 │ ∴ Lju {from 1}
6 └ ∴ ~Lju {from 3}
7 ∴ (∃x)Lxu {from 2; 5 contradicts 6}

3. Invalid

1 Oab
 [∴ Oba
2 asm: ~Oba

```
a,b
┌─────────────┐
│ Oab, ~Oba   │
└─────────────┘
```

To make it valid, we need the premise that "older than" is asymmetrical: "(x)(y)(Oxy ⊃ ~Oyx)" – "In every case, if a first person is older than the second then the second isn't older than the first."

5. Invalid

1 (x)(∃y)Dxy
 [∴ (∃y)(x)Dxy
* 2 asm: ~(∃y)(x) Dxy
3 ∴ (y)~(x)Dxy {from 2}
* 4 ∴ (∃y)Day {from 1}
5 ∴ Dab {from 4}
6 ∴ ~(x)Dxb {from 3}
7 ∴ (∃x)~Dxb {from 6}

```
a,b
┌─────────────┐
│ Dab, Dba    │
│ ~Daa, ~Dbb  │
└─────────────┘
```

Endless loop: we add further wffs to make the premise true and conclusion false. "~Dab, ~Dba, Daa, Dbb" also refutes the argument.

10. Valid

* 1 (∃x)(y)Lyx
 [∴ (∃x)Lxx
* 2 ┌ asm: ~(∃x)Lxx
3 │ ∴ (y)Lya {from 1}
4 │ ∴ (x)~Lxx {from 2}
5 │ ∴ Laa {from 3}
6 └ ∴ ~Laa {from 4}
7 ∴ (∃x)Lxx {from 2; 5 contradicts 6}

15. Valid

1 (x)((∃y)Lxy ⊃ (y)Lyx)
2 Lrj
 [∴ Liu
3 ┌ asm: ~Liu
* 4 │ ∴ ((∃y)Lry ⊃ (y)Lyr) {from 1}
5 │ ┌ asm: ~(∃y)Lry {break up 4}

6 │ │ ∴ (y)~Lry {from 5}
7 │ └ ∴ ~Lrj {from 6}
8 │ ∴ (∃y)Lry {from 5; 2 contradicts 7}
9 │ ∴ (y)Lyr {from 4 and 8}
10 │ ∴ Lur {from 9}
* 11 │ ∴ ((∃y)Luy ⊃ (y)Lyu) {from 1}
12 │ ┌ asm: ~(∃y)Luy {break up 11}
13 │ │ ∴ (y)~Luy {from 12}
14 │ └ ∴ ~Luj {from 13}
15 │ ∴ (∃y)Luy {from 12; 2 contradicts 14}
16 │ ∴ (y)Lyu {from 11 and 15}
17 └ ∴ Liu {from 16}
18 ∴ Liu {from 3; 3 contradicts 17}

20. Valid

1 (x)(Gx ⊃ (y)((Ey · Cxy) ⊃ Pxy))
2 (x)(Ox ⊃ (y)(Ey ⊃ Cxy))
3 ((∃x)(y)(Ey ⊃ Pxy) ⊃ ~(∃x)Ex)
* 4 (∃x)Ex
 [∴ (~Og ∨ ~Gg)
* 5 ┌ asm: ~(~Og ∨ ~Gg)
6 │ ∴ Og {from 5}
7 │ ∴ Gg {from 5}
* 8 │ ∴ (Gg ⊃ (y)((Ey · Cgy) ⊃ Pgy)) {from 1}
9 │ ∴ (y)((Ey · Cgy) ⊃ Pgy) {from 7 and 8}
* 10 │ ∴ (Og ⊃ (y)(Ey ⊃ Cgy)) {from 2}
11 │ ∴ (y)(Ey ⊃ Cgy) {from 7 and 8}
12 │ ∴ Ea {from 4}
* 13 │ ∴ ~(∃x)(y)(Ey ⊃ Pxy) {from 3 and 4}
14 │ ∴ (x)~(y)(Ey ⊃ Pxy) {from 13}
* 15 │ ∴ ~(y)(Ey ⊃ Pgy) {from 14}
* 16 │ ∴ (∃y)~(Ey ⊃ Pgy) {from 15}
* 17 │ ∴ ~(Eb ⊃ Pgb) {from 16}
18 │ ∴ Eb {from 17}
19 │ ∴ ~Pgb {from 17}
* 20 │ ∴ ((Eb · Cgb) ⊃ Pgb) {from 9}
* 21 │ ∴ (Eb ⊃ Cgb) {from 11}
22 │ ∴ Cgb {from 18 and 21}
* 23 │ ∴ ~(Eb · Cgb) {from 19 and 20}
24 └ ∴ ~Eb {from 22 and 23}
25 ∴ (∃x)(Nx · Exe) {from 5; 18 contradicts 24}

25. Valid

1 (x)(Dx ⊃ Ax)
 [∴ (x)((∃y)(Dy · Hxy) ⊃ (∃y)(Ay · Hxy))
* 2 ┌ asm: ~(x)((∃y)(Dy · Hxy) ⊃ (∃y)(Ay · Hxy))
* 3 │ ∴ (∃x)~((∃y)(Dy · Hxy) ⊃ (∃y)(Ay · Hxy)) {from 2}
* 4 │ ∴ ~((∃y)(Dy · Hay) ⊃ (∃y)(Ay · Hay)) {from 3}
* 5 │ ∴ (∃y)(Dy · Hay) {from 4}
* 6 │ ∴ ~(∃y)(Ay · Hay) {from 4}
* 7 │ ∴ (Db · Hab) {from 5}

8   ∴ Db   {from 7}
9   ∴ Hab   {from 7}
10   ∴ (y)~(Ay • Hay)   {from 6}
* 11   ∴ ~(Ab • Hab)   {from 10}
12   ∴ ~Ab   {from 9 and 11}
* 13   ∴ (Db ⊃ Ab)   {from 1}
14   ⌐∴ Ab   {from 8 and 13}
15   ∴ (x)((∃y)(Dy • Hxy) ⊃ (∃y)(Ay • Hxy))
       {from 2; 12 contradicts 14}

7.1a

1.   □G
3.   ~□M
5.   □(R ⊃ P)
10.   Ambiguous: (R ⊃ □R) or □(R ⊃ R)
15.   ~◇(G • E)
20.   □(G ∨ M)
25.   (R ⊃ □E)
30.   □(G ⊃ □G)

7.2a

1.   Valid
* 1   ◇(A • B)
    [∴ ◇A
* 2   ⌐ asm: ~◇A
* 3   │ W ∴ (A • B)   {from 1}
4   │ ∴ □~A   {from 2}
5   │ W ∴ A   {from 3}
6   │ W ∴ B   {from 3}
7   ⌐ W ∴ ~A   {from 4}
8   ∴ ◇A   {from 2; 5 contradicts 7}

3.   Valid
* 1   ~◇(A • ~B)
    [∴ □(A ⊃ B)
* 2   ⌐ asm: ~□(A ⊃ B)
3   │ ∴ □~(A • ~B)   {from 1}
* 4   │ ∴ ◇~(A ⊃ B)   {from 2}
* 5   │ W ∴ ~(A ⊃ B)   {from 4}
6   │ W ∴ A   {from 5}
7   │ W ∴ ~B   {from 5}
* 8   │ W ∴ ~(A • ~B)   {from 3}
9   ⌐ W ∴ B   {from 6 and 8}
10   ∴ □(A ⊃ B)   {from 2; 7 contradicts 9}

5.   Valid
* 1   (◇A ∨ ◇B)
    [∴ ◇(A ∨ B)
* 2   ⌐ asm: ~◇(A ∨ B)
3   │ ∴ □~(A ∨ B)   {from 2}
4   │ ⌐ asm: ◇A   {break up 1}
5   │ │ W ∴ A   {from 4}
6   │ │ W ∴ ~(A ∨ B)   {from 3}
7   │ ⌐ W ∴ ~A   {from 6}

* 8   ∴ ~◇A   {from 4; 5 contradicts 7}
9   ∴ □~A   {from 8}
* 10   ∴ ◇B   {from 1 and 8}
11   WW ∴ B   {from 10}
* 12   WW ∴ ~(A ∨ B)   {from 3}
13   WW ∴ ~A   {from 12}
14   ⌐ WW ∴ ~B   {from 12}
15   ∴ ◇(A ∨ B)   {from 2; 11 contradicts 14}

10.   Valid
1   □(A ⊃ B)
    [∴ (□A ⊃ □B)
* 2   ⌐ asm: ~(□A ⊃ □B)
3   │ ∴ □A   {from 2}
* 4   │ ∴ ~□B   {from 2}
* 5   │ ∴ ◇~B   {from 4}
6   │ W ∴ ~B   {from 5}
* 7   │ W ∴ (A ⊃ B)   {from 1}
8   │ W ∴ ~A   {from 6 and 7}
9   ⌐ W ∴ A   {from 3}
10   ∴ (□A ⊃ □B)   {from 2; 8 contradicts 9}

7.2b

1.   Valid
1   □(T ⊃ L)
* 2   ◇(T • ~I)
    [∴ ◇(L • ~I)
* 3   ⌐ asm: ~◇(L • ~I)
* 4   │ W ∴ (T • ~I)   {from 2}
5   │ ∴ □~(L • ~I)   {from 3}
6   │ W ∴ T   {from 4}
7   │ W ∴ ~I   {from 4}
* 8   │ W ∴ (T ⊃ L)   {from 1}
9   │ W ∴ L   {from 6 and 8}
* 10   │ W ∴ ~(L • ~I)   {from 5}
11   ⌐ W ∴ ~L   {from 7 and 10}
12   ∴ ◇(L • ~I)   {from 3; 9 contradicts 11}

3.   Valid
* 1   (C ⊃ □(T ⊃ M))
* 2   ~□M
3   □(~T ⊃ ~~T)
    [∴ ~C
4   ⌐ asm: C
5   │ ∴ □(T ⊃ M)   {from 1 and 4}
* 6   │ ∴ ◇~M   {from 2}
7   │ W ∴ ~M   {from 6}
* 8   │ W ∴ (~T ⊃ ~~T)   {from 3}
* 9   │ W ∴ (T ⊃ M)   {from 5}
10   │ W ∴ ~T   {from 7 and 9}
11   ⌐ W ∴ ~~T   {from 8 and 10}
12   ∴ ~C   {from 4; 10 contradicts 11}

5.   Valid
* 1   ◇(G • T)

2   □(T ⊃ E)
    [∴ ◇(G · E)

* 3 ┌ asm: ~◇(G · E)
* 4 │ W ∴ (G · T) {from 1}
5 │ ∴ □~(G · E) {from 3}
6 │ W ∴ G {from 4}
7 │ W ∴ T {from 4}
* 8 │ W ∴ (T ⊃ E) {from 2}
9 │ W ∴ E {from 7 and 8}
* 10 │ W ∴ ~(G · E) {from 5}
11 └ W ∴ ~E {from 6 and 10}
12 ∴ ◇(G · E) {from 3; 9 contradicts 11}

10. Valid

1   □((R · B) ⊃ ~N)
* 2   ◇(R · B)
    [∴ ~□(R ⊃ N)

3 ┌ asm: □(R ⊃ N)
* 4 │ W ∴ (R · B) {from 2}
5 │ W ∴ R {from 4}
6 │ W ∴ B {from 4}
* 7 │ W ∴ ((R · B) ⊃ ~N) {from 1}
8 │ W ∴ ~N {from 4 and 7}
* 9 │ W ∴ (R ⊃ N) {from 3}
10 └ W ∴ N {from 5 and 9}
11 ∴ ~□(R ⊃ N) {from 3; 8 contradicts 10}

15. Valid

1   □(~T ⊃ T)
    [∴ □T

* 2 ┌ asm: ~□T
* 3 │ ∴ ◇~T {from 2}
4 │ W ∴ ~T {from 3}
* 5 │ W ∴ (~T ⊃ T) {from 1}
6 └ W ∴ T {from 4 and 5}
7 ∴ □T {from 2; 4 contradicts 6}

7.3a

1. Invalid

* 1   ◇A
    [∴ □A

* 2 asm: ~□A
3 W ∴ A {from 1}
* 4 ∴ ◇~A {from 2}
5 WW ∴ ~A {from 4}

W	A
WW	~A

3. Invalid

* 1   ◇A
* 2   ◇B
    [∴ ◇(A · B)

* 3 asm: ~◇(A · B)
4 W ∴ A {from 1}
5 WW ∴ B {from 2}
6 ∴ □~(A · B) {from 3}
* 7 W ∴ ~(A · B) {from 6}

W	A, ~B
WW	B, ~A

8   W ∴ ~B {from 4 and 7}
* 9   WW ∴ ~(A · B) {from 6}
10   WW ∴ ~A {from 5 and 9}

5. Invalid

1   (□A ⊃ □B)
    [∴ □(A ⊃ B)

W	A, ~B
WW	~A

* 2 asm: ~□(A ⊃ B)
* 3 ∴ ~◇(A ⊃ B) {from 2}
* 4 W ∴ ~(A ⊃ B) {from 3}
5 W ∴ A {from 4}
6 W ∴ ~B {from 4}
** 7 asm: ~□A {break up 1}
** 8 ∴ ◇~A {from 7}
9 WW ∴ ~A {from 8}

10. Invalid

* 1   ~□A
2   □(B ≡ A)
    [∴ ~◇B

W	A, B
WW	~A, ~B

* 3 asm: ◇B
* 4 ∴ ◇~A {from 1}
5 W ∴ B {from 3}
6 WW ∴ ~A {from 4}
* 7 W ∴ (B ≡ A) {from 2}
* 8 W ∴ (B ⊃ A) {from 7}
9 W ∴ (A ⊃ B) {from 7}
10 W ∴ A {from 5 and 8}
* 11 WW ∴ (B ≡ A) {from 2}
* 12 WW ∴ (B ⊃ A) {from 11}
13 WW ∴ (A ⊃ B) {from 11}
14 WW ∴ ~B {from 6 and 12}

7.3b

1. Valid

* 1   (P ⊃ □(T ⊃ B))
* 2   ◇(T · ~B)
    [∴ ~P

3 ┌ asm: P
4 │ ∴ □(T ⊃ B) {from 1 and 3}
* 5 │ W ∴ (T · ~B) {from 2}
6 │ W ∴ T {from 5}
7 │ W ∴ ~B {from 5}
* 8 │ W ∴ (T ⊃ B) {from 4}
9 └ W ∴ B {from 6 and 8}
10 ∴ ~P {from 3; 7 contradicts 9}

3. Invalid

1   □(B ⊃ B)
    [∴ (B ⊃ □B)

	B
W	~B

* 2 asm: ~(B ⊃ □B)
3 ∴ B {from 2}
* 4 ∴ ~□B {from 2}
* 5 ∴ ◇~B {from 4}
6 W ∴ ~B {from 5}

7   ∴ (B ⊃ B)   {from 1}
8   W ∴ (B ⊃ B)   {from 1}

5.   Invalid

$$\boxed{\text{~R, ~F}}$$

1   □(R ⊃ F)
2   □(U ⊃ ~R)
 [∴ ~□(F ⊃ U)
3   asm: □(F ⊃ U)
4   ∴ (R ⊃ F)   {from 1}
5   ∴ (U ⊃ ~R)   {from 2}
6   ∴ (F ⊃ U)   {from 3}
7   asm: ~R   {break up 4}
8   asm: ~F   {break up 6}

10.   Invalid

W | ~D |
WW | D |

1   □(D ∨ ~D)
 [∴ (□D ∨ □~D)
* 2   asm: ~(□D ∨ □~D)
* 3   ∴ ~□D   {from 2}
* 4   ∴ ~□~D   {from 2}
* 5   ∴ ◇~D   {from 3}
* 6   ∴ ◇D   {from 4}
7   W ∴ ~D   {from 5}
8   WW ∴ D   {from 6}
9   W ∴ (D ∨ ~D)   {from 1}
10   WW ∴ (D ∨ ~D)   {from 1}

15.   Valid

* 1   (M ⊃ □(S ⊃ G))
* 2   ◇(S · ~G)
 [∴ ~M
3   asm: M
4   ∴ □(S ⊃ G)   {from 1 and 3}
* 5   W ∴ (S · ~G)   {from 2}
6   W ∴ S   {from 5}
7   W ∴ ~G   {from 5}
* 8   W ∴ (S ⊃ G)   {from 4}
9   W ∴ G   {from 6 and 8}
10   ∴ ~M   {from 3; 7 contradicts 9}

20.   Valid

* 1   (M ⊃ □(A ⊃ B))
* 2   ◇(~B · A)
 [∴ ~M
3   asm: M
4   ∴ □(A ⊃ B)   {from 1 and 3}
* 5   W ∴ (~B · A)   {from 2}
6   W ∴ ~B   {from 5}
7   W ∴ A   {from 5}
* 8   W ∴ (A ⊃ B)   {from 4}
9   W ∴ ~A   {from 6 and 8}
10   ∴ ~M   {from 3; 7 contradicts 9}

25.   Valid

* 1   ◇(W · D)
2   □(D ⊃ F)
 [∴ ◇(F · D)

* 3   asm: ~◇(F · D)
* 4   W ∴ (W · D)   {from 1}
5   ∴ □~(F · D)   {from 3}
6   W ∴ W   {from 4}
7   W ∴ D   {from 4}
* 8   W ∴ (D ⊃ F)   {from 2}
9   W ∴ F   {from 7 and 8}
* 10   W ∴ ~(F · D)   {from 5}
11   W ∴ ~F   {from 7 and 10}
12   ∴ ◇(F · D)   {from 3; 9 contradicts 11}

8.1a

1.   Valid in B or S5

* 1   ◇□A
 [∴ A
2   asm: ~A
3   W ∴ □A   {from 1}   # ⇒ W
4   ∴ A   {from 3}   need B or S5
5   ∴ A   {from 2; 2 contradicts 4}'

3.   Valid in S4 or S5

* 1   ◇◇A
 [∴ ◇A
* 2   asm: ~◇A
* 3   W ∴ ◇A   {from 1}   # ⇒ W
4   ∴ □~A   {from 2}
5   WW ∴ A   {from 3}   W ⇒ WW
6   WW ∴ ~A   {from 4}   need S4 or S5
7   ∴ ◇A   {from 2; 5 contradicts 6}

5.   Valid in S4 or S5

* 1   (□A ⊃ □B)
 [∴ □(□A ⊃ □B)
* 2   asm: ~□(□A ⊃ □B)
* 3   ∴ ◇~(□A ⊃ □B)   {from 2}
* 4   W ∴ ~(□A ⊃ □B)   {from 3}   # ⇒ W
5   W ∴ □A   {from 4}
* 6   W ∴ ~□B   {from 4}
* 7   W ∴ ◇~B   {from 6}
8   WW ∴ ~B   {from 7}   W ⇒ WW
9   asm: ~□A   {break up 1}
10   ∴ ◇~A   {from 9}
11   WWW ∴ ~A   {from 10}
12   WWW ∴ A   {from 5}
13   ∴ □A   {from 9; 11 contradicts 12}
14   ∴ □B   {from 1 and 13}
15   WW ∴ B   {from 14}   need S4 or S5
16   ∴ □(□A ⊃ □B)   {from 2; 8 contradicts 15}

10.   Valid in B or S5

* 1   ◇A
 [∴ ◇□◇A
* 2   asm: ~◇□◇A
3   W ∴ A   {from 1}   # ⇒ W

```
    4  | ∴ □~□◇A  {from 2}
*   5  | W ∴ ~□◇A  {from 4} any system
*   6  | W ∴ ◇~◇A  {from 5}
*   7  | WW ∴ ~◇A  {from 6} W ⇒ WW
    8  | WW ∴ □~A  {from 7}
    9  └ W ∴ ~A  {from 8} need B or S5
   10  ∴ ◇□◇A  {from 2; 3 contradicts 9}
```

15. Valid in S4 or S5

```
    1     □A
       [ ∴ □□□A
*   2   ┌ asm: ~□□□A
*   3   | ∴ ◇~□□A  {from 2}
*   4   | W ∴ ~□□A  {from 3} # ⇒ W
*   5   | W ∴ ◇~□A  {from 4}
*   6   | WW ∴ ~□A  {from 5} W ⇒ WW
*   7   | WW ∴ ◇~A  {from 6}
    8   | WWW ∴ ~A  {from 7}
        |   WW ⇒ WWW
    9   └ WWW ∴ A  {from 1} need S4 or S5
   10   ∴ □□□A  {from 2; 8 contradicts 9}
```

8.1b

1. Valid in S5

```
    1     □(N ⊃ □N)
*   2     ◇N
       [ ∴ □N
*   3   ┌ asm: ~□N
    4   | W ∴ N  {from 2} # ⇒ W
*   5   | ∴ ◇~N  {from 3}
    6   | WW ∴ ~N  {from 5} # ⇒ WW
*   7   | W ∴ (N ⊃ □N)  {from 1} any system
    8   | W ∴ □N  {from 4 and 7}
    9   └ WW ∴ N  {from 8} need S5
   10   ∴ □N  {from 3; 6 contradicts 9}
```

3. This side is valid in S5

```
    1     □(N ⊃ □N)
       [ ∴ ~(◇N • ◇~N)
*   2   ┌ asm: (◇N • ◇~N)
*   3   | ∴ ◇N  {from 2}
*   4   | ∴ ◇~N  {from 2}
    5   | W ∴ N  {from 3} # ⇒ W
    6   | WW ∴ ~N  {from 4} # ⇒ WW
*   7   | W ∴ (N ⊃ □N)  {from 1} any system
    8   | W ∴ □N  {from 5 and 7}
    9   └ WW ∴ N  {from 8} need S5
   10   ∴ ~(◇N • ◇~N)  {from 2; 6 contradicts 9}
```

The other side is valid in S4 or S5

```
*   1     ~(◇N • ◇~N)
       [ ∴ □(N ⊃ □N)
*   2   ┌ asm: ~□(N ⊃ □N)
*   3   | ∴ ◇~(N ⊃ □N)  {from 2}
*   4   | W ∴ ~(N ⊃ □N)  {from 3} # ⇒ W
```

```
    5  | W ∴ N  {from 4}
*   6  | W ∴ ~□N  {from 4}
*   7  | W ∴ ◇~N  {from 6}
    8  | WW ∴ ~N  {from 7} W ⇒ WW
    9  | ┌ asm: ~◇N  {break up 1}
   10  | | ∴ □~N  {from 9}
   11  | └ W ∴ ~N  {from 10} any system
   12  | ∴ ◇N  {from 9; 5 contradicts 11}
*  13  | ∴ ~◇~N  {from 1 and 12}
   14  | ∴ □N  {from 13}
   15  └ WW ∴ N  {from 14} need S4 or S5
   16  ∴ □(N ⊃ □N)  {from 2; 8 contradicts 15}
```

5. Valid in S4 or S5

```
    1     □T
*   2     ◇~L
*   3     (N ⊃ □(□T ⊃ L))
       [ ∴ ~N
    4   ┌ asm: N
    5   | W ∴ ~L  {from 2} # ⇒ W
    6   | ∴ □(□T ⊃ L)  {from 3 and 4}
*   7   | W ∴ (□T ⊃ L)  {from 6} any system
*   8   | W ∴ ~□T  {from 5 and 7}
*   9   | W ∴ ◇~T  {from 8}
   10   | WW ∴ ~T  {from 9} W ⇒ WW
   11   └ WW ∴ T  {from 1} need S4 or S5
   12   ∴ ~N  {from 4; 10 contradicts 11}
```

8.2a

1. (x)◇Ux
3. □Uj
5. (Ns • ◇~Ns)
10. (x)(Nx ⊃ □Ax)
15. ◇(x)(Cx ⊃ Tx)
20. (∃x)□Ux

8.3a

1. Valid

```
*   1     (∃x)□Fx
       [ ∴ □(∃x)Fx
*   2   ┌ asm: ~□(∃x)Fx
    3   | ∴ □Fa  {from 1}
*   4   | ∴ ◇~(∃x)Fx  {from 2}
*   5   | W ∴ ~(∃x)Fx  {from 4}
    6   | W ∴ (x)~Fx  {from 5}
    7   | W ∴ Fa  {from 3}
    8   └ W ∴ ~Fa  {from 6}
    9   ∴ □(∃x)Fx  {from 2; 7 contradicts 8}
```

3. Valid

```
       [ ∴ □(∃x)x=a
*   1   ┌ asm: ~□(∃x)x=a
*   2   | ∴ ◇~(∃x)x=a  {from 1}
*   3   | W ∴ ~(∃x)x=a  {from 2}
```

4   W ∴ (x)~x=a   {from 3}
5   W ∴ ~a=a   {from 4}
6   W ∴ a=a   {to contradict 5}
7   ∴ □(∃x)x=a   {from 1; 5 contradicts 6}

5.   Valid

* 1   ◇(x)Fx
    [∴ (x)◇Fx
* 2   ┌ asm: ~(x)◇Fx
3   │ W ∴ (x)Fx   {from 1}
* 4   │ ∴ (∃x)~◇Fx   {from 2}
* 5   │ ∴ ~◇Fa   {from 4}
6   │ ∴ □~Fa   {from 5}
7   │ W ∴ Fa   {from 3}
8   └ W ∴ ~Fa   {from 6}
9   ∴ (x)◇Fx   {from 2; 7 contradicts 8}

10.   Valid

* 1   (∃x)◇Fx
    [∴ ◇(∃x)Fx
* 2   ┌ asm: ~◇(∃x)Fx
* 3   │ ∴ ◇Fa   {from 1}
4   │ ∴ □~(∃x)Fx   {from 2}
5   │ W ∴ Fa   {from 3}
* 6   │ W ∴ ~(∃x)Fx   {from 4}
7   │ W ∴ (x)~Fx   {from 6}
8   └ W ∴ ~Fa   {from 7}
9   ∴ ◇(∃x)Fx   {from 2; 5 contradicts 8}

8.3b

1.   Invalid

1   Bi
    [∴ □(x)(~Bx ⊃ ~x=i)
* 2   asm: ~□(x)(~Bx ⊃ ~x=i)
* 3   ∴ ◇~(x)(~Bx ⊃ ~x=i)   {from 2}
* 4   W ∴ ~(x)(~Bx ⊃ ~x=i)   {from 3}
* 5   W ∴ (∃x)~(~Bx ⊃ ~x=i)   {from 4}
* 6   W ∴ ~(~Ba ⊃ ~a=i)   {from 5}
7   W ∴ ~Ba   {from 6}
8   W ∴ a=i   {from 6}
9   W ∴ ~(~Bi ⊃ ~i=i)   {from 6 and 8}
10   W ∴ ~Bi   {from 7 and 8}

a, i

| Bi |
| ~Bi, ~Ba |
| a=i |

W

3.   Valid

1   ~a=p
* 2   (((∃x)□x=p • ~(x)□x=p) ⊃ S)
    [∴ S
3   ┌ asm: ~S
* 4 │ ∴ ~((∃x)□x=p • ~(x)□x=p)
   │   {from 2 and 3}
5 │ ┌ asm: ~(∃x)□x=p   {break up 4}
6 │ │ ∴ (x)~□x=p   {from 5}
7 │ │ ∴ ~□p=p   {from 6}
8 │ │ ∴ ◇~p=p   {from 7}
9 │ │ W ∴ ~p=p   {from 8}

---

10 │ └ W ∴ p=p   {to contradict 9}
* 11 │ ∴ (∃x)□x=p   {from 5; 9 contradicts 10}
12 │ ∴ (x)□x=p   {from 4 and 11}
13 │ ∴ □a=p   {from 12}
14 └ ∴ a=p   {from 13}
15   ∴ S   {from 3; 1 contradicts 14}

5.   Invalid

1   □(∃x)Ux
    [∴ (∃x)□Ux
* 2   asm: ~(∃x)□Ux
3   ∴ (x)~□Ux   {from 3}
* 4   ∴ (∃x)Ux   {from 1}
5   ∴ Ua   {from 4}
* 6   ∴ ~□Ua   {from 3}
* 7   ∴ ◇~Ua   {from 6}
8   W ∴ ~Ua   {from 7}
* 9   W ∴ (∃x)Ux   {from 1}
10   W ∴ Ub   {from 1}

a, b

| Ua, ~Ub |
| Ub, ~Ua |

W

Endless loop: add "~Ub" to the actual world to make the conclusion false.

10.   Valid

* 1   ◇(Ts • ~Bs)
2   □(x)(Tx ⊃ Px)
    [∴ ~□(x)(Px ⊃ Bx)
3   ┌ asm: □(x)(Px ⊃ Bx)
* 4 │ W ∴ (Ts • ~Bs)   {from 1}
5 │ W ∴ Ts   {from 4}
6 │ W ∴ ~Bs   {from 4}
7 │ W ∴ (x)(Tx ⊃ Px)   {from 2}
8 │ W ∴ (x)(Px ⊃ Bx)   {from 3}
* 9 │ W ∴ (Ts ⊃ Ps)   {from 7}
10 │ W ∴ Ps   {from 5 and 9}
* 11 │ W ∴ (Ps ⊃ Bs)   {from 8}
12 └ W ∴ ~Ps   {from 6 and 11}
13   ∴ ~□(x)(Px ⊃ Bx)   {from 3; 10 contradicts 12}

15.   Valid (but step 11 requires S5 or B)

* 1   ◇(∃x)Ux
2   □(x)(Ux ⊃ □Ox)
    [∴ (∃x)Ox
* 3   ┌ asm: ~(∃x)Ox
* 4 │ W ∴ (∃x)Ux   {from 1}
5 │ ∴ (x)~Ox   {from 3}
6 │ W ∴ Ua   {from 4}
7 │ W ∴ (x)(Ux ⊃ □Ox)   {from 2}
8 │ ∴ ~Oa   {from 5}
* 9 │ W ∴ (Ua ⊃ □Oa)   {from 7}
10 │ W ∴ □Oa   {from 6 and 9}
11 └ ∴ Oa   {from 10}
12   ∴ (∃x)Ox   {from 3; 8 contradicts 11}

9.1a

1.   (L̲ ∨ S̲)
3.   (A̲ ⊃ W) *or, equivalently,* (~W ⊃ ~A̲)
5.   ~(A̲ · B̲)
10. ((x)Ax ⊃ Au̲)
15. (B ⊃ ~A̲)
20. (∃x)(Sx̲ · Wx)

9.2a

1.   Valid

   1   ~A̲
     [∴ ~(A̲ · B̲)
   2 ⌐ asm: (A̲ · B̲)
   3 └ ∴ A̲ {from 2}
   4 ∴ ~(A̲ · B̲) {from 2; 1 contradicts 3}

3.   Invalid |~B, A̲, ~A|

   1   (A ⊃ B̲)
     [∴ (~B ⊃ ~A̲)
* 2   asm: ~(~B ⊃ ~A̲)
   3   ∴ ~B {from 2}
   4   ∴ A̲ {from 2}
   5   asm: ~A {break up 1}

5.   Valid

* 1   ~◇(A̲ · B̲)
* 2   ~(C̲ · ~A̲)
     [∴ ~(C̲ · B̲)
* 3 ⌐ asm: (C̲ · B̲)
   4 │ ∴ □~(A̲ · B̲) {from 1}
   5 │ ∴ C̲ {from 3}
   6 │ ∴ B̲ {from 3}
   7 │ ∴ A̲ {from 2 and 5}
* 8 │ ∴ ~(A̲ · B̲) {from 4}
   9 └ ∴ ~A̲ {from 6 and 8}
  10 ∴ ~(C̲ · B̲) {from 3; 7 contradicts 9}

10.   Valid

* 1   ~(A̲ · ~B̲)
     [∴ (~A̲ ∨ B̲)
* 2 ⌐ asm: ~(~A̲ ∨ B̲)
   3 │ ∴ A̲ {from 2}
   4 │ ∴ ~B̲ {from 2}
   5 └ ∴ B̲ {from 1 and 3}
   6 ∴ (~A̲ ∨ B̲) {from 2; 4 contradicts 5}

9.2b

1.   Valid

* 1   (C̲ ∨ E̲)
   2   V
* 3   (V ⊃ ~C̲)
     [∴ E̲
   4 ⌐ asm: ~E̲

   5 │ ∴ C̲ {from 1 and 4}
   6 └ ∴ ~C̲ {from 2 and 3}
   7 ∴ E̲ {from 4; 5 contradicts 6}

3.   Valid

* 1   ~(D̲ · W̲)
   2   D̲
     [∴ ~W̲
   3 ⌐ asm: W̲
   4 └ ∴ ~W̲ {from 1 and 2}
   5 ∴ ~W̲ {from 3; 3 contradicts 4}

5.   Invalid |S, ~P̲, ~S̲|

* 1   ~(S̲ · ~P̲)
   2   S
     [∴ P̲
   3   asm: ~P̲
   4   ∴ ~S̲ {from 1 and 3}

10.   Valid

   1   N
   2   □(B̲ ⊃ D̲)
   3   □(D̲ ⊃ (N ⊃ S̲))
     [∴ (S̲ ∨ ~B̲)
* 4 ⌐ asm: ~(S̲ ∨ ~B̲)
   5 │ ∴ ~S̲ {from 4}
   6 │ ∴ B̲ {from 4}
* 7 │ ∴ (B̲ ⊃ D̲) {from 2}
   8 │ ∴ D̲ {from 6 and 7}
* 9 │ ∴ (D̲ ⊃ (N ⊃ S̲)) {from 3}
* 10 │ ∴ (N ⊃ S̲) {from 8 and 9}
  11 └ ∴ S̲ {from 1 and 10}
  12 ∴ (S̲ ∨ ~B̲) {from 4; 5 contradicts 11}

15.   Valid

* 1   (S ⊃ G̲)
   2   ~G̲
     [∴ ~S
   3 ⌐ asm: S
   4 └ ∴ G̲ {from 1 and 2}
   5 ∴ ~S {from 3; 2 contradicts 4}

20.   Valid

* 1   ~(B̲ · A̲)
     [∴ (~B̲ ∨ ~A̲)
* 2 ⌐ asm: ~(~B̲ ∨ ~A̲)
   3 │ ∴ B̲ {from 2}
   4 │ ∴ A̲ {from 2}
   5 └ ∴ ~A̲ {from 1 and 3}
   6 ∴ (~B̲ ∨ ~A̲) {from 2; 4 contradicts 5}

9.3a

1.   (A ⊃ O~B̲)
3.   (O~A̲ ⊃ ~A̲)
5.   □(A̲ ⊃ RA̲)
10. O~(B̲ · ~A̲)

15.　(~◇(x)Ax ⊃ O~A<u>u</u>)
20.　R(x)(~Tx ⊃ S<u>x</u>)

9.4a

1.　Valid

```
1     O~A
   [ ∴ O~(A · B)
* 2   ┌ asm: ~O~(A · B)
* 3   │  ∴ R(A · B)   {from 2}
* 4   │  D ∴ (A · B)   {from 3}
  5   │  D ∴ A   {from 4}
  6   │  D ∴ B   {from 4}
  7   └  D ∴ ~A   {from 1}
  8   ∴ O~(A · B)   {from 2; 5 contradicts 7}
```

3.　Valid

```
1     b=c
   [ ∴ (OF ab ⊃ OF ac)
* 2   ┌ asm: ~(OF ab ⊃ OF ac)
  3   │  ∴ OF ab   {from 2}
  4   │  ∴ ~OF ac   {from 2}
  5   └  ∴ OF ac   {from 1 and 3}
  6   ∴ (OF ab ⊃ OF ac)   {from 2; 4 contradicts
        5}
```

5.　Invalid

```
   [ ∴ O(A ⊃ OA)
* 1   asm: ~O(A ⊃ OA)
* 2   ∴ R~(A ⊃ OA)   {from 1}
* 3   D ∴ ~(A ⊃ OA)   {from 2}
  4   D ∴ A   {from 3}
* 5   D ∴ ~OA   {from 3}
* 6   D ∴ R~A   {from 5}
  7   DD ∴ ~A   {from 6}
```

10.　Valid

```
* 1     (A ⊃ OB)
   [ ∴ O(A ⊃ B)
* 2   ┌ asm: ~O(A ⊃ B)
* 3   │  ∴ R~(A ⊃ B)   {from 2}
* 4   │  D ∴ ~(A ⊃ B)   {from 3}
  5   │  D ∴ A   {from 4}
  6   │  D ∴ ~B   {from 4}
  7   │  ∴ A   {from 5 by indicative transfer}
  8   │  ∴ OB   {from 1 and 7}
  9   └  D ∴ B   {from 8}
 10   ∴ O(A ⊃ B)   {from 2; 6 contradicts 9}
```

15.　Valid

```
1     OA
2     OB
   [ ∴ ◇(A · B)
3   ┌ asm: ~◇(A · B)
4   │ ┌ asm: O(A · B)   {assume so we can
    │ │   derive the opposite using 3 and
    │ │   Kant's Law}
```

5   └ └ ◇(A · B)   {from 4 using Kant's Law}
* 6   ∴ ~O(A · B)   {from 4; 3 contradicts 5}
* 7   ∴ R~(A · B)   {from 6}
* 8   D ∴ ~(A · B)   {from 7}
  9   D ∴ A   {from 1}
 10   D ∴ B   {from 2}
 11   D ∴ ~B   {from 8 and 9}
 12   ∴ ◇(A · B)   {from 3; 10 contradicts 11}

20.　Invalid

```
  1     O(x)(Fx ⊃ G x)
  2     OF a
   [ ∴ OG a
* 3   asm: ~OG a
* 4   ∴ R~G a   {from 3}
  5   D ∴ ~G a   {from 4}
  6   D ∴ (x)(Fx ⊃ G x)   {from 1}
  7   D ∴ F a   {from 2}
* 8   D ∴ (Fa ⊃ G a)   {from 6}
  9   D ∴ ~Fa   {from 5 and 8}
 10   ∴ ~Fa   {from 9 by indicative transfer}
```

25.　Valid

```
* 1     (A ∨ OB)
  2     ~A
   [ ∴ OB
* 3   ┌ asm: ~OB
  4   └  ∴ OB   {from 1 and 2}
  5   ∴ OB   {from 3; 3 contradicts 4}
```

9.4b

1.　Valid

```
* 1     ~R(K · V)
  2     OV
   [ ∴ ~K
  3   ┌ asm: K
  4   │  ∴ O~(K · V)   {from 1}
  5   │  ∴ V   {from 2}
* 6   │  ∴ ~(K · V)   {from 4}
  7   └  ∴ ~V   {from 3 and 6}
  8   ∴ ~K   {from 3; 5 contradicts 7}
```

3.　Valid

```
  1     A
  2     O~A
* 3     ((A · ◇~A) ⊃ F)
   [ ∴ F
  4   ┌ asm: ~F
* 5   │  ∴ ~(A · ◇~A)   {from 3 and 4}
* 6   │  ∴ ~◇~A   {from 1 and 5}
  7   └  ∴ ◇~A   {from 2 by Kant's Law}
  8   ∴ F   {from 4; 6 contradicts 7}
```

5.　Invalid

```
   [ ∴ (OA ⊃ A)
* 1   asm: ~(OA ⊃ A)
```

2   ∴ O<u>A</u> {from 1}
3   ∴ ~A {from 1}
4   ∴ <u>A</u> {from 2}

10.   Invalid
* 1   R(∃x)A<u>x</u>
        [∴ (x)RA<u>x</u>
* 2   asm: ~(x)RA<u>x</u>
* 3   D∴ (∃x)A<u>x</u> {from 1}
* 4   ∴ (∃x)~RA<u>x</u> {from 2}
   5   D∴ A<u>a</u> {from 3}
* 6   ∴ ~RA<u>b</u> {from 4}
   7   ∴ O~A<u>b</u> {from 6}
   8   D∴ ~A<u>b</u> {from 7}

15.   Valid
* 1   (O~<u>K</u> ⊃ O~<u>I</u>)
* 2   (R<u>N</u> ⊃ R<u>I</u>)
        [∴ (O~<u>K</u> ⊃ O~<u>N</u>)
* 3 ⌐ asm: ~(O~<u>K</u> ⊃ O~<u>N</u>)
   4 │ ∴ O~<u>K</u> {from 3}
* 5 │ ∴ ~O~<u>N</u> {from 3}
* 6 │ ∴ R<u>N</u> {from 5}
   7 │ ∴ O~<u>I</u> {from 1 and 4}
* 8 │ ∴ R<u>I</u> {from 2 and 6}
   9 │ DD∴ <u>I</u> {from 8}
   10 └ DD∴ ~<u>I</u> {from 7}
   11   ∴ (O~<u>K</u> ⊃ O~<u>N</u>) {from 3; 9 contradicts 10}

20.   Valid
   1   N
   2   □(<u>B</u> ⊃ <u>D</u>)
   3   □(<u>D</u> ⊃ (N ⊃ <u>S</u>))
        [∴ O(<u>S</u> ∨ ~<u>B</u>)
* 4 ⌐ asm: ~O(<u>S</u> ∨ ~<u>B</u>)
* 5 │ ∴ R~(<u>S</u> ∨ ~<u>B</u>) {from 4}
* 6 │ D∴ ~(<u>S</u> ∨ ~<u>B</u>) {from 5}
   7 │ D∴ ~<u>S</u> {from 6}
   8 │ D∴ <u>B</u> {from 6}
* 9 │ D∴ (<u>B</u> ⊃ <u>D</u>) {from 2}
   10 │ D∴ <u>D</u> {from 8 and 9}
* 11 │ D∴ (<u>D</u> ⊃ (N ⊃ <u>S</u>)) {from 3}
* 12 │ D∴ (N ⊃ <u>S</u>) {from 10 and 11}
   13 │ D∴ ~N {from 7 and 12}
   14 └ ∴ ~N {from 13 by indicative transfer}
   15   ∴ O(<u>S</u> ∨ ~<u>B</u>) {from 4; 1 contradicts 14}

25.   Valid
* 1   (R<u>P</u> ⊃ O<u>S</u>)
* 2   ~◊S
        [∴ O~<u>P</u>
* 3 ⌐ asm: ~O~<u>P</u>
   4 │ ∴ □~S {from 2}
* 5 │ ∴ R<u>P</u> {from 3}
   6 │ ∴ O<u>S</u> {from 1 and 5}
* 7 │ ∴ ◊S {from 6 by Kant's Law}

   8 │ W ∴ S {from 7}
   9 └ W ∴ ~S {from 4}
   10   ∴ O~<u>P</u> {from 3; 8 contradicts 9}

10.1a

1.   u:~G
3.   ~u:G
5.   □(u:G ⊃ ~u:~G)
10. ~(u:A · u:~A)

10.2a

1.   Valid
* 1   ~◊(A · B)
        [∴ ~(<u>u</u>:A · <u>u</u>:B)
* 2 ⌐ asm: (<u>u</u>:A · <u>u</u>:B)
   3 │ ∴ □~(A · B) {from 1}
* 4 │ ∴ <u>u</u>:A {from 2}
   5 │ ∴ <u>u</u>:B {from 2}
   6 │ u ∴ A {from 4}
* 7 │ u ∴ ~(A · B) {from 3}
   8 │ u ∴ ~B {from 6 and 7}
   9 └ u ∴ B {from 5}
   10   ∴ ~(<u>u</u>:A · <u>u</u>:B) {from 2; 8 contradicts 9}

3.   Invalid
* 1   ~◊(A · B)
        [∴ (u:A ⊃ ~<u>u</u>:B)
* 2   asm: ~(u:A ⊃ ~<u>u</u>:B)
   3   ∴ □~(A · B) {from 1}
   4   ∴ u:A {from 2}
* 5   ∴ <u>u</u>:B {from 2}
   6   u ∴ B {from 5}
* 7   u ∴ ~(A · B) {from 3}
   8   u ∴ ~A {from 6 and 7}

5.   Invalid
* 1   ~◊(A · B)
        [∴ (<u>u</u>:~A ∨ <u>u</u>:~B)
* 2   asm: ~(<u>u</u>:~A ∨ <u>u</u>:~B)
   3   ∴ □~(A · B) {from 1}
* 4   ∴ ~<u>u</u>:~A {from 2}
* 5   ∴ ~<u>u</u>:~B {from 2}
   6   u ∴ A {from 4}
   7   uu ∴ B {from 5}
* 8   u ∴ ~(A · B) {from 3}
   9   u ∴ ~B {from 6 and 8}
* 10   uu ∴ ~(A · B) {from 3}
   11   uu ∴ ~A {from 7 and 10}

10.   Valid
* 1   ~◊(A · B)
        [∴ ~(<u>u</u>:A · ~<u>u</u>:~B)
* 2 ⌐ asm: (<u>u</u>:A · ~<u>u</u>:~B)
   3 │ ∴ □~(A · B) {from 1}

4 | ∴ u:A {from 2}
* 5 | ∴ ~u:~B {from 2}
6 | u ∴ B {from 5}
* 7 | u ∴ ~(A · B) {from 3}
8 | u ∴ ~A {from 6 and 7}
9 | u ∴ A {from 4}
10 | ∴ ~(u:A · ~u:~B) {from 2; 8 contradicts 9}

10.2b

1. Valid

1   □(A ⊃ B)
* 2   ~u:B
    [∴ ~u:A
3   ┌ asm: u:A
4 | u ∴ ~B {from 2}
* 5 | u ∴ (A ⊃ B) {from 1}
6 | u ∴ ~A {from 4 and 5}
7   └ u ∴ A {from 3}
8   ∴ ~u:A {from 3; 6 contradicts 7}

3. Invalid

1   u:A
    [∴ ~u:~A
* 2   asm: u:~A
3   u ∴ ~A {from 2}

5. Invalid

    [∴ (u:A ∨ u:~A)
* 1   asm: ~(u:A ∨ u:~A)
* 2   ∴ ~u:A {from 1}
* 3   ∴ ~u:~A {from 1}
4   u ∴ ~A {from 2}
5   uu ∴ A {from 3}

10. Invalid

    [∴ (A ⊃ u:A)
* 1   asm: ~(A ⊃ u:A)
2   ∴ A {from 1}
* 3   ∴ ~u:A {from 1}
4   u ∴ ~A {from 3}

10.3a

1. u:Sj
3. (x)~Eux
5. (Fu · ~u:Fu)
10. ~(u:(x)~Eux · u:Eut)
15. (u:Axu ⊃ Aux)

10.4a

1. Valid

    [∴ ~(u:A · u:~A)

* 1   ┌ asm: (u:A · u:~A)
* 2 | ∴ u:A {from 1}
3 | ∴ u:~A {from 1}
4 | u ∴ A {from 2}
5   └ u ∴ ~A {from 3}
6   ∴ ~(u:A · u:~A) {from 1; 4 contradicts 5}

3. Invalid

    [∴ (u:Ba ∨ u:~Ba)
* 1   asm: ~(u:Ba ∨ u:~Ba)
* 2   ∴ ~u:Ba {from 1}
* 3   ∴ ~u:~Ba {from 1}
4   u ∴ ~Ba {from 2}
5   uu ∴ Ba {from 3}

5. Invalid

1   u:(x)OAx
    [∴ u:Au
* 2   asm: ~u:Au
3   u ∴ ~Au {from 2}

10. Valid

1   □(A ⊃ B)
    [∴ ~(u:OA · ~u:B)
* 2   ┌ asm: (u:OA · ~u:B)
3 | ∴ u:OA {from 2}
* 4 | ∴ ~u:B {from 2}
5 | u ∴ ~B {from 4}
* 6 | u ∴ (A ⊃ B) {from 1}
7 | u ∴ ~A {from 5 and 6}
8 | u ∴ OA {from 3}
9   └ u ∴ A {from 8}
10   ∴ ~(u:OA · ~u:B) {from 2; 7 contradicts 9}

10.4b

1. Invalid

    [∴ (u:OAu ⊃ Au)
* 1   asm: ~(u:OAu ⊃ Au)
2   ∴ u:OAu {from 1}
3   ∴ ~Au {from 1}

3. Valid

    [∴ ~(u:(x)~Eux · u:Eut)
* 1   ┌ asm: (u:(x)~Eux · u:Eut)
* 2 | ∴ u:(x)~Eux {from 1}
3 | ∴ u:Eut {from 1}
4 | u ∴ (x)~Eux {from 2}
5 | u ∴ Eut {from 3}
6   └ u ∴ ~Eut {from 4}
7   ∴ ~(u:(x)~Eux · u:Eut) {from 1; 5 contradicts 6}

5. Valid

1   □(E ⊃ (N ⊃ M))

[∴ ~((u̲:E̲ · u̲:N) · ~u̲:M̲)

*   2   asm: ((u̲:E̲ · u̲:N) · ~u̲:M̲)

*   3   ∴ (u̲:E̲ · u̲:N) {from 2}

*   4   ∴ ~u̲:M̲ {from 2}

    5   ∴ u̲:E̲ {from 3}

    6   ∴ u̲:N {from 3}

    7   u ∴ ~M̲ {from 4}

*   8   u ∴ (E̲ ⊃ (N ⊃ M̲)) {from 1}

    9   u ∴ E̲ {from 5}

* 10   u ∴ (N ⊃ M̲) {from 8 and 9}

  11   u ∴ ~N {from 7 and 10}

  12   u ∴ N {from 6}

  13   ∴ ~((u̲:E̲ · u̲:N) · ~u̲:M̲) {from 2; 11 contradicts 12}

10.   Valid

[∴ ~(u̲:(x)(Mx ⊃ OE s̲x) · ~u̲:(Mf ⊃ E s̲f))

*   1   asm: (u̲:(x)(Mx ⊃ OE s̲x) · ~u̲:(Mf ⊃ E s̲f))

    2   ∴ u̲:(x)(Mx ⊃ OE s̲x) {from 1}

*   3   ∴ ~u̲:(Mf ⊃ E s̲f) {from 1}

*   4   u ∴ ~(Mf ⊃ E s̲f) {from 3}

    5   u ∴ Mf {from 4}

    6   u ∴ ~E s̲f {from 4}

    7   u ∴ (x)(Mx ⊃ OE s̲x) {from 2}

*   8   u ∴ (Mf ⊃ OE s̲f) {from 7}

    9   u ∴ OE s̲f {from 5 and 8}

  10   u ∴ E s̲f {from 9}

  11   ∴ ~(u̲:(x)(Mx ⊃ OE s̲x) · ~u̲:(Mf ⊃ E s̲f)) {from 1; 6 contradicts 10}

15.   Valid

    1   □(RAu̲ ⊃ O(x)Ax̲)

[∴ ~(u̲:Au̲ · ~u̲:(x)Ax̲)

*   2   asm: (u̲:Au̲ · ~u̲:(x)Ax̲)

    3   ∴ u̲:Au̲ {from 2}

*   4   ∴ ~u̲:(x)Ax̲ {from 2}

    5   u ∴ ~(x)Ax̲ {from 4}

*   6   u ∴ (RAu̲ ⊃ O(x)Ax̲) {from 1}

    7   u ∴ Au̲ {from 3}

    8   u asm: ~RAu̲ {break up 6}

    9   u ∴ O~Au̲ {from 8}

  10   u ∴ ~Au̲ {from 9}

  11   u ∴ RAu̲ {from 8; 7 contradicts 10}

  12   u ∴ O(x)Ax̲ {from 6 and 11}

  13   u ∴ (x)Ax̲ {from 12}

  14   ∴ ~(u̲:Au̲ · ~u̲:(x)Ax̲) {from 2; 5 contradicts 13}

10.5a

1.   Ou̲:Sj

3.   Ru̲:OSj

5.   (x)~Rx̲:G

10.   (Ou̲:x=x · (x=x · u:x=x))

15.   (Ou̲:A ≡ ~◇(u:A · ~A))

20.   (u:Ax̲u ⊃ OAu̲x)

25.   ((Ou̲:Bj · ~Du) ⊃ Ou̲:Fj)

10.6a

1.   Valid

    1   □(A ⊃ B)

*   2   ~Ru̲:B

[∴ ~Ru̲:A

*   3   asm: Ru̲:A

    4   ∴ O~u̲:B {from 2}

    5   D ∴ u̲:A {from 3}

*   6   D ∴ ~u̲:B {from 4}

    7   Du ∴ ~B {from 6}

*   8   Du ∴ (A ⊃ B) {from 1}

    9   Du ∴ ~A {from 7 and 8}

  10   Du ∴ A {from 5}

  11   ∴ ~Ru̲:A {from 3; 9 contradicts 10}

3.   Valid

*   1   R(~u̲:A · ~u̲:~A)

[∴ ~Ou̲:A

    2   asm: Ou̲:A

    3   D ∴ (~u̲:A · ~u̲:~A) {from 1}

    4   D ∴ u̲:A {from 2}

    5   D ∴ ~u̲:A {from 3}

    6   ∴ ~Ou̲:A {from 2; 4 contradicts 5}

5.   Invalid

    1   Oa̲:(C · D)

[∴ Ob̲:C

*   2   asm: ~Ob̲:C

*   3   ∴ R~b̲:C {from 2}

*   4   D ∴ ~b̲:C {from 3}

    5   Db ∴ ~C {from 4}

*   6   D ∴ a̲:(C · D) {from 1}

*   7   Da ∴ (C · D) {from 6}

    8   Da ∴ C {from 7}

    9   Da ∴ D {from 7}

10.   Valid

    1   Ou̲:(A ⊃ OBu̲)

[∴ ~(u̲:A · ~u̲:Bu̲)

*   2   asm: (u̲:A · ~u̲:Bu̲)

    3   ∴ u̲:A {from 2}

*   4   ∴ ~u̲:Bu̲ {from 2}

    5   u ∴ ~Bu̲ {from 4}

    6   ∴ u̲:(A ⊃ OBu̲) {from 1}

    7   u ∴ A {from 3}

*   8   u ∴ (A ⊃ OBu̲) {from 6}

    9   u ∴ OBu̲ {from 7 and 8}

  10   u ∴ Bu̲ {from 9}

  11   ∴ ~(u̲:A · ~u̲:Bu̲) {from 2; 5 contradicts 10}

10.6b

1. Valid

    1   Ou:G
         [∴ ~Ru:~G
    * 2   ┌ asm: Ru:~G
    * 3   │ D ∴ u:~G   {from 2}
      4   │ D ∴ u:G   {from 1}
      5   │ Du ∴ ~G   {from 3}
      6   └ Du ∴ G   {from 4}
      7   ∴ ~Ru:~G   {from 2; 5 contradicts 6}

3. Valid

         [∴ O~(u:OAu • ~u:Au)
    * 1   ┌ asm: ~O~(u:OAu • ~u:Au)
    * 2   │ ∴ R(u:OAu • ~u:Au)   {from 1}
    * 3   │ D ∴ (u:OAu • ~u:Au) {from 2}
      4   │ D ∴ u:OAu   {from 3}
    * 5   │ D ∴ ~u:Au   {from 3}
      6   │ Du ∴ ~Au   {from 5}
      7   │ Du ∴ OAu   {from 4}
      8   └ Du ∴ Au   {from 7}
      9   ∴ O~(u:OAu • ~u:Au)   {from 1; 6
             contradicts 8}

5. Valid

      1   □(E ⊃ C)
    * 2   R~u:C
         [∴ ~Ou:E
      3   ┌ asm: Ou:E
    * 4   │ D ∴ ~u:C   {from 2}
      5   │ Du ∴ ~C   {from 4}
    * 6   │ Du ∴ (E ⊃ C) {from 1}
      7   │ Du ∴ ~E   {from 5 and 6}
      8   │ D ∴ u:E   {from 3}
      9   └ Du ∴ E   {from 8}
      10   ∴ ~Ou:E   {from 3; 7 contradicts 9}

10. Valid

      1   a:F
      2   Oa:F
      3   ~F
      4   C
      5   a:(F ∨ C)
      6   ~K
         [∴ (((Oa:(F ∨ C) • (F ∨ C))
             • a:(F ∨ C)) • ~K)
    * 7   ┌ asm: ~(((Oa:(F ∨ C) • (F ∨ C)) •
             a:(F ∨ C)) • ~K)
    * 8   │ ∴ ~((Oa:(F ∨ C) • (F ∨ C)) • a:(F ∨ C))
             {from 6 and 7}
    * 9   │ ∴ ~(Oa:(F ∨ C) • (F ∨ C))   {from 5
             and 8}
      10   │ ┌ asm: ~(F ∨ C)   {break up 9}
      11   │ └ ∴ ~C   {from 10}
      12   │ ∴ (F ∨ C)   {from 10; 4 contradicts 11}
    * 13   │ ∴ ~Oa:(F ∨ C)   {from 9 and 12}

    * 14   │ ∴ R~a:(F ∨ C)   {from 13}
    * 15   │ D ∴ ~a:(F ∨ C)   {from 14}
      16   │ D ∴ a:F   {from 2}
      17   │ Du ∴ ~(F ∨ C)   {from 15}
      18   │ Du ∴ F   {from 16}
      19   └ Du ∴ ~F   {from 17}
      20   ∴ (((Oa:(F ∨ C) • (F ∨ C)) • a:(F ∨ C))
             • ~K)   {from 7; 18 contradicts 19}

15. Valid

      1   Ou:(M ⊃ F)
         [∴ ~(u:M • ~u:F)
    * 2   ┌ asm: (u:M • ~u:F)
      3   │ ∴ u:M   {from 2}
    * 4   │ ∴ ~u:F   {from 2}
      5   │ u ∴ ~F   {from 4}
      6   │ ∴ u:(M ⊃ F)   {from 1}
      7   │ u ∴ M   {from 3}
    * 8   │ u ∴ (M ⊃ F)   {from 6}
      9   └ u ∴ ~M   {from 5 and 8}
      10   ∴ ~(u:M • ~u:F)   {from 2; 7 contradicts
             9}

20. Invalid

      1   O~(u:A • ~u:B)
         [∴ (u:A ⊃ u:B)
    * 2   asm: ~(u:A ⊃ u:B)
      3   ∴ u:A   {from 2}
      4   ∴ ~u:B   {from 2}
      5   ∴ ~(u:A • ~u:B)   {from 1}
    ** 6   asm: ~u:A   {break up 5}
      7   u ∴ ~A   {from 6}

25. Valid

      1   Ou:(P ⊃ OAu)
      2   Ou:P
         [∴ u:Au
    * 3   ┌ asm: ~u:Au
      4   │ u ∴ ~Au   {from 3}
      5   │ ∴ u:(P ⊃ OAu)   {from 1}
      6   │ ∴ u:P   {from 2}
    * 7   │ u ∴ (P ⊃ OAu)   {from 5}
      8   │ u ∴ P   {from 6}
      9   │ u ∴ OAu   {from 7 and 8}
      10   └ u ∴ Au   {from 9}
      11   ∴ u:Au   {from 3; 4 contradicts 10}

30. Invalid   a, b

      1   (x)Rx:A   D ┌─────────────┐
         [∴ R(x)x:A   │ a:A, ~b:A   │
    * 2   asm: ~R(x)x:A   DD │ b:A, ~a:A   │
      3   ∴ O~(x)x:A   {from 2}   └─────────────┘
    * 4   ∴ Ra:A   {from 1}
      5   D ∴ a:A   {from 4}
    * 6   D ∴ ~(x)x:A   {from 3}
    * 7   D ∴ (∃x)~x:A   {from 6}
    * 8   D ∴ ~b:A   {from 7}

```
   9    Db ∴ ~A   {from 8}
*  10   ∴ Rb:A   {from 1}
   11   DD ∴ b:A   {from 10}
```

Endless loop: add "~a:A" to world DD to make the conclusion false. (You weren't required to give a refutation.)

11.6 (see footnote at end of Chapter 11)

```
1.    [ ∴ ~(u:RA · ~u:(∃F)(FA · ■(X)(FX ⊃ RX)))
*  1  ┌ asm: (u:RA · ~u:(∃F)(FA · ■(X)(FX ⊃
      │    RX)))
   2  │ ∴ u:RA   {from 1}
*  3  │ ∴ ~u:(∃F)(FA · ■(X)(FX ⊃ RX))
      │    {from 1}
*  4  │ u ∴ ~(∃F)(FA · ■(X)(FX ⊃ RX))
      │    {from 3}
   5  │ u ∴ RA   {from 2}
*  6  │ u ∴ (∃F)(FA · ■(X)(FX ⊃ RX))
      └    {from 5 by G5}
   7  ∴ ~(u:RA · ~u:(∃F)(FA · ■(X)(FX ⊃ RX)))
         {from 1; 4 contradicts 6}

2.    [ ∴ ~(u:Au · ~u:(∃F)(F*Au · ■(X)(FX ⊃
         MX)))
*  1  ┌ asm: (u:Au · ~u:(∃F)(F*Au · ■(X)(FX ⊃
      │    MX)))
   2  │ ∴ u:Au   {from 1}
*  3  │ ∴ ~u:(∃F)(F*Au · ■(X)(FX ⊃ MX))
      │    {from 1}
*  4  │ u ∴ ~(∃F)(F*Au · ■(X)(FX ⊃ MX))
      │    {from 3}
   5  │ u ∴ Au   {from 2}
   6  │ ┌ u asm: ~RAu
   7  │ │ u ∴ O~Au   {from 6}
   8  │ └ u ∴ ~Au   {from 7}
   9  │ u ∴ RAu   {from 6; 5 contradicts 8}
*  10 │ u ∴ (∃F)(FAu · ■(X)(FX ⊃ RX))
      │    {from 9 by G5}
*  11 │ u ∴ (GAu · ■(X)(GX ⊃ RX))
      │    {from 10}
   12 │ u ∴ GAu   {from 11}
   13 │ u ∴ ■(X)(GX ⊃ RX)   {from 11}
   14 │ u ∴ (X)(∃F)F*X   {by rule G11}
*  15 │ u ∴ (∃F)F*Au   {from 14}
   16 │ u ∴ H*Au   {from 15}
*  17 │ u ∴ (HAu · (F)(FAu ⊃ □(X)(HX ⊃ FX)))
      │    {from 16 by G10}
   18 │ u ∴ HAu   {from 17}
   19 │ u ∴ (F)(FAu ⊃ □(X)(HX ⊃ FX))
      │    {from 17}
*  20 │ u ∴ (GAu ⊃ □(X)(HX ⊃ GX))
      │    {from 19}
   21 │ u ∴ □(X)(HX ⊃ GX)   {from 12 and 20}
   22 │ u ∴ (F)~(F*Au · ■(X)(FX ⊃ MX))
      │    {from 4}
*  23 │ u ∴ ~(H*Au · ■(X)(HX ⊃ MX))
```

```
   24   u ∴ ~■(X)(HX ⊃ MX)   {from 16 and
           23}
*  25   uH ∴ ~(X)(HX ⊃ MX)   {from 24 by
           G8}
*  26   uH ∴ (∃X)~(HX ⊃ MX)   {from 25}
*  27   uH ∴ ~(HB ⊃ MB)   {from 26}
   28   uH ∴ HB   {from 27}
   29   uH ∴ ~MB   {from 27}
   30   uH ∴ (X)(HX ⊃ GX)   {from 21}
*  31   uH ∴ (HB ⊃ GB)   {from 30}
   32   uH ∴ GB   {from 28 and 31}
   33   uH ∴ (X)(GX ⊃ RX)   {from 13 by G7}
*  34   uH ∴ (GB ⊃ RB)   {from 33}
   35   uH ∴ RB   {from 32 and 34}
   36   uH ∴ MB   {from 35 by G1}
   37   ∴ ~(u:Au · ~u:(∃F)(F*Au · ■(X)(FX ⊃
           MX)))   {from 1; 29 contradicts 36}
```

13.2a

1. There are 32 such cards out of the 103 remaining cards. So your probability is 32/103 (about 31.1 percent).

3. Coins have no memory. The probability of heads is 50 percent.

5. The probability that Michigan will win the Rose Bowl is 80 percent times 60 percent times 30 percent, or 14.4 percent.

10. You get a number divisible by three 12 out of 36 times. You don't get it 24 out of 36 times. Thus, mathematically fair betting odds are 2 to 1 (24 to 12) against getting a number divisible by three.

15. In 100 such cases, Ohio State would pass 60 times and run 40 times. If we set up to stop the pass, we'd stop them 58 times out of 100 [(60 · 70 percent) + (40 · 40 percent)]. If we set up to stop the run, we'd stop them 62 times out of 100 [(60 · 50 percent) + (40 · 80 percent)]. So we should set up to stop the run.

13.3a

1. You shouldn't believe it. It's only 12.5 percent (50 · 50 · 50 percent) probable.

3. You shouldn't believe it. It's 37.5 percent probable, since it happens in 3 of the 8 possible combinations.

5. You shouldn't believe it. It isn't more probable than not; it's only 50 percent probable.

10. You should buy the Enormity Incorporated model. If you buy the Cut-Rate model, there's an expected replacement

cost of $360 ($600 times 60 percent) in addition to the $600 purchase price. This makes the total expected cost $960. The expected cost on the Enormity Incorporated model is $900.

13.4a

1. This is a poor argument, since the sample has little variety.
3. This is a poor argument, since the sample is very small and lacks variety.
5. This is a good inductive argument (presuming that you aren't in the polar regions where the sun doesn't come up at all for several weeks in the winter). In standard form, the argument goes: "All examined days are days when the sun comes up; a large and varied group of days has been examined; tomorrow is a day; so probably tomorrow is a day when the sun comes up."
10. This weakens the argument. Some students cram logic mainly for the Law School Admissions Test (since this test contains many logic problems). You might not have known this, however.

13.5a

1. This doesn't affect the strength of the argument, since the color of the book has little to do with the contents.
3. This weakens the argument. It's less likely that a course taught by a member of the mathematics department would include a discussion of analogical reasoning.
5. This weakens the argument. An abstract approach that stresses theory is less likely to include a discussion on analogical reasoning.
10. This weakens the argument. A book with only 10 pages on inductive reasoning is less likely to include analogical reasoning.
15. This weakens the argument, since it's a significant point of difference between the two cases.

13.7a

1. Using the method of agreement, we conclude that either having a few drinks causes a longer reaction time, or having a longer reaction time causes a person to have a few drinks. The second alternative is less likely in terms of our background information. So we conclude that having a few drinks probably causes a longer reaction time.
3. The method of agreement seems to lead to the conclusion that the soda caused the hangover. However, we know that scotch, gin, and rum all contain alcohol. So soda isn't the only factor common to all four cases; there's also the alcohol. So the method of agreement doesn't apply here. To decide whether the soda or the alcohol caused the hangover, Michelle would have to experiment with drinking soda but no alcohol, and drinking alcohol but no soda.
5. Using the method of agreement, we'd conclude that either factor K caused cancer or cancer caused factor K. If we found some drug to eliminate factor K, then we could try it and see whether it eliminates cancer. If eliminating factor K eliminated cancer, then it's likely that factor K caused cancer. But if factor K came back after we eliminated it, then it's likely that cancer caused factor K.
10. Using the method of disagreement, we'd conclude that eating raw garlic doesn't by itself necessarily cause mosquitoes to stop biting you.
15. Using the method of agreement, we'd conclude that either the combination of factors (heating or striking dry matches in the presence of oxygen) causes the match to light, or else the lighting of the match causes the combination of factors. The latter is implausible (it involves a present fire causing a past heating or striking). So probably the combination of factors causes the match to light.
20. By the method of variation, it's likely that an increase in the electrical voltage is the cause of the increase in the electrical current, or the electrical current is the cause of the electrical voltage, or something else caused them both. We know (but perhaps little Will doesn't) that we can have a voltage without a current (such as when nothing is plugged in to our electrical socket) but we can't have a current without a voltage. So we'd think that voltage causes current (and not vice versa) and reject the "electrical current is the cause of the electrical voltage" alternative. So we'd conclude that probably an increase in the electrical voltage is the cause of the increase in the electrical current, or else some other factor (Will's curiosity, for example) caused both increases.

25. By the method of difference, wearing a single pair of socks probably is (or is part of) the cause of the blisters, or the blisters are (or are part of) the cause of wearing a single pair of socks. The latter is impossible, since a present event can't cause a past event. So probably wearing a single pair of socks is (or is part of) the cause of the blisters. Since we know that we don't get blisters from wearing a single pair of socks without walking, we'd conclude that wearing a single pair of socks is only part of the cause of the blisters.

13.8a

1. The problem is how to do the experiment so that differences in air resistance won't get in the way. We could build a 100-foot tower on the moon (or some planet without air), drop a feather and a rock from the top, and see if both strike the ground at the same time. Or we might go to the top of a high building and drop two boxes that are identical except that one is empty while the other is filled with rocks. In this second case, the two boxes have the same air resistance but different weights.

3. We could study land patterns (hills, rock piles, eccentric boulders, and so on) left by present-day glaciers in places like Alaska, compare land patterns of areas that we are fairly sure weren't covered by glaciers, and compare both with those of Wisconsin. Mill's method of agreement might lead us to conclude that glaciers probably caused the land patterns in Wisconsin. To date the glacier, we'd have to find some "natural calendar" (such as the yearly rings in tree trunks, yearly sediment layers on the bottoms of lakes, corresponding layers in sedimentary rocks, or carbon breakdown) and connect it with Wisconsin climatic changes or land patterns.

5. We could give both groups an intelligence test. The problem is that the first child might test higher, not because of greater innate intelligence, but because of differences in how the first and the last child are brought up. (The last child, but not the first, is normally brought up with other children around and by older parents.) To eliminate this factor, we might test adopted children. If we find that a child born first and one born last tend to test equally (or unequally) in the same sort of

adoptive environment, then we could conclude that the two groups tend (or don't tend) to have the same innate intelligence.

10. See the answer to problem 3. Any data making statement 3 probable would make 10 improbable. In addition, if we found any "natural calendar" that gives a strong inductive argument concerning any events occurring over 5,000 years ago, this also would make 10 unlikely. [Of course, these are only inductive arguments; it's possible for the premises to be all true and the conclusion false.]

14.2a

1. "Cop" is negative. "Police" is more neutral.
3. "Heroic" is positive. These are negative: "reckless," "foolhardy," "brash," "rash," "careless," "imprudent," and "daredevil."
5. "Elderly gentleman" is positive. "Old man" is negative.
10. "Do-gooder" is negative. "Person concerned for others" and "caring human being" are positive.
15. "Booze" is negative or neutral. "Cocktail" is positive, while "alcohol," "liquor," and "intoxicant" are neutral.
20. "Babbling" is negative. "Talking," "speaking," and "discussing" are neutral.
25. "Bribe" is negative. "Payment" and "gift" are neutral or positive.
30. "Whore" is negative. "Prostitute" is more neutral.

14.3a

1. If you make a false statement that you think is true, that isn't a lie.
3. (1) One who believes in God may not make God his or her ultimate concern. (2) One may have an ultimate concern (such as making money) without believing in God. (3) "Object of ultimate concern" is relative in a way that "God" isn't: "Is there an object of ultimate concern?" invites the question "For whom?" – while "Is there a God?" doesn't.
5. Since "of positive value" is no more clearly understood than "good," this definition does little to clarify what "good" means. And there's the danger of circularity if we go on to define "of positive value" in terms of "good."

10. (1) If I believe that Michigan will beat Ohio State next year, it still might not be true. (2) If "true" means "believed," then both these statements are true (since both are believed by someone): "Michigan will beat Ohio State next year" and "Michigan won't beat Ohio State next year." (3) "Believed" is relative in a way that "true" isn't: "Is this believed?" invites the question "By whom?" – while "Is this true?" doesn't.

15. This set of definitions is circular.

14.3b

1. This is true according to cultural relativism. Sociological data can verify what is "socially approved," and this is the same as what is "good."

3. This is true. The norms set up by my society determine what is good in my society, so these norms couldn't be mistaken.

5. This is undecided. If our society approves of respecting the values of other societies, then this respect is good. But if our society disapproves of respecting the values of other societies, then this respect is bad.

10. This is true according to CR.

15. This is false (and self-contradictory) according to cultural relativism.

20. This is undecided, since cultural relativism leaves unspecified which of these various groups is "the society in question."

14.5a

1. This is meaningful on LP (it could be verified) and PR (it could make a practical difference in terms of sensations or choices).

3. This is meaningful on both views.

5. This is probably meaningless on both views (unless the statement is given some special sense).

10. This is meaningless on LP (at least on the version that requires public verifiability). It's meaningful on PR (since its truth could make a practical difference to Manuel's experience).

15. Since this (LP) isn't able to be tested empirically, it's meaningless on LP. [To avoid this result, a positivist could claim that LP is true by definition and hence analytic (see Section 14.7). Recall that LP is qualified so that it applies only to synthetic statements. But then the positivist

has to use "meaningless" in the unusual sense of "not empirical" instead of in the intended sense of "true or false." This shift takes the bite out of the claim that a statement is "meaningless." A believer can readily agree that "There is a God" is "meaningless" if all this means is that "There is a God" isn't empirical.] It's meaningful on PR (since its truth could make a difference to our choices about what we ought to believe).

14.6a

(These answers were adapted from those given by students)

1. "Is ethics a <u>science</u>?" could mean any of the following:
  • Are ethical judgments true or false independently of human feelings and opinions? Can the truth of some ethical judgments be known?
  • Can ethics be systematized into a set of rules that will tell us unambiguously what we ought to do in all (or most) concrete cases?
  • Can ethical principles be proved using the methods of empirical science?
  • Is there some rational method for arriving at ethical judgments that would lead people to agree on their ethical judgments?
  • Can a system of ethical principles be drawn up in an axiomatic form, so that ethical theorems can be deduced from axioms accessible to human reason?

3. "Is this belief part of <u>common sense</u>?" could mean any of the following:
  • Is this belief accepted instinctively or intuitively, as opposed to being the product of reasoning or education?
  • Is this belief so firmly entrenched that subtle reasoning to the contrary, even if it seems flawless, will have no power to convince us?
  • Is this belief something that people of good "horse sense" will accept regardless of their education?
  • Is this belief obviously true?
  • Is this belief universally accepted?
[In each case we could further specify the group we are talking about – for example, "Is this belief obviously true to anyone who has ever lived (to all those of our own country, or to practically all those of our own country who haven't been exposed to subtle reasoning on this topic)?"]

5. "Are values <u>relative</u> (or <u>absolute</u>)?" could mean any of the following:
- Do different individuals and societies disagree (and to what extent) on values?
- Do people disagree on basic moral principles (and not just on applications)?
- Are all (or some) values incapable of being proved or rationally argued?
- Is it wrong to claim that a moral judgment is correct or incorrect rather than claiming that it's correct or incorrect relative to such and such a group? Do moral judgments express social conventions rather than truths that hold independently of such conventions?
- Do right and wrong always depend on circumstances (so that no sort of action could be always right or always wrong)?
- In making concrete moral judgments, do different values have to be weighed against each other?
- Are all things that are valued only valued as a means to something else (so that nothing is valued for its own sake)?

10. "Is that judgment based on <u>reason</u>?" could be asking whether the judgment is based on the following:
- Self-evident truths, the analysis of concepts, and logical deductions from these (reason versus experience).
- The foregoing plus sense experience, introspection, and inductive arguments (reason versus faith).
- Some sort of thinking or experience or faith (as opposed to being based on mere emotion).
- The thinking and experience and feelings of a sane person (as opposed to those of an insane person).
- An adequate and impartial examination of the available data.
- A process for arriving at truth in which everyone correctly carrying out the process would arrive at the same conclusions.
- What is reasonable to believe, or what one ought to believe (or what is permissible to believe) from the standpoint of the seeking of truth.

[We could be asking whether a given person bases his or her judgment on one of the foregoing, or whether the judgment in question could be based on one of the foregoing.]

15. "Do you have a <u>soul</u>?" could mean any of the following:

- Do you have a personal identity that could in principle survive death and the disintegration of your body?
- Are you capable of conscious thinking and doing?
- Would an exhaustive description of your material constituents and observable behavior patterns fail to capture important elements of what you are?
- Are you composed of two quite distinct beings – a thinking being without spatial dimensions and a material being incapable of thought?
- Are you capable of caring deeply about anything?
- Are you still alive?

14.7a

1. Analytic.
3. Synthetic.
5. Analytic.
10. Analytic.
15. Analytic.
20. Most philosophers think this is synthetic. St Anselm, Descartes, and Charles Hartshorne argued that it was analytic. See examples 3 and 4 of Section 3.7b, and examples 9 and 26 of Section 7.3b.
25. Most say synthetic, but some say analytic.

14.8a

1. *A priori.*
3. *A posteriori.*
5. *A priori.*
10. *A priori.*
15. *A priori.*
20. Most philosophers think this could only be known *a posteriori*. Some philosophers think it can be known *a priori* (see comments on problem 20 of the last section).
25. Most philosophers think this could only be known *a priori*, but a few think it could be known *a posteriori*.

15.2a

1. Complex question (like "Are you still beating your wife?").
3. Pro-con. The candidate might be a crook. Or an opposing candidate might be even more intelligent and experienced.
5. Appeal to the crowd.
10. Genetic fallacy.
15. Appeal to authority.

20. None of the labels fit exactly. This vague claim (what is a "discriminating back-packer"?) is probably false (discriminating backpackers tend to vary in their preferences). The closest labels are "appeal to authority," "appeal to the crowd," "false stereotype," or perhaps "appeal to emotion." There's some "snob appeal" here too, but this isn't one of our categories.
25. *Post hoc ergo propter hoc.*
30. Appeal to opposition.
35. Appeal to emotion.
40. *Post hoc ergo propter hoc.*
45. *Ad hominem* or false stereotype.
50. *Post hoc ergo propter hoc.*

15.3a

(The answers for 3 and 5 are representative correct answers; other answers may be correct.)

1. There are no universal duties.
   If everyone ought to respect the dignity of others, then there are universal duties.
   ∴ Not everyone ought to respect the dignity of others.

3. If we have ethical knowledge, then either ethical truths are provable or there are self-evident ethical truths.
   We have ethical knowledge.
   Ethical truths aren't provable.
   ∴ There are self-evident ethical truths.

5. All human concepts derive from sense experience.
   The concept of logical validity is a human concept.
   ∴ The concept of logical validity derives from sense experience.

10. If every rule has an exception, then there's an exception to this present rule; but then some rule doesn't have an exception.
    Statement 10 implies its own falsity and hence is self-refuting.

15. If it's impossible to express truth in human concepts, then statement 15 is false. Statement 15 implies its own falsity and hence is self-refuting.

15.4a

(These are examples of answers and aren't the only "right answers.")

1. If the agent will probably get caught, then offering the bribe probably isn't in the agent's self-interest.
   The agent will probably get caught. (One might offer an inductive argument for this one.)
   ∴ Offering the bribe probably isn't in the agent's self-interest.

3. Some acts that grossly violate the rights of some maximize good consequences (in the sense of maximizing the total of everyone's interests).
   No acts that grossly violate the rights of some are right.
   ∴ Some acts that maximize good consequences aren't right.

5. Any act that involves lying is a dishonest act (from the definition of "dishonest").
   Offering the bribe involves lying (falsifying records, and the like).
   ∴ Offering the bribe is a dishonest act.

10. Science adequately explains our experience.
    If science adequately explains our experience, then the belief that there is a God is unnecessary to explain our experience.
    ∴ The belief that there is a God is unnecessary to explain our experience.

    Or: Science doesn't adequately explain certain items of our experience (why these scientific laws govern our universe and not others, why our universe exhibits order, why there exists a world of contingent beings at all, moral obligations, and so on).
    If science doesn't adequately explain certain items of our experience, then the belief that there is a God is necessary to explain our experience.
    ∴ The belief that there is a God is necessary to explain our experience.

15. The idea of logical validity is an idea gained in our earthly existence.
    The idea of logical validity isn't derived from sense experience.
    ∴ Some ideas gained in our earthly existence don't derive from sense experience.

Glossary

This includes terms introduced in **bold type** in the text (with section references in parentheses), plus a few other common terms. The reader should be warned that other authors may use some of these terms in somewhat different senses.

A posteriori **knowledge (empirical knowledge)**   Knowledge based on sense experience. (14.8)

A priori **knowledge (rational knowledge)**   Knowledge not based on sense experience. (14.8)

Actual world   The possible world that is true; the consistent and complete description of how things in fact are. (7.1)

Actualism   To be a being and to exist is the same thing – so there neither are nor could have been non-existent beings. (8.4)

Ad hominem **(against the person)**   Attacking a person instead of an issue. (15.2)

Affirming the consequent   The "If A, then B; B; therefore A" fallacy. (3.11)

Agreement method   A occurred more than once, B is the only additional factor that occurred if and only if A occurred, so probably B caused A or A caused B. (13.7)

Algorithm   Step-by-step procedure for answering a question (for example, "Is this propositional logic formula true in all cases?") that doesn't involve guesswork or intuition and would always give a definite answer in a finite number of steps.

Ambiguous argument   One that shifts the meaning of a term or phrase within the argument. (15.1)

Analogy syllogism   Most things true of X also are true of Y, X is A, this is all we know about the matter, so probably Y is A. (13.5)

Analytic statement   See **necessary truth**.

And-gate   Electronic device whose output has a given physical state (like a positive voltage) if and only if both inputs have that state. (3.14)

Antecedent   See **conditional**.

Appeal to authority   To base a conclusion on what some authority says. (15.2)

Appeal to emotion   To stir up feelings instead of arguing in a logical manner. (15.1)

Appeal to force   To use threats or intimidation to get a conclusion accepted. (15.2)

Appeal to ignorance   Arguing that what hasn't been proved must thus be false, or that what hasn't been disproved must thus be true. (15.2)

Appeal to the crowd   Arguing that something that most people believe must thus be true. (15.2)

Argument   Set of statements consisting of premises and a conclusion. A *deductive argument* is an argument combined with the claim (usually implicit) that the conclusion follows with necessity; an *inductive argument* is an argument combined with the claim (usually indicated by a word like "probably" in the conclusion) that the conclusion follows with probability. Arguments can have no premises, but not an infinite number of premises. Imperative arguments can contain imperatives. (1.2, 9.2, 13.1)

Aristotelian essentialism   There are properties that some beings have of necessity and some other beings totally lack. (8.2)

Aristotelian view   An approach to the validity of syllogisms that assumes that each general term refers to at least one existing being. (2.8)

Arithmetic   The set of truths and falsehoods that can be expressed using symbols for the positive numbers (1, 2, 3, ...), variables (x, y, z, ...), parentheses, *equals, plus, times, to the power of, not, and, or, if-then, every,* and *some.* (12.7)

Assumption   In a formal proof, a line consisting of "asm:" and then a wff. (4.2)

Axiom   Basic assertion that isn't proved but can be used to prove other things. In logical systems, a formula that can be put on any line, regardless of earlier lines. (6.2, 12.6)

Begging the question   See circular argument.

Belief logic   A branch of logic that studies patterns of consistent believing and willing; it generates consistency norms that prescribe that we be consistent in various ways. (10.0)

Belief world   Possible world, relative to a set of imperatives telling person X what to believe or refrain from believing, that contains everything that X is told to believe. The imperatives tell X to believe in a *consistent* way, provided that there is some non-empty set of belief worlds in which (1) whatever X is told to believe is in all the worlds, and (2) the denial of whatever X is told to refrain from believing is in at least one world. (10.2)

Beside the point   Arguing for a conclusion irrelevant to the issue at hand. (15.1)

Biconditional   Statement of the form "A if and only if B." (3.2)

Biting the bullet   Accepting an implausible consequence of a view. (15.4)

Black-and-white thinking   Oversimplifying by assuming that one or another of two extreme cases must be true. (15.2)

Calculus   See formal system.

Cause   What brings about something else (the effect). The term "cause" can express any of a cluster of related notions. (13.7)

Church's theorem   There is no possible mechanical strategy that in every case will give a proof or refutation of a relational argument in a finite number of steps. (6.4)

Circular argument (question begging)   Argument that presumes the truth of what is to be proved. (15.1)

Clarifying definition   One that stipulates a clearer meaning for a vague term. (14.4)

Coherence criterion   Other things being equal, we ought to prefer a theory that harmonizes with existing well-established beliefs. (13.8)

Complete system System in which every valid argument expressible in the system is provable in the system. (12.3)

Completely consistent believer Person who believes some things, believes a logically consistent set S of things, and believes anything that follows logically from set S. (10.2)

Complex question Question that assumes the truth of something false or doubtful. (15.2)

Complex wff In propositional logic, a wff that is neither just a letter nor the negation of a letter. (4.2)

Conclusion See argument.

Conditional proof One that derives an if-then conclusion by assuming the antecedent and then deriving the consequent. (4.7)

Conditional Statement of the form "If A, then B." The "if"-part (here "A") is the antecedent; the "then"-part (here "B") is the consequent. (3.2)

Conjunct See conjunction.

Conjunction Statement of the form "A and B." The parts are conjuncts. (3.2)

Conjunctivity principle You ought not to combine believing A and believing B and not believing (A and B). (10.7)

Conscientiousness principle Keep your actions, resolutions, and desires in harmony with your moral beliefs. (11.2)

Consequent See conditional.

Consistent believer See completely consistent believer.

Constant (individual constant) Letter standing for a specific person or thing. (5.1)

Contingent statement (synthetic statement) One that logically (that is, without self-contradiction) could have been either true or false. In propositional logic, a wff whose truth table has some cases true and some cases false. (3.5, 7.1, 14.7)

Contradiction (logical falsehood) See self-contradiction.

Contradictories A pair of statements so related that one must be true if and only if the other is false. In propositional logic, two wffs are (formal) contradictories if they are exactly alike except that one starts with an additional "~." (4.2)

Contrapositive Result of switching the antecedent and consequent of a conditional and negating both. The contrapositive of "(A ⊃ B)" is "(~B ⊃ ~A)." (3.8)

Counterexample method Refuting an "all A is B" by finding something that is A but not B, or refuting a "no A is B" by finding something that is A and also B. (15.4)

De dicto necessity Necessity ascribed to a statement – as in the claim that it's necessary that all bachelors are unmarried. (8.2)

De re necessity Necessity ascribed to a thing having a property – as in the claim that John has the necessary property of being unmarried. (8.2)

Decision procedure See algorithm.

Deductive argument Argument that claims that it's *logically necessary* that if the premises are all true then so is the conclusion. (13.1)

Definite description Term of the form "the so and so." (6.5)

Definition Rule of paraphrase intended to explain meaning. More precisely, a definition of a word or phrase is a rule saying how to eliminate this word or phrase in any sentence using it and produce a second sentence that means the same thing – the purpose of this being to explain or clarify the meaning of the word or phrase. (14.3)

Denying the antecedent The "If A, then B; not-A; therefore not-B" fallacy. (3.11)

Deontic logic A branch of logic that studies arguments whose validity depends on "ought," "permissible," and similar notions. (9.0)

Deontic world Possible world, in the sense of a consistent and complete set of indicatives and imperatives, in which (a) the indicative statements are all true and (b) the imperatives prescribe some jointly permissible combination of actions. (9.4)

Derived step In a formal proof, a line consisting of "∴" and then a wff. (4.2)

Difference method A occurred in the first case but not the second; the cases are otherwise identical, except that B also occurred in the first case but not the second; so probably B caused (or is part of the cause of) A, or A caused (or is part of the cause of) B. (13.7)

Direct proof One that derives a conclusion without making any assumptions. (4.7)

Disagreement method A occurred in some case, B didn't occur in the same case, so A doesn't necessarily cause B. (13.7)

Disjunct See disjunction.

Disjunction Statement of the form "A or B." The parts are disjuncts. (3.2)

Distributed letter Letter in a syllogistic wff that occurs just after "all" or anywhere after "no" or "not." (The traditional definition says that a general term is *distributed* in a statement if the statement makes some claim about every entity that the general term denotes.) (2.2)

Division-composition Arguing that something true of the whole must be true of all the parts, or that something true of all the parts must be true of the whole. (15.2)

Empirical knowledge See *a posteriori* knowledge.

Empiricist One who believes that we have no synthetic *a priori* knowledge. More broadly, one who emphasizes *a posteriori* knowledge. (14.8)

Endless loop Doing the same sequence of actions over and over, endlessly. See **loop, endless.** (6.4)

Ends–means consistency principle Keep your means in harmony with your ends. (11.2)

Exclusive "or" One or the other but not both. See **inclusive "or."** (3.2)

Existential quantifier See **quantifier.**

Expected gain of an alternative Sum of probability times gain of the various possible outcomes. (13.3)

Fallacy Deceptive error of thinking. (15.2)

False stereotype Assuming that members of a certain group are more alike than they actually are. (15.2)

Form of an argument See logical form.

Formal ethical principle Ethical principle that can be formulated using the abstract notions of our logical systems plus variables. (10.6, 11.2)

Formal logic (deductive logic) That part of logic that focuses on testing for validity – on determining whether the conclusion of an argument follows from the premises.

Formal proof Sequence of steps that uses the rules of a logical system to show that an argument is valid. In our propositional logic, a formal proof is a vertical sequence of zero or more premises followed by one or more assumptions or derived steps, where each derived step follows from previously not-blocked-off lines by RAA or one of the inference rules, and each assumption is blocked off using RAA. (4.2)

Formal system (calculus) Artificial language with notational grammar rules and notational rules for determining validity. There must be algorithms for determining whether formulas and proofs are correctly formulated. (12.7)

Formula of universal law Act only as you're willing for anyone to act in the same situation – regardless of imagined variations of time or person. (11.2, 11.5)

Free logic System of logic that is free of the assumption that individual constants like "a" always refer to existing beings. (8.4)

General term Term that describes or puts in a category. Adjectives, verbs, and phrases of the form "a so and so" are usually general terms. (2.1, 5.1, 6.1)

Genetic fallacy Arguing that a belief must be false if we can explain its origin. (15.2)

Gödel's theorem Arithmetic isn't reducible to any formal system. More precisely, any formal system that contains arithmetic will have either unprovable arithmetic truths or provable arithmetic falsehoods. (12.7)

Golden rule Treat others only as you consent to being treated in the same situation. More precisely, don't combine these two: (a) I do something to another, and (b) I'm unwilling that this be done to me in the same situation. (11.2, 11.3, 11.5)

Good argument Argument that is logically correct and fulfills the purposes for which we use arguments. A good argument is deductively valid (or inductively strong) and has all true premises; has this validity and truth be as evident as possible to the parties involved; is clearly stated; avoids circularity, ambiguity, and emotional language; and is relevant to the issue at hand. (15.1)

Hare's Law An "ought" entails the corresponding imperative. (9.4)

Hume's Law You can't deduce an "ought" from an "is." (9.4)

Hypothesis (scientific) Scientific conjecture with little backing. (13.8)

Identity statement Statement of the form "x=y." (6.0, 6.1)

Impartiality principle Make similar evaluations about similar actions, regardless of the individuals involved. (11.2, 11.5)

Imperative logic A branch of logic that studies arguments with imperatives (like "Do this"). (9.0)

Inclusive "or"   One or the other or both. See **exclusive "or."** (3.2)

Inconsistency in beliefs   To hold logically incompatible beliefs at the same time, or to believe something without believing what logically follows from it. (10.2, 11.2, 15.3)

Independent events   Events for which the occurrence of one doesn't affect the probability of the occurrence of the other. (13.2)

Indirect proof   One that derives a conclusion by assuming its opposite and then deriving a contradiction. See **RAA**.

Inductive argument   Argument that claims that it's *likely* (but not logically necessary) that if the premises are all true then so is the conclusion. (13.1)

Inference rule   Rule stating that certain formulas can be derived from certain other formulas. (3.10 , 3.11, 12.6)

Informal fallacy   Deceptive error of thinking that isn't covered by some system of deductive or inductive logic. (15.2)

Informal logic   The part of logic that deals with things other than testing the validity of deductive arguments or the strength of inductive arguments.

Interchange test   To test a lexical definition claiming that A means B, try switching A and B in a variety of sentences; if some resulting pair of sentences don't mean the same thing, then the definition is incorrect. (14.3)

Invalid argument   One in which it would be possible to have the premises all true and conclusion false. See **valid argument**.

I-rules   The six inference rules of propositional logic used to infer a conclusion from two other formulas. (3.11)

Kant's Law   "Ought" implies "can." (9.4)

Law (scientific)   Scientific principle with much scientific dignity and backing. (13.8)

Law of non-contradiction   A statement can't be both true and (taking it in the exact same sense) also not true: "~(A · ~A)."

Law of the excluded middle   Every statement is either true or false: "(A ∨ ~A)." (3.5)

Lexical definition   One that explains current usage. (14.3)

Literal golden rule   If you want X to do A to you, then do A to X. (11.3)

Logic   The analysis and appraisal of arguments. (1.1)

Logic gate   Electronic device whose input–output function mirrors the truth table of a propositional wff. (3.14)

Logical falsehood   See **self-contradiction**.

Logical form   Arrangement of logical notions (like "if-then" and "not") and content phrases (like "You overslept" and "You're late"). We can display an argument's logical form by using words or symbols for the logical notions and letters for the content phrases. In most cases (with perhaps exceptions like "This is completely red ∴ This isn't completely green"), an argument's logical form determines whether it is valid. (1.2)

Logical positivism The meaning of a synthetic statement is determined by what conceivable observable tests would settle whether the statement is true or false. (14.5)

Logical truth See **necessary truth**.

Logicality principle Avoid inconsistency in beliefs. More precisely, don't believe logically inconsistent things and don't believe something without believing what logically follows from it. (11.2)

LogiCola The computer instructional program intended to be used with this book. (See the appendix.)

Loop, endless See **endless loop**. (6.4)

Material conditional Statement using the simple "⊃" sense of "If A then B" (which just denies that we have A true and B false). (3.2)

Mathematical induction Suppose that something holds in the first case, and if it holds in the first n cases, then it holds in the n+1 case; then it holds in all cases. (12.3)

Mathematically fair betting odds Betting odds that are in reverse proportion to the odds of an event's occurring. (13.2)

Metalogic The study of logical systems and the attempt to prove things about these systems. (12.1)

Mill's methods Methods proposed by John Stuart Mill for arriving at and justifying claims about what caused what. (13.7)

Modal logic A branch of logic that studies arguments whose validity depends on "necessary," "possible," and similar notions. (7.0)

Modern view An approach to the validity of syllogisms that allows for empty general terms (terms like "unicorn" that don't refer to existing beings). (2.8)

Modus ponens **(affirming mode)** An inference that goes "If A, then B; A; therefore B." (3.11, 13.9)

Modus tollens **(denying mode)** An inference that goes "If A, then B; not-B; therefore not-A." (3.11, 15.4)

Mutually exclusive events Events that can't both happen together. (13.2)

Necessary truth (analytic truth) Statement whose denial is self-contradictory. Necessary truths are based on logic, the meaning of concepts, or necessary connections between properties. (7.1, 14.7)

Negation Statement of the form "Not-A." (3.2)

Ohm's Law The electrical law that $I = E/R$, where I = current (in amps), E = voltage (in volts), and R = resistance (in ohms). (13.8)

Opposition Arguing that what an opponent believes must thus be false. (15.2)

Or-gate Electronic device whose output has a given physical state (like a positive voltage) if and only if at least one input has that state. (3.14)

Philosophy Reasoning about the ultimate questions of life. (1.1)

Poincaré's Law   You can't deduce an imperative from an "is." (9.4)

Possible world   Consistent and complete description of how things might have been or might in fact be. A statement is *possible* if it's true in some *possible* world – and a statement is *necessary* if it's true in *all* possible worlds. In imperative logic onward, a consistent and complete set of indicatives and imperatives. (7.1, 9.4)

Post hoc ergo propter hoc **(after this therefore because of this)**   Arguing that, since A happened after B, thus A was caused by B. (15.2)

Pragmatism (pragmatist theory of meaning)   The meaning of a synthetic statement is determined by what practical difference the truth or falsity of the statement could make. (14.5)

Premise   Statement of an argument from which (perhaps when combined with other such statements) the conclusion is claimed to follow. In a formal proof, a line consisting of a wff by itself (with no "asm:" or "∴."). (1.2, 4.2)

Probability   Ratio of abstract possibilities or observed frequencies, or measure of actual or rational belief. (13.2, 13.3)

Pro-con   An argument that weighs the reasons in favor of and against an action. (15.2)

Proof   Non-circular, non-ambiguous, deductively valid argument with clearly true premises. The word "proof" can have somewhat different meanings depending on the context; see **formal proof**. (15.1)

Propositional logic   A branch of logic that studies arguments whose validity depends on "if-then," "and," "or," "not," and similar notions. (3.0)

Quantificational logic   A branch of logic that builds on propositional logic and studies arguments whose validity depends on "all," "no," "some," and similar notions. (5.0)

Quantifier   Symbol of the form "(x)" or "(∃x)," where any variable may replace "x." The universal quantifier "(x)" means "for all x," while the existential quantifier "(∃x)" means "for some x." Quantifiers express "all" and "some" by saying in how many cases the following formula is true. (5.1)

Question begging   See **circular argument**.

RAA ("*reductio ad absurdum*" or "reduction to absurdity")   A rule that says that we may derive the opposite of an assumption that leads to a contradiction. (4.1, 4.2)

Rational knowledge   See *a priori* **knowledge**.

Rationalist   One who believes that we have synthetic *a priori* knowledge. More broadly, one who emphasizes *a priori* knowledge. (14.8)

Recursive definition   One that first specifies some things that a term applies to and then specifies that if the term applies to certain things then it also applies to certain other things. (14.4)

Reductio ad absurdum   See **RAA**.

Refutation of a statement   Proof of the negation of the statement; see **proof**. (15.1)

Refutation of an argument Possible situation making the premises all true and conclusion false. (4.3)

Relational statement Statement about two or more persons or things (for example, "Romeo loves Juliet"). (6.0, 6.3)

Reliable (inductively) An inductive argument that is strong (the conclusion is probable relative to the premises) and has true premises. (13.1)

Sample-projection syllogism N percent of examined A's are B's, a large and varied group of A's has been examined, so probably roughly N percent of all A's are B's. (13.4)

Self-contradiction Statement that is false in every possible case. (3.5, 7.1)

Self-refuting statement Statement that makes negative claims so sweeping that it ends up denying itself. (15.3)

Simple wff In propositional logic, a letter or its negation. (4.2)

Simplicity criterion Other things being equal, we ought to prefer a simpler theory to a more complex one. (13.8)

Singular term Term that picks out a specific person or thing. Proper names and phrases of the form "the so and so" or "this so and so" are usually singular terms. (2.1, 5.1, 6.1)

Sound argument Valid argument that has every premise true. Equivalently, a sound argument is one in which (1) the premises are all true and (2) it would be contradictory to have the premises all true and conclusion false. (1.3)

Sound system System in which every argument provable in the system is valid. (12.3)

S-rules The six inference rules of propositional logic used to simplify a single formula into smaller pieces. (3.10, 4.2)

Star test for syllogisms Star the distributed letters in the premises and undistributed letters in the conclusion; then the syllogism is valid if and only if every capital letter is starred exactly once and there is exactly one star on the right-hand side. (2.2)

Statistical syllogism N percent of A's are B's, X is an A, this is all we know about the matter, so it's N percent probable that X is a B. (13.1)

Stipulative definition One that specifies how you're going to use a term (instead of one that explains current usage). (14.3, 14.4)

Straw man An argument that misrepresents an opponent's views. (15.1)

Strong (inductively) An inductive argument whose conclusion is probable relative to the premises. (13.1)

Syllogism Roughly, an argument of syllogistic logic. More precisely, a vertical sequence of one or more syllogistic wffs in which each letter occurs twice and the letters "form a chain" (each wff has at least one letter in common with the wff just below it, if there is one, and the first wff has at least one letter in common with the last wff). (2.2)

Syllogistic logic A branch of logic that studies arguments whose validity depends on "all," "no," "some," and similar notions. (2.0)

Synthetic statement See **contingent statement**.

Tautology (logical truth)   Statement that is true in every possible case. (3.5)

Theorem of a system   Formula derivable from zero premises. (12.5)

Theory (scientific)   Scientific principle with a moderate amount of scientific dignity and backing. (13.8)

Traditional proofs   A method of proving arguments that relies on a standard set of inference and equivalence rules. (4.7)

Traditional syllogism   Two-premise syllogism with no small letters. (2.6)

Truth table   Diagram listing all possible truth-value combinations for the letters in a propositional wff and saying whether the wff is true or false in each case. (3.2)

Truth trees   A method of testing arguments that decomposes formulas into the cases that make them true. (4.7)

Truth value   Truth ("1") or falsity ("0"). (3.2)

Turnaround arguments   Arguments that result from each other by switching the denial of a premise with the denial of the conclusion. (15.3)

Universal property   Non-evaluative property describable without proper names (like "Gensler" or "Cleveland") or pointer terms (like "I" or "this"). (11.4)

Universal quantifier   See quantifier.

Universalizability principle   Whatever is right (wrong, good, bad, etc.) in one case also would be right (wrong, good, bad, etc.) in any exactly or relevantly similar case, regardless of the individuals involved. (11.4, 15.3)

Universe of discourse   Set of entities that words like "all," "some," and "no" range over in a given context. (5.1)

Unsound argument   Argument that isn't sound. Alternatively, an unsound argument is one in which either (1) it would be possible to have the premises all true and conclusion false, or (2) at least one premise is false. (1.3)

Valid argument   Argument in which it would be contradictory (impossible) to have the premises all true and conclusion false. In imperative logic, an argument in which the conjunction of the premises with the contradictory of the conclusion is inconsistent. (1.2, 1.3, 9.2)

Variable   Letter standing for an unspecified member of a class of things. (5.1)

Variation method   A changes in a certain way if and only if B also changes in a certain way; so probably B caused A, or A caused B, or some C caused both A and B. (13.7)

Venn diagram   Diagram for testing syllogisms that uses three overlapping circles. (2.6)

Wff (well-formed formula)   Grammatical sentence of a system of logic. The exact definition of how to form a wff varies with different systems. (2.1, 3.1)

World prefix   String of letters that represents a possible world in a formal proof. In modal logic, a world prefix consists of a string of zero or more instances of "W." (7.2)

Index of Names